DEALING IN VIRTUE

Yves Dezalay *&* Bryant G. Garth

Foreword by

Pierre Bourdieu

DEALING IN VIRTUE

International

Commercial

Arbitration

and the

Construction

of a

Transnational

Legal Order

The University of Chicago Press
Chicago *&* London

YVES DEZALAY is a sociologist and director of research at the Centre national de la recherche scientifique, attached to the Centre de sociologie européenne of the Ecole des hautes études en sciences sociales and the Collège de France. His books include *Marchands de droit* (Fayard, 1992). BRYANT GARTH, trained as a lawyer, is director of the American Bar Foundation in Chicago. Prior to coming to the American Bar Foundation in 1990, he was dean of Indiana University School of Law (Bloomington).

The University of Chicago Press, Chicago 60637
The University of Chicago Press, Ltd., London

© 1996 by The University of Chicago
All rights reserved. Published 1996

Printed in the United States of America
05 04 03 02 01 00 99 98 97 96   1 2 3 4 5

ISBN: 0-226-14422-4 (cloth)

Library of Congress Cataloging-in-Publication Data

Dezalay, Yves, 1945–
    Dealing in virtue : international commercial arbitration and the construction of a transnational legal order / Yves Dezalay & Bryant G. Garth ; foreword by Pierre Bourdieu.
        p.   cm. — (Language and legal discourse)
    Includes bibliographical references and index.
    ISBN 0-226-14422-4
    1. Arbitration and award, International.   2. Dispute resolution (Law)   I. Garth, Bryant G.   II. Title.   III. Series.
    K2400.D49   1996
    341.5'22—dc20   96-15880
                                                                          CIP

Chapter 3, "Merchants of Law as Moral Entrepreneurs: Constructing International Justice out of the Competition for Transnational Business Disputes," is a modified version of an article that appeared in the *Law and Society Review*.

⊗ The paper used in this publication meets the minimum requirements of the American National Standard for Information Sciences—Permanence of Paper for Printed Library Materials, ANSI Z39.48-1984.

Contents

Foreword

This book might benefit from the current fashion (for indeed there is no other word for it) of highlighting and grouping together a series of loosely related phenomena under the rubric *globalization*. Although this can only have resulted from a profound misunderstanding, I am glad of it. For I am convinced that this analysis can bring about a real paradigm shift in an area until now given over to long-winded and dangerous approximations of "essayism."

To speak of a global—or, better, international—legal field is immediately to escape the temptation to explain the processes of unification observed in very different domains of practice in one of two ways: either as a quasi-mechanical effect of the intensification and acceleration of circulation and exchange, leading to an ecumenical reconciliation of all cultural traditions, or as an effect of imperialism exercised by a few great industrial powers capable of exporting and imposing, on a universal scale, not only their products but also their style of life. The notion of field (in the sense of fields of forces and fields of struggle to conserve and transform the relationship of forces) requires a position beyond the sophomoric alternatives of consensus and conflict, and thus permits us to understand and analyze the process of unification as a product of competition and conflict.

By collaborating in this research, Yves Dezalay and Bryant Garth have been able to combine their own familiarity (linked to their national origins and disciplinary training, involving two of the great legal traditions confronting each other) with their learned knowledge of a great number of national legal spaces (including their own). They have managed to show that conflicts between jurists of different countries seeking to impose their judicial forms, or their modes of producing law, contribute to the progressive (and unfinished) unification of the global legal field and the global market of legal expertise. The international is constructed largely from the competition among national approaches. Since lawyers and others are trained nationally, and for the most part they make their careers nationally, it is not surprising that they seek as a matter of course to deploy their ways of thinking and practicing in the construction of international institutions. This process makes the international the site of a regulatory competition between essentially national approaches. In the conquest of new markets for their legal services, the large law firms rely on the fact that legal capital plays a decisive role in the regulation of commerce and also in organizations for the defense of "human rights," organizations that, along with great international institutions like the IMF and the World Bank, are often the Trojan Horses of the "Chicago boys" and their strategies of legal-economic import-export—that associate ethical idealism and economic realism. But these new "bourgeois conquerors" must take into account the resistance of national legal fields threatened by the new world legal order or, more exactly, the balance of power and conflict—found within these national fields—between modernists, who take the position of the international, and traditionalists, who play for protectionist closure and the maintenance of national tradition.

Thinking in terms of "field" also allows one to recapture the global logic of the new world legal order without resorting to generalities as vague and vast as their object. Instead, one can observe and analyze the more concrete strategies by which particular agents, themselves defined by their dispositions (tied to a social position and a trajectory in a national field), their properties, and their interests, construct an international legal field while at the same time transforming their national legal fields. This approach leads, for example, to the discovery that within each national field the partisans of "global" and "local" are not distributed randomly, since international strategies are really accessible only to those with (very) privileged social origin, possessing dispositions and competences (notably linguistic) that do not come from classroom instruction.

The national members of this new international elite, a *noblesse de robe*, by exercising their talents in the major transnational entities, humanitarian organizations, or even great legal multinationals, help to bring juridical forms to a higher level of universalization in and by a confrontation of different and at times opposed visions. Always at play in this confrontation, both as weapon and as stakes, is the law (whether the rights of business, the rights of man, or the rights of businessmen)—that is, piously hypocritical reference to the universal.

Pierre Bourdieu

Acknowledgments

Our research has been facilitated by the generosity of many individuals and institutions. The American Bar Foundation's support has been indispensable, both in terms of material support and especially in providing a unique intellectual environment and set of colleagues. We have also received a substantial grant from the National Science Foundation (Grant No. SES-9024498) and a small but helpful grant from the Phillips Foundation.

We cannot name the nearly three hundred (mostly) lawyers that we have interviewed, but we want to single out a few of the individuals who facilitated our entry both into the general world of arbitration and to particular research sites. Our initial contacts and guides were especially James Carter and Lawrence Newman in New York, William Park in Boston, Pierre Bellet in Paris, Jacques Werner in Geneva, Albert Jan van den Berg of Amsterdam, Neil Kaplan and Carol Jones in Hong Kong, and Per Hendrik Lindblom in Sweden.

In the United States we have been aided in the organization and collection of archival material by a talented group of research assistants, including Tiffany Davis, Erika George, Duncan Kinkead, Rhonda Mundhenk, Corinna Polk, Victor Reinoso, and Jonathan Rosenblum. We thank NSF again for a program that enabled most of those individuals to come and work on our project at the ABF. Special thanks go to Carole Silver, who became an essential part of our research and writing effort, and to Brenda Smith, who has typed most of the manuscripts, handled the "faxing frenzies" we engage in to prepare our research trips, patiently dealt with numerous efforts to try to get the manuscript right, and in general managed to provide order and stability in the midst of a research and writing style that—perhaps borrowing from the style of the international arbitrators we studied—necessarily alternated between periods of frenzy devoted completely to the project and the more normal periods of academic and administrative life. We also are grateful for the support of the Board of the American Bar Foundation, and in particular for its encouragement of the director in his effort to bring the project to fruition.

Academic colleagues who have been especially helpful in reading drafts and providing suggestions include John Comaroff and Elizabeth Mertz, both of whom are half-time fellows at the American Bar Foundation; Robert Stevens, now at Oxford; and Garry Watson of Toronto. We are grateful to Nancy Reichman of Denver for encouraging and working with us on the article we published in the *Law and Society Review* (29:27–64), which became the basis for chapter 3 (and parts of chapter 1); and to Mack O'Barr for his role and insights as editor of the *Review*.

Finally, the international-arbitration community that is the basis for this study was extremely cooperative and helpful. We want to express our thanks to an impressive group of individuals—and our hope that the representation of their world that we have used them to produce helps them understand how their own struggles and positions relate to the construction of international business justice.

Part One
Dealing in Virtue

The two chapters in this part provide an introduction to the method and structure of the book, our research strategy, and the world of international commercial arbitration. The first chapter, which provides a preview of the entire book, also exemplifies our general strategy of presentation. We seek to build on the familiar, taking the reader on a journey that begins with the most easily understandable and accessible elements of the story and then moves to more complex relationships and more abstract theoretical questions. International commercial arbitration can in this manner provide a point of entry into more complex questions of the role of law, the relationship between the national and the international, and the relationship between business, state, and law. At the same time, however, any commonsense or conventional understanding of the point of entry must be questioned, since conflicts over *what* and *who* represent "international commercial arbitration" comprise a key part of the inquiry.

The second chapter begins the process described and mapped in the first chapter, providing a discussion of the kind of individuals who are named most often as international arbitrators. Again, they provide a logical point of entry, since they embody what is now accepted as international commercial arbitration; but again, as we shall see, the value given to what they embody—their "symbolic capital"—is the product of complicated historical developments, individual and group strategies, and institutional processes.

I

Exploring and Representing the World of International Commercial Arbitration

The "rule of law" has become one of the rallying cries for the post-cold-war era, and it is a phrase that moves easily across borders. But ideas do not circulate and take hold by themselves. However powerful, an idea, like any new invention or technology, still requires carriers to promote it in a new context. The abstraction of the rule of law, for example, draws from what could be termed the rule of business and especially from the rule of lawyers who serve business interests. Moreover, the increasingly important process of internationalization of the rule of law cannot be explained as if lawyers simply want and produce more law at all levels. Anyone who searches for a single lawyers' collective program—for good or evil—will be quite disappointed. Lawyers (assuming that the term even has the same meaning in different countries) come from very different national legal traditions and from different parts of the profession (judiciary, academy, practice, government), and they respond to different clients and constituencies. If they promote directly or indirectly the spread of internationalism in law, it is because their specific careers, ambitions, and interests lead them to make a personal investment at a particular time and place. The abstraction of international law is therefore closely tied to the activities of individuals and groups, who thereby give concrete meaning to the abstraction.

This study begins the process of understanding the internationalization of the rule of law by studying institutions that have been developed for the resolution of transnational business disputes. We can trace in the mechanisms of this increasingly global private justice the emergence of a transnational legal profession, institutionalized in new kinds of "courts"—international commercial arbitration—and a special body of "law"—the so-called *lex mercatoria*.

Internationalization, however, does not refer only to activity that takes place at the transnational level. The transnational level, in fact, is best understood as a virtual space that provides strategic opportunities for competitive struggles engaged in by *national* actors—struggles, for example, about whether international commercial arbitration should resemble litigation in court, and, if so, whose courts, or how much it should reflect a perspective of third-world

3

or Arab countries. The transnational opportunities and struggles, furthermore, tend to disrupt the established national categories and, as a result, are as significant for their impacts on the national landscapes of business disputing as they are in the creation of an international private justice. Our study, therefore, includes both transformations of the international through national actors and transformations of the national through the impact of the international.

We have written this book for at least three audiences: lawyers, legal academics, and social scientific scholars interested in the relationships between law, lawyers, business, markets, and the state. International commercial arbitration is an arcane domain, the subject to date of a literature produced mainly by insiders with their own particular understandings. Many lawyers and legal academics know something about the subject, but the world of arbitration remains rather mysterious, especially for those not fully initiated into it. One of our hopes is to provide readers with a descriptive account that will bring together information available only to a relatively small group of insiders. We hope also that our description will allow insiders to understand better the general picture and their position in it. At the same time, however, we do not wish to produce a primarily journalistic account. Our primary interest is in seeing what the study of international commercial arbitration can tell us with respect to more general theoretical questions about the role of law and lawyers.

The task of combining an accessible and interesting narrative with relatively complex and abstract theoretical concerns is never an easy one. Here it is made more difficult because our general approach is relatively new and unfamiliar to scholars who study the legal profession, alternative dispute resolution, and more generally the relations between law and business. Pierre Bourdieu—whose structural approach we use as a starting point—is very well known, but aspects of Bourdieu's approach central to our work will appear unconventional and novel to many of our potential academic readers. It is probably fair to say that Bourdieu's work is used mainly as a kind of ornamental reference by most "law and society" or "neoinstitutionalist" scholars. The structural and reflexive parts of the approach are forced into, or put aside in favor of, a more "scientistic" and positivistic framework.

Somewhat to our surprise, we have found that our approach typically encounters less resistance from legal practitioners than from legal academics. Practitioners, it seems, are relatively accustomed to thinking in terms of strategies and positions in the legal field, which is precisely what we are trying to do and to show. Academics, however, especially legal academics, tend to resist thinking in terms of the internal politics of the field of law (or, similarly, seeing their role in that politics). We do not suggest that more traditional academic positions should be displaced, but we are confident that our approach is the one best suited to our research agendas. Since it is relatively unfamiliar, we devote a number of paragraphs to explaining what we have done and what we hope to bring to studies of the role of law and lawyers.

We have sought to develop a method of presentation suitable to our research strategy and our potential audiences—and also to explain our choice. This introductory chapter both parallels the larger structure of the book and provides a fairly detailed narrative road map. The chapter's first section provides a brief description of what is generally understood as "international commercial arbitration." The second section turns to the arbitrators themselves, explaining their centrality both to arbitration and to our research strategy. The third section describes the structure and content of the book in relation to the research strategy. We then conclude this chapter with a somewhat more abstract and theoretical presentation of our research strategy. We focus more explicitly on the problem of studying a phenomenon whose boundaries must be part of the object of the study. As we shall emphasize repeatedly, even the subject of international commercial arbitration is the product of a complex process of social construction. The changing role of arbitration in business dispute resolution cannot be understood without examining that process of social construction.

International Commercial Arbitration

This book is not meant to be a technical study of arbitration, but some preliminary observations are necessary to provide the setting (for useful texts, see, e.g., Redfern and Hunter 1991; Craig, Park, and Paulsson 1990; Berger 1993; Mustill and Boyd 1989). When businesses enter into transnational relationships such as contracts for the sale of goods, joint ventures, construction projects, or distributorships, the contract typically calls for private arbitration in the event of any dispute arising out of the contractual arrangement. The main reason given today for this choice is that it allows each party to avoid being forced to submit to the courts of the other. Another is the secrecy of the process.

International arbitration can be "institutional," following the procedural rules of the International Chamber of Commerce in Paris (the ICC, which is the leading institution), the American Arbitration Association (AAA), the London Court of International Arbitration (LCIA), the World Bank's International Center for the Settlement of Investment Disputes (ICSID), or many others; or it can be ad hoc, often following the rules of the United Nations Commission on International Trade Law (UNCITRAL), used also for the arbitrations by the Iran–United States Claims Tribunal in The Hague. Arbitration hearings typically take place on a "neutral site" away from the countries of the disputants; but they may be set virtually any place where hotels and conference rooms can be found.

The arbitrators are private individuals, and usually there are three of them when the cases involve substantial amounts in controversy. The parties typically select one each; and the parties jointly, the arbitrators, or an institutional appointing authority will select the third. And while there are some debates about the role of arbitrators, it is generally agreed that all three should be neutral, even if they play different roles. The arbitrators act as private judges, holding hearings and issuing judgments. There are few grounds for appeal to courts, and the final decision of the arbitrators, under the terms of the widely adopted 1958 New York Convention, is more easily enforced among signatory countries than would be a court judgment. Indeed, the growing acceptance of the 1958 convention is one indicator of the success of this international private justice.

Over the past twenty-five to thirty years, international commercial arbitration has become big legal business, the accepted method for resolving international business disputes (Salacuse 1991).[1] Its success is reflected in the arbitrations of high-profile disputes, such as those arising out of the nationalizations of oil concessions in the 1970s and 1980s (Lillich 1993), huge international construction projects such as the tunnel under the English Channel ("ICC Panel" 1993), and international incidents like the French sinking of the *Rainbow Warrior* on its Greenpeace mission (Chatterjee 1992). Success is also evident in the tremendous growth since the late 1970s in the number of arbitration centers,[2] arbitrators,[3] and arbitrations.[4]

1. As stated matter-of-factly by a leading international practitioner, "in today's world the dispute resolution mechanism will invariably be arbitration" (Aksen 1990, 287).

2. The Parker School, affiliated with Columbia Law School, lists over 120 centers even if, consistent with the conventional account, we eliminate those concerned exclusively with maritime or commodities disputes (Parker School 1992). We know of centers not mentioned in that list as well. Some indicator of the action in new centers and rules is that in the two and one-half years from July 1991 to December 1993, the *World Arbitration and Mediation Report* published articles about at least 7 new international centers (Singapore, Oregon, North Carolina, Sydney, Bahrain, Vietnam, and Denver) and thirteen new or proposed rules or laws for international arbitration cases (Germany, Geneva, Singapore, Russia, Ukraine, Egypt, Tunisia, American Arbitration Association, Russia again, Bermuda, Finland, Algeria, and Italy).

3. One indicator of who the "recognized arbitrators" are is the "list of a thousand" self-identified arbitrators published by the Parker School (Parker School 1992), which they were compelled to double in size after the first edition in 1990.

4. There are no global statistics, nor could there be, since there are no agreed-upon criteria for what should be counted. We can also note that there are quite a number of

International commercial arbitration represents an international dispute resolution device of tremendous practical importance. The workings of international commercial arbitration have a considerable impact on the security of business investments and on the transaction costs of resolving transnational disputes. International commercial arbitration, therefore, should be seen as a key institution in the structuring of international markets (Granovetter and Swedberg 1992; Milgrom, North, and Weingast 1990; North 1990).

The growth of the market *in arbitration* is also evident in the competition that can be seen among different national approaches and centers.[5] Once the International Chamber of Commerce began to gain relatively large numbers of high-profile international commercial arbitrations in the 1970s, a process of competition began, aided by the forum-shopping possibilities of large U.S. multinational law firms able to pick and choose among laws, rules, institutions, and places according to the perceived interests of their clients (on the domestic origins of this legal technique, see Purcell 1992). Within Europe, first England in 1979, then France in 1981, Belgium in 1985, the Netherlands in 1986, and Switzerland in 1989 enacted new statutes to reform their arbitration laws to satisfy the business users of international arbitration; and the United States achieved the same result through Supreme Court action in 1985 (see Carbonneau 1989). This kind of "regulatory competition" (Charny 1991; Trachtman 1993) to gain the business of arbitration has helped promote a form of arbitration detached from the scrutiny and regulation of the national court systems.

---

ad hoc arbitrations—not affiliated with any arbitral institutions—that are not recorded anywhere. The growth of the International Chamber of Commerce docket, however, is probably indicative of the general trend, especially since its market share may be declining with the development of several serious competitors. The ICC had 333 cases in 1991, 337 in 1992, and 352 in 1993 ("ICC Court Reports Increase" 1994). The first three thousand ICC requests for arbitration came between 1923, when the ICC was founded, and July 1976. The next three thousand came in the next eleven years (Craig, Park, and Paulsson 1990, 4). The American Arbitration Association reported about 300 international cases for 1991, although the stakes are smaller in general than the ICC cases; and the London Court of International Commercial Arbitration reported about 30 to 40 (int. 95, 4) (references in this form refer to the number of our interview and the page of our transcript—or notes, if no transcript). There are also some 300 cases pending before the Chinese International Economic and Trade Arbitration Commission (Moser 1993, 41). As noted in the text, however, statistics are very misleading in this field, further distorting a subject that is difficult to capture.

5. "[I]nternational arbitration has become a field of intense competition: competition between arbitral sites; between the arbitral institutions; between counsel; between arbitrators; and even between the periodicals of international arbitration" (Werner 1988, 5; see Berger 1993, 1–6).

The Importance of Arbitrators

The large law firm both with its forum shopping and the general style of legal practice has been a key actor in the construction of an international justice system for commercial transactions. The important role of these law firms as agents of legal internationalization will be seen throughout this work. If we ask the central sociological question of how the legitimacy of this private justice in the service of merchants is maintained (Hunt 1993), however, we must turn our attention to the arbitrators who make the decisions. For students of the legal profession, moreover, the arbitrators represent a fascinating combination of professional achievement and personal reward.

The work of these arbitrators is a rather glamorous and—at least for the large cases—well-paid activity associated with nice places, like Paris or Geneva, and a first-class lifestyle. Only a very select and elite group of individuals is able to serve as international arbitrators. They are purportedly selected for their "virtue"—judgment, neutrality, expertise—yet rewarded as if they are participants in international deal-making. In more sociological terms, the *symbolic capital* acquired through a career of public service or scholarship is translated into a substantial cash value in international arbitration.

Not surprisingly, scholars are not the only persons interested in the somewhat mysterious world of international arbitration. Many lawyers would very much like to get into this line of work. A number of leading U.S. lawyers, for example, especially those who have attained a formal retirement age, have reacted to the subject matter of our research by inquiring how they can enter the world of international commercial arbitration, a world that they often perceive as a rather closed and arcane European club. We have pursued the question of how to get into this world, and our work should be of some use to outsiders who might wish to get in; but our purpose has been mainly to learn what the means of entry reveal about who becomes an arbitrator and how that fits into the international system of private justice.

Both the processes and the outcomes of particular cases and arbitration in general depend on the characteristics of the arbitrators. Unlike official court systems, where public judges are assigned more or less randomly to individual cases and are supposed to operate according to clearly established procedures and substantive laws, arbitration allows the parties to select their judges. As demonstrated by pathbreaking research conducted almost forty years ago by Soia Mentschikoff and Ernest Haggard on domestic arbitration in the United States, the selection is a key decision in winning or losing.[6] The attorneys for

6. They concluded, "Overall, who the arbitrator is in terms of expertise and prior experience is the most important single factor in both the decisional and the consensus

the parties well understand that the "authority" and "expertise" of arbitrators determine their clout within the tribunal. The operation of the market in the selection of arbitrators therefore provides a key to understanding the justice that emerges from the decisions of arbitrators.

The Organization of the Book and Its Relationship to the Research Strategy

Before describing the book and how it relates to the research strategy, it may be useful to describe the source material more generally. After some three years of research, we have conducted almost three hundred interviews, in eleven countries, with the average interview running almost two hours (with both of us present for virtually all of them). The informants have come from twenty-five countries—mainly Europe, the United States, and the Middle East, but also Asia, Latin America, and North Africa. We have interviewed most of the leading members of the international arbitration community and the representatives of the leading institutions, attended two conferences, and scanned the massive literature on this subject. Most of our interviews have been concentrated in Europe and the United States—the places where international commercial arbitration is relatively well established; but we have also visited, inter alia, the sites that are the subjects of part 3. We have not provided any detailed study of places where arbitration is only beginning to gain acceptance, such as Africa or Latin America.

This research began with an effort to learn the major names and institutions in international commercial arbitration. We first interviewed persons whom we had identified through their writings or reputations as experts in this field. We built up a list of names through the technique of snowballing, starting from very different origins—large law firms in New York and Chicago, in-house counsel in New York, American Bar Association committees, well-known Paris arbitrators, journalistic accounts of arbitration, editors of arbitration journals, and administrators of arbitration associations and institutions.

This starting point led to two initial and related discoveries. First, the much heralded competition for arbitration business favored a few institutions and settings. The International Chamber of Commerce was clearly the leading, even dominant, institution (see chap. 3). Second, the same, relatively few, names of arbitrators were repeated over and over on both sides of the Atlantic.

---

processes. *Who* he or she is determines the availability of both substantive and fact finding norms, conditions the procedural and role norms that are held, and raises or lowers the degree of influence in interaction with other arbitrators" (Mentschikoff and Haggard 1977a, 307).

These individuals are not tied to any single institution but rather handle arbitrations under the auspices of multiple institutions or as ad hoc proceedings. We could quite quickly see a senior generation—the "grand old men" of arbitration (which included no women)—and a younger generation of lawyers in their forties (which is characterized by slightly more diversity). And it was clear that this international arbitration community was relatively small and linked together pretty closely. Members of the inner circle and outsiders often referred to this group as a "mafia" or a "club."[7]

Our research gradually moved out from the inner core of this international commercial arbitration community. We have sought to map the main capitals of the international commercial arbitration world, but we have also sought to use the leads that have come from the interviews to move from the centers of arbitration to a variety of other sites and to issues that are necessary to situate arbitration in a broader perspective. As suggested below, we have tried to organize this book to reflect the process of gathering and examining the data.

Part 1 of this book, containing this chapter and the following one, reflects our point of entry and seeks to introduce the relatively small world of international commercial arbitration. Chapter 2 thus introduces the careers of arbitrators, showing what characteristics make them suitable for selection as arbitrators. We assess the symbolic capital that gives them particular value in the market for private judges of international business disputes.

Part 2 turns from the people to the process of construction of international private justice. It also begins with the most familiar and accessible, focusing on the role of a key institution, the International Chamber of Commerce in Paris, and exploring how "generational warfare" between the grand old men and the younger "arbitration technocrats"—aided by the U.S. multinational law firms—transformed an informal justice centered on the European grand professors into a U.S.-style "offshore litigation" (chap. 3). We see from a perspective internal to international commercial arbitration how the center of gravity—and the relative values of symbolic capital—changed substantially over a period of about two decades.

---

7. In the words of a well-informed New York partner, "The more you see of international arbitration, the more you know the people who are involved, and they tend to be repetitively involved" (int. 47, 9). Another expert noted that "especially in the ICC, it's a club of friends [with the] same names coming up all the time" (int. 6, 18). According to another insider, "It is a club. They nominate one another. And sometimes you're counsel, and sometimes you're arbitrator" (int. 50, 8). Another very successful arbitrator put it even more strongly: "It's a mafia because people appoint one another. You always appoint your friends—people you know" (int. 85, 27).

The reshuffling of hierarchies and alliances played out in institutional palace wars is only a part of the story of the construction of transnational private justice. The internal story must be related to economic and political transformations that can be seen as outside of the international commercial arbitration world.[8] The construction and transformation of international private justice can be traced through the large oil arbitrations and the mega–construction disputes that followed the huge petrodollar projects of the 1970s and 1980s (chap. 4). These north-south disputes, which have at times assumed almost mythic proportions, in many respects provided the raw material and resources necessary to build a transnational law—*lex mercatoria*—and a private justice that could purport to be universal, applicable to business disputes around the world. They set in motion the transformations that we traced within the field of international commercial arbitration.

We conclude part 2 by looking at the trilateral arrangement, involving U.S. law firms and litigators, European arbitrators and their learned law, and third-world governments, through an extended case study (chap. 5). The case study provides a concrete example of the simultaneous and interrelated impacts of developments described in the preceding two chapters. The chapter also shows that the large-law-firm litigators who played such a key role are themselves not a static phenomenon. The corporate litigator seen especially in the 1970s and 1980s is a recent development rooted both in the specific history of the United States and in international factors.

The chapters in part 3 explore specific outposts for international commercial arbitration. England (chap. 7), the United States (chap. 8), and Sweden (chap. 9) are obvious sites, given that the London Court of International Arbitration, the American Arbitration Association, and the Stockholm Chamber of Commerce are always named as leading competitors of the ICC. Egypt (chap. 11), while less obvious, has a well-known Cairo arbitration center, a long legal tradition, and a number of the major arbitrators from the south. Hong Kong (chap. 12), finally, combines an ambitious arbitration center with an entry into the question of the role of China and "Asian methods" of business disputing.

These chapters focus on national developments, but they are essential to our study of internationalization. The international developments in part 2 are inseparable from the national developments in part 3. International com-

8. The terms *internal* and *external* are somewhat artificial, since the external developments in politics and economics may very well be constituted in legal terms or in relation to legal constructions. Nevertheless, it makes sense to distinguish internal developments from occurrences that in a general sense are outside of the field of international commercial arbitration, such as decolonization and the oil crisis.

mercial arbitration is a way to see how internationalization disrupts and transforms the boundaries and hierarchies evident on the national legal scene—and
therefore reconstructs the markets in business disputing and in legitimate
authority. The landscape of business disputing is transformed in each country,
but the resulting scenes depend on specific local features. These transformations take place, we emphasize, whether or not an individual country is successful in gaining a large market share for international commercial arbitration. Our primary interest is in the process, not who is winning the arbitration
competition.

It is interesting to see the differences and similarities as we move out of
the Western world to the Arab world and to Asia—moving from places where
law is thoroughly institutionalized to places where the role of law is itself a
key aspect of the story. We can see increasingly that the politics of law—and
the relationship of law to families, political parties, and bureaucracies—is
heavily implicated in the story of arbitration, which is itself a key part of the
story of the internationalization of legal practice. As we move away from the
established core of international commercial arbitration, our chapters accordingly reach out more explicitly to broader questions of the role of law and
lawyers. Most obviously, the chapter on Hong Kong and China must confront
the question of the role of law in Hong Kong after 1997, when Hong Kong
returns formally to China.

Part 3 also contains three more abstract and theoretical chapters. The first
introduces part 3 (chap. 6) and the general theme of the continuing transformation of business justice in national settings—sometimes pulled toward law,
other times toward business. It highlights the very close connections between
international commercial arbitration and domestic arbitration and indeed domestic legal systems.

After the three chapters on Western, developed legal systems, we outline
(chap. 10) two models for the handling of business disputes through law—
delegated justice, as seen especially in England, and *parallel justice,* exemplified by Sweden. We also raise the intriguing question—at the same time national and international—of why Paris became the national site for the development and institutionalization of international commercial arbitration. This
question requires a closer look at parallel justice, leading to further explorations of legal education and the role of law-educated individuals in the fragmented and compartmentalized parallel justice found in Paris (and, with variations elsewhere).

The final chapter in part 3 (chap. 13) then turns to the question of the role
of international commercial arbitration in the "periphery," exemplified by

Egypt and Hong Kong. We focus on lawyers' roles as "double agents," signified
by such terms as *comprador* and *courtier*. And we explore the role of patron-
client relations in the unequal network of personal relations essential to international commercial arbitration. We can see how lawyers through these networks gain distance from their local legal environments. The role of large law
firms in transforming legal fields on the periphery is also addressed. The firms
tend to replicate in the periphery what also happened in Paris—attacking a
local and fragmented justice, and promoting a more universal (and more
profitable for them) business justice.

The concluding chapter (chap. 14) explores a question that is not asked
systematically elsewhere in the text—what is the future of the world of international commercial arbitration? The question may seem out of place, since
the ICC has in effect defined the model for international business disputing
and that model is flourishing in a growing number of places around the world.
Indeed, most of the analysis in the book serves to explain why the world of
the ICC dominates its potential competition. Nevertheless, we suggest that
we may be entering a new era, characterized by more involvement of states
in business competition and prefigured by complex bi- and multilateral trade
arrangements such as GATT (General Agreement on Tariffs and Trade) and
NAFTA (North American Free Trade Agreement). The specific features that
have allowed international commercial arbitration to develop and thrive by
avoiding the state, we suggest, may also render it incapable of adapting effectively to a new and very different regime in business disputes.

The order and style of the chapters, as we suggested above, reflect closely
our research approach. We have not imposed a rigid framework either on the
material or on the reader. In particular, it is essential to our approach to *avoid*
a strict definition of the research domain. If, for example, we had started with
a narrow definition of international commercial arbitration as the subject of
the study, seeing it, for example, only as a set of established institutions and
players who "go by that name," we might have gained in precision. But we
would have missed the way in which those established players and institutions
gained the ability to define and institutionalize this particular type of international arbitration. We also would have missed the way arbitration—in both
national and international settings—reveals the shifting and unstable relationship between business and law—and the role of the legal profession in defining
and shifting that relationship. From a different perspective, if we had started
only with a very broad research domain—like, for example, the general relationship between business and law—we would have remained at a far too
general level. It would have been difficult to know how to get beyond some

kind of superficial opinion poll. We use the general domain of international commercial arbitration to get into questions of law and business and internationalization.

As a point of entry, international commercial arbitration provides a means for uncovering the different landscapes of business disputing and how they are being transformed—sometimes to a great extent, sometimes not very much—in relation to internationalization. Since we have used arbitration as a point of entry, our research has necessarily been cumulative, and we have tried to preserve this aspect in our presentation. Readers can see how we have constructed a representation from the self-representations produced by the actors in the field of international commercial arbitration.

The same approach and goal characterizes our more theoretical interpretations and hypotheses about international commercial arbitration in particular and business disputing more generally. The theoretical chapters are not written to be the last word, the final truth that emerges out of descriptive chapters organized and written to underscore the validity of the last word. We think we would mislead our readers—including those with general theoretical interests—if we were to force all the narrative material into such a limited framework.

Certainly there are trade-offs in any research strategy, but we are convinced that much can be gained through a research method—and a line of exposition faithful to that method—that begins with centrally placed individuals and moves outward, combining micro- and macrolevel analyses, individuals and institutions, narratives and structures. Our multileveled approach may appear to give an unfinished quality to the book, and there may be some repetition, but it is important to show the numerous structural links characteristic of a reality where things happen precisely because of a number of connections and factors.[9]

To borrow from the authority of the field of art, we note that, despite initial academic controversies over the works of the impressionists, we now recognize in art that a finished work—in the sense of a completed representation of reality—is not necessarily the one that removes all the messy juxtapositions and color combinations. With respect to the changing landscapes of business disputing, we hope that our own representations—of the world of law, business, the state, and even globalization—will give readers a fresh (and

9. We thus see that U.S.-style large-law-firm litigation appears almost at the same time as a result of international developments, as a major international contributor to the changes in the ICC and in national legal fields, and as a target of the ADR movement produced from the success of international commercial arbitration.

hopefully even "truer") perspective than might a tidier and more linear representation.

Research Strategy: How to Study Law and Other Symbolic Phenomena

We conclude this introduction with a more general section about our research strategy. Despite the networks, relationships, and institutions that can be found around the topic of international commercial arbitration, it is important to recognize that there is no objective thing called "international commercial arbitration." More importantly from a social scientific perspective, we must study the question of boundaries in order to see how a given domain—in this case, transnational business relationships—is regulated and how institutions develop and change. The problem is a general one in the study of topics that exist only symbolically, such as law, the legal profession, or the state (Bourdieu and Wacquant 1992, 240–47); but the problem is especially apparent with topics that are relatively new and weakly embodied in institutionalized forms. As Bourdieu observes, a term like *profession* is "the *social product* of a historical work of construction of a group and of a *representation* of groups that has surreptitiously slipped into the science of this very group" (243).

It is important in social research, therefore, not to reproduce uncritically the discourse of those who proclaim that transnational business disputing or international commercial arbitration *by definition* refers to the particular representation that supports their position. Success in international commercial arbitration, indeed, comes in part by persuading others that the position of particular groups and individuals *does* represent international commercial arbitration. There is therefore an incentive—not unusual in law or, for that matter, in any marketing exercise—to try to "make it by faking it," exaggerating the experience of individuals and institutions in order to allow them to gain acceptance because of their success. Contests about definitions and details of practice, in short, must be part of the object of study. Otherwise, scholarly efforts tend too easily to become entries on behalf of one or another competitors seeking acceptance as legitimate.

We use the analytical tool of a legal field, or, more particularly for international arbitration, an international legal field. While not without its own problems, we believe that the use of Bourdieu's tool of the *field* is the approach best suited for this particular object of study. This approach has affinities with the "new institutionalism" in sociology (e.g., Powell and DiMaggio 1991), with network analyses of economic and social relations (Nohria and Eccles 1992), and with recent scholarship in political science identifying and studying international "epistemic communities" (Haas 1992) or "transnational issue networks" (Keck and Sikkink 1994). These approaches tackle the similar issue of how an object such as international commercial arbitration (or the international environmental and human-rights movements) emerges and changes. So far, however, these scholars have paid little attention to the role of law and lawyers. More importantly, perhaps, they have also tended to downplay the conflict and competition that the notion of field makes evident. International commercial arbitration, we find, is partly an epistemic community or issue network organized around certain beliefs in an ideal of international private justice, but it is also an extremely competitive market involving big business and megalawyering. To understand it requires an understanding of both the ideals *and* the competition for business (Gordon 1984).

By national or international legal field, we refer to a symbolic terrain with its own networks, hierarchical relationships, and expertise, and more generally its own rules of the game, all of which are subject to modification over time and in relation to other fields (Bourdieu and Wacquant 1992, 94–100). While a researcher inevitably constructs the object of study by imposing some boundaries, the concept of field is sufficiently open and sufficiently systematic to facilitate the exploration of what Bourdieu terms "relatively autonomous social microcosms, i.e., spaces of objective relations that are the site of a logic and a necessity that are *specific and irreducible* to those that regulate other fields" (Bourdieu and Wacquant 1992, 97). The Bourdieu model also recognizes the role of conflict. Within a field, "agents and institutions constantly struggle, according to the regularities and rules constitutive of this space of play (and, in given conjunctures, over those rules themselves . . .)" (Bourdieu and Wacquant 1992, 102).

A legal field is not the same as a legal order. One purpose of referring to a legal field is, in fact, to avoid confusing it with the institutions that are found in existence at any given time and place. As Bourdieu observed in "The Force of Law," it is necessary to underline the difference between the institutions of a field (such as the ICC or the *lex mercatoria* examined in this book), and the "social space" in which these institutions are created, rendered obsolete, or reinvented. In Bourdieu's terms, "a symbolical order of norms and doctrines [i.e., the institutions of the legal field] . . . does not contain within itself the principles of its own dynamic . . . whereas the [legal or] juridical field itself contains the principles of its own transformation in struggles" (Bourdieu 1987, 816).

This observation explains why the point of departure of our research is individuals and their relationships, rather than institutions. We start with individuals to better understand institutions—to show how institutions impose themselves on actors while the institutions themselves are also the product of the actors' continuing struggles. Institutions have no reality other than the strategic use that is made of them by different social groups. Our approach, therefore, is concerned more with the social space or structure of positions than what might be seen as a more institutional vision, and for this reason it differs both from the classic approach of lawyers and from most law-and-society research.

The unfamiliarity of the approach risks some confusion. When we speak in terms of positions, we may be read—and criticized—as if we are speaking in terms of institutions. It is necessary to keep in mind, for example, that there can be an international legal field—a space for positions and struggles—without there necessarily being an international legal order—sets of established international institutions.

Our interviews were used to construct a map of the field of international commercial arbitration. In part the map is a matter of learning the networks and relationships organized around international commercial arbitration. As we have already noted, it is surprising how easy it was to identify the major players around the world on the basis of their reputations and contacts. Lengthy and semistructured interviews, in addition, are critical to an understanding of the structure of the field. They reveal, in particular, the social capital and personal trajectories of individuals in the field, that is to say, what they bring concretely to international arbitration, as well as the principles and ideas underlying the field in the minds and strategies of the people who operate in and around it. Not surprisingly, respondents tend to use us to present their own pictures of this legal field, but we encourage it. It serves to identify what they seek to appear to be and what they reject, thereby serving to define the principles of opposition that structure the field and shape change over time.

Our concern is to identify the ways in which internationalization, and in particular international commercial arbitration, reveals and contributes to the reorganization and reshuffling of hierarchies of positions, modes of legitimate authority, and structures of power. The story therefore should not be read as one of total winners and losers in a contest to become a leading arbitrator or a leading arbitration institution. Relative losers on the periphery of the world of international commercial arbitration may still be affected powerfully by the activities around commercial arbitration. Nor is this a simple story of business turning away from law to a form of business justice for international transactions. Rather, as suggested above, our research approach is built on the necessity not only to question conventional categories—winners and losers, law and economy, law and politics, litigation and arbitration, core and periphery—but also to see the contests about definitions and categories as part of the object of study.

2

Becoming an Arbitrator: Building and Exchanging National and International Symbolic Capital

This chapter will serve primarily to introduce a selection of arbitrators. Since the arbitrators are the key actors in the field of arbitration, one reason to introduce them is simply to provide examples of who these people are. Second, an examination of the careers of successful and somewhat less successful arbitrators allows us to develop the concept of symbolic capital that we use throughout this study. The arbitrators selected for this chapter exemplify the major forms of symbolic capital that we see in the field of international commercial arbitration. As we shall see in chapter 3, the symbolic capital allows us to decode the competition between arbitrators—even those more or less solidly entrenched in the arbitration "club."

Indeed, international lawyers in the field of international commercial arbitration must constantly evaluate the stature and authority of potential arbitrators who come from different legal traditions and backgrounds. They must see who will have clout with other arbitrators and with the parties who must obey the decision. Lawyers trying to select arbitrators must therefore determine who from France is equivalent to a retired justice of the House of Lords, or who in Sweden is equivalent to an elite professor of contracts and commercial law from the United States. What this means is that arbitration must create a market in symbolic capital—the social class, education, career, and expertise that is contained within a person.

The key to symbolic capital is "recognized power" (Bourdieu 1991, 72). In Bourdieu's words, "the weight of different agents depends on their symbolic capital, i.e. on the *recognition*, institutionalized or not, that they receive from a group." Educational degrees and formal positions in the legal, economic, or political system have a certain value as capital, depending upon the purpose and audience for which they are assessed. Particular experiences, expertises, and connections likewise have a capital value to the extent that they are recognized as having such a value.[1]

1. Or as Bourdieu says, the symbolic capital has power to the extent that "categories of perception . . . misrepresent the arbitrariness of its possession and accumulation" (Bourdieu and Wacquant 1992, 119).

The values of specific forms of symbolic capital and their market equivalences, we should note, are not necessarily stable. Different kinds of symbolic capital may gain or lose in value over time. Indeed, as we shall see, change within the field of international commercial arbitration can be examined through contests about the value of various forms of symbolic capital—academic standing, scholarly publication, particular kinds of practical experience, training in alternative dispute resolution, connections to business, connections to political power, particular language skills, proficiency in technical aspects of arbitration practice. Most of the remaining parts of this chapter will describe individuals who have "made it"—which is always a relative status—into the arbitration world. It will be apparent that there are alternative routes and that the routes themselves will help to decode the contests that take place about the relative value of particular approaches and attributes.[2]

It is also important to note that, since the values of capital change over time, the strongest position in law and elsewhere is to hold a diversified portfolio. The retired judge with solid academic credentials and an of-counsel relationship with an international law firm, for example, can satisfy the requirements of a number of existing arbitration constituencies and be ready to adjust, or even profit from, changes in the relative value of the assets in the portfolio.

Finally, it is characteristic of the legal field generally that substantial value is typically assigned to those who reinforce the universal claims of law. Recognized high status within the legal field is given to those who help to build the universality that is essential to the legitimacy of law. We can see this easily within the field of arbitration, but it is also a phenomenon that comports more generally with law.

We can start this inquiry with Pierre Lalive, a Swiss professor and lawyer, who occupies a key place in the history of international commercial arbitration in the 1970s and 1980s (and beyond). Everyone with a rudimentary knowledge about international commercial arbitration knows his name,[3] and most have met him at one time or another (or will say that they have). While

2. The centrality and difficulty of studying symbolic capital is described by Bourdieu and Wacquant as follows: "People are at once founded and legitimized to enter the field by their possessing a definite configuration of properties. One of the goals of research is to identify these active properties, these efficient characteristics, that is, these forms of *specific capital*. There is thus a sort of hermeneutic circle: in order to construct the field, one must identify the forms of specific capital that operate within it, and to construct the forms of symbolic capital one must know the specific logic of the field. There is an endless to and fro movement in the research process that is quite lengthy and arduous" (Bourdieu and Wacquant 1992, 108).

3. Most recently, his prowess and his 4,697,258 pounds sterling fee for the Westland arbitration was the subject of a cover story in *Legal Business* (Edwards 1994a).

nothing about his energy or intellect suggests that he is old, he belongs to the generation of the "grand old men" of arbitration. His résumé gives some indication of his stature at the top of the field. Indeed, it is worth looking at in some detail because it *defines* stature in arbitration.

He is the president of the ICC's Institute of International Business Law and Practice, which organizes the best-known colloquia of arbitrators, and he is a member of the London Court of International Arbitration. He was the president of the Swiss Arbitration Association until 1990. He is also a member of the elite International Council for Commercial Arbitration (ICCA) and the Milan "Club of Arbitrators." He has lectured to the Hague Academy of International Law and is a member of the Institute of International Law—the most prestigious organization of international law scholars. He was a professor at the law school in Geneva until he retired in 1986, and he has served as visiting professor at Columbia University, Cambridge University, and the University of Brussels. He has written numerous books and articles.

A quite notable accomplishment in the field of arbitration is the fact that he chaired the first "annulment proceeding" of an ICSID arbitration, and the result was that his panel overruled the decision of the original tribunal (*Klochner-Industrie-Anlagen v. Republic of Cameroon*, 1985). Finally, with his older brother Jean-Flavien Lalive, another of the top senior arbitrators, he is a partner in the leading Swiss arbitration law firm. The portfolio of symbolic capital therefore covers the national and the transnational, pure international law and practical business law, practice and academia, all added to a good family pedigree.

The career path of Professor Lalive prepared him for arbitration but could as easily have led to distinction in other areas. He began with a cosmopolitan education in Geneva and subsequently at Cambridge University, where he graduated in 1950 with a dissertation on the subject of "private international law." He practiced law beginning in 1951 and became a law professor at the University of Geneva in 1955. He first became involved with international arbitration at that time when he served as *greffier*—a kind of law clerk, also called secretary—in one of the relatively few arbitrations of the time, the Buraimi matter between Saudi Arabia and the United Kingdom. He also served as an expert in a matter before the World Court, and then he served as the secretary-general from 1955 to 1958 in the famous Aramco oil arbitration, which concerned Aramco and Saudi Arabia. By the mid-1960s he had enough academic prominence to gain admission to the prestigious Institute of International Law as an associate, and his expertise in a famous oil arbitration helped also to cause him to be invited to give a Hague lecture to the Academy of International Law in 1967 on the subject of commercial arbitration.

It is important to see that even a résumé that focuses on arbitration shows that it was an "add-on" to a career already made in international law and in a successful legal practice. The cosmopolitan symbolic capital represented by Professor Lalive—including the apprenticeships in major international arbitrations—made him able to move easily into any national or international field that required the services of legal professionals. And it would be natural for him to be one of the persons thought of as a potential leader in such matters. He could enter at the top because his presence would lend prestige to whatever organization or activity he elected to enter. The growth of arbitration in the 1970s and 1980s pulled him increasingly into arbitration, but he could as easily have moved into other areas. All this does not mean that his success in arbitration did not also come from talent and hard work, but the point here is to observe the career pattern and the capital brought to international commercial arbitration and further accumulated there.

An insightful partner in a New York law firm observed, "You've got to have a platform," such as an academic position or a partnership in a "significant law firm," or "you can't get into the game" (int. 38, 22). From another perspective, "You have to be one of the people who would be thought of as people to do that" (id., 23). The platforms can be very different, but the generation of the grand old men tended to develop their platforms outside of arbitration and then enter the field at a very high level.[4] Professor Lalive became mainly an arbitration specialist, in part because of the importance of Switzerland as a neutral site, but his kind of portfolio is characteristic of similar individuals who remained "distinguished amateurs" in commercial arbitration.[5]

Judge Gunner Lagergren from Sweden provides an example of a very well known arbitrator whose other activities remained central to his career. Like Lalive, he comes from a good family pedigree, and indeed he is married to one of the Wallenbergs. After graduation from the University of Stockholm in the late 1930s, he began a career in the judiciary. The International Chamber of Commerce at that time was connected very closely to Sweden. In fact, during World War II, the ICC was moved temporarily from Paris to Stockholm. Work-

4. As a relatively young arbitrator noted, "In the old days, . . . people thought you were the kind of person whose judgment . . . I respect you and you respect him. So let's . . . ask him to be our arbitrator" (int. 82, 10).

5. The contest between amateurs and experts is addressed in chapter 3. One prominent member of the newer generation of experts in arbitration states, "I think it's bad for international arbitration for people to approach it in an amateurish way. . . . There are far too many people who consider that becoming an arbitrator is part of the things that happen to you when you become a senior respected lawyer in your community. And no particular preparation or rethinking is required at that stage. That I think is unfortunate because it's a difficult thing to do to be an arbitrator" (int. 132, 36).

ing in Paris after the war, Judge Lagergren served as a secretary to an arbitration tribunal as a young judge, and he began to serve as arbitrator in ICC cases as early as 1949. He became president of the Commission on International Commercial Practice of the ICC in 1951 and served to 1967. In the meantime, he served in various public-law capacities, such as member of the International Court at Tangier, 1953–56, and as the neutral member of the French-German Arbitration Court in Saarbrucken, 1957–72. He became the arbitrator in several notable boundary disputes between states, culminating in the Taba case between Egypt and Israel in the late 1980s.

Judge Lagergren occupied several of the most important positions in the development of international commercial arbitration, including sole arbitrator of the British Petroleum-Libya Concession Tribunal in the early 1970s, one of the arbitrators in the first ICSID case, and president of the Iran–United States Claims Tribunal from 1981 to 1984. At the same time, however, he probably never devoted more than a fraction of his time to commercial arbitration. He continued to be a judge, serving as president of the Court of Appeal for Western Sweden, 1966–77, and he took on other positions, most notably perhaps as a judge of the European Court of Human Rights in Strasbourg from 1977 to 1988. Commercial arbitration—with the exception of perhaps the BP-Libya case—has occupied a secondary position in his activities in the field of law.

Judge Lagergren's career is that of the distinguished gentleman lawyer to whom governments and businesses will entrust their very complex and politically controversial disputes. His stature—the symbolic capital of a leading international public arbitrator and cosmopolitan Swedish judge—enabled him to drop in and out of commercial arbitration as he chose.

The career pattern of William D. Rogers, a partner in the Washington, D.C., law firm of Arnold and Porter, provides a U.S. version of this blue-chip "amateur" who can drop in or out of arbitration. His credentials include Princeton, Yale Law School, and a Supreme Court clerkship, a substantial number of appointments for the government, including undersecretary of state for Economic Affairs, and special emissary for President Carter to El Salvador. He has taught at Cambridge University, served as president of the American Society of International Law, and published many articles and at least one book. He now serves also as vice-chairman of Kissinger Associates, Inc., the consulting firm of Henry Kissinger. Like Judge Lagergren, he has not invested much of his own time in building capital and relationships within the arbitration community. From his position of eminence as a cosmopolitan U.S. lawyer with ties to government and business, he is in demand as an arbitrator. His service as arbitrator reinforces his prestige and authority and allows him to deploy his services in whatever is the most high-profile, significant international matter of the moment.

The careers of these notable individuals recall accounts of the medieval church. The son of a nobleman could become a bishop of the church simply because of family background and social prominence. Others would shave their heads, take vows of celibacy, devote everything to the church, and yet have no chance to rise to a position of eminence, such as bishop. Their hard work would help maintain the institutional structure that made the position of bishop attractive to the son of a nobleman, but they lacked the social platform to gain the top position.

There is a similar phenomenon in arbitration. Without a suitable platform, defined now as more than social class (which is nevertheless useful), the arbitration devotee can never get selected as an arbitrator. There are individuals who, for example, teach at low-prestige schools, work in unknown law firms, or produce scholarship that is deemed to be too marginal, who cannot gain access to this world no matter how much they write, attend conferences, or in general profess the faith. Others need not even profess the faith or write about arbitration to enter the field more or less at the top. One of those who fits the profiles of those just described stated simply, it is "not that hard to get into the club" (int. 22, 3).

It is not a coincidence that these *kinds* of people move into arbitration, but it often appears to be a coincidence that a particular individual with such credentials becomes an arbitrator. The first arbitration may result from a friendship or connection that has no relationship to arbitration, or it may relate to a particular case or kind of legal practice. A prominent London solicitor thus stated, "I started roughly twenty years ago" with an ICC case in Geneva: "The chairman of the tribunal was Claude Reymond, who has now become a firm friend. Our opponent was Pierre Lalive, who's also become a firm friend. Michael Mustill . . . [now Lord Mustill of the House of Lords] was one of the other arbitrators. And it was quite a good introduction . . . to the mafia" (int. 85, 1). And now that this lawyer has "gray in the hair," he said, he is "getting appointments" as arbitrator at an increasing rate. The coincidence of a good arbitration case early in a legal career helped ensure that, when this lawyer reached a certain age and stature, the community would seek him out to serve as arbitrator.

The career of Jan Paulsson, a partner in Freshfields in Paris and one of the leaders of the emerging generation, illustrates a different track than that of the grand old men. In contrast to the strong national platforms that established the basis for the international careers of individuals like Lagergren or Lalive,

Jan Paulsson's career is the essence of transnationalism. He was born in Swe-den; grew up primarily in Liberia, where his parents were missionaries; and went to Harvard College and Yale Law School. Now an American citizen, he is a partner and chair of the litigation department with Freshfields, a British firm of solicitors, in their Paris office.

Paulsson's career so far is that of the arbitration specialist ("Profile of Arbi-trator, Jan Paulsson" 1992), beginning with work as a new associate for Coudert Brothers in 1975 on one of the Libyan oil nationalization cases. It is fair to say that, currently, he is the closest equivalent in his generation to Pierre Lalive of the older generation. As counsel, he has represented parties in seven ICSID cases—many more than any other lawyer. He has coauthored the leading book on International Chamber of Commerce arbitration (Craig, Park, and Paulsson 1990), published countless articles in English and French, is the general editor of *Arbitration International*, and a vice president of the London Court of International Arbitration. He is also a member of the Interna-tional Olympic Committee's Arbitral Committee for Sports. He is very visible at the leading conferences on international commercial arbitration, usually as one of the featured speakers. He thus has excellent connections to the major institutions and journals, a strong base in practice as arbitrator and lawyer, and the capital that comes from major publications.

The symbolic capital of a member of Jan Paulsson's generation, in contrast to the older generation, comes almost entirely from activities in the field of international commercial arbitration. There is no link to public international law, government, or even any particular national legal tradition (except through education). He is a specialist in a field of law, and he is an internation-alist. His portfolio is well diversified within arbitration but so far is mainly limited to arbitration. Paulsson, still in his midforties, "arrived" in interna-tional commercial arbitration at an age when most of the members of the older generation of arbitrators—the grand old men—had hardly even turned to it. Paulsson is an expert who has grown up with arbitration. Like other members of his generation, including perhaps most notably, Albert Jan van den Berg, the editor of the *Yearbook on Commercial Arbitration* and a lawyer/professor in the Netherlands, his capital is based above all on his arbitration know-how.

The same is true of the growing number of individuals who enter the field of arbitration through connections with the major institutions, especially the ICC. One leading example is Yves Derains, a very active Parisian arbitrator with a boutique arbitration law firm. He began his legal career in 1971 in the legal department of the ICC, and through a series of promotions became the secretary-general of the ICC Court of Arbitration and director of the legal department of the ICC in the late 1970s. He has been practicing law as an arbitration specialist since 1982, has published numerous articles and books, and is listed on almost every arbitration panel imaginable around the world.[6] He also is at the core of the ICC and the world of arbitration, but his base again was expertise in the field of international commercial arbitration.

The relatively few well-known arbitrators from third-world countries, such as Professor Ahmed El-Kosheri from Cairo; Judge Mohammed Bedjaoui, the Algerian judge on the World Court; Judge Khaled Kadiki of the Supreme Court of Libya; and former judge of the World Court Eduardo Jiminez de Arechaga, from Uruguay, have profiles very much like those of the "grand old men"—with one crucial difference, discussed below.

Judge Bedjaoui, for example, has a cosmopolitan education with a French doctorate and experience practicing law in France. His career includes dean of the Faculty of Law at the University of Algiers, minister of justice, and permanent representative of Algeria to UNESCO. He has published countless articles in the field of international law, including many in the 1970s calling for a New International Economic Order more sensitive to the needs of third-world countries, has lectured in the Hague Academy in 1970 and 1976, and is a member of the Institute of International Law. He has very high status in Algeria and in the field of international law generally, culminating in his appointment to the World Court. His national career, as noted before, resembles that of the grand old men. The difference is that an arbitrator from the third world must find a way to gain access to and credibility with the center. National stature is probably not enough without close connections to Paris, London, or elsewhere in the legal center. Indeed, one of the characteristics of the successful third-world arbitrators is that they get pulled to the center, spending much of their time residing in places like Paris.

There is another kind of platform available for a new generation of individuals in the international commercial arbitration community from third-world

6. According to the Parker School guide to arbitrators (Parker School 1992) and the recent profiles of members of the Swiss Arbitration Association (Swiss Arbitration Association 1994), he is on the editorial board of *Arbitration International* and the *Revue de l'Arbitrage*, is a member of several prestigious organizations—ICCA, the Club of Arbitrators, the ICC Commission on International Arbitration, and the ICC Institute of International Business Law—and is listed on the following panels or groups of arbitrators: AAA, ICC, French National Committee, Regional Center for Arbitration at Kuala Lumpur, Cairo Regional Center for International Commercial Arbitration, the Indian Council of Arbitration, the British Columbia International Commercial Arbitration Center, the Vienna Arbitration Center, the Greek Arbitration Association, the Hong Kong International Arbitration Center, and the Polish Chamber of Commerce Arbitration Court.

countries. The best example perhaps is Ibrahim Shihata, since 1983 the vice president and general counsel of the World Bank and the secretary-general of the World Bank's International Center for the Settlement of Investment Disputes. He also is the editor of *ICSID Review*. He has done much from his position to legitimate and promote arbitration as a means of encouraging investment in third-world countries. Dr. Shihata is Egyptian, a graduate with three degrees from Cairo University Law School and an S.J.D. degree in 1964 from Harvard Law School. Unlike Judge Bedjaoui, however, he has made his career through the opportunities available outside of his home country. He served therefore as director-general of the Vienna-based OPEC Fund for International Development (1973–83) before coming to the World Bank. Focusing on third-world concerns for economic development, his voluminous writings—recognized by his election to membership in the Institute of International Law—have consistently taken what might be termed a "realist" third-world perspective. Thus in the 1960s and 1970s, when third worldism was enjoying its greatest influence in the United Nations and elsewhere, he was a strong proponent of the concerns of a New International Economic Order, while recently he has defended the role of the World Bank while working to provide recognition in the investing world of the interests and needs of the host countries. Dr. Shihata's role in arbitration continues to be important, but his focus remains on a broader concern in which arbitration is a part: economic development and, above all, the role of law in economic development.

Another U.S. profile that merits attention is what might be called the specialist in alternative dispute resolution (ADR). We can see this profile in the career of Joseph Morris, a lawyer and former federal judge whose career in dispute resolution has taken off recently in the United States. He began his career as a lawyer in the oil industry in the 1950s, working for Shell and then as general counsel for Amerada Petroleum Corporation. Reflecting the growing importance of the oil industry in the 1960s and 1970s, especially in states like Oklahoma and Texas, and building on the academic capital established by Judge Morris's ability to write and publish while a practitioner, he became dean of the University of Tulsa School of Law and soon thereafter a federal district court judge for the Eastern District of Oklahoma.

His reputation as a judge and his connections with the oil industry led Shell to invite him to serve as general counsel. He resigned from the bench and served in that position from 1978 to 1984. He also gained stature through connections to the Southwestern Legal Foundation, an institution closely tied to the oil industry and linked also to the international world of arbitration, and to the American Bar Association, where he chaired the section on natural-

resources law. As a retired judge with important experience as in-house counsel, he became closely connected to the Center for Public Resources (CPR),
which has been the U.S. forum for in-house counsel to promote alternatives
to litigation. He starred as the judge in the first minitrial promotional video
of CPR, and he is on CPR's National Panel of Distinguished Neutrals, as
well as the American Arbitration Association's Large, Complex Case Panel of
Arbitrators.

After his retirement in 1984 at a relatively young age through Shell's mandatory retirement program, he began to be asked to serve as an arbitrator in
petroleum-related cases. For many reasons, the symbolic capital he possesses
for national dispute resolution has grown dramatically and his portfolio of
cases diversified. The reputation in alternative dispute resolution and CPR
both became much more important in the United States in the decade of the
1980s. When these factors are added to the stature brought from the law school
deanship, a number of publications, close connections to oil, and especially
from retirement as a federal judge, it is easy to see why he has become very
much in demand for arbitration and for alternative dispute resolution.

Stature in the United States has also led to appointments in several transnational cases, including cases administered by the ICC, and the increasing international value of ADR is evident from the fact that he taught ADR at the
International Development Law Institute (founded and chaired by Ibrahim
Shihata) in Rome in 1991. Judge Morris was mentioned to us frequently by
U.S. lawyers whom we asked to name leading arbitrators and activists in
dispute resolution, including the leading members of the international-
arbitration community in New York.

It is fair to say, however, that Judge Morris's platform has not yet made
him a key player in international commercial arbitration. The expertise in
alternative dispute resolution, the links to the in-house counsel movement,
and the particular link to CPR, we would suggest, have at present much more
recognized value within the United States than in Paris, the home of the ICC
and still the center of international commercial arbitration.

One other profile gives the situation of someone who is seeking to gain
recognition as an arbitrator but has not been successful. Here we shall not use
the name and shall use interview data to supplement the curriculum vita. The
individual is Swiss and practices law in Zurich. He is midforties in age, has
an American L.L.M., and comes from a distinguished legal family. Prior to
studying in the United States, he became acquainted with international commercial arbitration by serving as a secretary for an arbitration. After a series
of legal positions with a multinational company, he set up his own practice

in Zurich as part of a small law firm. He stated that, after he set up his own practice, he joined the Swiss Arbitration Association and approached the ICC in Paris.

"I liked arbitration. . . . And they started giving me little cases where I was working as a sole arbitrator in small cases which it was financially absolutely not rewarding. . . . It was a lot, a lot of work . . . [for] lots of honors. . . . I went to arbitration seminars of ICC and I tried to get cases. And I knew from the very beginning that it is very difficult to get into this very exclusive and closed circle of arbitrators" (int. 176, 2). He was also referred a number of cases through the Zurich Chamber of Commerce, but he was not getting the big, visible cases. "Still it's difficult to get the real good cases where you can, where it's first of all interesting on the legal issues and secondly interesting financially, because I have to run a law firm with a substantial cost" (id., 3).

Speaking of the leading arbitrators in Zurich as friends, even old friends, he said, "They are the top shots. They call the shots in Switzerland. And I am of course not one of them, not yet. But I would like to do more arbitration. I, but it's hard to get into these circles because they tend to use, you know to hand cases among themselves. So it's quite difficult to get into these very closed arbitration circles." Yet "people at the ICC always promise to give me bigger cases" (id., 2, 4).

It is interesting that this individual has had difficulty breaking into the core of the Swiss arbitration community, but it is also quite interesting that he has the desire and expectation of being granted entry. He says that he is *not yet* one of the "top shots." Moreover, he continues to insist on his fondness for arbitration: "How should I say it, it's more sophisticated. It's more sophisticated than just being a lawyer. I mean that, I don't want to be degrading, but it's on a legal point of view it's more sophisticated" (id., 40).

Yet, as he also notes, "Not many of my generation . . . are very much interested in arbitration." They are more interested in making money. The arbitration cases "have generated new arbitration cases . . . not other business" (id., 5, 6). What is clear is that this individual is not looking only for short-term profits (and can afford to wait). He is "very much involved in the Zurich Bar Association," "like[s] to publish," considers himself a "generalist of the economic world," and is seeking to build an international law firm as his "own legal factory" (id., 11, 9, 8). The commitment to arbitration makes sense as part of an effort to assume an expected place at the top of the legal profession, not merely to maximize income over the short term. In ten years, in fact, the story of this individual may look like another "natural" transfer of symbolic capital into the field of international commercial arbitration. But the story to date shows that it takes some work to break in even among family and friends.

These profiles show how relatively prominent individuals have succeeded or are trying to succeed in converting local and international symbolic capital into success in the arbitration world. The contests about the importance of particular skills and experience are important to the development and the constitution of the field. It will suffice for present purposes, however, to note only that we have seen different generations, one formed mainly in national settings outside of arbitration and one formed in the international arena and within arbitration. We have seen judges, academics, and practitioners. We have seen also that lawyers from the third world can gain recognition as arbitrators, but they must gain recognition from the individuals and institutions in the center. We have also seen how the U.S. growth of the in-house counsel movement and alternative dispute resolution has made an impact, but they are not yet valued very highly in the European centers of arbitration. And while there have been nonlawyers or non-law-trained individuals who have played a role in national and sometimes international commercial arbitration, at present entry into the field requires legal credentials.

Finally, it is clear even from the profiles that the players in the arbitration field do not simply possess certain credentials. The arbitrators and would-be arbitrators themselves operate within this field. They learn the rules of the game—what accounts for success. They see the relative values given to publication, to links to institutions, to alternative dispute resolution, and the like, and those who seek success in the field act accordingly. They not only promote the forms of symbolic capital that give maximum value to their personal characteristics, but also they try to build symbolic capital that will allow them to prosper and succeed in the changing environment. As suggested before, they may diversify their portfolios.

The main point, however, is simply that the concept of symbolic capital can be used to explore the field of international commercial arbitration. The basic question is simple: what are the characteristics of the people who are *recognized* as having authority to handle these high-stakes, complicated disputes. By examining those characteristics, and the conflicts over the relative value of those characteristics, we can see how this field operates and is changing.

Part Two

Constructing Transnational Private Justice and Legalizing Business Conflicts

The three chapters in this part focus on the construction of an international private justice. We ask how international commercial arbitration became the accepted and legitimate way to resolve transnational business disputes and why it has the specific features that we found. Chapter 3 situates the actors on the field of international commercial arbitration in relation to each other and to the major institution, the International Chamber of Commerce in Paris. We see an intense competition among the players for preeminence in the "club" and in the arbitration field. While they struggle mainly over legitimacy, that is, what arbitration ought to be to become accepted, players also compete over the relative values of the specific forms of symbolic capital each possesses. Through the dynamic of this competition, we can trace the growth, transformation, and increasing institutionalization of international commercial arbitration. Institutionalization came with a shift in the practice of arbitration from an informal justice dominated by Continental academics to offshore justice dominated by U.S. litigators.

It is not sufficient, however, to examine only the internal story, even though it is perhaps relatively easy to see and to present as a story of institutional transformation. The internal process, we suggest, occurred in harmony with transformations that are best understood as external to the field of international commercial arbitration and even law more generally. Events in the political and economic fields, especially decolonization, the oil crisis, and the petrodollar megaprojects, intersected with the legal developments, including those described in chapter 3. Chapter 4, accordingly, reaches out to situate the legal story in the larger political and economic context. The result of the dynamic seen in the two chapters has been to produce an "autonomous" law—with pretensions of universality and specific features aligned with U.S. legal practice—that is at the same time in perfect harmony with the power and interests of transnational business.

In order to bring these two chapters together, we conclude this part with a case study of one of the large petrodollar construction disputes. The case study illustrates both the political-economic aspects of these disputes and how international commercial arbitration was transformed through the intersection of U.S. litigators and the European arbitration elite. Finally, it shows that the "national" approach—U.S. litigation—that helped develop and transform international business disputing is itself a social construction that is also, in part, a product of international developments.

3

Merchants of Law as Moral Entrepreneurs: Constructing International Justice out of the Competition for Transnational Business Disputes

A central theme in sociolegal research is how the legitimacy of law is maintained so that it can provide a basis to govern matters that involve powerful economic and political entities (Hunt 1993).[1] The study of international commercial arbitration allows us to see how international private justice—lacking the legitimacy of the state court system—has become established and recognized almost universally as legitimate for business disputes. Competition among key actors and groups, as we shall see in this chapter, serves to construct legal legitimacy and at the same time promote law in the service of merchants. The competition, however, is not simply a matter of striving for business by offering better services. International commercial arbitration is a symbolic field, and therefore the competitive battles that take place within it are fought in symbolic terms among moral entrepreneurs. Battles fought in terms of legitimacy and credibility then serve a double role. They build careers and markets for those who are successful in this competition, and they build the legitimacy and credibility of international legal practices and international institutions (cf. the "schizophrenia" of the legal profession as described by Gordon 1984).

This is not to say that the construction of this global justice for transnational business disputes was "caused" only through some dynamic within the field of international commercial arbitration. The relationship is much more complex. The relative positions and indeed even the entry onto the field of many key players, as will be seen below and in chapter 4, relate to other factors of considerable importance—in particular, decolonization, the growth of international trade, and the power of Anglo-American law firms (in turn bolstered by their clientele). Our ambition, however, is not to confirm the simple promotional story of the inevitable growth of international commercial arbitration in response to the growth of international trade and commerce. It

---

1. Our study of legitimacy is mainly of arbitration entrepreneurs who promote the legitimacy of particular conceptions of arbitration. For empirical support for the proposition that the subjects of legal regulation also act in part out of beliefs in legitimacy, see Tyler and Mitchell (1994).

is to explain why the phenomenon termed international commercial arbitration has become more institutionalized and has a particular set of characteristics that, we submit, are not mere details but rather are important aspects of the emerging global economy.

Oppositions and Complementarities in the Field of International Commercial Arbitration

The field of international commercial arbitration is given its structure and its logic of transformation through oppositions and complementarities that we shall now begin to map. The key source of conflict, and also of transformation, is that between two generations—"grand old men" versus "technocrats." We therefore begin this section by showing what this conflict and the symbolic battles around it reveal about international commercial arbitration. We shall then focus on a related conflict, between academics and practitioners. After these oppositional relationships have been described, we shall turn in the next sections to the way that the conflicts have been managed in the case of one key institution, the International Chamber of Commerce in Paris, and to the role of large Anglo-American law firms in the transformation of relatively informal arbitration into "offshore litigation." The conflicts, the management, and the power of the large law firms are key ingredients in the success and current status of international commercial arbitration.

Grand Old Men and Technocrats

The starting point of the generational warfare is diverging ideas of arbitral competence—the characteristics that qualify one to be an arbitrator. For the pioneers of arbitration, exemplified especially, but not only, by very senior European professors imbued with the traditional values of the European legal elites,[2] the dominant opinion has been that arbitration should not be a profession: "Arbitration is a duty, not a career" (int. 173, 3). For true independence of judgment, in the words of another senior insider, "The person who goes into this business as an arbitrator to make a living should not be encouraged" (int. 37, 2). Arbitrators, they insist, should render an occasional service, provided on the basis of long experience and wisdom acquired in law, business,

---

2. A good discussion of the European aristocratic values is in Osiel (1989, 2033–39). This is not to say that the values do not echo in the United States, only that in the United States there has been, as Osiel notes, "a relatively unqualified embrace of the modern world of commerce and corporations" (2046). Compare Kronman 1993, which seeks to reassert the aristocratic values.

or public service.[3] Those who hold this opinion are, indeed, individuals who have risen to the top of their national legal professions and gained financial independence before being asked to serve as arbitrators.

The specific criteria for these "grand notable" arbitrators allow for numerous variations. Different countries and legal systems have different hierarchies in their legal professions. The great professors and a few high judges have for a long time controlled the arbitration terrain of Continental Europe,[4] while the comparable role is assumed in the Anglo-American system by the most respected of the practitioners, senior barristers or Queen's Counsel (QCs), or senior partners in firms of solicitors or U.S. law firms. Retired judges such as Lord Wilberforce have been important as well to England. The arbitration market has selected those at the top of their domestic professions to become senior arbitrators: "high profile, high visibility . . . national aura behind them" (int. 51, 18).

These relatively few grand old men,[5] as they are often referred to (there were no women), have played a central role in the emergence and the recognition of arbitration,[6] and they continue to have a quasi monopoly for very large matters. As a U.S. litigator stated, "There are some categories of disputes where you're going to need the grand old men who are known to each other" (int. 38, 18). Stated another longtime observer of the field, "In these big, big

3. Jean Robert, one of the respected founding fathers of international commercial arbitration, reportedly stated that "arbitrators are the well-paid unemployed." One leading member of the pioneering generation noted that to be "really independent," one had to be over seventy-five years of age and not dependent on further arbitration business (int. 158, 8).

4. This generation in Europe could also be defined as somewhat marginal in the sense that they were not content to simply work their way up national hierarchies through their patience and technical skill. They used their personal qualities and social characteristics to redefine the traditional careers and maintain an openness to new opportunities and approaches that were not strictly "legal," but rather at the crossroads of law, politics, and business.

5. Figure 1 gives numbers of the individuals we interviewed according to general characteristics, but we would define ten to fifteen of the senior individuals we interviewed as the most perfect embodiment of the characteristics of the pioneering generation.

6. More generally, it is typically the case that when a new symbolic field is being constructed it requires the personal legitimacy of "grand old men" or their equivalent to provide it with sufficient legitimacy to survive. Almost by definition, this process will apply to a specific time in the history of the legal field. Our preliminary research suggests that we can find precisely the same phenomenon in the early development of the field of international human rights.

cases, you go for people who have already years of experience" (int. 10, 12).[7]
But these "divas"—sometimes defined also as dinosaurs—are increasingly
criticized by a new generation of practitioners who came to arbitration because
of the rapid growth of this market in the 1980s.

To the aura or the charisma of their elders, these new arrivals oppose their
specialization and technical competence. In the words of a Swiss member of
the new generation, "Arbitration was characterized by a limited, small group
of impeccable, outstanding professionals—characters known around the
world. . . . Today I have difficulty in seeing the outstanding personality [among]
a big crowd of people" (int. 166, 33).[8] Put in more aggressive terms by a member of the same cohort, an arbitrator cannot now just step in "with all . . .
[the] glorious past" and provide the "great old man's opinion" (int. 184, 6).
Indeed, charisma is said even to be a source of error. In the words of an ICC
insider, "Some of the biggest problems that we see are probably with some of
the big names" (int. 134, 14). Why? "They're probably just more full of themselves than other people" (id., 14). Furthermore, "Sometimes an eminent arbitrator feels he doesn't have to explain things" (id., 25). A leading figure of
the younger generation thus describes his generation as "technically better
equipped in procedure and substance" (int. 148, 6).

They present themselves in this new generation as international arbitration
professionals,[9] and also as entrepreneurs selling their services to business practitioners, contrasting their qualities[10] to the "amateurism" or "idealism" of

7. "I have two lists . . . two ways of thinking. I have what I call the big hitter . . .
a grand monsieur . . . a man of sixty-five or seventy—a professor. . . the French- or
German-style professor, or the ex-judge—retired judge" (int. 82, 14). The grand old man
is for "a case that has political ramifications. . . . You need him for his eminence and
respect" (id., 17).

8. Virtually all of the thirty-three arbitration specialists that we interviewed and
noted graphically in figure 1, as well as many of the "arbitration bureaucrats," are major
players in this generation.

9. The international characteristics of this generation are also captured in the following quotation: "[W]e had recently an arbitration and we did it in English. Place of
arbitration was Vienna. And the way we conducted it was very much influenced by our
common background of time in the United States. That was the one thing we had in
common. Next thing we had in common was that we all knew some Latin. And some
knowledge of Roman law. Third thing that we had in common was the German legal
theory, which in Turkey, Switzerland, and Germany was also a common thing. And
the fourth thing was that we all watched CNN and read the *Financial Times*, and you
know" (int. 108, 45).

10. Several young Swiss arbitrators highlighted the difference between generations,
in their opinion, by stating that, while they would stay awake all night to finish an

their predecessors.[11] This idea of change is well captured in an article by Jan Paulsson, a leading member of the new generation (also described in chapter 2):

> the age of innocence has come to an end . . . [and] the subject has inevitably lost some of its charm. Once the delightful discipline of a handful of academic *aficionados* on the fringe of international law, it has become a matter of serious concern for great numbers of professionals determined to master a process because it is essential to their business. They labor, but not for love. (Paulsson 1985, 2)

Indeed, now that arbitration has become accepted in commercial international mores, they assert, even citing Max Weber in one instance, that the time has come for the "routinization of charisma" essential to the transition from the stage of artisans to that of mass production (int. 104). This transition requires the "rationalization" of arbitration know-how.

These technocrats play key roles now in institutions like the International Chamber of Commerce, which they not only have come to direct but also have used for their education in arbitration. The quick route to arbitration expertise is through the major institutions, which hire young lawyers to administer the arbitrations.[12] These organizations, which the pioneers used for evangelical purposes to promote arbitration, now have added a more technical involvement in the administration of the arbitrations themselves.

The large Anglo-American law firms, which dominate the international market of business law, are also central to this conflict between grand old men and technocrats. With the growth of trade and the success of the pioneers in building international arbitration, they now consider it important to include this speciality in the gamut of services that they put at the disposition of their

---

arbitration and produce an award, the senior Swiss arbitrators would terminate the hearing at 5:00 P.M. for dinner and an evening at the opera.

11. We find this same opposition elsewhere, for example in economics. Engineers and also lawyers at a certain moment began to define themselves as economists to align themselves with the new expertise, but they were later dismissed by a new generation trained in the more technical aspects of economics (see Wade 1990).

12. The method is not only quick, but also one of the only ways to resolve the catch-22 of arbitration: It is necessary to have a reputation in international arbitration to gain access to arbitration. The new generation can through these institutions gain a control over the production of producers—arbitrators and arbitration lawyers. There are other ways to enter, but they are difficult. For example, the large law firms offer possibilities to younger lawyers, but they tend still to treat arbitration as only part of general litigation. It is hard to become a recognized expert.

multinational clients. The attitude of the large law firms has been to favor overtly this "banalization" and rationalization of arbitration, which permits them to introduce themselves into the closed "club" and to introduce the legal techniques that are at the basis of their preeminence. As a U.S. lawyer stated about the Swiss, "It's the younger generation that I like, because all of them have gone to school in the United States. They all speak fluent English. They know how to deal with Americans and English, and they move cases along" (int. 37, 34). Another U.S. expert, describing a particular individual of the new generation, is quite revealing:

> He'll make a fortune in this work if he keeps growing. And one of the reasons is he's not in the sense that you use that word, a "star," because he's never going to act like that. What you see is what you get. He'll do his work, he'll do it well, and people will keep coming back to him. But he won't be a pontificating presence. (Int. 7, 26)[13]

This opposition between grand old men and young technocrats—supported by Anglo-American firms—is one of the keys that permits decoding a great number of the debates and the fights—in scholarship as well as in institutions—that affect this field of practice. One controversy, discussed further below, is whether the major institutions, the ICC notably, are now too involved in the actual work of the arbitrators. A second is whether arbitration is becoming too much like litigation. The perspective of the senior generation is highly critical of both of these trends. A leading senior arbitrator thus reported that procedural infighting was "suicidal" to arbitration and that he was likewise "absolutely opposed to drowning arbitration in paperwork" (int. 173, 6). With respect to the ICC, the same individual noted that the weakness of the ICC was that its arbitration was "overly regulated" by the secretariat[14] who had "never seen arbitration from the inside" (id., 6).[15]

13. The new president of the Swiss Arbitration Association, succeeding one of the great stars of the senior generation, Pierre Lalive, makes the same point in his description of what he aspires to in arbitration: "a continuing challenge to overcome obstacles and to grow—not to grow to a 'super arbitrator,' but to an arbitrator with dignity, an open heart and mind and, above all: modesty" ("Profile of Arbitrator, Marc Blessing" 1991, 253).

14. A published article by Gillis Wetter (1990) of Sweden is unique for articulating these concerns in strong language. For example, he states that the "ICC Court . . . is an administrative institution that engages in rather far-reaching involvement in arbitration proceedings, yet offers relatively little administrative or intellectual support to arbitration tribunals" (1990, 95). Stephen Bond, then secretary-general of the ICC and a member of the new generation, wrote an equally strong response, published in the same journal (1990).

15. A criticism that can also be made of our work. An older, but fascinating, account of arbitration, which supports our attention to symbolic capital and the role of authority and expertise within the arbitral tribunal, is Mentschikoff and Haggard 1977.

This cleavage about the conduct of arbitration is also present in debates that appear much more academic. The best known of such debates concerns the so-called *lex mercatoria,* conceived by many as a return to an international law of business—a new "law merchant" independent from national laws (see generally Carbonneau 1990; de Ly 1992). Avoiding open criticism of the power-ful grand old professors from France and Switzerland who, as discussed in chapter 4, reinvented this theory and applied it to commercial arbitration, the new generation prefers to focus on how it is applied by "other" arbitrators. A U.S. arbitration expert in a large law firm in Paris thus stated about the *lex mercatoria,*

> It's something that can be subject to abuse where an arbitrator doesn't feel like going through a difficult choice of law . . . or simply decides that something is *lex mercatoria* because that's an answer he feels is right. . . . The question is . . . whether commercial parties feel that it provides sufficient security and predictability—and how well arbitra-tors who don't have the abilities of [Berthold] Goldman [a senior French professor and the "father" of the *lex mercatoria*] are able to apply the theory and come up with suitable answers that are per-ceived as fair and reasonable by both parties. (Int. 104, 23; see also Paulsson 1990, 68; int. 10, 14)

It is as if only a few arbitrators with incontestable authority have the right to invoke the notion of *lex mercatoria.* All others must restrain themselves and carefully explicate the legal reasoning that prevents their decision from being condemned as arbitrary. As the quotation also indicates, Anglo-American prac-titioners tend not to support the Continental, academic *lex mercatoria* (see the lineup in Carbonneau 1990; Mustill 1987).

But beyond the contest between generations about what and whose charac-teristics should be at the center of international commercial arbitration, this fight for power contains the true transformation that is taking place—the passage from one mode to another for the production of arbitration and the legitimation of arbitrators. As is the case for the entire field of business law, the Anglo-American model of the business enterprise and merchant competi-tion is tending to substitute itself for the Continental model of legal artisans and corporatist control over the profession (Dezalay 1992). In the same way, international commercial arbitration is moving from a small, closed group of self-regulating artisans to a more open and competitive business.

The arrival of new generations and greater competition, beginning in the late 1970s, can be seen as part of this process. We must be careful, however, not to overlook the personal dimension in this story. The break between the

small group of artisans and today's arbitration professionals is not as pronounced as it might appear. A good number of these "angry young men" of
arbitration are "new" arrivals only in the strict sense of the term. They are
also the inheritors—or more precisely the disciples—of the grand old men.[16]
They have been able to avoid waiting patiently for the retirement of their
mentors in order to succeed them, which was the tradition in the artisanal
model (and also in the classic Continental academic model). They have sought
to jump these stages and profit from a boom in arbitration that created a
demand that exceeded the capacity of the grand masters and the artisanal
mode of production. The desire to promote their own technical competencies
has led them to a position that devalues the wisdom and generalist experience
of their notable mentors, whom they now characterize as dinosaurs. Since
they are for the most part too young to compete with the charisma of grand
old men, they must emphasize their technical sophistication.

The positions in these contests, however, are more tactical than permanent. It is not at all clear that these young technocrats are ready to renounce
completely the attractions of charismatic arbitration, which present advantages both for the arbitrators and for the parties in conflict. Not surprisingly,
a certain number of these technicians are seeking to take the prominence
gained as international arbitration specialists and reinvest it in a more generalist professional profile.[17] The strategy of diversification may permit them to

16. It will suffice to note that many of the leaders of the new generation were closely
connected to the most well known senior arbitrators. Among other examples, we may
point to the close connections between Albert Jan van den Berg and Pieter Sanders in
the Netherlands; the connection of numerous Swiss arbitrators to Pierre Lalive and the
Lalive firm; the numerous disciples of the great French professor, René David, including
Yves Derain, Julian Lew, and van den Berg; prominent French disciples to Pierre Bellet
and Berthold Goldman. Indeed, the observation can be generalized. Even within U.S.
law firms, we found that leading arbitration notables of the new generation, such as
James Carter and David Rivkin, were promoted by notable mentors—Jack Stevenson
and Robert von Mehren. The systems of patronage may no longer be as extreme as the
European legal dynasties of the past, but there are artificial recreations of the same
phenomenon. Because of the small size of the groups we investigated and the early stage
of the development of the field, our project has noted connections that we are certain
would be revealed in similarly detailed studies of other areas of legal practice.

17. A formerly quite active Swiss arbitrator, now involved in electoral politics, thus
noted,
    I used to be fairly legalistic as an arbitrator. Give me the facts. Give me the
    law. And I'll decide it, okay. . . . I was impressed . . . when I was . . . secretary
    at several panels, for several arbitration panels where Pierre Lalive was the
    chairman. He . . . hardly ever decided a case. They would all be settled at
    some point. And that takes a lot of skill . . . from the chairman—skills which

come back into arbitration (or go elsewhere) as new versions of a senior arbitration elite, combining the qualities of expert and the social capital and experience of the charismatic notables.[18]

While it is useful to decode the contests through which the field and the markets of arbitration are constituted, the opposition between notables and technocrats may lead to confusion. The risk is that an objective content will be given to notions that exist only in their opposition. The notables and the technocrats are defined only in a relative manner, the one by relation to the other and also in a quite specific context. The same caution applies to the other major cleavage, which opposes practitioners and academic jurists.

Academics and Practitioners

The polarization between academics and practitioners has elements in common with that between notables and technocrats, but the practice-versus-academia conflict exists also on its own. It provides another key principle for understanding the positions and fights for influence in a field of practice in great measure conceived by and for (mainly Continental) academics but dominated increasingly by (mainly Anglo-American) practitioners. The controversy around the *lex mercatoria* is indicative also in this respect. The Anglo-American practitioners are nearly unanimous in their denunciation of a doctrinal construction that, according to them, allows academics to avoid the rigorous analysis of the facts, the formal law, and even the terms of the contract.[19]

In this controversy as well, it is clear that each side seeks to promote the value of the know-how or the competence that it has mastered the best. Academics—with a competitive advantage in theory—emphasize the *lex mercatoria* elaborated in countless academic books and articles. Practitioners promote the virtues of solid case law and thorough analysis of the facts. But this opposition is also only a relative one. The practitioners of arbitration even in

I clearly didn't have some years ago. And I think maybe I'm developing them a little more now. Probably a matter of aging. (Int. 178, 5)

18. An ambitious U.S. arbitration expert we asked about "future grand old men" replied, "The people my age who are clearly extremely good lawyers and who've devoted a good chunk of their career to international arbitration and so as a matter of course enter in the public eye" (int. 38, 22).

19. A well-known English QC from the commercial bar captures the feeling: "These people are just deciding by the seat of their pants. There's no such thing as the *lex mercatoria*" (int. 87, 34). An American lawyer in Paris makes the same point: "And we don't want *lex mercatoria*. We want to know what law it is. In fact we want to know which procedural law it is. We don't want to leave it up to the arbitrator" (int. 100, 12).

the Anglo-American countries carefully cultivate an intellectual image through publication and university affiliations. Lord Michael Mustill, for example, one of the leading English commercial judges, took the time to master the subtleties of the *lex mercatoria* in order to criticize it at a suitably high level (Mustill 1987). On the other side, the academics who are in the arbitration world—including the Continental ones—are often described as far from the pure academic model. One French academic imbued with the values of the academy thus looked down on academic arbitrators: "abundance of arbitrations" is not "abundance of intelligence" (int. 209, 1).

As a result of the contests for preeminence in the field, each of the competing groups seeks to gain a diversified portfolio of arbitration capital. That is to say, professors must show they can master business practicalities, and practicing lawyers must seek to show competence in sophisticated academic theories. Each group, in short, is in fact closer to the other than appears in the first place, and they complement each other admirably. The academic theorization of arbitration—"developed by the French and Swiss professors largely" (int. 85, 28)—gave the field its *lettres de noblesse* as a sophisticated legal expertise suitable for high-level practitioners. This academic pedigree has helped promote the acceptance and recognition of arbitration throughout much of the world.

In the same way, this rapprochement (or homologation) between professors and practitioners has served to open a market of arbitration well beyond what could have been created by a small group of learned jurists more preoccupied with doctrinal advances than with marketing. Transformations promoted by practitioners, similarly, have overcome the professors' resistance to basic Anglo-American conceptions of litigation—especially more attention to questions of fact and more openness to procedural tactics. Accordingly, the large Anglo-American law firms have become more willing to invest in this process. Anglo-American arbitrators have also changed through some rapprochement, becoming more open to Continental practices such as active judicial questioning and limits on pretrial discovery (Lowenfeld 1985).

The opposition and the complementarity between these different poles structures the field of arbitration, creating a dynamic that, we can see in retrospect, has allowed this field of practice to change and renovate itself over the past two decades. At the same time, the diversity of resources and competencies among the available—and competing—"private judges" has allowed different kinds of conflicts—great or small, exceptional or routine—to call on different types of arbitrators. As a result, international arbitration can reap the symbolic benefits and material prosperity of its generally accepted legitimacy in international business transactions.

The Management of Antagonisms and the Production of Universals: The International Chamber of Commerce

We can pursue these themes and hopefully avoid the problems of a simplistic or objectifying schematization by focusing in more detail on the emergence of modern arbitration around international commercial arbitration's preeminent institution—the International Chamber of Commerce in Paris (Ridgeway 1938). The success of the missionary enterprise of the founders[20] led to the diffusion of the ICC arbitration clause into business transactions around the world. With a rapid growth of international trade and commercial conflict, the resultant case boom challenged the ICC's structure. According to one of the key figures in this period of the ICC,

> in the late seventies [the ICC] started having problems because the number of cases increased quite dramatically. And the ICC, I think, at the time still only had five or six people in the secretariat. And that's when, I guess in 1980 or '81, there was this very significant effort by the ICC to organize itself administratively, to hire more people. (Int. 104, 2)

The ICC, as we shall see, necessarily became a more bureaucratic institution.

New Arrivals and the Expansion of the Market

The ICC had to administer the influx of new cases and, more importantly, to respond to the new problems posed by the arrival of a new clientele and, to a lesser degree, new arbitrators. The new arrivals were unfamiliar with the usages of an international arbitration coterie that was at the same time learned, militant, and a little marginal because of its shared hobby. The expansion of the market of Eurodollars, then the manna of petrodollars thanks to the oil crises in the 1970s, both enlarged and *reoriented* international trade. North-south conflicts became more important as the ICC became the focal point for the major arbitrations tied to the very large construction projects located especially in the Arab countries.

This opening to north-south conflicts coincided, somewhat paradoxically, with an accelerated American involvement in the practice of arbitration. One

20. Among countless examples of the role of the ICC in universalizing arbitration, we can point to the travels by ICC leaders around the world to sell the concept of arbitration, the role of the ICC in the 1958 New York Convention, which set the stage for the easy enforcement of arbitral awards in all signatory countries, and the relationship of the ICC to the International Council for Commercial Arbitration (ICCA), which sponsors the most important conferences and uses them to gain new terrain for arbitration.

reason is that, since the North American exporters were confronted with problems in the execution of their contracts, their law firms invested in the forum already accepted for these contracts—international arbitration, typically in Paris or Switzerland (and later through the Iran–United States Claims Tribunal operating in The Hague).[21]

Another reason for increased American (and English) involvement is that the multinationals of law arrived on the arbitration scene with technical facilities that were unique in the market. Serving both multinational enterprises and not infrequently third-world countries, they were well equipped for the mass of facts characteristic of these megalitigations with gigantic sums in controversy. As a result, the ICC saw both new parties from the south and new law practices from the north. And the market expanded considerably.

Competition in the Field

This rapid expansion of the market of arbitration naturally awakened new appetites (Clow and Stewart 1990). The ICC thus found itself more and more in competition with new arbitral institutions aiming at such or such segment of this very diverse market. One segment of the market could be defined in geographical terms, like East-West or Euro-Arab relations. Stockholm, for example, made its reputation with Soviet-U.S. disputes in particular and East-West in general (see chap. 9). Another segment might involve a type of specific case, like those concerning intellectual property. There are also efforts to promote alternative technologies for the administration of business disputes.[22]

The multiplication and diversification of places and institutions of arbitration promotes further competition. The ICC, for example, has been forced to adjust its general fee schedule downward to attract business clients, and some institutions seek to gain the favor of arbitrators by emphasizing that they allow the arbitrators to negotiate any fee arrangement they can obtain. Multinational law firms accelerate this competition by their ability to forum shop—both in contractual negotiations and after disputes arise—among institutions, sets of rules, laws, and arbitrators (Purcell 1992).

---

21. According to a British lawyer with a multinational law firm, referring to ICC arbitrations, "In the Middle East with the oil explosion and the huge contracts that were let in the late sixties and seventies, they gave rise to a good number of disputes. And there were a number of us in Western Europe who made a lot of money resolving them" (int. 85, 17).

22. Ironically, the promoters of alternative dispute resolution represent an echo, now from a new place, of precisely the arguments that the arbitration community once used to challenge the hegemony of the formal state justice systems (see chap. 8).

The ICC and the Universality of Arbitration

Even if the ICC has lost its position of quasi monopoly, it remains the central institution. A longtime British observer thus points out, "But the ICC is a great institution. I mean it's the leading arbitral, international arbitral institution in the world by a long way" (int. 85, 18; see also int. 91, 16; int. 66, 26; int. 52, 12; int. 95; int. 69). Potential clients see the ICC as trustworthy and respectable because of its senior status, and because it has preserved the missionary idealism of its origins. An American critic of the ICC agrees: "The ICC has of course the great advantage that they were in it from the beginning. And they have created this aura that if you have an ICC arbitration that the award is good and it will be enforced everywhere" (int. 57, 6).

As the status of the ICC indicates, history is a key legitimator in the legal field. No one can compete with tradition without ending up underscoring that one group is a new arrival and another the established elite, akin to the aristocracy. The passage of time also tends to obscure the politics that created an institution, thereby giving it an aura of naturalness. And this kind of legitimacy is probably especially important in a field where it is important to be able to claim a distance from business and politics.[23]

The ICC is the most universal of the arbitration institutions, able to brag even about having become a sort of United Nations (int. 106, 4) of commerce and of international arbitration. With members from some one hundred nations and national committees in sixty, it offers a powerful image of neutrality and legitimacy. In addition, ICC arbitration benefits from a double sponsorship—that of the world of business, since the parent organization remains a major business group, and that of the world of learned jurists, to which belong the founding fathers and an important fraction of arbitrators today. Finally, we can also note that the ICC has benefited from a close relationship with the state, evident in both the support it obtained from the French government and the "public-private" career profiles of key figures in the arbitration community (e.g., the retired French judge, Pierre Bellet).

The ICC has therefore become one of the principal places where the "politics" of arbitration is elaborated and expressed. There are innumerable committees and multiple networks of influence that gravitate around this institution. The court, for example, which is really an oversight committee that reviews arbitration appointments and decisions, appears to be particularly sensitive to the business clientele; the Institute of International Business Law

---

23. It is similarly interesting that one feature of the *lex mercatoria* is that it builds links to medieval times, suggesting that it is quite normal to have a special merchant law.

and Practice focuses on the academic side; and the secretariat guides the court and seeks to manage growth and change. Through exchanges and contests expressed in these and other ICC forums and networks, the ICC is able to make policy to regulate the relations of arbitration with the worlds of national law (essentially the new legislation and jurisprudence in matters of arbitration) and politics.[24]

The emergence of institutional networks around the ICC can also be seen as a true microcosm of the legal field. Between the first generation of charismatic pioneers and the experts of the ascending generations, one finds a sort of striking abridgment of the principal stages in the grand Weberian canvas (Weber 1978, 246–54, 784–816). We see first the legal *honoratiores*, embodying the wisdom of law and the social legitimacy necessary to the management of social conflicts. We then find institutionalization and the creation of a division of labor, which permits the development of a collective legitimacy dependent not on individual notables but rather on "the ICC" or even "law" or "international commercial arbitration."[25]

It is clear, however, that this project of routinization—even judicialization—of arbitration, supported strongly by the ICC bureaucracy while denounced as treason by the founding fathers, cannot be completely accomplished. Despite the changes, there remains a vital element of personal relations in this field. The system of selection and self-regulation of arbitrators created by the pioneers and resembling a club has remained quite essential to the prosperity of international commercial arbitration.

Despite the conflicts and differing positions taken with respect to the conduct of arbitration, the participants in the debates are still in key respects members of a common community. This community, like all organizations where professional relations are reproduced through an extraordinary network of personal ties, has a tendency to fix itself by ensuring that social interests are organized to make themselves heard better. The main organs of the ICC, by allowing this more personal debate and interchange, contribute crucially to the management of conflicts toward the success of international arbitration.

24. One recent example was the question of the appropriate attitude to adopt with respect to contracts and arbitration threatened by sociopolitical disturbances, such as was the case recently with the destruction of the Soviet bloc. Another is the difficult problem of what to do with the bribes, or baksheesh, that surface in accounts of much of international trade and investment. The ICC provides committees and forums to debate and resolve such issues.

25. An insider of the secretariat during the time of change thus noted, "When I started then it was more or less a group of friends, for the club. . . . And then with the expansion of the number of cases [it] was not any longer possible just to deal on a personal basis" (int. 108, 18).

Between the Club and the Market

The secretariat of the Court of Arbitration of the ICC makes no secret of its desire to open the market of arbitration beyond the narrow circle of the grand old men.[26] Certainly these efforts can be justified by the growth in the number of cases submitted to the ICC, as well as by their great geographical diversity (see Bond 1990). The arrival into arbitration of the third world and of the Anglo-Americans rendered necessary the recruitment of new arbitrators who did not fit the profile of the Continental academic or the other pioneers (Bond 1990, 120). Many new users are bound to nominate arbitrators—and a fortiori lawyers—from their own legal settings. According to Stephen Bond, then the secretary-general of the ICC, "In such instances, given the importance of party autonomy and consensus as basic principles of international commercial arbitration, the ICC has not refused confirmation of such persons, even when they are unknown to the Court itself " (Bond 1990, 121).

These newcomers, however, are by definition not the progeny of the club. Their entry into the practices and norms of the club cannot be ensured by a long apprenticeship or by an informal process controlled by a small group of senior men. The institutionalization of these tasks of enlisting new arbitrators and observing their performance, in fact, justifies the growth and transformation of the ICC bureaucracy (the secretariat) and also the Court of Arbitration. This "bureaucratization" of the ICC, and also the retention of two of the most controversial aspects of the ICC procedure—the terms of reference and the review of the arbitrators' opinions by the court—can therefore be seen as part of the effort to bring in newcomers, accommodate their situation, and preserve the universality of the ICC and arbitration.[27]

26. As one key representative of the secretariat mentioned, "There was an effort to broaden the pool." And new nationalities were also brought in partly because "it's important for the perception of the ICC as being international. And it's important in the perception of international arbitration as an institution, it's being universal" (int. 104, 7).

27. The terms of reference are a document that the parties must develop at the outset of the arbitration. Even those generally critical of the terms of reference, which includes most American and British lawyers, state that the terms of reference are "helpful if you've got inexperienced arbitrators or unprofessional arbitrators or those who might be likely to misbehave in some way" (int. 53, 8). Similarly, an English barrister notes that the English "hate the terms of reference. Now that is because they've never been exposed to an arbitration where there is some deficiency or some imbalance between the parties or their legal representative whether it's cultural or legal" (int. 93, 7). We suggest that this kind of process, which serves to produce belief in the rules of the game at the outset and build a common language, is quite common in places where the system has not yet been routinized.

The ICC court reviews decisions and has the power to ask arbitrators to rewrite.

This set of events helps to explain better the current ambivalence of the founding fathers with respect to the ICC—seen in their attitude toward "bureaucratization." It is an organization that they helped to build, and that celebrates them at all conferences and ceremonial occasions. But, at the same time, it is now dispossessing them from what constitutes a large part of their power. They are losing the informal control they could assert on a community of disciples, where loyalty could be rewarded by suggesting names for arbitration or for the activities of legal representation. We have here the classical scenario of an institution that is devouring its founding fathers in order to better follow their work.

The ICC and the Recentering of the Field of International Commercial Arbitration: The Arrival and Role of the Anglo-American Law Firms

The tensions implicated by these transformations are not explained only by a crisis of growth. They are also the corollary of displacement from the center of gravity of arbitration. The recentering favors the world of Anglo-American law firms, who have used their power in the international business world to impose their conception of arbitration and more largely of the practice of law.[28] It is thus no accident that, within the ICC itself, the politics of rationalization has been conducted since the beginning of the eighties by young Anglo-American lawyers recruited from outside of the club, and whose key words have been transparency, rationalization, and competition.[29] The Anglo-Americans, including the two most recent secretaries-general of the ICC (from the United States), have clashed with leading members of the senior arbitration club over a number of issues, including the necessity of bureaucratization. A recent example, which provides a good illustration of the conflict and the trend in management, has been the effort of the ICC to expand the requirements of ICC arbitrators to disclose relationships with counsel and other arbitrators.

Conflicts of Interest, Independence, and Transparency

According to an observer sympathetic to the controversial approach taken by the ICC secretariat,

---

According to an ICC insider, the ICC court returns to the arbitrators for revision about 15–20 percent of the awards rendered.

28. Arbitration is only one example of a recentering in favor of the Anglo-Americans that we find more generally through the internationalization of legal practice (Dezalay 1992; Garth 1980, 130–42).

29. As stated from the more recent perspective, "That frustration from the American community has to some degree gotten soft. And I think it's been helped a lot because . . . [of an] American secretary-general of the ICC" (int. 100, 8).

The court took the view that the "declaration of independence" which is required to be signed by all proposed arbitrators should include a mention of any significant relationship between arbitrators proposed and counsel for parties in the arbitration. And there, what the Swiss [and many Europeans] objected to . . . is that the relationships that may exist between counsel and arbitrators are irrelevant, because they cannot possibly call into question the independence of the arbitrator. It's only the relationships with parties that arise. (Int. 134, 6)

The senior generation wants no disclosure of relationships between counsel and arbitrators. The ICC, supported by U.S. lawyers, has opted to support greater disclosure (compare Lowenfeld 1991; see Lalive 1991).

Conforming to the liberal logic that the new Anglo-American generation embodies, it is partly a matter of introducing competition in a market that was strongly cartelized. This objective can be pursued by multiplying the number of producers, and the large Anglo-American firms have had a role in increasing the number of arbitration suppliers (e.g., London, Sweden, Vienna) competing with the ICC. But it is even more essential and also more difficult to introduce a minimum of transparency in a community of specialists characterized by personal relations so complex and so entangled that they interdict access to this market by nonspecialists.[30] Broad disclosure can provide that kind of transparency.

Because of a mixing of roles, the same individuals who belong to the networks around the central institutions of arbitration are found in the roles of lawyers, coarbitrators, or chairs of the arbitral tribunal. The principal players therefore acquire a great familiarity with each other, and they develop also, we suspect, a certain connivance with respect to the role held by the adversary of the moment. The extraordinary flexibility of this rotation of roles contributes greatly to the smooth running of these mechanisms of arbitration.[31] It promotes the reaching of acceptable awards under a regime where the players do not speak of contradictions and antagonisms that, if formulated explicitly and disclosed, would create some difficulties of legitimation. "Adversaries" can protect the processes that provide their legitimacy and prosperity.

30. We do not mean that outsiders do not participate in ICC arbitrations, only that the repeat work and most effective representation will be within the club.

31. These kinds of relationships, discussed also in chapter 4, contribute to the smooth functioning generally of legal means of resolving disputes, since the advocates can both represent their clients forcefully and avoid dramatic clashes through their personal relations with opposing counsel (e.g., Eisenberg 1976; Mnookin and Kornhauser 1979). Certainly the English system of barristers who know each other well arguing before judges who come also from barristers' chambers is another example.

The potential problem confronted by outsiders and invoked by the ICC secretariat is evident in the words of a leading arbitrator of the new generation:

> This is a mafia. There are about, I suppose, forty to fifty people in Western Europe who could claim that they make their living doing this. I'm one of them. It took me, oh, probably close to fifteen years to get to the point that when I go as I do regularly to the Swiss Arbitration Association meeting twice a year, or I go to an ICC gathering, or an ICCA gathering that I will know and be recognized, and know and talk to a number, you know, the leading figures. And if you . . . that's how you just get into it. Now why is it a mafia? It's a mafia because people appoint one another. You always appoint your friends— people you know. It's a mafia because policymaking is done at these gatherings. (Int. 85, 27)

A self-identified U.S. "associate member" of the club stated, "They nominate one another. And sometimes you're counsel and sometimes you're arbitrator" (int. 50, 9).[32]

At the same time, it is clear that this somewhat mysterious accumulation and confusion of roles represents a formidable handicap for the occasional players. In order to risk playing on the field of international arbitration, it is necessary to be one of the initiated or to draw on the services of one of the initiated. In fact, the majority of specialists of arbitration earn much more from their activity as lawyers than from their activity as arbitrators. Service as arbitrator helps above all to build and to keep up prominence in the arbitration world.[33] By contrast, the activity of lawyer represents a quite profitable activ-

32. A U.S. litigator stated, "I've appeared in Scandinavia, in the U.K., in France, in Switzerland, and in Italy, and I run into the same lawyers everywhere it's the same names. . . . And so there are people who are almost always involved in some fashion or other if there's an arbitration involving a national event of their country. . . . [O]nce you go offshore, . . . it is a very fungible group and it's the same people over and over [as lawyers and arbitrators]" (int. 51, 11). A senior English arbitrator noted the dilemma: "You're often appointed a party arbitrator by someone with whom you have worked before," and "You know you're going to work with him again. Does that unconsciously bias one? I think that's a difficult one." But "not everybody is 100 percent honest and you know it's a very great advantage to find someone whose character you really do know and can depend on" (int. 97, 13–14).

33. This division between arbitrators and counsel, where the counsel is compensated more materially and the arbitrator more symbolically, is a general phenomenon of the legal world. For example, British QCs, when they are named to the bench, gain the prestige of becoming judges, lose some of their income, and fulfill the function of judging that is necessary for the survival of the system. And those who will take the cut in pay are typically those who are more interested in promoting the universals and

ity for the almost obligatory specialists who serve outsiders confronted with the procedure of arbitration. The approach of the ICC secretariat to some extent challenges this subtle mixing of roles, but clearly personal relations and membership in the "club" remain quite important to success in this field. The ICC is working on behalf of its view of legitimacy to give outsiders a little more access to the otherwise hidden connections between the arbitration players.[34]

Anglo-American Law Firms and Arbitration Insiders

This problem for outsiders highlighted by the ICC secretariat can apply not only to individuals from areas new to international commercial arbitration, but also to the large international law firms themselves. As noted above, the insiders' club of arbitration, while expanded since the days of the pioneers, still enjoys a quasi monopoly on the functions of arbitrator. This monopoly is difficult for multinational law firms to support. When large multinational law firms decided to intervene on the scene of arbitration, they could not be content with folding chairs around a table dominated by others. It is not simply a matter of gaining access to and learning the rules of the game; they insist—and have the power to insist—also on being able to play according to their own terms. That is to say, they insist on utilizing their language and the legal technology that assures their preeminence in the international market of business law. It has therefore been necessary for them not only to enter the closed club of ICC arbitration, but also to impose a redefinition of the rules of the game.[35]

While this strategy is perfectly rational from a strict economic and professional point of view, we believe there is also a more subjective dimension to the contests. The Anglo-American practitioners seek revenge with respect to

---

legitimacy of the system. From a more economic perspective, Richard Posner makes precisely the same point about U.S. judges (1995, 133).

34. This handicap, according to the ICC insiders of the current generation, causes distrust as well. "Appearance is very important. . . . I think one can assume in many international cases the level of mistrust, suspicion of the other party is greater than in a domestic situation." The mandatory disclosure of relationships between counsel and arbitrators could thus have real impacts: "If there is a party who, if there is disclosure of something and the court is more or less uncertain as to whether or not there is really a problem of independence. . . , the court, I think, is more willing to say let's replace the person. . . . Because what we want in the end is for parties to comply with the awards that are rendered" (int. 134, 7).

35. The terminology fits the perceptions of participants: for example, according to a senior observer, "The [U.S.] lawyers are changing the rules of the game" (int. 10, 7).

the intellectual Parisian salons. To understand the importance of the sociocultural shock that promotes this desire, it is necessary to consider the context of the 1970s, the time of the first great arbitrations tied to the construction of large factories in the oil-producing countries. On both sides of the arbitration world the level of incomprehension was total (see case study in chap. 5). The professional groups in effect could not recognize each other, nourishing solid prejudices with respect to each other.

The litigators debarked at Paris (or later The Hague for the Iran–United States Claims Tribunal) with a certain condescension about the procedure of arbitration—in their eyes nothing but a bastard form of process, a sloppy litigation. They were confronted by a community of learned patricians who, while they considered themselves to be cosmopolitans, were more familiar with the theory than with the legal practice of the Anglo-American world (int. 136, 4). They knew little of a recent evolution under the influence of a young generation of litigators, whose aggressive tactics, a "vulgar justice," were gaining ground in what was a gentlemen's world on Wall Street (see Caplan 1993, 121–75)

The divide was therefore not only between two cultures, but also between two generations—even two social classes. A sophisticated U.S. lawyer long active in international arenas put it this way:

> You take the sort of dyed-in-the-wool, hard-edge, brass knuckles American litigators whose style varies from region to region and, you
> know, put them into a sort of conventional, somewhat European, international arbitration and that's like inviting that thing off the street
> into a grand salon—makes about the same impression sometimes.
> (Int. 7, 6)

These pretentious litigators sought to impose the barbarian manners of the far West and the marginal East in the salons of old Europe. They were received as completely ignorant of the proper European ways of combining business disputes with the lofty production of jurisprudence, doctrine, and legal theory. They also tended to misjudge the Europeans because arbitration, in the opinion of the Americans, was associated with the relatively low status and perceived intellectual content of U.S. domestic arbitration (the less formal, compromise-oriented arbitration largely practiced in labor and smaller commercial conflicts under the auspices of the American Arbitration Association).

Arbitration, we could say, was mistranslated. The misunderstanding was total between these litigators, on one side, who wanted to fight on their own terrain of facts with their usual arms of adversary procedure, discovery, cross-examination; and the arbitrators on the other, for whom the noble terrain was that of law (see int. 49). Certainly after the first misunderstanding each side sought to bridge the gap. But in this private justice in the service of merchants, the relation of the forces was such that one made more inroads than the other.

The European arbitrators, including some of the most notable, were converted to the English language and to the usages of Anglo-Americans. Berthold Goldman, for example, one of the most famous pioneers, learned English at forty years of age; and his flexibility was noted as follows: "Cross-examination is not accepted in France . . . barbaric . . . primitive. And except for people like Goldman, . . . he's been cross-examining" (int. 136, 8). An American litigator with considerable arbitration experience noted that the senior arbitration experts "began to realize that clients seemed to like this [cross-examination and expert testimony,] and it was clearly affecting their business, and so I mean there were only two things they could do. . . . And I found again in my experience they embraced it" (int. 51, 32). Leading arbitrators allowed the tactical maneuvers that permitted winning or losing through contested searches for facts.

The multinational law firms recognized on their side that the arbitration game in the European context was rather more sophisticated than the domestic variant that they looked down upon in the United States, and they chose to invest in this new legal terrain. They attached themselves to the services of the initiated in order to avoid faux pas and to dress up their arguments in the distinguished language of *lex mercatoria*. But one can understand the resentment of these litigators, who were forced to pay the fees of the initiated under the pretext that one must have the required expertise in the learned language that was then de rigueur in the Parisian club of arbitration. From this perspective we can see the vigor of the offensive brought by the American lobby to enlarge the club and to rationalize the practice of arbitration such that it could become offshore—U.S.-style—litigation.

This warlike terminology may promote confusion. The fact that it does not appear as aggression is critical in this operation of redefinition and of recentering. Even if the attacks and the relations of force were quite real, the violence would remain symbolic in this symbolic field. The exportation of legal technologies involves less gunboat politics than the strategy of the fifth column. This operation began in the interior of the club and with the support—at least the connivance of the founding fathers. The fifth column in this process has been the Parisian offices of the American firms. For a small number of expatriate lawyers, often married to Europeans, the practice of international arbitration represented an excellent opportunity. It permitted them to profit from their double expertise and to serve as *courtiers* between two cultures.

Interest in arbitration helped to recruit top local talent, contributing to the local implantation of these large Anglo-American firms and favoring the constitution of a nucleus of Eurolawyers. In the 1970s, this establishment in Paris did not provoke the local barriers that tend to result from such efforts today. The bar did not then feel at all concerned by the quite limited international market. A few modernists—even visionaries—saw there an opportunity and incitement to reform legal practice and to develop Paris as an offshore legal market. They welcomed the chance to help reshape the domestic legal field.[36]

On their side, the founding fathers of arbitration could only enjoy these efforts of the *courtiers* who, by opening arbitration to all the North American markets, enlarged considerably the demand for an expertise that they had mastered better than anyone. The Americanization of arbitration thus occurred with much less reticence than has been perceived, since, at least in the beginning, it appeared to the pioneers as a recognition of the merits of arbitration and an investment in the practical field (see ICC 1984). The new consumers permitted the pioneers (finally) to receive very handsome dividends on their arbitration capital—a savoir faire and an experience accumulated for decades.

Arbitration as Litigation

But the reality of the relation of forces between this small club of learned artisans and these great conglomerates of legal experts was that, rather quickly, those who had opened the doors of their club to the Anglo-American practitioners became bothered by the transformation of approaches to arbitration under the influence of the "American lobby." Perhaps the trees had initially hidden the forest. The "Americans in Paris" may actually have fallen for the charm of arbitration in the Continental manner. But behind them was lined up an army of great law firms who, by the simple fact of their mode of organization, could only throw into profound disorder a game of arbitration conceived essentially by and for the civilian academic. As a British solicitor long active in arbitration observed, "If you ever want a bunch of lawyers who are completely inflexible about international arbitration and how to conduct it, it's the Americans" (int. 85, 21). Electing arbitration, says an American close to the new generation, "doesn't mean that I necessarily want to give up

36. The first efforts to reform the French legal profession, which culminated only in some higher status of the *conseils juridiques* and a merger of *avocats* and *avoués*, took place at this time. The image of a grand unified profession had to wait until the end of the eighties.

all the trappings of full-scale litigation and what might come with it" (int. 134, 16). And indeed, the Americans have imposed many of those trappings.

As a result, noted a prominent U.S. arbitrator, "American style practice has taken off. . . . A lawyer comes with a team—more attention to fact, motions, objections, delays. Beginning to look more like litigation" (int. 50, 3). A French leader of the older generation made the same point: "The role of the U.S. firms is growing," and they "utilize more and more Anglo-American devices" (int. 115, 4). It is no surprise that the leading arbitrators of the new generation emphasize their skills of case management. The most common statement about a very popular arbitrator today, Karl-Heinz Bockstiegel, is that he is "great in procedural management" (int. 148, 9).

The artisan and the factory cohabit with difficulty. As with respect to the general-practitioner physician and the modern hospital, the model of specialization and differentiation found in the great corporate structures inevitably puts into question the traditional Continental approach. With respect to the arbitration club, there has been pressure on the more or less cooperative mixing of roles that characterized the specialists of arbitration. We have seen the impact in the issue of conflicts of interest, but it goes deeper. The new protagonists have made the problem even more serious by refusing to consider the practice of international commercial arbitration as a specialty into itself. Only a handful of law firms installed for a long time in Paris, and for that reason rather marginal in the hierarchy of U.S. litigating firms, have chosen to invest in arbitration in the more traditional manner by constituting small teams of specialists.

The large American law firms continue to consider international arbitration as but one kind of "litigation" (or, more recently, "dispute resolution") among others. As a partner in a leading New York law firm observed, "Arbitration is considered by us to be an adjunct to litigation—litigation in the courts. It's simply a different forum" (int. 47, 3). In reaffirming their competence to treat this type of matter (at least after the litigators gained ascendancy), these large law firms reject the specificity of the terrain of arbitration. They repeat that it is but one in a menu of competences and solutions that they can propose to their clients in a case of difficulty. That at least is the approach of the litigators, who have acceded in the past several years to a dominant position in the large law firms (Nelson 1988). This territorial demand is easily understood. One does not renounce voluntarily, when in full vigor, a rather prestigious and lucrative practice, especially if this form of competence appears indispensable to success in the market of international transactions. But their insistence on their own approach and their refusal to make international arbitration a specialty make it necessary for the law firms to translate arbitration to fit the knowledge and self-conception of the litigator.

This category of practitioners has been constituted by borrowing but also by opposition between the two great groups that had dominated the field of legal practice in the United States: the corporate lawyers, who held the upper hand in the large firms of Wall Street thanks to their competence as negotiators in the creation of contracts; and the trial lawyers, whose talent was exercised essentially in conducting jury trials. Since enterprises began to change the legal scene through mergers and acquisitions, and also as a result of antitrust and other litigation, a new knowledge has been developed, that of specialist in taking charge of conflict situations (e.g., Caplan 1993). The art consists precisely in knowing how to combine judicial attacks and negotiation behind the scenes in order to lead to an optimal solution from the point of view of the interest of the client. These experts in the tactical administration of disputes consider judicial recourse not as an end in itself, but only as an argument and a means of pressure (cf. Margolick 1993). The negotiators consider judicial recourse as one of the weapons that can be deployed in a conflict that will almost surely end prior to a trial (e.g., Galanter 1985).

The specialists of this parajudicial negotiation are then at the antipode of the traditional Continental model found, not surprisingly, within the club of international commercial arbitration. That model is of an "auxiliary justice," where the duty of counsel is to clarify and aid the judge in rendering good justice. The conflict specialists from the United States (or elsewhere) do not feel any responsibilities except to their client. Furthermore, they offer their clients the ability to operate for tactical reasons in many jurisdictions or types of proceedings at once. This "legal superarmament" of multiple attacks and forum shopping escalates the warfare considerably on behalf of clients able to afford it. And for various reasons, it is a service that was successful in building the power and success of U.S.-style litigation for corporate clients in the 1980s.[37]

The large law firms have tended to practice the very same strategy when handling international disputes. Yet this pragmatic and tactical approach is opposed to the tacit usages of the arbitration club. In the community of the initiated, the proximity and interchangeability of roles makes the advocates comport themselves in a very subtle manner as auxiliaries of the arbitral tribunal. Defending the interests of their clients does not in a case push them to actions that jeopardize their own credibility or, worse still, the social legiti-

---

37. It is now somewhat under attack by proponents of a truce to the "arms race," such as the Center for Public Resources.

macy of arbitration.[38] Such an attitude would have been equivalent to professional suicide in building the practice of international commercial arbitration.

But it is not the same for the litigators. Their reference group and their criteria for success are different. While the career of arbitrators is in large part dependent on the goodwill of the grand old men who control access to and prominence in the field of arbitration, litigators depend only on their capacity to satisfy important clients. That is what determines their position in the hierarchy of the law firm (Nelson 1988). In short, where one group is obliged to be quasi-referential with respect to the dogmas and the customs upon which is reposed the collective faith in arbitration, the others have but one ambition—that is, winning a good result. To get that result, they are ready to exploit any procedural tactics and forums available to them. They are willing to create difficulties for their colleagues and the arbitral tribunal and even to damage the image of this justice—which had pretended to be rapid and less costly because informal.[39] One understands the irritation of the founding fathers confronted by these newcomers who permit themselves to transform the nature of arbitration by multiplying the incidents of procedure and technical appeals.

The litigators respond matter-of-factly that it is only a matter of fulfilling their duty as lawyers and protecting, by all legal means at their disposal, their clients' interest. Even to win some time, after all, is not of negligible value economically. At the same time, this general strategy, which conforms so perfectly to their mission as defenders of the interests of their clients, permits them also to promote their own conception of arbitration. If arbitration is no longer a last resort but rather one tactical recourse among others, it is no longer correct to make of it a protected preserve for a group of initiated. On the contrary, specialists or law firms that can play simultaneously in many places are in the position of strength.

The International Field Transformed: Toward a Delocalized Market for the Management of International Commercial Disputes

Competition and rationalization, especially as promoted by U.S. litigators, leads to the judicialization of international commercial arbitration. Some commentators, especially from the senior generation, see in this evolution toward the judicialization of arbitration the preview—and the cause—of its decline.

---

38. Examples of this role abound. Recent documentations of this kind of practice in the civil-law world include Olgiati 1995.

39. A lawyer for a large U.S. firm in Paris says simply: "You know the first advice you give to a defendant in an ICC case is take your time. When they ask for the deposit, don't pay it" (int. 129, 10). The skill is "to spin out the dispute for years" (id., 9).

What good, they say, is it to opt for arbitration when this alternative is at the same time slower and more costly, but also more uncertain, than recourse to the courts? This pessimistic vision, which is in fact a plea for a return to the sources, appears overstated. It is true that the system has been transformed, and the qualities that made arbitration successful for the pioneers seem to be little in evidence. But arbitration is far from withering away. It is in full vigor.[40]

Far from dissolving itself, it seems the community of arbitration specialists has moved a long way toward forming the nucleus of a sort of offshore justice. This expression, which alludes to fiscal paradises exploited by the operators of the great financial centers, is rather far from the unified international private system of justice—organized perhaps around one great *lex mercatoria*—that might have been imagined by some of the pioneering idealists of law. The current model can be understood much better as simply a delocalized and decentralized market for the administration of international commercial disputes, connected by more or less powerful institutions and individuals who are both competitive and complementary.

Conclusion

In this chapter we have mapped the relative positions of groups and individuals in the field of international commercial arbitration. We have been able to see both oppositions and complementarities. The players on the field compete vigorously, but in terms of the universals accepted—as a ticket to admission[41]—by all the players. Examples have included the grand old men and the technocrats, the Continental professors and the U.S. litigators, each promoting

40. Not surprisingly, the current state is celebrated by U.S. litigators in part because arbitration has been "judicialized." A recent U.S. volume "designed as an intellectual pause for reflection" on the state of international commercial arbitration and entitled *Towards "Judicialization" and Uniformity* brought one of the editors, a prominent member of the arbitration community, to the following conclusion: "International arbitration thus is in large measure a substitute for national court litigation," necessary only because the parties from different nationalities do not wish their "rights and obligations to be determined by the courts of the other party's state of nationality" (Brower 1993, x). From this perspective, the closer arbitration is to the general model of courts, the better.

41. The moral tenor of the debates comes in part from the fact that potential arbitrators must invest over a long period of time, promoting a kind of cult of disinterestedness, and because the potential arbitrators must demonstrate a distance from the parochial and particular aspects of their national portfolios. Persons with strong moral beliefs and an interest in universals are attracted. At the same time, the tendency of those in the field to try to diversify their portfolios to accommodate new positions and entrants allows the field to enlarge its coverage to become more universal in another sense.

its own mix of symbolic capital—for example, age and experience, technical know-how, theoretical sophistication, ability to represent clients vigorously, prestige in a particular national legal culture. What each group represents tends also to be what they contend is best suited for the legitimation of arbitrators and therefore for the long-term success of international commercial arbitration. The competition among these different actors in the field of international commercial arbitration—and, we submit, in law generally—thus simultaneously builds the market for particular legal services and the legitimacy of the resultant law.

This intense competition among merchants of law acting as moral entrepreneurs, in addition, requires some institutional management. Our research suggests that the International Chamber of Commerce, once the preserve of a small group of arbitration aficionados, was able to play that role and help to facilitate the transformation of the field in the 1980s. International commercial arbitration has to a great extent now been institutionalized as the generally accepted private legal process applicable to transnational business disputes.[42]

The transformation of the field, represented in figure 1, can be examined in both a general and a particular sense. First, there is a general story of rationalization and institutionalization, and second, an equally important story of details of the transformation. Those details are bound to exert a powerful influence on the conduct of international dispute resolution and on competition in the market for legal services.

The boom in the market for international commercial arbitration, the arrival of new players, and the competition and power of the large multinational law firms contributed to break the traditions of the small, learned, cosmopoli-

---

42. This account of the phenomenon of institutionalization, while based on Bourdieu, obviously has similarities to certain aspects of the "new institutionalism" in American sociology. There are many similarities, for example, between our approach and that taken by Paul DiMaggio to the process of "constructing an organizational field as a professional project" with respect to art museums in the United States (DiMaggio 1991). We share an emphasis on the complex interactions between professionalism and institutionalism, and on the transformation and institutionalization that takes place with its growth. The most notable differences between his study and our approach are first, since his research was based on archival records, it did not examine the importance of social capital despite its obvious relevance to the story; second, the effort to document the development of an institution in the DiMaggio account tends to avoid probing connections to the larger world around the processes he studies, for example, the changes in municipal politics or in the role of foundations; and third, while our approach fits reasonably well with the one he describes, our focus is on conflict found in the discourses and strategies of the relevant actors rather than specifically on institutions.

tan group that built the International Chamber of Commerce and the basic institutions of international commercial arbitration. The growth and accelerated competition, we have seen, were reflected in an accelerated Weberian transformation—the routinization of charisma and the ascendancy of legal rationality.

The general or Weberian line of this story, we suggest, will be repeated elsewhere in the successful development of an international or other legal field. The social capital and charisma (and even idealism) of elite lawyers respected for their careers and accomplishments helps to legitimate the legal institutions and approaches that they favor.[43] International businesses and national commercial entities, for example, have been more likely to accept the idea of arbitration by lawyers if the chosen lawyers are recognized members of an elite with credibility in the worlds of business and politics. Once the idea of arbitration is sufficiently established, however, it can become more rationalized and generalized as it gains further economic and numerical success.

It must be remembered, however, that even when successful over a long period of time, such a Weberian transformation is only a matter of degree. The conflicts that produce the transformation continue to have an impact on the field. The grand notable arbitrators are still influential, for example, and their services are called upon when disputes are outside the routine, requiring more political sensitivity and indeed more of the authority and clout that comes with their status.

Further, as noted before, the retrospective logic of the successful Weberian scenario should not be invoked to imply that the specific characteristics of this international legal field were natural or inevitable—the product of a slogan like globalism. The particular features cannot be understood if we limit ourselves to a retrospective account suggesting the inevitability of today's "more rational" version of international commercial arbitration. The fact that international commercial arbitration currently combines a certain amount of Continental legal theory, a major Parisian institution at the core of the field, and a practice that resembles offshore litigation as promoted by U.S. litigators—rather than, for example, a less adversarial Continental style of litigation or a central focus on London or New York's institutions for arbitration—comes from the specifics of the international legal field as it was first constituted and later transformed.

While international commercial arbitration has become more formal and expensive, more like U.S. litigation, it does not make sense to describe arbitra-

43. The social capital and charisma, especially in Europe, was also necessary to overcome the resistance to the involvement of lawyers in practices closely connected to business.

tion as a given process inevitably like U.S. litigation (or otherwise, as in the pioneer days of a less formal, more "gentlemanly" international arbitration). Arbitration has evolved in response to particular social factors, and the competition we have seen *continues* about the meaning and legitimacy of particular aspects of international commercial arbitration. Any resolution of the debates about arbitration—as with respect to law—is bound to be provisional.

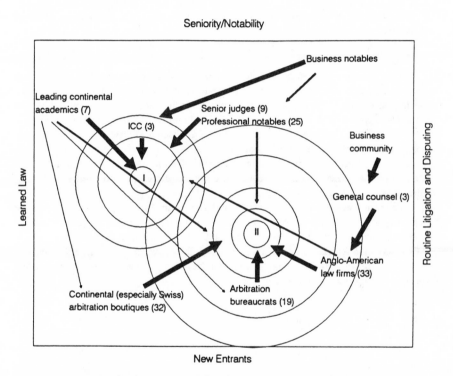

Figure 1. International Commercial Arbitration as a Field of Structured Opposition

NOTES: The shift toward new entrants, routine arbitration, and Anglo-American conceptions is represented by a move from I to II (roughly 1970–1990) in the "center of gravity" in the field of international commercial arbitration. This figure is limited to one period of transformation and largely to the central actors within the arbitration field. It seeks to show how the different actors are positioned with respect to the core of international commercial arbitration around 1970 and around 1990. The arrows show the direction of influence. The thin arrows show the more or less "disciple" relationship between two generations. The two thicknesses of other arrows show the relative strength of the influence. The numbers in parentheses are the number of people we interviewed who can be placed in these positions.

Phase I.

1. This phase is characterized by the reinvention, promotion, and institutionalization of international commercial arbitration out of the contributions of leading Continental academics, the International Chamber of Commerce, senior judges, and professional notables. We call this pioneering generation the "grand old men."

2. The leading academics contributed the "technology," especially the *lex mercatoria*.

3. The International Chamber of Commerce provided the institutional support and legitimacy in the world of business.

4. Senior judges brought the acceptance and recognition of the official justice system.

5. Professional notables brought connections and legitimacy with the domestic legal professions.

6. The Anglo-American law firms played a relatively small role.

Phase II.

1. This phase is characterized by the routinization and general acceptance of international commercial arbitration for business transactions, and its conduct as a form of "offshore litigation." The new center of gravity is farther from academic law and hostile to the *lex mercatoria*. A more precise division of labor can be seen in the new phase.

2. The Continental boutiques, containing many disciples of the earlier generations, provide the core of arbitrators for most cases.

3. The arbitration bureaucrats (including the ICC today), many of whom are also disciples of the earlier generation, contribute specific arbitration know-how and management.

4. The senior academics, senior judges, and professional notables continue to provide credibility and stature for the very high-stakes and politically sensitive cases. (Notables from areas new to arbitration also help to establish arbitration in new areas.)

5. The Anglo-American law firms provide much of the resources, clients, emphasis on fact-finding, and adversarial lawyering, and they also provide the major connections to general counsel and the business community.

4

Setting the Legal Scene for North-South Conflicts and the Collective Construction of the Universality of Law

The construction of transnational legal institutions evokes a national historical process that resulted simultaneously in the construction of both royal authority and the autonomy of law (Kantorowicz 1961). The difference is that the transnational process has been distinguished by the pervasive presence of conflict. Royal legalists constructed their own legitimacy from the power of legitimation conceded to them by the monarchy, but their distant, transnational successors gained their position by drawing on the realities of international commercial conflicts. In order to coexist with the modern holders of economic and political power, international legal experts did not have to invent[1] the notion of a "public" service entrusted entirely to legal experts. They needed only to propose their own services, developed in national settings, to defend the legal interests of the new social operators in international economic relations. New conflicts therefore became the raw material for the construction of a transnational legal order.

As suggested in the preceding chapter, a boom in international arbitration business was a key factor in fueling the changes that took place in the field of international commercial arbitration, beginning in the 1970s and accelerating in the 1980s. As revealed from the study of the conflicts and complementarities that now structure the field, international commercial arbitration has clearly moved along a Weberian path to a more routine, judicialized form of dispute resolution, and the center of power of the field has shifted from the small group of Continental professors to the increasingly powerful transnational law firms dominated by the Anglo-Americans. Part of this change, we also suggested, involved a relative decline in the role of the *lex mercatoria*.

This chapter explores the same time period from a different, but closely related and indeed parallel, perspective. It focuses on north-south conflicts, which made up most of the celebrated arbitrations of the period. The main question is how political and economic conflicts between north and south

1. As had Aguesseau, in a celebrated discourse in the Paris parliament (see Karpik 1992).

became translated into general business conflicts that could be managed by a transnational legal order, and in particular by the institutions of international commercial arbitration. How was the law—or more precisely, the law that developed along with the field of international commercial arbitration—able to extend authority over countries that had no developed legal traditions, no trust in Western-dominated institutions, and in particular no faith in some new form of transnational law? Without this achievement, the boom in international commercial arbitration would not have taken place.

It is too easy—and vastly oversimplified—to say that the power of the developed capitalist countries of the north was sufficient to impose their institutions on the countries of the third world. It avoids the key question of which institutions were able to be successful and to gain legitimacy. It is also important to see how specific national and international factors relate to and structure that success and legitimacy. The particular outcomes, as we have repeatedly emphasized, were not inevitable, and they in turn have their own impacts on the constitution of economic and political relationships.

It is also not sufficient to conclude with the observation that the result was that the economic relations of north and south were gradually "legalized." While it is true that the disputes came to be handled through the domain of law, law does not exist as a distinctive thing. It is necessary therefore to explore the set of power relationships implicated by the particular constructions of law that come to be applied within the transnational legal field. Only detailed study can reveal the space that is occupied by law in relation to economic and political power.

This chapter will address the issues of north and south in five parts. The first part will again provide the short story, describing how, through a relatively straightforward process—when seen in retrospect—the legal scene for north-south relations was set. An escalation of conflict took the form of law, requiring both sides to invest in the law and legal practice, especially U.S.-style adversarial legal practice, thus building comparable sides in an adversary proceeding that, in turn, served to provide the independence, neutrality, and legitimacy that enabled the law and lawyers to prosper.

The second part shows that, in the construction of this adversarial arrangement, part of the success of the U.S. style of advocacy came from the situation in which a certain group of lawyers found themselves. It was not just that the U.S. adversary system made it relatively easy to legitimize aggressive advocacy on behalf of countries with radically divergent interests. It was also important that developments inside the United States generated a group of lawyers eager to seek out just such opportunities and, therefore, to play the double role of promoting third-world perspectives and extending the power of U.S. legal practice—indeed, giving it roots in third-world countries that were politically opposed to the United States.

The third part focuses on the major oil arbitrations and their role in the construction of an international legal order. It suggests, on the basis of interviews with many of the lawyers and arbitrators involved in the historic oil arbitrations, that the arbitrations should be considered "founding acts" for the international arbitration community, serving to build reputations and beliefs in the law that went well beyond the importance of those arbitrations in the particular disputes that generated them.

The fourth part explores the invention and role of the transnational law that grew out of the oil arbitrations and served in a crucial way to build and legitimate the field of international commercial arbitration both to business and to national legal fields. The now controversial *lex mercatoria*, seen in the previous chapter in relation to the internal politics of the international arbitration field, must be examined from a broader perspective. It should be seen as an aspect both of the autonomy and universality of the international legal field and its subordination to economic and political power.

Finally, the conclusion seeks to relate the construction of the universality of international commercial arbitration to the development of an international legal field and law more generally.

Independence and Legal Adversarialism: The General Picture

The legitimacy of the transnational legal order rests on the way representation is structured. In simple terms, one side defends the established interests, others speak for the dominated interests; and this opposition serves collectively to produce the universality of law and make prosperity for the intermediaries. That, in short, is the story of the setting of the legal scene for north-south conflicts.

A useful starting point to trace this general story is the effort, beginning especially after World War II, of what became known as third-world countries to increase their sovereignty and share of the wealth from natural resources. When multinational businesses found their mineral concessions undermined or nationalized, they turned loose lawyers who had until then been kept in a relatively secondary, even marginal, role.[2] As described by a former in-house counsel, after the Libyan nationalization in the early 1970s, the "chairman [of

---

2. As we shall see, the companies did not only, or even principally, rely on the law at this stage of north-south conflicts over natural resources.

the company] . . . was very cross," and said, " 'You bloody lawyers are sitting up out there in the stables eating your hay and your corn all the time. You never do anything! Now's your chance. Do the law.' So from that moment on virtually, through the executive, . . . we didn't exactly have carte blanche, but very close to it" (int. 70, 8). And as we shall see, in these and other north-south conflicts, the lawyers unleashed on behalf of one side quite often found colleagues from similar law firms and legal practices on the other side.[3]

This tactic of a legal escalation, however, initially placed the young governments of the third world at a handicap, since they were uniformly underequipped in matters of legal competence. For some countries, including those of the Persian Gulf, nonreligious legal traditions were more or less nonexistent (Kelly 1980, 225). Other new regimes distrusted their lawyers, since they were seen as part of the comprador bourgeoisie closer to the interest and the culture of the West than to the groups who led the nationalist movement. The army of Nasser's Egypt exemplified this fairly widespread hostility to the local legal profession.[4] Furthermore, also as exemplified by Nasser, the most prestigious members of the government were increasingly technocrats, especially engineers and later economists.[5] Even where lawyers had once been important, they lost a considerable portion of their power and prestige (Lynch 1981; Reid 1981, 165–71). Moreover, even if there were competent national jurists in whom the third-world leaders had confidence, that would not have helped

3. As a New York lawyer noted about his opponent representing a third-world government in a major arbitration in Paris, "Our offices weren't even all that far apart" (int. 49, 23).

4. According to a long-time practitioner in Egypt, "When Nasser came in . . . up to that time most of the leaders of Egypt had been lawyers. . . . [E]ngineers, army officers, medical doctors, those became the important professions, and law was relegated to the bottom of the pile. Plus there were mass admissions to Egyptian universities, so everybody who graduated from high school was entitled to go to the university. . . . [T]hose who got the lower scores . . . went to law school" (int. 188, 13).

A practitioner with long experience in Indonesia made a similar observation about Sukarno: "I guess he saw lawyers as being a conservative drag on the kinds of revolutionary development that he thought Indonesia needed. . . . [L]aw had fallen into disrepute, lawyers had fallen into disrepute" (int. 46, 5).

5. According to Donald Reid, "Nasser and his Revolutionary Command Council systematically destroyed the features of the political system that had brought lawyers to the fore" (1981, 165). Further, "The orientation of the new regime was not yet clear in 1954 when lawyers placed third in occupational prestige—behind only doctors and bank directors—in a survey of 249 higher civil servants. . . . And by 1966 only 12% of Egyptian secondary students in a survey thought law a high status occupation. Law barely edged out secondary teaching at 10% and trailed far behind engineering at 64% and the military at 30%" (1981, 168).

very much in ensuing legal battles, since they typically took place on the terrain of their adversaries.[6]

Indeed, multinational companies who felt threatened by actions in the developing world most often sought action initially within their own and kindred legal systems. Domestic legal remedies provided a ready means to attack the countries with whom they were in conflict. When Iran national-ized—or tried to nationalize—the Anglo-Iranian Oil Company in the early 1950s, for example, the British company proceeded on a number of fronts in legal systems outside of Iran. A lawyer involved noted that one legal strategy was to "arrest . . . a cargo in Asia." Another was to bring "proceedings in Japan and Italy" (int. 70, 5). Similarly, when Libya nationalized British Petroleum in 1971, according to the same lawyer, "we were running the arbitration in paral-lel with litigation in Italy and . . . thirty-five cases" (id., 4).

The third-world countries were then obliged to defend themselves in some fashion or another. They turned to "legal mercenaries" from Europe or the United States.[7] One way to account for this approach was that, as a prominent Arab lawyer pointed out, they thought they had to pick "the best lawyers," and they assumed them to be Western (int. 101, 3).[8] In the competition to provide legal counsel to the (rich) countries of the third world, the U.S. law firms enjoyed several obvious advantages. First, the young nationalist leaders who had recourse to their services could avoid returning to the colonial powers against whom they had recently been contending for independence. Second, large U.S. law firms were better equipped than most of their competitors on the Continent and elsewhere to administer complex disputes that, as noted before, often took place simultaneously in many countries. Third, they were familiar with the contentious, aggressive tactics that the adversaries were deploying, and they did not hesitate to employ the same tactics to show clients that their interests were well defended.

Finally, the rhetorical education of the U.S. lawyers (the famous Socratic

6. While the legal terms in the contracts or concessions remained relatively brief, they tended to exclude all recourse to local legal systems in cases of conflict.

7. This process can be found even in the early 1950s in the nationalization of the Anglo-Iranian Oil Company. Mosadeq employed several Belgian lawyers to help build the legal argument against the British and the company (Elm 1992, 209). With respect to Libya, the major business that went to Curtis, Mallet, for example, commenced in 1977 when the firm "was hired to defend Libya in a breach of contract suit . . . stemming from Libya's nationalization" (Bruck 1982, 1).

8. As a British lawyer noted generally about north-south legal conflicts, they had to participate in "a process which they think they did not understand. . . . And in order to do so they had to deliver themselves into the hands of Western European lawyers—not just Western European arbitrators—but Western European lawyers" (int. 85, 17).

method in the law schools) probably helped to prepare them to play just such a more or less reversible role in defense of clients from completely antagonistic social positions (Mertz forthcoming). Their professional ideology presented this characteristic of legal practice—the adversary system—as the best proof of the neutrality of their legal institutions. Serving opposing social interests could only enrich these lawyers and further promote the autonomy of the legal practice they pursued.

This emphasis on conflict in the U.S. legal culture was perfectly suited for "setting the legal scene" for north-south conflicts. As noted in chapter 3, European "jurists"—typically considered auxiliaries of a justice supposed to embody the general interest—were trained to maintain a distance from the claims of clients. The U.S. "lawyer," in contrast, has no hesitation in demonstrating legal inventiveness and tactical aggressiveness. The cause of the client is defended by any available means. Far from considering the role of mercenary as a liability, U.S. lawyers are proud of their effectiveness on behalf of their clients. Far from seeking to minimize tensions, therefore, the U.S. lawyers unapologetically exacerbate and magnify them (see case study in chap. 5).

This characteristic U.S. focus on conflict, not surprisingly, appealed to the antagonistic situation in which the third-world leaders found themselves. It is not that the leaders embraced the law. They distrusted the norms of a justice that pretended to be universal but, in their opinion, did nothing but dress up the interests of the rich countries and a Western conception of the world in a universalizing discourse (see Asante 1993; Snyder and Sathirathai 1987).[9] Nevertheless, they felt it necessary to fight on legal terrain. In such a fight, the third-world leaders could at least employ mercenaries who would, without any qualms, practice the tactics of total legal warfare—"scorched earth" litigation. In this way, the leaders could feel that their cause and their interests were defended as vigorously as possible.

From a third-world perspective, however, it was not just a fear of bias that understandably made them nervous about battles on legal terrain. Even if they could fight with the very best legal weapons, seemingly devoted to their position, they knew that they could not easily control those who were conducting the legal battles and who could, in their own interests, either work

9. According to a justice of the International Court of Justice from Senegal, Keba M'baye, in 1984, "For a while the notion that there is a system of international justice will not be shared by some countries, notably those of Africa, Asia, and Latin America, who still see arbitration as a foreign judicial institution which is imposed upon them" (International Chamber of Commerce 1984, 295).

things out between themselves or unduly prolong the legal activities—in either case, at a cost to the clients.[10]

A fear of a dispossession by experts is quite common, but here it is exacerbated by the geographic and cultural difference between the site of the legal dispute and the place of actual conflict. Since there exists no formal institution embodying neutrality—no World Court, for example—in the disputes of private international law, this distance between actual conflict and legal conflict is both a condition and a manifestation of the neutrality of the legal process. Many of the north-south arbitrations have been held, for example, in places emblematic of neutrality, like Switzerland. Or, if not set in a place that symbolizes neutrality, the arbitration takes place in one or another of the competing sites offering arbitration "detached" or even "floating free" of national legal systems. The independence of the place, whether Austria, Belgium, France, Holland, Switzerland, or elsewhere, therefore becomes an aspect of the independence of the arbitral process.

For many reasons, therefore, the setting of arbitration gives the impression of a legal scene held meticulously aside from the place of all the social relations that produced the actual conflict. All the protagonists, moreover, have an interest in constructing this scene. The lawyers on both sides use this distance to promote their autonomy. The political or economic leaders—even if distrusting arbitration—use the distance to avoid putting themselves in a position where, because of local sensitivities, they would have to risk alienating irreversibly an adversary who remains a potential, even obligatory, commercial partner.[11] These leaders gain because they can act more reasonably, even from an economic point of view, away from the pressures of their specific business or political constituencies. The secrecy of arbitral awards further helps remove them from the close scrutiny of too many interested parties.

This simple story is true as far as it goes, but it also makes the story seem inevitable—political and economic conflicts caused one side to escalate legal tactics, and the other side had no choice but to respond by hiring the lawyers best suited for their needs. And the result was a legal order legitimated by the

10. They were also handicapped because they had to conduct the battle in terms of a law developed by academics to embody universals—which serves to disarm the contestants as the conflict is moved to the symbolic realm.

11. An example is the *Government of Kuwait v. Aminoil* arbitration. According to one of the lawyers involved in the arbitration, "It was a very friendly arbitration . . . a topnotch tribunal." This same lawyer also described the relationship between the lawyers on either side of the case as very cordial, with correspondence among them continuing to the present. Further, there has been consultation by one party to the dispute with a lawyer who represented the opposing party, on unrelated matters arising after the dispute (int. 64, 10).

adversary system. The complexity of the story will be seen in the subsequent sections of this chapter, but it is useful to begin by restating the problem of international commercial arbitration, which is also the problem for law more generally.

Leading the Way: Legal Missionaries and Double Agents

In conflicts where the political and economic stakes are considerable, the difficulty is to manage the delicate combination of proximity and distance between the holders of power and those who embody the legitimacy of justice. For those who hold the upper hand in terms of economic power, the question is how they can protect their position of strength while delegating authority elsewhere. For the lawyers and their justice, the question is how to affirm the autonomy necessary for legitimacy while at the same time manifesting sufficient fidelity to the economic powers who must in the end find these services worth purchasing and deploying. Once again, it is the diversity of the positions held by the lawyers in their professional roles that permits the resolution of this apparent contradiction between autonomy and control.[12] A coincidence of interests, accordingly, between the holders of economic power and the lawyer-representatives has accounted for an evolution that has allowed the seemingly irreconcilable to be reconciled. A conflict determined in critical respects by political and economic conditions can be reenacted on the legal stage as independent of political and economic power.

We have emphasized already that lawyers are the professionals of a double game, serving clients and the construction of a particular legal order. The story of the legal scene for north-south conflicts, however, cannot be understood as one simply of lawyers playing out a natural role. Despite initial appearances, the representative roles that lawyers played in this setting of the legal scene for north-south conflicts were not, in fact, completely interchangeable.

The credibility of the representation given to the interests of the third world depended on the existence of a connection—a kind of homology—between the interests of the lawyer-intermediaries and those of their clients. When, for example, those responsible for the oil industry of countries like Algeria, Iran, Libya, or Saudi Arabia sought legal counsel, they looked for

12. As noted in part 3 of the book, it is also important to see that, within the third-world countries, there were "local converts" who could serve also in the role of double agents—promoting local interests at the same time as the interests of the international-arbitration community and law in general. Part 3 also explains how the diversity of approaches to arbitration and the relative fluidity between them facilitated these developments.

individuals with a suitable profile and career. Given the intensity of the political feelings and the stakes involved, they were attracted to potential allies, not just mercenaries. They sought lawyers who had demonstrated an opening toward the problems of international economic relations and a sympathy, or at least a sensibility, with respect to the position of the third world.[13] The availability of such "turncoats," who put their talent in the service of the third world, was especially important early in the setting of this legal scene.[14] It is therefore useful to see how these lawyers sympathetic to third-world interests were produced.

The tremendous growth in the 1970s in the vocation of asserting the legal interests of the third world was facilitated, even provoked, by the arrival of the petroleum manna, but this economic logic cannot explain it all. This success was by no means assured at the beginning of the 1970s. The pioneers of these developments—as is often the case—reveal a mixture of socioprofessional determinism and of idealism. Here, as elsewhere, there is nothing like the exclusion—objective or subjective—from elite career paths to incite individuals to explore less frequented options and paths. But those new paths are as likely to reveal themselves as cul-de-sacs as openings that lead to major successes.

Strategic choices that appear in retrospect to have been the most evident were often also the most risky. They attracted only the excluded or the idealists, who were often the same individuals. Sometimes they succeed and sometimes not. All we can suggest is that those who happened to take the path we shall describe in retrospect made a good strategic choice—important for their own careers and for the contributions made to the establishment of an international legal order for international commercial disputes. The example of the

13. An early example was Frank Hendryx, an Exxon attorney after World War II who became legal adviser to Abdullah Tariki, the oil minister of Saudi Arabia around 1960; he later was described as "legal adviser to the Libyan Oil Minister" (Hirst 1966, 62). Hendryx helped develop legal arguments for the renegotiation of the oil concessions and played an important role, therefore, in helping develop the legal approach for OPEC. For example, according to Hendryx, "The idea that oil concessions are 'something inherently sacred in origin and operation, separate and distinct in law from other commercial agreements and to be governed by special and separate legal rules'—this idea, which was deliberately fostered by the oil companies, is a legal 'fable and fancy' " (Hirst 1966, 63). The importance of his role was mentioned by one of the early leaders of OPEC (int. 181) as well as a prominent British lawyer active in the Middle East at the time (int. 69). It is significant that Hendryx, while adopting a perspective favorable to changes in contracts, did not support local law. He insisted that his interpretation was of international law.

14. E.g., Samuel Goetjkian of Surrey and Morse in 1976, who represented Sonnetrach (int. 49, 19).

U.S. lawyers is especially revealing, since they played such an important role in representing clients in the north-south disputes.

Our focus is on the generation that graduated from U.S. universities in the 1960s touched by the third-world fever found in those universities.[15] Not only were they "idealistic" (int. 26, 36) and predisposed to defend the new legal claims of the third world, but also their personal itineraries—Peace Corps, missions of cooperation and development, work with AID—had familiarized them with the generation of political leaders produced by decolonization. Others had shown an interest—quite rare during this epoch in the law schools—in international law and politics. All or nearly all belonged to this liberal intelligentsia, strongly critical of the conservative establishment and such individuals as John Foster Dulles, who had dominated the U.S. State Department since World War II and imposed their political orientation in the name of "the defense of the free world" (Barnet 1973).

Their criticisms were all the more virulent since many of them belonged to the same social and professional milieu. Like the others, they had been educated in Ivy League law schools.[16] Also like them, they considered themselves invested with a messianic task—to spread among all the world the political ideal that, in their eyes, America embodied. But rather than seeking to realize this imperial objective through the force of arms, as their predecessors had, they placed their hopes on the force of law (see Gardner 1980).[17]

Unfortunately for these missionaries of the "rule of law," the possibilities of employing themselves in accord with their convictions were limited.[18] The

15. One prominent U.S. lawyer, who represented an Arab government in the 1970s and 1980s, got an early start in 1960 when he took a leave from a Wall Street law firm to accept a Ford Foundation fellowship—a pilot program that influenced the subsequent Peace Corps—to assist an attorney general's office in West Africa (int. 13). A lawyer a few years older described how members of his generation "got the bug—you know the New Frontier" (int. 26, 56). Another, who graduated from law school in 1970, built his interest on earlier academic travel and the training of Harvard's China law specialist, who found him a fellowship through the International Legal Center to go to Indonesia (int. 46, 3).

16. The possession of social capital is part of what allowed them to succeed in facilitating major changes and then embedding them in the U.S. legal system. These developments parallel the transformations that took place in the New Deal in the United States (see Shamir 1993). This phenomenon is more general, as shown by Bourdieu's discussion of Manet and the break from French academic painting (Bourdieu 1993).

17. "This law and development [movement] was the second . . . post–World War II generation of lawyers" (int. 26, 35).

18. According to an international lawyer who graduated from Harvard Law School in the mid-1960s, "But if you wanted to work and be an international lawyer, forget it.

State Department was dominated by the hawks—and offered no access to other legal careers in any event. The provincialism of law schools condemned specialists of comparative law to a very marginal position. Finally, aside from a few matters of international arbitration and some cases before the Court of Justice of The Hague, international cases were almost nonexistent. Under these conditions, if they wanted to avoid the pressures and uncertainties of the competition for partnership (Galanter and Palay 1991) in large law firms, which were unlikely at that time to have offices abroad, these internationalists had no real choice but that of expatriation through the agencies of international aid or development.

This choice of alliances with economic-development agencies conformed both to their commitment to public service and their cosmopolitan interests, but it was quite risky at the time from the point of view of their careers. The economists who controlled this sector paid little attention to the law and tended to relegate the lawyers to the role of administrator or teacher. According to one of the lawyers in AID at the time, "AID had no tradition by the way of supporting law. There are a lot of lawyers in AID, but no tradition. Lawyers were not program officers, you follow me? They were legal advisers. And it was very hard to get money . . . [for the law] from AID in those days" (int. 26, 33). Another recalled that it was as if the lawyers were saying to the economists, "what about us?" with the economists replying that policy, not law, was what counted (int. 31, 4).[19]

Nevertheless, many of these lawyers found a way to legal internationalism, and it is easy to see how the new disputes tied to the problems of development were attractive to this cosmopolitan elite. Threatened with marginalization, they could instead make their idealistic ventures and attitudes relevant to a high-visibility and well-paying clientele. For example, according to one member of that generation, "AID became a place where you could be in practice, go to government, come out and develop a commercial practice involving the developing countries. And then slowly but surely these lawyers began to get

---

There was no way to be one in the law firm and there was no way to go. . . . [P]eople were told that if you want to be an international lawyer the only thing to do is you go to the State Department. . . . And then the general feeling was that will be it—terminal, dead end" (int. 26, 106).

19. The domain of development was dominated by engineers and economists both in the United States and elsewhere, including in the third world, which explained also why third-world countries were "underdeveloped" in matters of international business law. Examples include the role of the "Chicago boys" and their students in Latin America, especially but not only in Chile (Latin American Bureau 1983; Silva 1991) and the "Berkeley Mafia" in Indonesia (see generally Markoff and Montecinos 1993 on "the ubiquitous rise of economists").

involved with . . . lawyers overseas" (int. 26, 37). The interest in these disputes came not only from those ready to put themselves in the service of the third world, but also, in a manner more indirect, those who could use these initiatives to contribute to revitalizing a sector of legal knowledge that had been at that point very little exploited.[20]

Large law firms had neglected this international economic area because they had little strategic interest in the potential clients for these services. The rare business enterprises that invested outside of the Western world relied more on relations with their clientele than on the force of law to guarantee their access to resources or to markets. Many of the businesses, in addition, occupied such a position of strength that they could economize on law (see Elm 1992, 33). They could prevail without resorting to legal tactics and weaponry (see Ellickson 1991 on the topic of "order without law").

The upgrading of the offensive and defensive capacity of the developing countries on the terrain of law—fortified with the new generation of lawyers—then obliged many companies to increase their legal investment. Indeed, as shown by the example of the oil conflicts, described below, the conflict relation went further in constructing a legal order. The conflicts between north and south "valorized" the knowledge of lawyers in framing the leading tactical argument in international economic relations. These conflicts, therefore, not only constituted a specific know-how, which went on to serve as a model for the regulation of different kinds of disputes, but also allowed the winning of *lettres de noblesse* in matters like the *lex mercatoria*—the ongoing effort to formalize an international "law merchant" for these new conflicts.[21]

The Paradoxes of Arbitration in Petroleum Disputes

In the representation of international commercial arbitration, the great petroleum arbitrations occupy a quasi-mythical position.[22] Opposing the north and the south, important multinationals and third-world states; combining important political stakes, in terms of sovereignty and commercial interests of considerable size—they are the perfect example of the great, complex con-

---

20. It is interesting that a distinguished Harvard professor of international law, Richard Baxter, put Libya in contact with the New York law firm that represented the country in the 1970s and 1980s (int. 13; see Bruck 1982).

21. This doctrine, as we shall also see, served to provide the necessary *droit savant*, a learned law developed by specialists as "doctrinal, theoretical (work of theoreticians) or scientific, systematic" (Oppetit 1992, 344) (quoting H. Capitant).

22. See, e.g., Barton and Carter (1993, 543).

flicts that this type of international legal system appears to have been designed to handle. They also provide a kind of showcase. If this institution can demonstrate publicly its utility for disputes involving such exceptional circumstances, a fortiori it must be capable of resolving the more mundane commercial differences that arise every day in ordinary economic dealings.

The observers potentially attracted to arbitration, moreover, are not only the potential consumers of arbitration. They include also the potential producers. If the highest magistrates or the most eminent professors will put their talents in the service of this justice for merchants, a fortiori their less prestigious colleagues will be eager also to follow them. The great petroleum disputes represent this way at the same time both the "nobility" and the facade of arbitration.

The petroleum disputes were founding acts. They made arbitration known and recognized. The importance of the financial, political (the redefinition of colonial relations), and legal (the relationship between sovereignty and the respect of contractual obligations) stakes incited a certain number of important actors from the legal field (high judges, noted practitioners and academics, leading law firms) to become interested and to invest in this mode of dispute resolution. The efforts and intellectual activity that they deployed for resolving these new, exceptional conflicts in a legal manner served to construct the minimum base of knowledge necessary to build a field of practice. They furnished an occasion for a series of investments in knowledge, institutions, and political relations that permitted the basic "equipping" of this new market. The basic equipment also required rules and the constitution of institutions capable of handling the work of international arbitration. All this occurred as if, through the mechanism of great conflicts, a small portion of the profit of the petroleum industry was converted into symbolic capital in the form of a new legal order.

At the same time, however, these great arbitration matters occupy only a marginal, even negligible, place in the history of the petroleum industry.[23] Their tremendous importance in the history and folklore of arbitration is not at all matched by importance at the time of the oil nationalizations. The petroleum industry may therefore have produced the legal order, but it did so merely by accident and without self-awareness.

23. The resort to arbitrations in the major oil nationalization disputes is not even mentioned by most of the accounts of the history of that period, e.g., Kelly 1980; Yergin 1991; Goodman 1981; Hirst 1966.

Law, Lawyers, and Conflict in the Petroleum Industry Prior to the Era of Nationalization: Companies as Quasi States

Until very recently, law and lawyers occupied only a very small position in the petroleum industry. Practical management and strongly personalized relationships handled the power differences of the different protagonists. In this world of engineers, entrepreneurs, and even diplomats, lawyers had scarcely any choice but to be "confidence men" used to gain effectiveness and flexibility rather than for legal rigor. They were in any event small in number and occupied positions mainly of secretary or of notary (int. 70, 11). They could be brought in at the last minute to formalize agreements concluded without their participation. In practical terms, it was necessary for them to choose between the law and business. At that time the majority of their colleagues working in in-house positions in commercial enterprises were in the same situation. Lawyers for businesses were synonymous with lawyers of second class (cf. Rosen 1989).

In such a context of economic relations, law was of marginal importance for the leaders of the companies and their spokespersons. The engineers or diplomats who dominated these enterprises gave little importance to lawyers in producing their contracts.[24] As a former general counsel observed, "Virtually everything got settled by negotiation. People knew each other, they were relatively responsible, they were mostly big actors rather than small and middle size" (int. 70, 39). An experienced U.S. practitioner described the situation as follows: "These are rough, tough people who have gone out there and made deals with the sheiks and the emirs, and there was a very large Texan component. These are rough guys, and lawyers, you know, 'You wrap that up.' The lawyers were seen much more as Japanese use lawyers, you know, as notary publics" (int. 13, 7).

Contracts in their eyes were never more than provisional pieces of paper, of secondary importance. Contracts could always be amended or renegotiated according to circumstances. A former in-house counsel described the attitude: "The big boys can say, 'Well, I may do this on the swing, but I'll get it on the roundabout somewhere else'" (int. 70, 40). In this delocalized industry, which had become with time a sort of "great family of expatriates," all that really counted was written in a network of personal ties. This distrust for the law

---

24. It is interesting that the most famous lawyer serving oil clients from a law firm in the 1960s and 1970s, John J. McCloy, was retained initially in 1961 in response to the formation of OPEC and in order to avoid antitrust exposure in the United States (Bird 1992, 517).

is explained also by the power relationships.[25] Linked by secret agreements, the "Seven Sisters" (Sampson 1991) were assured of monopoly profits that permitted them to pursue a political strategy of "clientelism," both around their own governments and in the countries where they operated.

These huge companies became so much the bastions of the establishment that they considered themselves in one sense above the state and in another quasi-statelike with respect to their attitudes to the populations "under their responsibilities." While somewhat self-serving and exaggerated, an Aramco executive was quoted as stating, "What we did for Saudi Arabia is a story that's never been told. We brought them into the world. We buried them. Oil was almost just a sideline. I've never seen anything so paternal" (Robinson 1988, 86).[26] As part of those responsibilities, they welcomed a small, selected contingent from among the local elite to their schools and universities (int. 70, 28). This was largely a matter of training a cadre of engineers who would ideally be both competent and devoted.[27]

These huge companies also contributed to the emergence of a small nucleus of administrators and of lawyers who had become their intermediaries—even ultimately their adversaries—within the local departments occupied with petroleum matters. Indeed, a list of "who's who" in the movement to establish OPEC and assert more control over the national petroleum industries would include many who obtained legal educations abroad, especially in the United States. Examples of legal backgrounds include Fouad Rouhani, the first secretary-general of OPEC;[28] Isa Huneidi, legal counsel for Kuwait Oil;[29] Suleiman Maghrabi, Libya's first prime minister under Gadhafi;[30] Sheik

25. "The oil companies had been spoiled for years. And in their market, I mean when I first began to learn about it [in the 1960s], they were just, they could do what they wanted to do. And [in the late 1970s] the tables had been turned so now the seller was saying no, we want to do it" (int. 13, 6).

26. According to an Aramco lawyer, "We had our differences, but they appreciated that they did need the help of a company such as Aramco. And we wanted to be that company and tried to be good citizens and were so recognized" (int. 64, 2).

27. Yergin notes that during negotiations with oil companies in 1971, OPEC was represented by Iranian finance minister Jamshid Amouzegar, educated at Cornell and the University of Washington; Saudi Arabian oil minister Zaki Yamani, with law degrees from New York University and Harvard; and the Iraqi oil minister, Saadoun Hammadi, with a doctorate in agricultural economics from Wisconsin (1991, 581).

28. From Iran, English educated, and for a time employed by Anglo-Iranian Oil Company.

29. An English-educated Palestinian and longtime legal counsel for Kuwait Oil Company.

30. Who had a doctorate in economics from George Washington University and had worked as a lawyer for Exxon (see Sampson 1991, 252).

Zaki Yamani, the famous Saudi Arabian oil minister;[31] and, from Venezuela, Juan Carlos Perez Alfonso, one of the founders of OPEC.[32]

The leaders of the companies considered it in their interests to arrange matters in a friendly fashion and avoid direct challenges to this discreet system of patronage. They could protect their positions by, in effect, "throwing some ballast" periodically by accepting slight reevaluations of the portion of profits conceded to local leaders, and the local leaders in turn could be used to help control individuals and groups showing tendencies toward independent activities.[33]

Impetus for Change

The rise of nationalism and the challenges to the international oil cartel put the paternalistic arrangements in question. Prior to that time, great companies had a tendency to consider themselves as the tutors of these young countries, just emancipated from colonial domination.[34] The company leaders now felt betrayed by their protégés and compelled to reconsider their attitude with respect to the pieces of paper drafted by their lawyers. In spite of their attitudes of indifference or hostility to legal approaches to problems, the company leaders were thus brought again to "discover"—as they had in past controversies

31. He studied in Cairo, then law at NYU and international law at Harvard. He opened the first law office in Saudi Arabia (Yergin 1991, 640). Note also that his predecessor, Abdullah Tariki, studied geology and chemistry at the University of Texas, working also as a trainee geologist in Texas. The relationship of Tariki to the U.S. lawyer Frank Hendryx has already been noted.

32. He studied medicine at John Hopkins University, subsequently studying law in Venezuela. He went into exile in the United States after World War II, using the time to make an extensive study of the international oil cartel, antitrust enforcement, and regulation of oil in Texas (Goodman 1982, 148–52).

33. For example, Aramco and Saudi Arabia were evidently able to make mutual adjustments. According to Hirst, the producing countries were "forever" enjoining the companies "to keep up with the spirit of the times" (1966, 60). The perspective from the producer countries is given by Fouad Rouhani: "It has been said, in defense of the major oil companies, that they have shown themselves willing to make changes in concession terms from time to time in the interests of the governments and peoples of the countries in which they operate. . . . [T]he companies have submitted to change only when they have considered this to be inevitable. . . . The fact that none of the concession agreements . . . has remained unchanged proves the compelling nature of circumstances rather than the accommodating attitude of the concessionaires" (Rouhani 1971, 272).

34. Put in the terms used after the controversies began, Abdullah Tariki noted that "They treat us like children" (Hirst 1966, 58).

(Elm 1992)—the force of law and the virtues of strictly construing contractual obligations.[35]

In the meantime, the economic conditions of exploitation of oil had also profoundly changed. The fact of the rapid growth of demand for oil was a part of the story, but the changes were more profound. In the place of a cartel of great bureaucratic companies, who managed their domain in a patriarchal manner and provided security for their investments over the long term, there emerged a highly competitive and unstable market. Competition came from bidding wars involving both the producers of oil and the oil companies.

In effect, the arrival to power of new generations of nationalist leaders, characterized by third-world ideology and a desire to gain mastery over their natural resources, coincided with the arrival in the Middle East of the "independents"—the small producer companies not belonging to the cartel of the Seven Sisters. This convergence was not by accident. Because they wanted to launch new programs and notably more ambitious economic development, the new leaders had many new requirements—financial as well as administrative. They wanted not only to participate in the capital and then also the profit of the companies operating on their territory, but also to control the timing of exploitation (Sampson 1991).

This new politics corresponded perfectly to the strategy of the independents, who had been gaining ground since the 1950s.[36] Not having access to the reserves controlled by the cartel of the great companies, these small producers were willing to negotiate for rights of exploitation under conditions that were much more advantageous for oil-producing countries, especially those adept at "playing the competition." The balance of power had changed. It had become a sellers' market even before OPEC had really entered the scene.

Libya had gained several advantages from the independents in the 1950s and 1960s. Under the Gadhafi regime, which came to power in 1969, the Libyans sought to exploit this advantage systematically, dictating conditions to small entrepreneurs who had no real alternative solution (Sampson 1991, 249–56). The other Arab states were very attentive to this show of strength

---

35. Discovering the law again did not necessarily mean abandonment of other strategies. Even after the Libyan expropriation, for example, the lawyers who were unleashed to fight the nationalization were told in one instance not only to "do the law," but also "don't bump the enemy. But bump them gently so that you don't get into trouble" (int. 70, 8).

36. According to Fouad Rouhani, "the independents found favor with the developing countries, because they showed willingness to accept the new conditions these countries desired to establish for the development of their resources, and which the major companies were by no means ready to concede" (Rouhani 1971, 51).

and used it for their own profit as well. The other governments also sought to increase their resources, therefore aiming to join with their peers in emancipating themselves from foreign domination.

The events then followed a simple pattern. It sufficed to denounce concession agreements that for the most part borrowed from archaic legal forms of the colonial period. The nationalist leaders could build their arguments on economic modernity and third worldism. They denounced the political legitimacy of the colonial and patriarchal structure, and they highlighted also the economic costs of cartel agreements inconsistent with free competition. Finally, while they certainly did not concentrate their approaches on the law,[37] they did not neglect legal argument. According to Rouhani, for example, "Support can, if needed, be found in legal theory for the mutability of contractual provisions in order to establish their harmony with changed economic circumstances" (1971, 274; see Robinson 1988, 103, citing Yamani). The few law-trained leaders, fortified with the early generation of "turncoats,"[38] could put their arguments also on the terrain of law.

The strategy of the Seven Sisters had led to an underexploitation of their reserves in order to preserve their freedom to maneuver. The independents, in contrast, had every interest in accelerating the rhythm of prospecting and exploitation necessary for them to obtain a profit. Bidding wars took place, aggravated by the Israeli-Arab tensions, as the occasions of potential conflict multiplied. The small independent producers served as detonators: first, because they increased the pressure on the companies of the cartel; and later, because the weak position of the independents made them the first victims of the aggravation of tensions (Yergin 1991, 577–80).

Before attacking the majors, the leaders of the oil-producing countries tested the new arrangements on the small oil companies (Kelly 1980, 332–36). The independents had neither a fallback position nor a network of influence that could be mobilized effectively for their defense. They had practically no choice but to concede or to bring the matter onto the terrain of law. There was not great hope on that terrain either, however, since the contracts that they had signed reflected the weakness of their negotiating position. But it was still only a matter of skirmishes.

---

37. Legal training, as noted elsewhere, especially outside of the United States and the common-law world, did not traditionally lead to careers that drew heavily on technical legal expertise. It did, however, allow these individuals to include the law among other strategic approaches.

38. Especially Frank Hendryx.

The great battles were not really engaged in until Libya, fresh from the first easy victories, attacked the majors and notably British Petroleum in the early 1970s. From the misadventures in Iran, in the early 1950s, BP had accumulated a certain experience in legal battles.[39] It was considered in fact somewhat of a leader of the petroleum industry on the terrain of law. The other OPEC countries, as noted before, were quite attentive to the Libyan example and ready to fall in line behind Gadhafi. They could act by nationalizing, as in Iraq, or by more moderate means to move toward majority participation. For both sides, in short, the engagement in Libya had important symbolic value.

The Consequences in Constructing the Legal Scene

The analysis of this situation draws on the scheme developed by Braudel. Braudel contrasted the legal logic of the impersonal market with that of a mode of quasi-domestic production where exchange relies more on personal ties (1982). In his scheme, the "global" operates like the "domestic," with the market in between the two domains. The north-south situation, however, reveals that the separation between the impersonal and the quasi-domestic stages or floors of the economic house is far from complete. There may be a greater or lesser interaction, even competition, between these different modes of structuring economic activity. The law and the market may prevail on terrain that has been domestic and personal, but law and the market could also lose. In either of the two situations, the process has its own dynamic.

In the example just described of the petroleum industry, exemplified especially in Libya, a generation of newcomers, including politicians and small independent producers exterior to the system of patronage, played the role of detonator. The shock waves unleashed by the resultant confrontation then went on to change progressively the entire edifice of clientele relations constructed by the earlier generations of petroleum operators in the Arab countries.

This process of destruction, however, created its counterpart. The investment in the law—strengthening law departments, hiring counsel, litigation, and arbitration—financed the construction of a legal apparatus that served as a substitute for disrupted personal relations.[40] But more precisely, the legal apparatus complemented and complicated the play of social relations by the

39. BP's legal department, according to a retired member, was in fact founded to handle the litigation against Iran in the early 1950s (int. 70, 11). Both Iran and BP were considered by their peers to have special insights because of the earlier experience, which can be seen as part of an investment in law (see 181).

40. See also chapter 11.

introduction of a new dimension and new intermediaries. As a result of the conflicts, the practitioners of law entered into the network of personal relations in order to reestablish *on another plane* the interrupted communication between partners who provisionally became adversaries.[41]

The success of this building of connections, as noted before, stems from the ability to play a double game. The lawyers exacerbate the conflict, all the while proposing their good offices as intermediaries to resolve it. They speak the law, and they produce it. They also do not neglect the importance of their own personal relations. They cultivate precisely the relations of clientele that the law pretends to ignore—notably, first of all, the relations between lawyers on all sides, and especially through the strong ties of apprenticeship between mentors and disciples.[42] Indeed, at the heart of the arbitration system today is this flexibility and the multiplicity of professional and personal ties between those who are relatively initiated.[43] The "club" members constantly promote

41. The lawyers' double role has been recognized, for example, by Eisenberg, who noted that the opposing lawyers tend "to take on a Janus-like role, facing the other as an advocate of his principal, and facing his principal as an advocate of that which is reasonable in the other's position" (1976; also Mnookin and Kornhauser 1979). A recent history of Coudert Brothers provides a fascinating example of how U.S.-British relations at the time of the World War I blockades by the British were mended in part by the fact that the key players in the disputes were all part of a "small and tightly knit" international law community: "Thus, by common instinct, they strove to smother the sparks of controversy in what Lansing [for the United States] called lawyers' verbosity and Coudert [for the British] referred to as lawyers' haggling." Furthermore, "As friends or friendly acquaintances, . . . they could, within limits, speak frankly with each other" to restrain their clients (Veenswijk 1994, 178).

42. In arbitration practice, quite often the arbitrators, the clients, and their counsel gather around a table in an anonymous room of a grand hotel—for many days, even many weeks. Despite the banalities of the decor, however, the charisma of the great arbitrators permits them to embody the authority of law. Their own authority makes up for the lack of formalities and connections to the state. Furthermore, the very close ties that exist in arbitration between the principal actors facilitate a successful presentation of this ceremony behind closed doors to a very restricted audience. The personal dimension therefore bolsters the formal authority available for the resolution of disputes through arbitration. The example illustrates the general point, discussed in part 3, that it is false to see relational capital built on personal relations and the rule of law as different models. They can also be complementary.

43. This role of lawyers is hardly controversial, but it may be useful to note what it means for the oil arbitrations. The Libyan arbitrations, of course, had representation only on the side of the claimants, but more recently, the arbitration following Kuwait's nationalization of Aminoil property led to a full-scale arbitration. Among the very well known members of the international arbitration community involved were, for Kuwait, Alan Redfern and Martin Hunter, British solicitors and the authors of the leading British text on international commercial arbitration; and Professor Ahmed El-Kosheri, probably

and support other members and potential members, whether or not in the particular interest of the client. While the club may be criticized as a cartel or even mafia, its selective and progressive openness has allowed this personal dimension of arbitration to continue and adapt to new interests, conditions, and entrants.[44]

The personal networks that are both reflected in and grew out of the great oil arbitrations are an essential part of the modern success of international commercial arbitration. The fragility of international commercial arbitration, nevertheless, obligates it to be more than just an international club. In rendering their decisions, arbitrators do not rely solely on their personal careers and authority, which would suffice to get them taken seriously, but also on the social capital of a particular international system of justice. This system of justice, moreover, must constantly provide evidence of its credibility. The legitimacy and the success of international commercial arbitration, therefore, rest on the combination of personal relations and the legitimacy of the justice applicable to arbitration.

The Paradox Examined

The paradox of the great petroleum arbitrations, which echo so faithfully the political history of this industry, can be explained by this analysis. The starting point for this analysis, however, is the recognition that the celebrated arbitrations appear to have played only a very secondary role; the leading actors and their chroniclers, as noted above, have essentially ignored them (e.g., Engler, Goodman, Kelly, Yergin, Sampson). During the crisis period of the 1970s, recourse to arbitration did not at all impede the principal protagonists from confronting each other on more public terrain, nor from negotiating, collectively or individually, in a parallel fashion. It even happened that the leaders of a company would reach an agreement in which they would concede points that an arbitral tribunal was clearly about to decide in favor of the company. One lawyer-participant thus lamented, "I have been confronted by situations in which oil companies have shown quite pathetic disinclinations

---

the best-known Egyptian in the arbitration field; for Aminoil was William Owen, formerly in-house counsel for Aramco and involved in the well-known Aramco arbitration with Saudi Arabia; the Lalives; William Ballantyne, an English QC with a long Middle East specialty; and Berthold Goldman (int. 64, 10).

44. Chapter 13 explains the functioning of this process, which uses a network of clientele relations to build a distance between the "initiated" and their national origins and to produce the universals necessary to legitimate this private justice in new territories and domains.

to see cases through to the end. . . . [T]he hearings . . . had got to the point
. . . to give a massive award. . . , but they threw it away" (int. 81, 16).[45]

The celebrated Aminoil arbitration is an interesting example of the relationship of a noted international arbitration to the actual petroleum dispute.[46]
According to sources involved in the dispute, Kuwait had already nationalized—without any fanfare—the major concessions operating in Kuwait, BP
and Gulf. The oil in the zone where Aminoil was operating was "very poor
quality, sulfurous, and heavy" (int. 79, 6). It was difficult, therefore, to figure
a fair way to split the profits. Kuwait's government, delicately balancing the
pressures of nationalistic movements, decided it had to nationalize, but the
sides could not agree on the amount of compensation. Since the arbitration
clause in the concession agreement was of uncertain validity, both parties
decided to agree to arbitration at the urging of the Aminoil side (int. 64, 9–10).
It turned out to be a "very friendly arbitration" (id., 13; Redfern 1984; int. 79,
4). It was hard fought as a matter of legal practice, but it was merely a sideshow
in terms of Kuwait's nationalization of foreign oil concessions.

One is tempted by these stories to suggest that the law and indeed the
dispute resolution practices were only a reflection of social relations. Justice,
we could say, is but a theater of illusion in these examples, an effort to distract
attention from the realities of power; this "legal" activity was only a distrac-
tion from conflicts that were resolved mainly by negotiation or, in the case
of Libya, by power politics. The error, however, would be to oppose the "legal"
battle with "political" negotiation, for they form one whole. Furthermore, in
this type of conflict, where the decisions are not automatically enforced, the
decisions of the arbitrators can often be the point of departure for a new
negotiation in which political and economic arguments can also be given an
appropriate or even determinant weight.

45. The question of who controls the termination of the dispute is part of the tension
between business and law. In litigation, for example, lawyers probably have more
control.

46. The also famous Aramco arbitration in the late 1950s was similar. It did not
involve in any fundamental way the relationship between Aramco and Saudi Arabia,
only an agreement that the government had made to allow shipping by Aristotle
Onassis. According to one account, "The government pointed out, look, we have already
committed ourselves to Onassis. And our reply was, well, you've committed yourselves
prior to that to us. Well, we don't interpret the agreement that way covering the transportation of oil. And we will certainly be liable to Onassis if we don't do everything in
our power to have him enjoy the fruits of which we promised him, and for which
he's already made certain concessions, and then give him a certain consideration"
(int. 64, 2).

The parties could not agree, especially with Onassis in the middle; but "it was a
friendly difference. So the parties decided they would go to arbitration" (int. 64, 2).

Finally, we cannot neglect the power of the symbolic capital that the decisions themselves represent because of the autonomy manifested by those who have rendered them. The fact of the decisions, promoted and celebrated subsequently by the participants, is part of what builds the legal order. It is instructive, therefore, to contrast the realist account of the Aminoil dispute—a friendly disagreement about how much value to place on poor-quality oil of peripheral importance in relation to concessions already nationalized amicably—with the legal, retrospective account of one of the lawyers for Kuwait, a partner in Freshfields of London:

> [A]t the core of the dispute was one of the most difficult and politically sensitive problems of State contracts—the public right of a developing country to exercise sovereignty over its natural resources, set against the private rights of a foreign corporation under a concession agreement. (Redfern 1984, 74)

In sum, the distance between the legal and the practical—or political—terrains of operation, in fact, makes them complementary, and it also makes arbitration strategically useful in the evolving administration of the structural, complex antagonisms that oppose industrialized countries and countries that are essential to supply their needs. Arbitration creates a distance and a language that can legitimate this form of justice applied to both friendly disputes and more politically controversial ones.

The history of economic relations between the West and the countries of the Middle East cannot be limited to the activities of the petroleum companies. The great petroleum arbitrations in the 1970s and beyond marked the end of the era of concession agreements characteristic of the postcolonial period, but they also marked a beginning: the construction of legal bases for a new commercial order that permitted the West to recuperate through great construction projects a large part of the profits lost by the Seven Sisters. In their own way, as we shall see, lawyers have contributed more than the financiers of the City of London and Wall Street to recycle petrodollars, and to prolong the economic domination of the West, because they helped to permit it to continue on other bases. The investment in law seen in the petroleum arbitrations has paid off over the long term and in a global manner.

The Invention of the *Lex Mercatoria*

The legal importance of the great petroleum conflicts depended on the fact that they coincided with a dramatic increase in international commerce and the emergence of new states insisting on their legal sovereignty. As long as the economic exchange between north and south proceeded essentially under a more or less colonial regime, the issue of the applicable law was hardly posed. Market domination was accompanied, and reinforced, by legal domination, and the supreme authority of the judges of the key metropolises was the best guarantor of the overseas investments by their fellow citizens. The appearance of the independent states, coupled with the internationalization of production and exchange, raised the question of the applicable law. As we shall see, this fundamental question was behind the development of the *lex mercatoria.*

The Internationalization of Private Law

The question of applicable law arises especially with respect to investments in construction projects, such as factories, power plants, or airports, since traditional legal principles would relate such projects to the courts and law of the states where the construction has been undertaken. Foreign investors, through recourse to a forum such as that of arbitration, in fact sought to avoid those local tribunals at any price. Nevertheless, if the companies wanted to protect their interests effectively, it was not sufficient to exclude recourse to the local judges—under the pretext that judges were part of the local political system. It was also necessary to prevent all risk of recourse to the laws of these countries. The companies and their governments would then be able to slip away from laws and regulations unfavorable to Western interests. Given this situation, and the reluctance of developing countries to agree to the law of the contracting Western country, we can see why there was so much strategic interest in the invention of this notion of "general principles of international commerce," put in issue in the petroleum conflicts, and later receiving its Continental doctrinal respectability under the name of *lex mercatoria.*[47] Subsequent attacks on this doctrine should not detract from its achievements (see chap. 3).

This general notion had developed already in the 1930s in the arbitration clauses in contracts for petroleum exploitation, enabling the negotiators to avoid having to determine the applicable law. The 1954 Consortium Agree-

47. A longtime English adviser of the oil companies emphasized the connection of the petroleum arbitrations to the more formalized *lex mercatoria* attributed by many to the writings of Berthold Goldman commencing in 1964. Citing the terminology in the concession agreements, the adviser stated that the "concept . . . had been presented, though in different terminology. . . . And Goldman has picked up something and I, I must admit, given it . . . an academic dressing" (int. 81, 2). In the Anglo-American world, there were also other legal doctrines that emerged around the same time to promote the internationalization of development contracts with state entities (see, e.g., Lillich 1993).

ment with Iran, for example, was to be governed by "principles of law common to Iran and the several nations in which the other parties were incorporated and, in the absence of such common principles, then by and in accordance with principles of law recognized by civilized nations in general, including such of those principles as may have been applied by international tribunals" (Lauterpacht 1993, 4). Given that Western jurists considered themselves the only legitimate interpreters of civilized law, and in fact controlled the leading institutions for international law,[48] this rather vague formula appeared to them sufficient to preserve the interests of their clients and to assure to them a margin of maneuver in case of conflict.[49] At the same time, it enabled the governments of these young states to avoid losing face by too easily abdicating their legal sovereignty. Finally, since the jurists of the new countries were educated in the great European legal tradition, in local universities or abroad,[50] they tended to believe that their own law was consistent with that tradition. In short, as in the colonial system but in a more discreet manner, the interests of Western merchants were protected by the affirmation of the universality of their system of law—and of their rights.

This pretension was put in question in the political conflicts of the 1960s and the 1970s. In forums like the United Nations, the third world demanded its own law (e.g., Jones 1983; Krasner 1985; Snyder and Sathirathai 1987).[51]

48. Advisers to oil companies were in fact close to the centers of international law. For example, Rene Dupuy was quite close to the Hague academy; and Eliju Lauterpacht was an international-law scholar and the son of another major international-law scholar.

49. Interestingly, according to one influential legal adviser with strong credentials in public international law, the Libyan language that led to arbitration was the same as that found in Iran. The reason is that the pre-Gadhafi monarchy had sought help in drafting from Shell, which through this adviser picked up the Iran language (int. 81, 3). In this manner, we can see, the seeds of the *lex mercatoria* were planted rather self-consciously by international lawyers.

50. For example, we counted five of the leading Egyptian members of the arbitration community, including Ahmed El-Kosheri, with degrees from Paris. The leading Algerian figure, Mohammed Bedjaoui, now a justice of the World Court, was also educated in France. Of course, as noted elsewhere, the younger individuals tend to go abroad to the United States.

51. The New International Economic Order thus fed into these debates through such doctrines as "permanent sovereignty over natural resources." The key proponents of the NIEO, it should be noted, were third-world economists (e.g., Raul Prebisch of Argentina) and Western sympathizers, with lawyers in developing countries playing a subordinate role (consistent with the hierarchies already noted) (int. 56). Prominent lawyers in the third world who promoted aspects of the NIEO, however, have played important legal roles, including appointment to the World Court and integration into the arbitration world (e.g., Bedjaoui, M'Baye, Jiminez de Arechaga).

Some, like Algeria, Libya, and Saudi Arabia, followed the example of Latin America by contesting even the principle of submitting their disputes to arbitration.[52] When they finally accepted the idea of arbitration, such countries wanted to fight the legal battles with all the more determination. As noted before, they recruited from among a growing number of benevolent champions available to serve the cause—and the market—that these countries represented. Like the multinationals who faced them—with petroleum companies and the great construction companies on the front row—they spared no resources in defending any norm of interpretation advantageous for them. Accordingly, "everyone and his brother" among the specialists of international law mobilized in the battles that took place around these famous "principles" of international commerce. Until then, these principles had been protected from precise definition of content or effects.

As its inventors had anticipated, the ambiguity of this notion made it an ideal terrain for these rearguard battles to which the oil companies had surrendered to gain time in the face of the demands of producing countries. The companies could relate the demand for economic sovereignty to the right to alienate as part of freedom of contract.[53] They could argue, in short, that the third-world countries had given up through "stabilization clauses" the possibility of nationalization or expropriation (as did Aminoil in its dispute with Kuwait). Then, when this first barrier had fallen, the lawyers could argue that, even if states had the right to nationalize, they must furnish prompt, adequate, and effective compensation that could not in any manner be determined by their own courts. And so on.

A Sociology of the Lex Mercatoria as It Relates to North-South Conflicts

Rather than focusing our account on the rhetorical powers demonstrated in this legal repartee, with more or less acquiescence in or critique of the doctrinal work, it seems to us more important to the sociology of the legal field to follow another line. In particular, we note that, in constructing this doctrine for the account of their clients, the promoters did not forget their

52. Saudi Arabia passed a law prohibiting "the Government and all Saudi Public Corporations from submitting either to a foreign law, the jurisdiction of foreign courts or to foreign arbitration" (Mustafa 1984, 248). The prohibition was evidently relaxed in 1983 (Mustafa 1984, 250; see also Bedjaoui 1992, 11). The Latin American hostility is described in Siqueiros (1990).

53. One proponent of general principles in one of the Libyan nationalization arbitrations (in which Libya did not appear) stated, "I mean the point we were making really was whatever system of law you take, you can pick out a few really basic norms. For instance, murder is wrong, genocide is wrong, contracts are to be honored rather than breached, you know" (int. 70, 15).

own interests. The recognition of great principles under the name of *lex merca-toria* (and other international-law doctrines) revealed itself as an extraordi-narily useful tool of promotion for this new market in handling international commercial conflicts. The history of this doctrine furnished also a beautiful illustration of the effect of homology between the field of arbitration and that of international economic relations. The flexibility of the *lex mercatoria* not only permitted Western enterprises to win time when confronted with the escalation of demands of the third world, but allowed its inventors to gain time as well, preserving their position when confronted with the new law firm offensive in this market.

A principal merit of this doctrinal construction was that it furnished a double legitimacy—political and learned—that the European pioneers of arbi-tration needed, in a new field of practice at the crossroads of the worlds of merchants and learned jurists (see Oppetit 1992). The collective image of neu-trality of the academy permitted these notables of law to intervene in a very delicate domain—that of postcolonial economic relations—by invoking great principles that could justify a middle way.[54] They thus found a way to protect themselves from the most extreme demands of one side or the other.

In order to construct legal reasoning capable of convincing two parties authoritatively, it would have been necessary to be supported by a body of texts or of well-established jurisprudence. This was hardly the situation in the case of international commercial arbitration. There was no authority to turn to for this doctrine other than "academic dressing" (int. 81, 2). The charis-matic notables, therefore, found it that much easier to invoke grand principles of law in support of their decisions, and the principles became embodied in those notables in the eyes of their colleagues and their potential adversaries. Their colleagues, as noted before, were as a general rule too respectful to these high judges or academic grand masters to dare contest their right to speak in the name of law. In the first generation of jurists of the third world, there was also scarcely any opposition on this point to the grand professors—of whom quite often they had been disciples.[55] As a French-educated Syrian lawyer

54. There is a parallel to the way that the traditionally brief and general civil-law contracts allowed a middle way between business and law. The approach allowed law-yers to maintain a distance from the details of business, and if there was a conflict, the courts could fill in the needed specifications to handle the dispute.

55. According to Audit, "the investor sees in it a guarantee; the host State concurs because his conception of international law is not the same as co-contractor's. In prac-tice, therefore, such clauses only referred the difficulty to the arbitrators. It will be seen that, on the whole, the private party's aim has been reached from this point of view" (1988, 100).

stated, "All believed in the *lex mercatoria* in the period 1960–70" (int. 122, 2). There was an illusion of consensus.

In contrast, neither the new nationalist leaders nor the large law firms that served them were disposed to accept a discourse of authority that, as with respect to all symbolical power, has no other value than that recognized by those to whom it is addressed. The relative decline of the *lex mercatoria* is therefore in part the product of its success. The rapid growth of the market of arbitration led to the arrival of new recruits from outside of the world of the grand professors. They had neither the status that permitted recourse to this type of argumentation nor the predisposition to accept it from others.

The *lex mercatoria* continues to be criticized by the Anglo-American legal community for its perceived lack of precision and the discretion it gives to the arbitrators. They are also willing to argue the case against the *lex mercatoria* on behalf of the south.[56] One U.S. leader of the younger generation stated that "developing countries . . . generally don't like *lex mercatoria* because they see it as another way . . . to avoid the application of the law . . . that was chosen in the contract" (int. 104, 23). Participants from the south do indeed make this criticism. A leading Egyptian lawyer and arbitrator thus stated critically that some European arbitrators "set aside local law" (int. 197, 7; see Sornarajah 1989; int. 198; int. 101; Audit 1988, 103; Asante 1993). An Arab leader in the arbitration community was blunt: it allows them to "break the contract from local law" (int. 101, 2).

These criticisms do not mean, however, that this doctrine has lost all strategic or practical interest.[57] It continues to preserve a good part of the influence of the grand masters of arbitration, even if it becomes more and more secondary with the arrival in force of the Anglo-American practitioners. Entering in this doctrinal debate, even if only to criticize the *lex mercatoria*, places the contestants on the terrain of the grand professors in defining the rules of the game and the legitimate arms. It therefore remains important within the international arbitration community.

The preeminence of learned debate in the little world of arbitration contrib-

56. Such criticisms on behalf of the south also pave the way for approaches such as bilateral investment treaties and GATT, which are much more detailed—akin to the detailed contracts traditionally favored by U.S. law firms.

57. Even promoters of Islamic arbitration may at times ground their arguments in terms of the *lex mercatoria* (int. 199). They argue that the *lex mercatoria* and Islamic law are perfectly consistent. And current Continental defenders of the *lex mercatoria* continue to keep it very much alive in scholarly debates and probably in arbitrations where the choice of law is unclear. For the suggestion that the doctrine can serve to accommodate important third-world concerns, for example, see Leboulanger (1991).

utes to select the most lettered among the new generations of practitioners in this market. The new entrants then maintain the market value of the form of specific competence that the grand masters possessed—and still possess— better than anyone else among their potential competitors. The preservation of the value of learned capital assures a measure of continuity in the passage of power from the generation of the notables to that of the technicians of arbitration. It excludes also the noninitiated, and notably those too "political" or "merchant," who would rather have "arbitration without law" or would undermine the legitimacy of arbitration.

In addition, the control that European professors have over the sites for the production of learned discourse on international law is also one of the better guarantees of Western domination in the market of north-south arbitration. Western lawyers are able all the more easily to concede a few places to the lawyers of the third world in order to protect their control of the discourse defining the orthodoxy of arbitration. Strength of their learned position permits them to make a few apparent concessions that serve also to reinforce their strength and control.

If it has served to prolong the hegemony of the learned jurists, the particular doctrine of *lex mercatoria* has by contrast lost much of its utility in actual commercial negotiation. Practitioners have conceived of other terms, which are no doubt more complex and more technical—and also even more opaque— for getting around or putting in parentheses the controlling question of the applicable law in international conflicts.[58] One of the leading senior arbitrators from Switzerland thus volunteered that the "time of *lex mercatoria*" is ending (int. 180, 6).[59]

The Changing Approach to Investment Contracts

The growing practical skepticism about the *lex mercatoria* does not mean, however, that the lawyers for the multinational companies are ready to concede the legal sovereignty of the developing countries—or that the leaders of these states have abandoned their nationalist demands with the decline of

58. Indeed, the contest over the terminology for problems of law and business is part of the process to be studied. We see the recent emphasis, for example, on antidumping, antitrust, and the importance of bilateral trade agreements. While there is no longer a vacuum, these approaches can be seen as competitors to the regime of international commercial arbitration.

59. According to El-Kosheri and Riad, in the oil industry one no longer sees contracts referring to "general principles": "The modern petroleum agreements not only omit such partial internationalization, but also go a step further by positively expressing a choice of the national law of the contracting public entity" (1986, 270). For a common-law perspective on the same phenomenon, see Lillich (1993).

third-world ideas. Nothing has fundamentally changed on this point. It is just that the positions of both sides are now less entrenched. The fight is no longer for the principle but rather for conserving tactical advantages in case of conflicts. And the possibilities have multiplied.

The great arbitrations of the 1970s and 1980s gave practitioners of international law an experience and knowledge that they put to work in the drafting and the negotiation of international contracts. The most qualified—or the most specialized—have put in place a panoply of contractual terms and jurisprudential rules or practices that permit them to protect quite effectively the legal interests of their clients. The principal merit of these new terms comes from their pragmatic side and their flexibility in utilization,[60] which makes them able to hide from any political judgment that is too simplistic. They become all the more difficult to denounce as pro-West or third worldish since they do not aim to exclude a priori one law or the other.

Refusing to let themselves be locked up in a debate on principle, the experts define their object in a manner much more pragmatic. It is a matter of optimizing the strategic position of their client in a case of conflict and of minimizing the disputing risk.[61] They do not hesitate to put to use a contractual montage that can combine different legal systems with their respective advantages and inconveniences with respect to the different phases of a transaction or the process of production.

In this new context, the inequality of the legal positions in north-south relations is no longer given in advance. It depends on the capacity of each of the parties to procure for itself the advice of the best specialist—and to place it in operation. It no longer suffices to negotiate a "good" contract; it is necessary to be capable of assuring the follow-up. But, as will be discussed below, this is often at the stage where the developing countries are the most handicapped by the absence or insufficiency of local legal expertise. For this reason, as suggested below, multinational companies gain an advantage on legal terrain, at least statistically.

The statistical advantage is important in two senses. First, in losing its predictable and systematic character, Western domination on the terrain of law has gained in legitimacy (on the importance of this statistical reproduction of hierarchies, see Bourdieu 1989). Second, with respect to the lawyers, they

---

60. It is not only about substantive terms, since, as shown in the chapter on the United States (chap. 8), there are numerous new and blended approaches that, for example, combine public and private, mediation and arbitration.

61. The writings of Jan Paulsson—directed often to the third world—emphasize precisely this approach (e.g., Paulsson 1987).

have gained further in terms of credibility. No one can doubt any more their utility to business interests in the prevention or the settlement of international commercial conflicts. Even better, the lawyers have proceeded to impose their own needs. That is to say, for example, they have progressively put into play the rules of the game of arbitration. The multinational companies are in this way investing in the construction of these legal services that serve them. And they participate in the directing committees of the arbitration community, where strategies that take into account all the complexity of local legal situations are elaborated.[62]

The legal risk therefore tends to become a risk like all others, that is to say susceptible of being analyzed and managed in a manner that is nearly rational. The rationality is available at least for the companies that have experience with these international commercial relations, or have the means to avail themselves of the advice of experts who have acquired this knowledge.

The Development of Third-World Legal Expertise

With certain variations, a similar evolution can be found in the countries of the third world. More particularly, it can be found in those countries that, thanks to the riches of their underground, have become the repeat players of arbitration. The appetites raised by the multiplication of petrodollars, coupled with the lack of experience of the leaders of these young states in the administration of contracts, proliferated north-south conflicts.

One typical scenario is well known.[63] In order to win the contracts in the first place, the Western enterprises underestimate their costs, and they then try to recover them later by claiming substantial damages for breach of contract. An experienced American litigator—typically representing a third-world country—summarized the situation as follows:

> A lot of it had a certain similarity. Construction projects for natural, liquefied natural gas plants, refineries, fertilizer plants, pipelines. Typically Western contractors, U.S., French, Italian, Japanese, always

62. There are numerous user committees, for example, connected to the arbitration centers. A concrete example in the ICC world is Nicolas David, general counsel of Elf and an active participant in the arbitration world.

63. The case study in the following chapter is an illustration. A U.S. lawyer who represented both sides in major arbitrations of the 1970s and 1980s remarked, "And by the way, that was a classic example of what happened a lot during that era, which was the contractor, multinational, goes and bids, and how does it win the bid? By bribing several of the local developing-country officials. Then they get the contract at a low bid, and they make it up by the experts in the course of the contract" (int. 49, 34) (Yemen-Dutch).

ICC arbitration clauses. In all of these cases I've just described, Switzerland, whether Lausanne or Geneva as the forum, turnkey projects where the project is not finished on time and the cost overruns are substantial, well in excess of, you know, 50 percent of the contract price. I mean, astronomical cost overruns usually and then a dispute about whose fault it was. The contractor would almost inevitably argue . . . that conditions . . . were impossible. The labor force was not reliable. The permits that were supposed to be available were never available to buy sand and gravel and get water and transportation and all that. The owner would always take the position that the contract required them to complete the project within a certain period of time and for a certain price and if they wanted an amendment there was a process for getting an approval of an amendment. It had to be in writing signed by both sides and approved by the, usually by the . . . ministry of oil and gas. And their response, if you will, to the contractor's arguments were usually you assumed the risks of local conditions which you investigated before the project and so that would be the clash and then you could see building around that the *lex mercatoria* arguments that all of these contracts were actually subject to revision based on some international *lex mercatoria* that said basically that terms and conditions change—well then, the contract should change. (Int. 51, 21)

It would not be uncommon for the contractors to build, often from the opening of the project, a legal dossier that catalogued all the difficulties encountered in fulfilling the contractual obligations. For example, they would note every time that the responsible local administrative persons charged with oversight refused their demands, judged them excessive, or acted to avoid losing face with local hierarchies. The disputes could rapidly become inflamed. Bad faith was often attributed to the other side. The work slowed or stopped; the payments were blocked or retarded; and finally the enterprise would decide to invoke the arbitration clause provided for in the contract.

This arbitration would begin hostilities, or tactical maneuvers and reactions: "Both sides would . . . launch sallies, . . . little attacks from their legal positions" (int. 51, 22). The attacks were all the more numerous, since the inventiveness of lawyers was stimulated by the importance of the financial stakes for them as well as for their clients. This type of contest, however, is nevertheless unequal. One side supports itself solidly on all the doctrinal and jurisprudential traditions available to advance claims that have been carefully documented over a long period of time by specialists. In contrast, lacking the equivalent technological infrastructure, the local administration is often forced to build a defense on force majeure or their good faith.[64] Important evidence is missing, and it is often too late to reconstitute it. The result is all the tactical maneuvering of the talented legal mercenaries does little more than gain time. The time, however, is not a negligible benefit. Delay does enable them to put pressure on the claimant and to renegotiate for a somewhat smaller obligation.

The legal situation has evolved from the repetition of this and similarly catastrophic scenarios. Even the political leaders most hostile initially to the formation of a legal profession for such economic matters have learned to recognize the strategic importance of this form of legal and practical expertise. Certain ones, like Algeria and Libya,[65] have created a specialized group of lawyers to administer international commercial disputes. There is some agreement that the repeat players from the south, like Algeria, no longer lose with "depressing regularity" (int. 132, 26; Paulsson 1987).

Limitations of the Market in Local Expertise

The local effect of the new market in north-south arbitration, however, was mainly to the profit of the university faculties of law and a small cosmopolitan fraction of the bar (chap. 11). They may assist, as experts in local law, the large international law firms whose capacity to handle a huge dossier gives them the lead position in the arbitrations, or they may be chosen as arbitrators by the authorities of their countries or those of a nearby country.

This market for their services, however, remains nevertheless very narrow. More precisely, the lawyers of the third world take little more than crumbs—relatively speaking—from it. Rare are the arbitrations that take place in their countries and still more rare are the ones where they are named as presidents of an arbitral tribunal. According to one Arab, the ICC thinks "Arabs are all together," while Europeans are neutral with respect to other Europeans outside their country (int. 121, 1). Quite often the two party-appointed arbitrators are Western (Bedjaoui 1992, 15–16). A leading Arab arbitrator thus complained

64. According to a Swiss arbitrator who saw many of these cases, "The host country did not have the people to administer the contract" (int. 180, 3). A French lawyer with much experience representing third-world countries states that they had "bad dossiers" and "always lose" (int. 114, 1). Noting that in the Eurotunnel case "four lawyers started on the first day to build a file for arbitration," another French expert stated that the third-world countries in contrast had "too often nothing but good faith and a sense of being hurt" (int. 117, 5). A lawyer close to Kuwait said that the "Kuwait government lost every . . . commercial case that came to ICC, whether in London or Paris" (int. 79, 17).

65. The Libyan department was part of the response to the litigation unleashed by the nationalization of oil in the 1970s (int. 70, 8).

that "Arabs appoint arbitrators who are not Arabs" (int. 111, 1). Consultation about local law represents only a tiny fraction of the rewards available from this market—the number of consultations and their importance remains limited. In short, the hegemony of the Western lawyers on this market of north-south arbitration is difficult to contest. While often denounced, it has successfully been prolonged.

These third-world countries in any event have only a very small number of legal notables with both the linguistic competence and the cosmopolitan experience required to be recognized in the milieu of international arbitration. They belong for the most part to the generations in which only a small faction of the elite benefited from a cosmopolitan education. This education typically commenced in the best local establishments, frequented by the *héritiers* of the colonial bourgeoisie, then continued in the universities of the metropolis. This elite generation is in the process of disappearing. Distrust by third-world leaders of this legal culture modeled on colonial culture has prevented it from having a successor.

Among the new generations of lawyers in these countries, it is quite rare to find individuals able to combine this double capital—social and scholarly—necessary to belong to the cosmopolitan legal culture. It is true that, for at least ten to fifteen years, the countries of the West and notably the United States have multiplied the number of scholarships offered to the lawyers of the third world. After a long period of neglect, the institutions charged with supporting development—most notably the World Bank—have recognized the importance of legal technology (int. 23). They are now working to reduce this deficit of expertise. But the demand is strong for these hybrid experts, capable of serving as legal *courtiers* between the center and the capitalist periphery. Many of these hybrid lawyers are tempted by the huge offers that are made to them by the large international law firms (e.g., Egypt) and by institutions like the UN or the World Bank that must hire individuals from the third world to maintain their image of neutrality. The salaries in these settings—and the career boost—simply are beyond the scale they could imagine if they elected to reenter their own country.

Far from being reduced by the market in north-south arbitration, the deficit in these countries in international legal expertise is becoming aggravated. The elder representatives of the cosmopolitan legal elite are themselves approaching closer and closer to the European centers of arbitration.[66] By install-

---

66. The leading individuals from the developing world named as arbitrators to us have thus typically served or are serving as judges on the World Court in The Hague (e.g., Jiminez de Arechaga, Bedjaoui, M'Baye). We saw in Egypt that many of the best-known international lawyers spent increasing amounts of their time in Paris. It is interesting

ing themselves provisionally or semipermanently in the great capitals of international law like London or Paris, these notables from the periphery proceed on a path that has a social as well as professional and commercial dimension. They rejoin there a diaspora formed by the other *héritiers* of the comprador bourgeoisie, a number of them having been exiled with the arrival of the nationalist regimes. This displacement from legal nationalism favors their integration into the cases and milieu of arbitration.[67]

Their presence, even if in very small numbers, places in question the pretensions to universality of these institutions, which purport to embody international justice. They may feel like provincial cousins, but they receive some compensations when they are admitted, for example, to the prestigious "academies of international law." They become peers of their venerated masters.

Finally, and perhaps above all, the symbolic recognition is not without material rewards. The notoriety and the contacts secured through arbitration bolsters quite substantially a career of intermediary in north-south economic relations. The learned and honorable practice in the service of international prosperity and peace represents also the best "cover" for an activity of *courtage*, well remunerated but little valued, since it touches the more or less occult world of baksheesh and influence peddling.[68]

Conclusion

As in the preceding chapter, we conclude by relating our examination of international commercial arbitration to the legal field more generally. We suggested in chapter 3 that the competition and complementarity among moral entrepreneurs interested in business provides a dynamic that helps to account for the specific transformations that take place in law, legal institutions, and legal practices. In this chapter we have seen how transnational economic and political conflicts catalyzed by decolonization became the impetus and the raw material for the construction of a transnational legal order. Both perspectives are necessary to account for the specific features and role of international commercial arbitration.

---

also how this drift affects the perspective of the members of this legal elite. The best-known Egyptian lawyer-arbitrator, Ahmed El-Kosheri, for example, served in the famous *S.P.P. (Middle East) v. Arab Republic of Egypt* arbitration on the side of the claimant against the Egyptian government, arguing that international principles prevented national legal action.

67. This process of distancing from local milieus is discussed especially in chapter 13.

68. Examples are in chapter 13. One respondent from an Arab state also noted that his contacts in arbitration allowed him to gain legal work in facilitating the investment of Gulf states in Asia (int. 135).

The division between internal and external perspectives, however, while convenient for the exposition and analysis, should not be taken too far. Our chapters make it obvious that each is constantly feeding back into the other, and in any event the boundaries are far from clear. Even the oil crisis of the early 1970s, which is best studied as a "political and economic"—not legal—event with a huge impact on the legal field, drew in some measure on the legal experience and education abroad of the founders of OPEC. Similarly, as we see elsewhere, a business reaction to the costs of litigation or arbitration could lead to important changes in business activities.

We have insisted on the importance of exploring the details of the transformations, since they are crucial to understanding major aspects of the "rules of the game" for international commercial transactions. Still, as noted in the preceding chapter, there are some general legal patterns worth noting. For example, chapter 3 could be seen as an accelerated Weberian transformation that could be described as the "rationalization of charisma." Weber's depiction could be seen in arbitration's evolution, although we asserted that, contra Weber, we do not see the evolution as inevitable or irreversible.

In this chapter, similarly, we saw how the autonomy of the law, which is necessary to its legitimacy, is not inconsistent with serving the needs of political and economic power. The law and legal practices directed to the north-south disputes, for example, developed to reflect the interests of Western businesses in avoiding national courts and laws. And merchants found the services useful and valuable also because the perceived autonomy and universality of the *lex mercatoria* enabled the Western merchants to ensure—at least statistically—their domination and their profits in their business relations with ex-colonial governments. Stated simply, autonomy and universality are not only consistent, but also closely related to the subordination of law to economic and political power. From a general perspective, drawing on both chapters, we can say that the internal competition on the field of law, in relation to events that take place outside of the legal field, allows the field to "keep up" with—and remain relevant to—political, social, and economic changes.

The new relations of power, however, cannot be homologous with the law except through a lengthy judicial and doctrinal process, which produces the impression of a law that is perpetually "behind" social transformations. This slippage, however, is a principle of legitimacy of this symbolic field. It permits it to keep its distance from particular excesses provoked by political events. The appearance of autonomy and neutrality does not at all prevent following and integrating—but at its own rhythm—the forces that at bottom shape social relations. This is, a fortiori, still more true with respect to structural transformation—habitus, organization of work, hierarchization of competences—which can effectuate themselves only through the rhythm of genera-tions. It is not a surprise, therefore, that the disintegration of the Communist world has not yet manifested itself on the field of arbitration except in an anecdotal manner at the periphery of the field. And in a notable contrast, the tremors of decolonization and of the petroleum crisis are still felt very strongly in the field of arbitration.

5

U.S. Litigators, Continental Academics, Petrodollar Construction Projects, and the *Lex Mercatoria*: A Case Study

Large U.S. law firms, and in particular their litigators, played a key role in the development and transformation of international commercial arbitration. The case study in this chapter allows us to see that role through a major north-south dispute, involving a very large construction project financed by petrodollars. The themes of the preceding two chapters can also be seen in a concrete example taken from a period when U.S. litigators, faced with many of these north-south disputes, encountered the "grand old men" and their *lex mercatoria*—which ended up serving well the interests of the large Western construction companies.

The case study also provides a bridge to part 3 of this book, which focuses on how internationalization transforms the landscapes of domestic disputing. We have already suggested that U.S. litigators invaded the small club of pioneers, helped it to prosper, and shifted its center of gravity toward U.S. approaches to litigation. The "international justice" that handles business disputes is itself a product of competition among "national" approaches, including that of U.S. litigators.

But the national approaches are not static, as we show repeatedly in part 3. It is useful, therefore, to show how the approach of the U.S. litigators also relates to the international events discussed in the preceding chapter. As we shall see, the development of "business litigiousness," especially in the 1970s and 1980s (Galanter and Palay 1991), which has been the subject of considerable attention in the United States and in the world of international commercial arbitration, can best be understood as part of a new and more competitive market in legal services created by transformations originating in the business world. Litigators were able to profit from the changes in the business world and move from a subordinate to a leading status in large U.S. law firms. This case study, therefore, shows both the development of a "national" approach and its almost simultaneous impact on the world of international commercial arbitration.

From Business Miscommunications to Legal Battles: The Rise of Business
Litigation and Arbitration

In the early 1970s, according to one of the New York lawyers who plays a
central role in our case study, "I was trying cases in the federal court" for a
three-person law firm (int. 49, 4). The legal environment then began to change.
He described a "crazy period" when "companies were buying everything that
they didn't know anything about" (id., 4), and he assisted a client owned by
one major corporation in the acquisition of another corporation.[1]

The acquired entity, it turned out, engaged in major construction projects
facilitated by the boom in oil revenues: "they had contracts all over the world"
(id., 4). Since the small law firm had assisted in helping acquire the company,
it in effect acquired a client. The litigator became the principal outside counsel
for the acquired company, replacing a large New York law firm. The predecessor firm, it turned out, had promoted arbitration in its representation of the
client. Because of successful experiences in nationalization cases, the firm
"believed strongly in ICC arbitration" (id., 5) for contracts with third-world
countries. The numerous construction contracts all called for ICC arbitration
of disputes. The fortuity of these arbitration clauses turned the disputes into
arbitrations rather than ordinary litigation.

The new owner of the construction company "put in newer, tougher
management" (id., 5) that no doubt resembled their own aggressive managers.
New management took an instant dislike to the loose and informal arrangements that characterized these fixed-price construction contracts. They saw
the contracts as unprofitable and began to push for assurances and changes:
"Problems erupted all over the world" (id., 5), leading to a number of arbitrations.

The arbitration we shall discuss concerned Algeria. The new management
was not very appealing to the Algerians involved in the construction. According to the New York informant, the new management was

> crew cut, Californian, white Anglo-Saxon, Harvard Business School.
> They came over to Algeria, they stayed in the best hotels, they flew
> in with their private jets. They flew out a couple of days later. . . .
> They looked down a bit at the Algerians . . . [who had been used to
> old-style engineers] who went a long way by taking the client out to
> dinner, a lot of drinks, entertaining them, . . . good old boys, and we'll
> do business together. Don't you worry if the contract says this and

1. Similar examples are in Lederman (1992).

you can't do it, well don't worry about it. We'll take care of you.
(Id., 10)

The new management simply spoke a very different business language, that of the Harvard MBA, and Algerian engineers and government officials were not at all used to it. The personal and economic relationship completely fell apart. In 1975 the Algerians threw out the company and went on the offensive. They immediately initiated ICC arbitration.

The Algerian party, as it turned out, was already quite familiar with the ICC and international commercial arbitration. It is interesting to note how that familiarity began. We do not know all the details, but we have some indications.[2] Leading Algerian lawyers and legal academics, typically educated in part in France, were involved in decisions to set up an arbitral tribunal around 1963 to deal with the problems that arose in French-Algerian relations after Algerian independence. The experience, according to an Algerian long involved in international commercial arbitration, went very well, and it provided the basis for some acceptance and even recognition of arbitration in contracts entered into later in the decade (int. 101, 3). At the ICC, in the meantime (1971–75), the secretary-general, Robert Thompson, spent considerable time developing ties with Arab countries.[3] For a combination of reasons, therefore, including the negotiating position of the businesses dealing with Algeria, a group of Algerian lawyers was relatively familiar with the international commercial arbitration world and the ICC by the early 1980s.[4]

Indeed, the Algerians were represented by a leading New York law firm with offices in Paris. They quickly appointed a well-connected Algerian law professor as their contribution to the panel of arbitrators, and the process commenced. The Algerian party, according to the New York respondent, "thought they had the advantage over us. . . . [T]hey thought they were just going to wipe us up. . . . [T]hey had a local French office and they had a big name firm, and the Algerians were very important to the ICC then" (int. 49,

---

2. While we cannot explore all the potential connections, it may be useful to note that French oil companies in the 1960s had ties to leading international-law professors in France, who advised them from time to time (int. 109, 1) and probably helped keep relevant some of the ideas of international commercial arbitration.

3. "He had a talent for speaking to Arabs" (int. 213, 6).

4. According to Lloyd Cutler, describing the origins of the Iran–United States Claims Tribunal, the familiarity of the Algerians was quite relevant in the negotiations: "some of the Algerian intermediaries also were skilled lawyers. The skills of these lawyers and their professional confidence in one another enabled us to overcome the obstacles of complexity and communication we faced" (Cutler 1981).

22).[5] The New York litigator at that point was quite clearly ill equipped to mount a defense in an ICC arbitration conducted by insiders.

At this point, according to other studies, large law firms were beginning to get heavily involved in big litigations (Nelson 1990, 414–15; Nelson 1988, 57–58, 61, 109–10; Galanter and Palay 1991, 50–52, 115–16). The basic methods of such litigation already existed—intense document production, aggressive fighting, huge amount of paperwork and pretrial skirmishing. Litigators were gaining more visibility within law firms because of their participation in lucrative defense work, particularly in the area of antitrust (Galanter and Palay 1991, 33; Neal and Goldberg 1964; Nelson 1988, 109–10). But litigators were still a relatively marginal group within their law firms and in the profession (Heinz and Laumann 1982; see Margolick 1993). There was not yet the legal climate that led to businesses routinely suing other businesses (Galanter and Palay 1991, 43, 115). Our example sheds some light on the process that led to the boom in business litigation and to increasing competition for the business of litigation (Nelson 1990, 58).

The arbitration case had huge potential damages, perhaps as high as $650 million, since the project would have to be finished at considerable expense. The Algerians sued not only the construction company but also the parent company, which was itself normally represented by a large Wall Street firm. Because of a conflict of interest, however, the major Wall Street law firm could not provide the representation needed for the parent company. The general counsel of the parent company then approved a list of nine other major New York firms who would be deemed suitable for the case, and the litigator for the construction company began to contact them. He "was turned down by eight of them in a row" (int. 49, 13). The attitude was

> look, we're very busy, this is an area we don't understand, and it's a
> one-shot transaction. It's just a transactional piece of business.
> There's no opportunity to get the institutions. We all know . . . that
> [the Wall Street firm is the normal] outside counsel. Therefore we'd
> just be pinch-hitting. We're not interested. We'd be wasting our en-
> ergy. . . . Firms were not like they are now. . . . That was the era of
> collegiality. And they didn't need any more business. And they didn't
> want it! And it was strange to them. It was in Europe, it was the Inter-
> national Chamber of Commerce, they were unfamiliar with it, and
> they basically didn't care about it. And I couldn't persuade them.
> (Id., 13)

5. According to one source, the Algerian oil company Sonnetrach went through a period where they were spending "over a million dollars a year on arbitral fees, not lawyers fees, arbitral fees" (int. 129, 6).

These firms remained quite happy with the status quo in New York. Finally, the litigator succeeded, through a personal friendship, in getting a commitment from the last New York firm on the list. That firm also was reluctant to take the case.[6]

The interesting question is why this "litigator's dream"—a huge case—was unattractive to big New York law firms at the time. Unfamiliarity with the ICC world certainly mattered in 1975, but by the early 1980s all the major firms had "decided to get into this field" (id., 26). What changed? The informant again offered a hypothesis.

> Money. . . . [F]irst of all, the change in the legal profession in New York and the United States. All of a sudden it was harder to keep these institutional clients. I think you might . . . if you check back you'll find that when Skadden, Arps started raiding other firms for their clients, saying that we're experts on takeovers and you might be taken over, sign up with us, that broke a lot of institutional relationships. And so you'd find company X hiring Skadden, Arps in addition to its outside counsel. And little by little Skadden, Arps would worm its way in and start doing a lot of work for them. (Id., 26)

Both international commercial arbitration and big litigation became more important to large law firm practice at that time (Galanter and Palay 1991, 50–52, 115–16). It is further instructive to note the experience of the litigator in our case study, after the law firm transformations in the 1980s:

> From my own selfish point of view I saw it hard to remain in my small law firm. . . . And that's why in '84 I merged into . . . a firm that I had originally spoken to in Paris. And they had an existing arbitration practice, and I merged with theirs. Then about a year and a half later [a larger firm] came along and swallowed up [the second firm]. [The new firm] has ever since then had a strong interest in international arbitration. So I had the group here in New York. And we have a strong Paris group, and we have some strong arbitration lawyers in Washington, D.C. (Int. 49, 27)

Both the rise of Skadden, Arps and of this litigator's career in international arbitration and megalitigation relate to an important transformation in large law firms. While our data generally concern arbitration, we may offer some generalizations about this transformation.

In what has been termed the "golden age" of New York law firms (Galanter and Palay 1991), the stability of clients coincided with a dominant position

6. The partner who handled the case for the large law firm, however, made a reputation in this area and "loved the case right down to the bitter end" (int. 49, 14).

within law firms of the corporate lawyers. They were the principal "partners with power," because they dealt with the clients, socialized with them, and in general occupied their world (Nelson 1988). The litigators in the firms, like the smaller litigation firms, did not as often come from upper-class backgrounds (see Heinz and Laumann 1982; Margolick 1993), and they were used only when called upon by corporate lawyers who in general looked down on litigation (Galanter and Palay 1991, 33). Certainly, there were outstanding litigators, but, since clients were generally loyal and did not shop for firms, litigation lacked the pressure of competition for business, and litigators did not have the opportunity to deploy their skills whenever *they* could persuade clients that litigation would be useful. The corporate lawyers controlled access and, quite naturally, did not want clients to interact too often with what the top partners perceived as the less impressive members of the firm. Litigation was thus kept at bay.

As the story of this very large arbitration suggests, national and international business relations were also based more on the gentlemanly practices of loyalty cemented by personal relations. While we should not exaggerate these ties, they no doubt played an important role. As the MBAs came on the scene, in conjunction with the opportunities presented by the growth of Eurodollars and later petrodollars, they imported a different set of operating principles and techniques learned in school. Mergers and acquisitions and a new set of economic relationships undermined the stable relations of law firms and their clients, again as the example illustrates. Competition developed among law firms, and quite naturally within the litigation departments. Firms like Skadden, Arps could wrest away clients because of their reputation for aggressive tactics in takeover strategies and litigation (e.g., Heymann and Liebman 1988, 106–35), and takeovers themselves undermined loyalties and promoted new rounds of business litigation.

The competition forced the complacent elite firms of New York to sharpen further their own or acquire top litigation skills. They began to acquire individuals such as the litigator described in the case study; and they necessarily allowed litigators to demonstrate their powers in order to win portions of an increasingly fragmented and competitive legal business. Clients became more familiar with litigators and what they could do, making litigation a much more frequently used tool in the increasing economic warfare (Nelson 1990).

Looking backward from the perspective of the mid-1990s, in fact, it may be that the "golden age" of U.S. lawyers was much more the 1980s than the 1960s. Law firms rapidly expanded, fueled by litigation revenues. At the same time, the litigators naturally gained much more prominence within the law firms. They gained crucial legal business through their litigation reputations (e.g., Pollock 1990, 243–47). And as "partners with power" through their client relationships, they became also the leaders of the large law firms.

We have many examples today of litigation as an accepted tactic in economic warfare (cf. Margolick 1993). The *New York Times* thus recently described lawsuits as "competitive tools to help a company keep its edge—or to blunt others" (Slind-Flor 1993, 34). An account of the corporate legal strategy of Intel referred to characterizations of the general counsel as "a relentless aggressor who attacks companies, particularly smaller companies, with weak lawsuits that serve to buy his company time in the marketplace" (Kostal 1992, 99).[7]

It is clear, as we show in the chapter devoted to the United States (chap. 8), that there is now a counterattack on the arms race of litigation that accelerated in the 1980s. The counterattack is promoted through alternative dispute resolution and led by general counsel acting largely through such institutions as the Center for Public Resources in New York. But there is no question that the acceleration in aggressive litigation tactics in the 1980s—motions to disqualify, civil conspiracy suits—represented to a great extent the fruits of competition for the business of "litigation as economic warfare." And the counterattack should not be taken to mean that general counsel have given up litigation as warfare when it suits their purposes.

To return to the case study, no doubt litigators, now in positions of leadership and hungry for very big cases, would have behaved differently in the 1980s or the 1990s than they did when confronted with this case. They would have fought for the case, not rejected it. It would have been a chance to show their stuff and enhance the reputation necessary to win further litigation and arbitration business.

New York Litigation Meets the International Chamber of Commerce

The transformation of the setting for business litigation in the United States was still under way in the mid-1970s, and U.S. lawyers, and in particular litigators, had very little contact at that point with the international-arbitration community centered on the ICC in Paris. There was some interaction between members of the legal profession in the United States and the international-arbitration community, and there was some expertise in international commercial arbitration that developed primarily out of the oil and other

7. A recent suit by Union Pacific against Santa Fe Pacific was described matter-of-factly by a spokesperson as aiming to let the defendant's board of directors "know that we are serious about our [takeover] offer. . . . It's a strategic move for us" (Yates 1994, 1).

nationalization cases. The American Arbitration Association maintained its own relations as well with the International Chamber of Commerce.

The continuing story of the Algerian construction arbitration illustrates how U.S. litigators reacted in their first encounters with the ICC. As noted before, the New York-Paris-Algerian team started with an advantage from familiarity with the ICC. The litigator for the U.S. company recognized that the forum was unfamiliar, and he set about, in his words, "brushing up on my Shakespeare. . . . And it didn't take much. I mean it didn't take long before I thought I understood what was going on" (int. 49, 5). A French firm he had worked with helped him see that he needed access to an insider, recommending Berthold Goldman, the very well known French academic arbitration lawyer identified with the *lex mercatoria,* and he retained Goldman as a consultant, in part to keep the other firm from putting him on their side. The U.S. litigator, however, did not use Goldman very much at first.

In order to name an arbitrator, the litigator for the construction company read the major writings of the arbitration community, took a Berlitz course in French, "interviewed dozens of people . . . and in the course of it learned a lot about the club—who they were, what their interests were, what their limitations were" (id., 15). The U.S. side picked as an arbitrator an American lawyer practicing in Paris and familiar with arbitration. The third arbitrator, or chair, was a Swiss lawyer, picked by the Swiss under ICC rules. The U.S. side also picked new local French counsel, settling on a U.S. firm in Paris with a good reputation that, it turned out, was not very helpful—"a great disappointment" (id., 20). The lawyers in the firm were neither top litigators nor top experts on what was distinct about French law or on arbitration.

At this point the professor-dominated, civil-law-oriented arbitration community was aggravating to a U.S. litigator:

> They were very insular. I thought that they had a very fixed set of prejudices. A lot of them were contrary to American legal training. Like totally gave lip service to the facts, just kind of assumed they knew the facts. They would make off-the-cuff judgments as to who was right or wrong based on who they had lunch with last week and told them something. I just was very upset with them. . . . [T]hey were very strong on the law. The trouble was they would get off on a debate on the law, and you could lose them for days. And they'd get involved in internecine fights with each other over some esoteric interpretation of French law which was applicable in my case, because it was Algerian law, which was really French law. And you'd have to pull them back. It was like a ringmaster in a circus with a whip try-

ing to get them back to pay attention to what was really going on.
And they wouldn't pay attention to the facts. (Id., 16)

A key strength of the U.S. litigators was in mustering the facts, while the
civilian system focused almost exclusively on the law (int. 136, 7–8).

The extent of this mismatch was illustrated by the question of transcripts
of the oral testimony. While the arbitration took place in Paris, the leading
lawyers were litigators from midtown Manhattan:

> Our offices weren't even all that far apart. So we had a mind-set of do-
> ing the thing in kind of the way an American would approach it. And
> we went ahead and we even took some depositions. We talked a lot
> about possible discovery. And we went ahead and held these hear-
> ings—we had witness hearings. And we brought over a court reporter,
> an American court reporter. . . . And we missed. You know how you
> can get when you are working out of the same cultural background.
> We missed. But the panel—we'd forgotten about the panel. We
> thought the panel would have surely appreciated all this effort. And
> what we both missed was that the chairman went along with us. He
> let us all do it, because he thought we wanted to do it and thought it
> would make us happy. But he had absolutely no interest. And it was a
> disaster. We didn't realize that. How I found out was months later
> one day when we were filing some stuff from the hearing. I said to the
> chairman, I said, well, Mr. Chairman I guess we're disappointed to tell
> you unfortunately the court reporter couldn't get the last volume of
> the transcript here in time, so we can't argue that point to you be-
> cause we don't have the transcript. And you don't have the transcript.
> And he said to us, why in the world would I want this transcript?
> This transcript is for you two gentlemen. We don't ever read it. . . .
> And I found out later on he'd never read them. So that was elimi-
> nated. We emphasized the facts to the witnesses. We learned that the
> Europeans don't ever believe their ears. And we wasted a lot of time
> in oral testimony. I think it helped them a little because we had ex-
> pert witnesses, and I think they learned a little. But I don't think they
> paid a lot of attention to it. What counted was the writings. . . , and
> the final arguments . . . that was the tour de force. (Int. 49, 23)

The Americans in Paris tried out their own legal weapons, but the arbitration
panel—civil-law experts and ICC insiders—paid very little attention to the
facts and to the oral examination and cross-examination. The U.S. litigators
knew perfectly well how to fight each other. They had no difficulty with
intensive fact-gathering, vigorous cross-examination, and even with fighting
in multiple forums, through simultaneous litigation commenced in the United

States. But neither lawyer knew how to communicate to the ICC world in Paris.

The Algerian side had also made a misjudgment, thinking that their knowledge of and access to the ICC would overwhelm the other side. But the New York litigator for the construction company had made a good decision to retain Goldman, and he strengthened the team by also retaining Pierre Lalive from Geneva, another major figure already in international arbitration: "The combination of Lalive and Goldman was . . . indescribable. . . . I was a conductor of virtuosos and prima donnas" (int. 49, 22). Recognizing the skills of his experts and their relevance to the ICC arbitration, the litigator began to rely on them more and more: "I switched subtly" (id., 20), bringing Goldman to the meeting on the "terms of reference." And he began also to pay more attention to the subtle issues of French law and the *lex mercatoria* so closely identified with Goldman's academic writings. At that point the Algerian side recognized that it had underestimated the opposition.

The Algerian side

> got worried, and they raced out and they hired Jean Bredin to counter Goldman, who was one of Goldman's former students. And that was a great break for me because Bredin was terrific—very good—but it really energized Goldman. But this made my case the most important case in his world, because his former student was now arrayed against him. . . . Not just any student. This was a battle of titans for him, and he was thrilled with it. He enjoyed it, and so I got his first-class attention. And it made a big difference in our case. (Id., 20)

Now the Paris community had individuals who could make the arguments at the highest possible level in the French academic language of ICC arbitration (but spoken in English). About Goldman, the father of the *lex mercatoria*, the lawyer noted, "He was the guy who could do it based on the *lex mercatoria*. But his standing and his reputation in that little world, and before . . . the . . . arbitrators, were golden" (id., 15).

The arbitration eventually came to an end with a substantial award that was only a portion of the requested damages. As suggested in the preceding chapters, it is clear that the *lex mercatoria*, communicated by the leading academic supporters and inventors of the doctrine, facilitated the avoidance of local law in favor of principles favorable to the Western construction company. The *lex mercatoria* overcame a strict interpretation of construction contracts that might have made it difficult to justify cost overruns. From that perspective, this most academic of doctrines served in part to hold down the claims of the developing countries. The main point here, however, is not so much the outcome as the nature of the encounter between New York litigators and civilian academic lawyers. As discussed below, this encounter allows us to see how arbitration was transformed in the 1980s, and the role that it played in regulating north-south disputes.

Three other general observations can be offered. First, this kind of megadispute arises only when there is a massive breakdown in the systems of communication that can "contain" a dispute in the interests of all parties (cf. Nelson 1990). Here we have breakdowns at many different levels, beginning with a new generation of managers unable to work with the Algerian engineers. There were also misjudgments about how much to invest in the elite of the ICC world, with the Algerian side thinking at the outset that the case could be handled to their advantage fairly routinely; then the Americans thought that their litigation skills could be deployed successfully in the Parisian ICC setting. These miscommunications helped make a large dispute much more difficult to bring to a conclusion and resulted in an estimated $9 million in legal fees alone. There was not a way to move easily to a common language for the resolution of disputes of this particular profile, even with lawyers from New York law firms on both sides.

From another perspective, however, we should note that the lawyers on both sides got along very well with each other, as did the academic experts on both sides. They loved the competition. The New York lawyer who was persuaded to take the case because of a friendship ended up "loving the case." It was a dream case, because each side let their lawyers and legal teams fight with all available legal technologies.

We suggest that the same kind of interactions helped fuel the explosion of corporate litigation in the 1970s and 1980s, much of which in fact involved parties from different countries (Nelson 1990, 446–48). The clients new to this kind of warfare quickly learned the benefits gained in terms of time and potential settlement value, but they did not have the expertise initially to control the costs or select among the possible legal strategies. Lawyers were given a virtual carte blanche, and the ranks of the contending armies of litigators naturally grew.

And it may have been that some of the countries with a head start in the ICC world, such as the Algerians, began with an advantage. But, as a perceptive Algerian noted, they had academic "knowledge" about international arbitration, but they lacked in their own country the "technology" of how to manage a construction project in order to be prepared to win a litigation or arbitration (int. 101, 4). As we noted in the preceding chapter, third-world countries may have ended up at an even greater disadvantage.

Large Law Firms and the Routinization of Arbitration

The rapprochement of civil law and common law, or more precisely civil law and U.S. litigation, began to take place through numerous encounters akin to the case just described (Lowenfeld 1985). Depositions, for example, tend not to be used today in international commercial arbitration (int. 38, 30). Oral testimony is somewhat more limited than in domestic U.S. litigation, but it does take place and includes cross-examination—admired by one French lawyer in the preceding example because it is "so cruel" (int. 51, 15). Pretrial skirmishing, intense fact-gathering, and adversary experts, however, are now common in international arbitration. Europeans, as suggested in the previous chapters, agree that arbitration is now more "procedural," even as it has become more routine and more judicialized.

Yet, from the point of view of the major New York law firms, the story is not so simple. Our knowledgeable observer from a New York law firm opined,

> In my view it's been much harder for American lawyers to get into this field in the last couple of years. I think the Europeans have been much stronger. The British have been extraordinarily competitive in this area—the solicitors firms, the Dutch. I, myself, am not as active as I used to be because our clients just have not been there. I'm back doing more U.S. litigation now. And I don't get . . . you know, I've been called on a couple of times to serve as arbitrator, which is a completely different role. But we don't have any big arbitrations, and we wonder why. And I've talked to the guys at the ICC or our Paris partners. They tell me a lot of the cases now are more computer tech rights, computer rights, different types of cases, Japanese companies involved, Korean companies involved. I really don't know European countries. I drew a blank. I've tried to figure it out. I mean I sit on all the committees here in New York . . . you will find forty partners of major American law firms chasing two cases. I mean that's my simplistic view of those meetings. I sit on the [another] committee. . . . Same thing. You've got every major law firm represented. I don't think they have more than three cases in the whole damned room. (Int. 49, 29)

Upon further reflection, the same commentator suggested that from the perspective of all the offices of his large, transnational law firm,

> yes, the actual number of cases may be the same, but the caliber and the quality of the cases is different. And a lot of them settle shortly after being filed. And they don't go all the way. . . . [T]he nature of

the cases are . . . they're smaller. There's just, you know, a . . . it's viewed under a supply contract, a patent, know-how dispute, you know, $10 million, $8 million involved. (Id., 30)

Again, it is possible to generalize to litigation in the United States. The phenomenon found with respect to the very large international commercial arbitrations may have sources that will affect large-litigation practice as well. For example, a recent article in the *Wall Street Journal* made this point explicitly: "Corporate takeover work turned many lawyers into millionaires in the 1980s, but the current takeover boomlet isn't expected to be quite so lawyer friendly" (Pollock 1993b). Part of the explanation, provided by a partner in a large New York firm, was the following:

In the old hostile takeovers, which often were fueled by junk-bond financing, "the litigation component was at least 50%" of the legal work. . . . In the recent friendly deals, there is often more corporate work to be done, "but that still doesn't make up for the very frenetic litigation time. . . . The overall legal time is probably less because you don't have the litigation." (Id.)

In addition, as noted in the same article,

While outside counsel had the lead role in many of the '80s deals, in some instances lawyers from high-powered law firms now are sharing more responsibility with in-house lawyers. . . . [C]ompany legal staff "is very much part of the management and very much caught up in getting the deal done." (Id.)

The cutback in litigation, presided over by the in-house counsel, has persuaded the managing lawyers quoted by Stephen Brill that large law firms in 1993 are operating with "one-third over-capacity." They simply do not have the litigation business to support their litigation departments: "buyers are making better decisions about what needs a top-dollar, full-court press and what doesn't" (Brill 1993, 81).

These observations suggest that business communication is now better, even on such contentious matters as takeovers. The parties are again more likely to deal amicably than to litigate. The rise of in-house counsel has allowed more effective monitoring of the expenses of litigation, and the tailoring of the litigation investment to the relevant dispute. In-house counsel can also talk to each other in a common business/law language. Finally, the technology for managing disputes has developed in other ways. There are now experts available, for example, who can monitor the documentation during a construction project such that any lawsuit will practically be a matter of routine (int.

136, 8). Individuals for oil companies, in the same way, handle any potential disputes through an ongoing communication system (int. 186, 1).

There may be many more international commercial arbitrations "filed," therefore; but they are not as likely to break out into full-scale litigation as they were in the highly unsettled period of mergers and acquisitions and the new era of north-south investment—both aspects of a major restructuring that took place in the wake of the oil crisis of the early 1970s. Arbitration and litigation have become more routinized and manageable as part of business relations. Large law firms helped produce the dynamics that made international commercial arbitration more rational and technocratic, but in doing so they also curbed the huge disputes that fueled their prosperity. We now turn specifically to other ways in which the growth and institutionalization of international commercial arbitration affects the national landscapes of business disputing.

Part Three
Internationalization and the Transformation of the Landscape for Handling Business Conflicts

The chapters in part 3 focus on the relationship between the development of international commercial arbitration and national transformations in the landscape of business disputing. We build on the basic observation that the transformations in the international arena lead to a kind of reconfiguring of the hierarchies and positions found in the national domain, which in turn affects the way that business disputes are handled. We see this impact through chapters that address England, the United States, Sweden, Egypt, and Hong Kong.

After an introductory chapter, described below, we begin appropriately with England and its well-developed commercial law, seen in both the more or less integrated system of arbitration and a closely connected Commercial Court and commercial bar (chap. 7). The first three of these national accounts—including the United States (chap. 8) and Sweden (chap. 9), in addition to England—focus mainly on how arbitration and business disputing are changing in countries where the basic legal institutions are more or less intact. As we move out of Europe and the United States to places more distant from Western legal centers, such as Egypt and Hong Kong (chaps. 11 and 12), we reach out much more explicitly beyond the established institutions identifiable with arbitration and the law. It becomes all the more important to situate the position of international commercial arbitration in relation to the changing position of law and lawyers in the fields of economic power and even state power. The story of Hong Kong arbitration, most obviously, is inextricably connected to the politics of law in Hong Kong and even in China.

The chapters in this part also provide the occasion to consider more general theoretical issues and questions. This consideration—and our general research strategy—also requires that we not force our presentation to adhere too rigidly to the line between the international and the national. It is true in a general analytical sense that the international is structured out of the national (or competition among national approaches) and that the national is transformed by the international, but these spaces of activity are implicated in each other in numerous ways, feed each other, and constantly change. One of the issues that resists the national-international dichotomy, in particular, is why international commercial arbitration took institutional root in Paris, where the International Chamber of Commerce became the leading international arbitration center in the world. Other places, especially London, might have seemed to be the more logical site. We address the dilemma of Paris as part of the discussion of the more general chapters that follow.

The introductory chapter (6) in this part provides a theoretical framework that can be used to orient the reader to the national studies, some general issues that inform them, and some of the connections between them. After the chapters on England, the United States, and Sweden, another more general and abstract chapter (10) develops models for the relationships between business, law, and the state judicial systems. The discussion of Continental parallel justice, as opposed to the delegated justice seen especially in England, also allows an extended analysis of the respective roles of business and law—and the state—in the civil-law world and especially in France, helping to explain the role of Paris in allowing international commercial arbitration to find a home. The chapter concludes by introducing the topic of internationalization and commercial arbitration in places where law has been relatively marginalized.

We conclude part 3 with a chapter (13) that focuses on questions of core and periphery. We do not mean by the use of these terms that the periphery is outside the main story of international commercial arbitration—even when peripheral arbitration centers may have relatively few cases. Our interest is not in which arbitration centers have the most cases, or indeed are "successful," but rather how they relate to the general story. The field of international arbitration is very complex. It includes a changing network of personal relationships that serves to produce the universals of an international justice that was the focus of part 2, and it promotes the national transformations that take place in relation to personal relations organized around a relative core and a relative periphery. The local transformations, we also recall in this chapter, relate to the role of the large multinational law firms.

Finally, the chapter revisits the role of Paris, suggesting that the elements of success of international commercial arbitration in Paris—the mix of the Continental academics, the large multinational law firms already in Paris, and the fragmented and compartmentalized French legal landscape in relation to business disputes—account also for the success of the model elsewhere. They facilitated both the export of international commercial arbitration and the transformation of the role of law and lawyers in the terrains where international commercial arbitration has gained ground.

6

Between the Worlds of Law and Business: The Contradictions of Business Justice and Its Permanent Reconstruction through Dispute Resolution Mechanisms

This chapter provides a preview and an analytical framework for those that follow. It proceeds in four sections, beginning with a relatively abstract model of the mechanisms at work in the construction and reconstruction of mechanisms of business justice—pulled at the same time toward business and law, toward relatively informal, business-oriented dispute resolution and control by formal lawyers. The second section emphasizes the close connections and systemic relations in any given setting between private arbitration and the official state courts. What happens in one sphere inevitably affects what happens in the other. This close, systemic connection also applies to the position of *international* commercial arbitration with respect to the national court systems. The third section suggests that the blurring of the categories between domestic and international commercial arbitration merits attention for other reasons. The blurring itself is part of what sustains both the national and the international. The fourth section then turns more specifically to the general theme of how the international leads to the recomposition of the national fields of business justice. Suggesting that the impact is not merely a matter of building on existing practices and institutions, but rather of restructuring the field of business justice, it begins also to explore why international business practices led to the location of the "capital" of international commercial arbitration in Paris, and not elsewhere.

The Permanent Tension between Holders of Economic Power and Legal Practitioners

According to Max Weber, the increasing importance of particularism in law, especially in commercial law (1978, 882), comes from pressure exercised by merchants to have their legal affairs treated by specialized experts. Arbitration responds effectively to this need, since it permits merchants to choose arbitrators who are either directly or indirectly familiar with their business problems. The arbitrators may even be predisposed to listen sympathetically to business arguments of the major players in order to protect their careers as arbitrators. The quite obvious suitability of arbitration, however, does not mean that it provides the only possible response to the business demand noted by Weber. Those responsible for public judicial institutions, for example, may respond to the success of private justice by creating special jurisdictions, like commercial tribunals or a special commercial court,[1] in order to prevent the world of business from escaping the state's justice.

The different methods and approaches for handling business disputes reflect a permanent tension between holders of economic power, who exert pressure to control the way their conflicts are handled, and a relatively small number of legal practitioners who seek to gain a large share of the lucrative market represented by commercial disputes. This tension does not necessarily develop into an antagonism. Arbitration, as we have seen, may evolve through a process of "judicialization" into a kind of private justice with all the features of state courts; and state courts can move in the other direction, offering within the courts what is essentially a "private justice," custom made and reserved for business enterprises. These typical compromise solutions, however, are unstable. Centrifugal forces and diverging interests prevent stable solutions from emerging.

We see recurring patterns to this process. One is for actors close to the side of business to denounce the evolution of arbitration toward a formal quasi justice. They follow this criticism by launching new—or newly packaged—products on this market.[2] The new offerings purport to return arbitration to the simplicity of its origins as an informal way for businesspeople to resolve their disputes. These efforts also serve at the same time to reaffirm the desire of the holders of economic power—for present purposes termed "merchants"—to preserve their control over a market that may pass too much under the control of lawyers.

In contrast, those who have only legal capital to offer—as opposed to broader social capital available to resolve disputes—will naturally play the only card they have, the law, invoking the importance of the official state law. Promoters of law, however, are in an ambiguous position, for the recognition of a private justice by state legal systems—and a fortiori the creation of a "private enclave" within the official justice system—clashes with law's universalist ideology. The legal system is supposed to be the same for all, weak

---

1. The de facto specialization of the state of Delaware in the domain of corporate law responds in part to this same logic, constituting a form of business justice apart from the state justice system. There are also examples of new business courts in the United States designed to focus on commercial conflicts. Delaware is in fact making an effort to create special mechanisms for business litigation ("Quick and Clean" 1994).

2. The most recent are those presented under the colors of alternative dispute resolution, or ADR, beginning in the United States (see chap. 8).

or powerful. Furthermore, practitioners of business law must confront a professional world in which they occupy a small minority position. The silent majority of lawyers is typically quite willing to play the role of "guardians of the
temple," invoking universalism to refuse to give merchants the "privilege" of
a "custom-made justice" that happens also to represent a "privileged market"
dominated by the minority of business practitioners.

Located at the intersection of the world of business and that of law, these
business lawyers serve as "lawyer-compradors"—double agents serving their
own interests as lawyers and those of the merchants who retain their services.
They are perpetually torn between the requirements of their peers in the legal
profession and those of their business clients. The legal profession seeks to
pull private justice into the ordinary legal system. The business response is
in effect that, if that is the case, they will bypass the courts and the lawyers
of the state altogether by arranging to regulate their conflicts between themselves.[3] They may rely on associations of business, like the chambers of commerce and industry, which permit them to draw on business solidarity or on
"moral sanctions" available to business peers.

The merchants could even take the option of producing their own "law,"
outside of the official legal system. One way to do so would be to utilize
corporate counsel, who are both numerous and for the most part relatively
indifferent as to whether they act as lawyers or business agents. Further, while
house lawyers may lack credibility in some matters, it is quite easy for leading
economic powers to look temporarily toward universities or even toward notables who embody the authority of the justice of the state. Business could in
this way develop a private justice outside of the legal system that draws selec-
tively on the same guarantees of legal legitimacy available to the state. In
sum, while we can name only a few of the possibilities, business has many
viable options. Depending on the context, business could even create its own
justice.

Those responsible for the official legal institutions are capable of appreciat-
ing the substantial resources available to business for these activities. Thus,
when the managers of the state justice system endeavor to provide justice
custom made for the holders of economic power, it is because they understand
the limits of their own power. The holders of economic power are able, at any
moment, to buy their own "legal system" from the justice of the state. Efforts
to "legalize" business disputes must always confront the limited power to act
without business cooperation and support.

---

3. As Auerbach recalls, "For centuries merchants and businessmen have been the
most outspoken proponents of non-legal dispute settlements" (1983, 5).

Arbitration and Official State Courts as a System

The different private and state mechanisms for dispensing business justice represent the products of competition in the market for handling commercial conflicts. Competitors in this field sometimes promote legal capital, sometimes social capital. This competition promotes a continuing definition and redefinition not only of commercial courts, but also of arbitration, mediation, and the new forms of ADR presented by their primarily U.S. promoters as the ultimate in the technology of conflict resolution. Contrary to the pretensions of the scholarly—but, above all, promotional—literature that insists on defining the "proper" characteristics of each form, the differences between competing forms or technologies are both uncertain and changing. Their instability is exacerbated by the fact that the promoters—or at least the most successful ones—wear multiple hats and employ different approaches when it serves their own or their clients' strategic purposes. The promotion of ADR, for example, can be a strategy to seek modification of the rules of the game for arbitration or litigation. And in the same manner, the promotion of arbitration practices typically serves also to put pressure on the official state courts.

As the examples suggest, the different places and modes of commercial conflict resolution exist only in relation to one another. They are best understood as forming a system. While the international dimension complicates the story, international commercial arbitration also must be situated as part of interconnected national systems. Its promoters tend naturally to insist on the fundamental differences between international commercial arbitration and national systems, whether public or private. They emphasize the international, neutral forum provided to parties equally reticent to submit their matters to the law and judges of their adversary. This sharp distinction between national and international, however, is vastly overstated.

Indeed, the connections between national and international are often quite obvious. First, the individuals from the countries that dominate or have dominated international economic exchange have often succeeded in imposing their own courts in their contracts. The Commercial Court in London, discussed in the following chapter, is often said to be an international court. The majority of the cases that come to the court have at least one party from outside the United Kingdom.[4] A certain number of countries of the third world also have succeeded from time to time in affirming their own legal nationalism, whether by using economic power to impose their own courts in a con-

---

4. We can say that the Commercial Court is formally, but not culturally, international. The zone of influence of the Commercial Court remains limited to territories that were once under British domination.

tract, by insisting on their courts even at the price of a contractual surcharge, or by gaining jurisdiction de facto in the absence of contractual provisions. It is, moreover, nearly always possible to invoke state court jurisdiction as a dilatory or tactical maneuver either by filing a related lawsuit or contesting the enforcement of an arbitral decision. Practitioners of international commerce cannot therefore ignore the complex, ambiguous, and changing relations between international arbitration and national jurisdictions.

The close connections between national and international are especially notable among the providers of these services. The most successful of the operators in international dispute resolution wear two hats. Traditionally, as we have seen in chapter 2, authority acquired in their respective national legal fields provided the ticket for admission to the practice of international arbitration. The cosmopolitan fame acquired through arbitration then reinforced their local positions. Recently, due to the increase in the "judicialization" of arbitration practice, we can also see a small current of inverse mobility. An apprenticeship in international arbitration allows one to acquire a familiarity with a range of legal cultures and state court systems. This familiarity facilitates entry into the more general career of international business lawyer, which, in turn, leads naturally to an enhanced national stature.

This personal dimension of relations between international arbitration and national legal fields facilitates the management, but not resolution, of the tensions between private and state justice. Despite the international aspect of the arbitration proceedings, the tensions remain between international commercial arbitration and state court systems. The monopoly of *legitimate* violence—coercion to enforce awards—possessed by the state assures the continuation of this tension, although it is manifested in a somewhat different manner with respect to international arbitration than with respect to private justice at the state level.

The geographic and social distance between the parties in international commercial arbitration creates a strong need to be able to mobilize the legitimate and legitimating authority of national courts. This phenomenon becomes more important as international commerce extends outside of the circle of large Western multinationals. While not often noted, it is important to see that the Court of Arbitration of the ICC has long benefited greatly from the quiet oversight of the Court of Appeal of Paris. This discrete oversight has been important for another reason. The merchant users of ICC arbitration would be wary of the loss of control to French lawyers and French laws were they to believe that the Court of Appeal was likely to appear actively on the scene.

The ideal formula, which combines arbitral autonomy with state court

legitimacy, is for the courts to maintain a distance, overseeing but not interfer-
ing with the proper functioning of private justice. But this equilibrium is not
as easy to realize in the domain of international conflicts as it is in internal,
national, conflicts. Instability tends to come from the natural propensity of
judges to want to extend their sphere of influence. This potential judicial
imperialism coincides also with the efforts of practitioners to develop their
market.

Lawyers as *litigators* consider it a matter of professional responsibility to
employ all the arguments and procedures possible to defend the interests of
their clients—or at least to gain time for them, which often means the same
thing—when the financial stakes are sufficiently great. This effort leads them
to push to enlarge the limited means of appeal and therefore expand the control
of the courts over private justice.

Judges do not typically like to give up their ability to supervise private
proceedings through some kind of review. This tendency is all the more understandable when the assertion of jurisdiction would permit them to familiarize
themselves, even if indirectly, with a field of practice—like business disputing—that represents a substantial potential market.[5] They may also confuse
this personal interest with the interest in law. Since business enterprises are
typically reluctant to turn to the courts, court proceedings growing out of
arbitrations may provide one of the principal sources for the renovation and
enrichment of legal jurisprudence applicable to commercial matters.

This approach historically has permitted many arbitration matters in London to reach the Commercial Court, where a point of law can be resolved in
a way that furthers the development of the common law (chap. 7). There is a
problem with such an approach, however. At the same time that it enriches
the law—and the senior commercial barristers, or QCs—the existence of this
procedure of appeal also gives London arbitration the image of proceedings
that are very legalistic, long, and costly, and dominated by a small group of
barristers expert in English commercial law and commercial practice.

This control of the courts over arbitration is, then, a double-edged sword.
On one side, it permits a small group of practitioners of law to develop their
expertise in matters of commercial relations, even to assure to themselves a
sort of quasi monopoly with respect to their competitors—domestic or foreign—in the arbitration market. But there is another side: this monopoly and
the rent generated by the situation promotes competition by those who can
develop other options. In particular, excluded from the market of London, or

5. Even if it is necessary for them to wait until retirement for this anticipated
market.

at least condemned to secondary roles, the large law firms that now dominate the market in international law are quick to exploit the negative image of London to steer their clients away. They thus contribute directly to the development of competing places. Those places, however, cannot offer the wealth of capital or experience and learning in international commercial law found in London.

The new offerings in international arbitration are built around a strategy opposite to that which both built international arbitration in London and handicapped its growth. The new strategy emphasizes the autonomy of arbitration with respect to the state courts. In countries from the civil-law tradition, this strategy is especially attractive since, in fact, neither the judiciary nor the bar have many specialists in commercial law. This dearth of specialists in domestic commercial law was a fortiori even more obvious in international matters. In other words, the autonomy of *this* private justice was bound to be better protected since it developed at the margins of the legal field, out of the way of judicial institutions. Potential mechanisms of control over this specialized kind of proceeding were therefore quite limited.

This quite particular context explains the process that, in the course of the 1980s, led the majority of Continental countries to recognize the existence of an arbitral justice, while according to it a relatively large degree of autonomy with respect to national courts. This "monitoring at a distance," which recognized the legitimacy of private justice, did of course encounter the principle of universal justice profoundly inscribed in the civil-law systems (as well as the common-law systems). It therefore remains a matter of a precarious compromise. The formal powers of control by the legal system have been preserved in proportion to the rare use of these powers. Again, however, the situation is unstable. As the courts have gradually developed their expertise, so too have they developed their appetites.

The equilibrium of this system, which requires state justice and private justice to function in a parallel fashion, has to date been assured mainly through the existence of a small group of individuals who have accumulated positions of authority in both universes of practice. They are able to embody the guarantees of legal legitimacy and bring them to private justice. And their participation in the field of international arbitration helps to ensure that its autonomy is not threatened by an excess of zeal by the courts.

The "Noblesse" and the Routine of Arbitration

The existence of national institutions of arbitration adds another dimension to the relationship between national and international. The majority of the national institutions functions at a double level. They maintain a distinction between international and other arbitration, but the distinction is based essentially on the different financial and professional stakes of the two types of cases. It is true that international arbitrations are often more complex and require a particular expertise, but the boundary between domestic and international is not fixed. As in the case of the distinction between sports teams that play in the premier and in the second division, the game is fundamentally the same except for the stature and prestige of the players. Domestic arbitration is relatively low in prestige, partly because it is perceived to be too close to business and lacking in much law. In contrast, international arbitration claims to be learned, in part because it involves relationships with many legal systems. It is also more chic because it permits one to rub shoulders with a more cosmopolitan elite, even to identify with it. It gains further in prestige from its relationship to the more or less mythical world of great arbitrations that involved important political and economic concerns. As is true elsewhere in legal practice (Heinz and Laumann 1982), a clientele of high status is reflected in the prestige of the individuals serving it.

Arbitrators naturally seek then to belong—or to pretend to belong—to this international aristocracy of arbitration. And "membership" does not prevent a good number of them from exploiting their international notoriety—or its perception—in order to sell their services in the market of local disputes. International arbitration is able to serve this way as a facade or a locomotive for more down-to-earth, but also more regular, legal practices, whether focused on arbitration, litigation, or business advice in making deals.

While less prestigious and less visible, this domestic arbitration market permits national arbitration institutions to preserve a minimum core of matters to cover their basic operating and promotional expenses. These relatively small matters are also useful to test new recruits. They permit the new recruits to try their hand at arbitration without risking the always fragile credibility of private arbitration.

The national institution also can serve as a place of exchange. The grand masters of arbitration may use it to reinforce the patronage and clientele system that assures their notoriety and their nomination—or that of their peers—as arbitrator or lawyer. It is good arbitration politics to thank business lawyers or other acquaintances who bring nice arbitration matters by letting them have limited access to the arbitration market. This system of exchange of favors is essential to success in arbitration, a career dependent on personal relations.

Domestic arbitration, lacking the foundation in learned law of international arbitration and involving relatively small claims in which there is little incentive to invest in much law, is much closer to the pole of business than to that of law. This proximity permits the maintenance at the local level of numerous contacts in the world of business. The persons responsible for the national rosters of arbitrators are naturally consulted by local businesspeople or their lawyers when they must name arbitrators for an international conflict. The national arbitration leaders are then in a position to suggest the names of foreign colleagues—which then will bring return favors.

Symbolic mastery of an arbitral territory—which can be geographic, sectorial, or institutional—leads quickly to a position of strength in the "favor bank" upon which the prosperity of arbitrators depends. In effect, the possibility of controlling and orienting a potential flow of arbitration business permits these "provincial suzerains" to accumulate symbolic credits with respect to the "princes" of arbitration.

This strategy, which can also be seen as that of "local concessionaire in the arbitration market," is certainly not the privileged route for access to the community serving large international arbitrations. With a few exceptions, that service is reserved to national notables of law. The notables, qualified by their elevated status, are co-opted and granted access to the arbitration nobility. The national strategy of arbitration concessions, however, represents an alternative solution for those seeking access to the international market despite the absence of prestigious national titles. The national institutions of arbitration, similarly, offer strategic bases suitable for senior legal notables who want to reconvert themselves for the arbitration market. Working through national institutions, they start the process of converting their local legal capital into international commercial arbitration.

These domestic practices, even the most "vulgar," are then indispensable to the prosperity of "noble" international arbitration. For those responsible for the national institutions, the trick is to play on the confusion between the matters in order to build reputations and augment statistics. And if the statistics are too numerous, as is the case of the American Arbitration Association, one must construct some distance between routine matters by creating a double organization: one charged with the administration of domestic arbitrations and the other occupied exclusively with the "elegant" matters. The institutional duality, which the AAA illustrates, makes official the de facto segmentation of the arbitration market between domestic and international, small and large matters. In a different way than the practice of augmenting statistics, this practice also obscures the continuity and the complementarity between the two spaces of practice.

In sum, one is not able to study the great places or institutions of international arbitration without describing precisely how each of them positions itself, as much in relation to domestic arbitration as to the state legal institutions. In addition, it is necessary to consider the connections between domestic arbitration and state courts. The complexity of this ensemble of practices of commercial disputes is not, however, as great as it at first appears. The general logic of this system is determined in each country principally by the structure of relations between the legal field and that of economic power. This structure of relations provides the key to understanding the diversity of situations encountered among the great sites of international arbitration.

This central hypothesis about the relationship between the legal field and economic power has a corollary. In each of these countries where arbitration has gained some importance, the small circle of specialists of international arbitration exercises an influence in the legal profession and legal practice disproportionate to the numerical importance of international arbitration matters. The reason is that this field of practice is one of the privileged places where the ambiguous relationships between business and professional, and between law and money, are redefined. This special and privileged position of arbitration is characteristic of all the different national legal cultures we have studied, even if the relative degree of privilege varies.

International Commercial Arbitration and the Recomposition of the Field of Business Justice

International commercial arbitration serves as a prototype—and a lever—in the recomposition of the field of business justice, but it is also the reflection—and the product—of particular national histories of the interaction between economic power and state justice. In order to understand the details of the renaissance of arbitral justice that began in the 1960s, it is important to examine how national legal professions are structured, since the structures define the possible forms for the handling of business disputes and the place that arbitration occupies.

This effort to trace the emergence of the international in relation to particular national approaches faces a central paradox. We might have expected a new form of international justice—such as international commercial arbitration—to develop and take hold in countries like Great Britain, Sweden, or even the United States, where, in one way or another, we can point to an ensemble of traditions and know-how focused on the judicial or quasi-judicial handling of business conflicts. In fact, however, the new form took root and flourished in France, a country where the worlds of law and business maintained a distance, even a reciprocal disdain for each other.

This enigma provides a guiding theme for this part of our study. We can suggest here, however, some of the basic lines of the argument. It is not simply a matter of building on national experiences and models transported to the international field. As noted earlier, the inherent contradictions in arbitration practice—and more generally in business justice (or justices)—explain both the forms that it has borrowed and its possibilities for future development. The inevitably ambiguous relations between law and business are essential to the construction and prosperity of a custom justice built up halfway between these two universes. But this position of equilibrium between two fields of power is by definition precarious. Pulled between two logics and two ideologies, this business justice cannot develop according to a strict logic of the market. New forms are born and develop as a complex function of new opportunities in the international scene.

This complex relationship may explain why the new version of international commercial arbitration in the 1960s developed and flourished on the banks of the Seine. It was invented—or reinvented—in response to the new stakes posed by international economic developments, the political challenge of the third world, and the problem of managing East-West commercial relations. While the practice of arbitration had already prospered for a very long time in the City of London in the shadow of the Commercial Court, its legal practitioners did not find a way to handle the new situation emerging in the 1960s. Even when they seek assiduously to serve business, as we shall see, legal practitioners of business are limited by the symbolic field to which they belong. Their membership in the domain of law is deeply inscribed in their institutions, their learning, and, even more, in their habitus. Moreover, if they are inclined to forget their position, their peers are bound to bring them back to the legal order.

In short, for all these reasons, the new market of arbitration has tended to break from those who—as in the English and U.S. domestic arbitration systems—had been considered specialists. It has reconstructed elsewhere for the greater profit of competitors around the ICC who have seized the opportunity to place a new product on the market of justice—a product better suited to the new elements of international commerce. Recent evidence of this general pattern is easy to find in other examples from arbitration. In Sweden, for example, as we shall see in chapter 9, the structural qualities that gave value in international arbitration to the notables of Swedish law on the market for East-West conflicts—seniority, unquestionable independence—are precisely the qualities that prevented them from exploiting their reputation through learned and promotional investments, both of which would have been necessary to gain an advantageous position in the larger market of international commercial conflicts. The larger question, which we discuss in the general conclusion, is whether this pattern of disruption in the market for business disputes will characterize the future, especially if, as appears to be the case, the conditions that promoted international commercial arbitration in its present form are changing dramatically.

Finally, we note that the same or a similar rule holds for the principal protagonists of the market that has emerged over the past several decades. It has not been a matter of simply taking an established model and reproducing and marketing it internationally. The developments in international commercial arbitration took some part of the small learned circle of European pioneers to create an instrument and a forum—among other forums—for American-style litigation, conducted according to the usages of the new dominant players on the international legal field. But while the Americans succeeded in imposing their tactics—and then their arms—in Europe and elsewhere, they have not been able to bring the arbitrations to the United States or to U.S. arbitrators. And even if international commercial arbitration now strongly resembles the North American practice of business justice, it is far from being simply a forum where U.S.-style litigators have free rein. The logic of the symbolic field, we suggest, is imposed even on those whose economic superiority is accompanied by a more specifically legal advantage. The logic compels some concessions, which often take the form of alliances with the "dominated" in the field—in the particular case of arbitration, the small European producers of legal learning and of quasi-judicial authority. This exercise of restraint in the interest of an alliance between dominant and dominated, in fact, is also a strong source of legitimacy—and of flexibility.

More generally, the constraints inherent in arbitration—and international business justice—as it has been structured contribute to its credibility by leading the actors to put into practice some of the universal logic that the law seeks to embody. The structure also permits business justice to continue to renovate itself. None of the players, after all, can pretend to a monopoly on the market of justice, and, in any case, the market of justice does not coincide with the logic of the market. The structure of the field of international business justice defines the terms and logic of the competition in justice.

7

England: The Contradictions and Limits of an International and Reformist Strategy

Prior to 1979, according to a leading arbitrator in Paris, "No one but an Englishman would recommend London as a place of international arbitration" (int. 132, 7); yet at that time there were countless arbitrations in London with international parties. International arbitration involved a relatively stable set of arbitral practices dominated by shipping, commodities, insurance, and construction and by the legal institutions of the commercial bar. The types of large commercial disputes handled by ICC arbitration were typically within the domain of the Commercial Court in London.[1] There was only an avant-garde connection to the international-arbitration community located around the ICC in Paris, and it was limited to some sophisticated practitioners of shipping arbitration, a few solicitors who were beginning to develop an arbitration practice, and a few notable barristers and judges who, through personal inclination, had taken an interest in the French-dominated institutions of the ICC. London's attitude for the most part was complacent and, as often alleged, insular. Its internationalism was limited to the fact that many non-English parties participated in English practices.

As of this writing, the situation looks very different. The English legal profession has had to come to grips with the global practice of law and disputing, and with international commercial arbitration as recognized by the ICC community. There have been reform efforts in English legislation and in leading court decisions. England, as we shall see, has succeeded in producing more individuals capable of serving as international commercial arbitrators in non-English settings, and considerable effort has been expended to develop the London Court of International Arbitration as an arbitration center capable of competing with the ICC.

The results of the effort to bring these large arbitrations to England, however, have been mixed. As we shall see, internationalization is indeed transforming legal practice in England, but England's strength—its commercial law

---

1. In the words of a knowledgeable French arbitrator, "The commercial court takes care of what would be in arbitration here" (int. 108, 9).

centered on the Commercial Court and the bar—is also its weakness, since the "internationalism" of the court is at the same time quite local. The current situation, in one sense, is almost a stand-off between those favoring more—but still somewhat limited—openings to internationalism and those more zealously protecting the role of the courts. Still, it is clear that internationalization is breaking down the categories that have traditionally held together the closed world of English arbitration. The past twenty years have seen major changes in both the terms of the battles over how to handle business disputes and the characteristics of the contestants.

Essex Court and the Legalization of Arbitration

A key site for the transformation of legal practice and arbitration is London's sophisticated commercial bar, which is at the heart of the legal system as it applies to business disputes. Numbers 3 and 4 Essex Court (which is now Essex Court Chambers), 7 Kings Bench Walk, 1 Brick Court Chamber, and a few others represent the best-known chambers of the commercial bar, which has been growing numerically but even today comprises less than 10 percent—some 550 out of 6,500—of the bar in general. For complex reasons, Essex Court's Cambridge-dominated chambers have provided the largest number of key figures in international arbitration in recent years. A more Oxford-dominated chambers, 7 Kings Bench Walk, has also contributed a disproportionate share.

These sets of commercial chambers, which developed out of London's long dominance in the shipping industry, helped to develop a remarkable system for promoting forum London, English law, English standard form contracts, and English-style arbitration. It fostered the growth of a huge system of arbitration in shipping, insurance, and commodities, and a powerful commercial court that oversees the system; and London's bar helped also to maintain a huge—but somewhat distinct—construction arbitration system as well.

The symbiotic system in the interest of English commercial law and practice has revolved around the senior barristers, or Queen's Counsel (QC). In the 1960s and 1970s, commercial barristers represented the disputants whenever a shipping dispute raised a serious legal question. Otherwise, at least for smaller or less-complicated disputes, the shipping industry would handle its own disputes through lay-dominated arbitration. The London Maritime Arbitration Association then, as now, had lists of lay arbitrators highly knowledgeable about the details of shipping, and they would serve expertly as arbitrators. When disputes arose about the interpretation of one of the standard terms of contract, the shipping business would take the dispute to one or another specialist chambers. There the QCs would be learned in commercial law in general (based, in fact, largely on reported shipping cases) and shipping in particular. Under these circumstances, they would quite naturally turn the arbitration proceeding into one that resembled closely the adversary practice of the English High Court.[2] The parties would select two arbitrators, typically businesspeople, and the referee would be an experienced QC arbitrator, also from the commercial bar. The skills of English advocacy would sharpen the issues and bring to bear the legal precedents, often cases that the barristers had handled themselves as advocate or arbitrator; and the result would be an unpublished arbitral award.

The next step was appeal of major issues to the Commercial Court, a branch of the High Court created in the late nineteenth century. The Commercial Court could further contribute legal and business expertise to the development of the standard form contracts. Estimates of the percentage of the work of the Commercial Court directed to arbitration appeals, which came until 1979 in the form of "special cases," range from 40 to 50 percent in the 1970s (Kerr 1987, 114). Unlike other cases, moreover, these cases required no witnesses or cumbersome testimony.[3] The barristers would argue the points of law, focusing on how best to interpret standard form contracts in light of legal precedents and the needs of the shipping world. The courts and arbitration networks could thus be thought of as a very close partnership.

The relative intrusiveness of the courts should therefore not be seen as a public-court hostility to private arbitration. Indeed, the labels are misleading on both counts: the public courts watched out for the interests of the shipowners who depended on the standard form contracts; and the private system was in turn assimilated into the public one. An extraordinary bond ran from the shipping industry through Essex Court and others to the trial and appellate courts across the street and in the House of Lords.[4]

The bond was cemented by the QCs who occupied all the major positions of advocacy, adjudication, and arbitration. For example, from 4 Essex Court came Justice Michael Mustill, now Lord Mustill of the House of Lords; Sir

2. "Those arbitrations are conducted in the historically English fashion" (int. 91, 3).

3. As one QC observed, "These are very nice cases to decide. There were no witnesses. It's all law. There's no fact. And it's the powerhouse of English law" (int. 93, 15).

4. According to a leading QC's description of the system, "The community was quite small because they would meet the judges, and it was a very symbiotic relationship. I'll mention other names in a minute. But Wilberforce would actually meet them; he'd talk to them. They'd invite Wilberforce to their dinners and tell him their problems. They'd discuss cases which Wilberforce had decided and had got it completely wrong—this causing commercial havoc the way they decided cases in the House of Lords. . . . They were shipowners—shipowners and charterers. I mean . . . the main special casework then was shipping" (int. 93, 11).

Michael Kerr, now retired from the Court of Appeal, then president of the London Court of International Arbitration (LCIA) (then back to Essex Chambers), Sir Johan Steyn, recently promoted to the Court of Appeal from the Commercial Court; and Sir Anthony Evans, now chief justice of the Commercial Court. Lord Goff of Chieveley, now of the House of Lords, followed the same pattern from 7 Kings Bench Walk, and retired judge Lord Denning also came from 7 Kings Bench Walk in the 1940s. Lord Roskill and Lord Donaldson came from 3 Essex Court, and Lord Diplock also came from the commercial bar (3 or 4 Paper Building).

Certainly the list of names of commercial judges could be multiplied. These are all individuals, however, who became central to the London arbitration world in the 1980s and 1990s. The only apparent exception among key activists was Lord Wilberforce, who came to the judiciary from a Chancery practice, but his practice there had become much like that of the commercial bar.

The commercial bar would thus bring cases to persons they knew and who were themselves formed in their practices through work on the same sets of issues in the same chambers.[5] All understood the importance of a situation that enabled high-quality expertise to promote certainty and to adapt English law to the needs not just of the shipping world but more generally to the commercial world. According to Sir Michael Kerr, "something like 50 percent of the modern leading decisions [of any major English casebook on the law of contracts] will be found to stem from [appeals from arbitration]" (1987, 114). Indeed, one QC described how the situation worked. Noting a problem that "everybody in these chambers and the other shipping chambers . . . advised on," he said that "everybody knew when that went to arbitration that the case would go to the House of Lords" (int. 71, 20).

The participants all had an interest in maintaining a system that saw many of them acquire *Mr. Justice, Sir,* and ultimately *Lord* as their title and badge of status. Certainly England had the advantages of the British Empire and historical dominance of shipping, but this system also attracted much of the rest of the world to London to have disputes resolved according to English law as applied to English contracts. Everyone around this situation insists still that "it is the best commercial court in Europe, and probably the best commercial court in the world. And that is reflected in the fact that the judges are all

5. Describing the current Commercial Court, one judge noted that all eleven judges, "when they were barristers, would have done some arbitration work. I think about half of them come from these . . . should I say shipping sets of chambers, I mean the original ones. And those would have done some arbitration work right throughout their careers" (int. 75, 9).

top-class commercial lawyers who were leaders of the commercial bar" (int. 85, 4).

Forum London in the 1970s could understandably be complacent about its dominance in international commercial disputing and arbitration that involved parties from throughout the world. While shipping provided most of the raw material for the production of new commercial law, the other kinds of arbitration also fed well into this system. The insurance industry used standard form contracts with English law and arbitration, although until the 1980s relatively few disputes from the close-knit insurance world found their way to the courts. Commodities arbitration under the auspices of the Grain and Feed Association (GAFCA), the Liverpool Cotton Association, the Metal Exchange, and others, successfully processed thousands of "look-sniff" and other informal arbitrations about the quality of commodities (Kerr 1987, 114).[6] Barristers mainly stayed out of these disputes. The industry groups in fact policed these systems to help keep barristers out of ordinary disputes; but, as with respect to shipping, the barristers and their institutions were available for key legal issues that would arise from time to time.

They were also available to keep some control over arbitration that was not as respected as the shipping arbitration. As stated by one prominent QC, "The old view I think was that arbitrators were quite likely taken out of a class to make dreadful mistakes of law, procedure, and everything. And so it was right that the courts would have to pass control" (int. 87, 9).

This more hostile attitude also fit the construction industry, which had its own specialized chambers, like 10 Essex Street and 1 Atkin Building, and a specialist court not quite of the status of the Commercial Court (Flood and

---

6. As described by one commercial QC,
They get through literally thousands of arbitrations every year. . . . They are governed entirely by English rules. The arbitrators are all drawn from the commodity association, and although some of them were not British citizens, the majority of them obviously will be. They are conducted very much in accordance with the English procedure. If they are attended by lawyers at all, it's almost always by English lawyers. And to a very large extent, they are not . . . lawyers don't play any part in them at all. Typically they have a two-tier arrangement where there is an initial arbitration, which very often takes place simply on the documents before a three-man tribunal. And most of them have an appeals stage before a panel—usually of five—and the rules of many, if not most of them, exclude attendance by solicitors or barristers. . . . It was very difficult to get permission from the Boards of Appeal to get legal representation. They would only in practice do it where there was a real point of law and the matter was likely to go to the court. Most of them have their own legal advisers who sit in on appeals, and they get their legal input from that and through their own very considerable experience of the laws that affect their own tribe. (Int. 71, 3)

Caiger 1993).[7] Thousands of construction disputes continue to be handled annually by the Chartered Surveyors Institute, which conducts its own arbitration regime. If there is an appeal, it goes to the Referees Court, composed of judges at the circuit level—lower than the High Court. The appeals do not therefore get decided by the Commercial Court. Again, however, the system has long provided for numerous arbitrations handled mainly by lay arbitrators, and again there has been a filtering system that allows appeal to judges with good knowledge of the system.

All the arbitrations that went to this commercial-bar community, whether construction, shipping, or commodities, national or international, were handled "in the English way." The proceedings were dominated by oral testimony, English rules of evidence, English law, and English advocates. Arbitration and litigation in the commercial area were for all practical purposes the same if members of the commercial bar ran the show. Otherwise, as was the case of the great mass of arbitrations, the proceedings were more informal and lay-dominated—often handled by a different class of people. And the entire system, as noted by a French observer, "assimilated the arbitrators into their system," in effect creating arbitrators who acted "by delegation of the judiciary" (int. 108, 10).

Shocks to the System and International Pressures for Reform

In the 1970s, English arbitration had to confront the ICC world and a crisis in its own cozy system. Transformations in the international economy and in international legal practice were major factors in both these developments. The special-case procedure generated more appeals in the 1970s than before in part because of larger amounts in controversy, a high inflation rate that made it strategically more useful to drag out cases through appeals, and a series of political shocks such as the U.S. soybean embargo. The result was an increased number of appeals, and evidently the courts struggled with how best to handle them (Kerr 1987, 118). The restructuring of the world economy was felt in a kind of litigation crisis.

The English litigators—solicitors and the barristers they instructed—may also have been infected already by the tactics becoming more prominent in the burgeoning litigation departments of large U.S. law firms. Indeed, according to one source, solicitors connected to some of the major oil arbitrations were among the first to see the possibilities of the new, document-intensive litiga-

7. "If you take people like engineers or architects, and I've seen a little bit of this in action, they really have no idea (I'm generalizing terrifically) . . . how to handle a legal dispute. They probably haven't got a very good feel of things like natural justice" (int. 87, 9).

tion. According to a leading commercial QC, referring to two of the first solicitors involved in major commercial arbitrations outside of England,

> I think that in fact they may have been one of the first people— Martin Hunter and Alan Redfern—were the first people to see that there was serious money to be made in litigation and arbitration and that it shouldn't be left to the unqualified. . . . [L]egal executives . . . were unqualified people who did it as a service to the other major departments in the law firm. And that was why the bar played such an important role in those days because they were the only specialists in the case. . . . They weren't law graduates or anything. What happened I think in the last twenty years is that solicitors not only got very interested in litigation/arbitration generally, but the quality of the individual has changed enormously in solicitors, and they are very, very good litigators. (Int. 93, 36)

Not surprisingly, according to Kerr, "there was a . . . dramatic increase in interlocutory [pretrial] work in England during this period" (1987, 118).

The proliferation of appeals and litigiousness fueled the idea that at least some fine tuning was required to control the overuse of the "case stated" procedure. There was also a U.S. influence on reform. American lawyers, already with branches in London, pointed out the early success of the ICC in the growing number of large transnational commercial disputes, including huge construction projects of clients such as Kellogg and Bechtel. These American lawyers, including Lloyd Cutler of Wilmer Cutler, noted the number of these large cases that were arbitrated in France or Switzerland and suggested that their clients would prefer arbitration in London except for the excessive involvement of the courts.[8] They asserted that ICC arbitration in Paris or Switzerland was less likely to get tied up in the courts and would therefore give the clients a quicker, enforceable, judgment.

This criticism strengthened the related concern that, throughout the 1970s, the ICC had refused to designate London as the site of an arbitration unless the ICC contract clause specified London.[9] London thus was losing any chance to get a share of the ICC cases that, to at least a small but influential group, belonged in London. The potential number of such cases was not huge, but

8. According to one commentator, Lloyd Cutler "wanted to do more in London" with respect to international construction arbitrations (int. 80, 4). Another commentator said that the American firms in London simply made it clear that "they were not going to recommend that anyone arbitrate in London" without some changes in the relationship between arbitration and the courts (int. 132, 29).

9. The ICC court has discretion to place cases where the site is not specified in the contract.

the cases themselves could be expected to be quite significant. Thus, "The commercial establishment became convinced that London was losing business and people were going elsewhere" (int. 85, 8).

The activists promoting reform comprised a very small group. A few solicitors—mainly those who had experience in major oil arbitrations—belonged to this group. They were attracted, in part, because they could handle an ICC arbitration as a lawyer from start to finish (as could U.S. lawyers). Many of these key solicitors, not surprisingly, were also drawn to ICC-style arbitration because of their own cosmopolitan, hybrid backgrounds—for example, they were born or educated abroad, including especially German immigrants; or they had foreign, typically French, spouses.[10]

Similar characteristics help to explain the avant-garde posture of the members of the House of Lords, who in fact orchestrated the 1979 reforms.[11] Lord Wilberforce, a cosmopolitan, well-bred man with a French wife (the daughter of a French judge), was already drawn to the ICC in the early 1970s. As a law lord, he declared a judgment that suggested the London courts might not apply the special-case procedure to an ICC arbitration (*James Miller and Partners Ltd. v. Whitworth Street Estates [Manchester] Ltd.*, 1970 App. Case 583, 616). A later case undermined that dictum, but the earlier case showed an effort to support the ICC in London. The other major figures included Lord Roskill, who is fluent in French; and Lord Diplock, who had long been involved with arbitration, including a stint (1977–80) as president of the Institute of Arbitrators, and who had ties to the leading Americans. From the perspective of these individuals, in the words of one of them, it was the general feeling at that time "in about '79 that the ICC . . . could be more related and interesting work, and more ought to be done to make London attractive as an arbitration center—as a part of which I had to get rid of the case stated, which was very much sort of disliked by international commercial lawyers" (int. 97, 3).

New Legislation and Court Interpretation

These law lords and their allies took advantage of their leadership in the profession and the waning days of a Labour government. They argued, among other things, that increasing the number of international arbitrations in Lon-

---

10. Part of the mission of these pioneers from among the leaders of the bench and bar was to revalorize arbitration. One noted that in the sixties he began talking about the value of arbitration "at dinners and things. And I think that had quite an influence on the relative standing of arbitration and litigation in this country" (int. 97, 3).

11. Another example of the avant-garde is Robert Macrindle, who moved in the 1970s from Essex Court to Shearman and Sterling in Paris. He has now reestablished formal ties with the new Essex Court Chambers.

don would generate as much as £500,000,000 of revenue ("International Arbitration London," 1978, 114). They succeeded in getting a hastily drafted, compromise bill through Parliament. As law lords, they could introduce legislation themselves. The key features of the legislation, now well known, included a revision of the special-case procedure to turn it into an actual appeal, and a provision that parties could in their contract or later opt out of the general appellate review that was otherwise available. This feature would permit ICC cases as a matter of course to avoid most of the grounds of review on law, even if review would still be available for "arbitral misconduct."

The opt-out provision was limited by a compromise feature. In three key areas, shipping, insurance, and commodities, the parties could not opt out in advance by contract. The feature was designed to preserve the special relationship of barrister, courts, contracts, and English law, which has already been described. The idea was to keep the basics of forum London alive, which was consistent with the generally conservative aims of the commercial bar and the Commercial Court—anxious to preserve "their bread and butter" (int. 93, 15).

Once the legislation was in place, Lord Diplock *as a judge* succeeded in going beyond what had been expected by most of the supporters of reform (Kerr 1987, 126). In a series of judgments in the early 1980s, he cut down dramatically the opportunities for appeal to the courts. In a relatively short time, the number of appeals from arbitration, *including* shipping, went from a very high percentage to a trickle (int. 71, 16). The court simply limited appeal mainly to cases confronting the standard terms, refusing to get involved with what they term "one-off" cases (cases where the dispute is only of concern to the parties, not about the standard contract terms).

These cases, together with the opt-out provision, changed both the policy of the ICC and, for the most part, the attitude of the international arbitral community generally about the possibility of London arbitration.[12] Cosmopolitan members of the commercial bar elite thus joined forces with American law firms and some solicitor-litigators to induce the London world of international commercial arbitration to respond to the competitive pressures of ICC arbitration.

Reinforcing the Position of the Promoters of Arbitration Reform

The situation after 1979 reveals considerable development of the sector devoted to international commercial arbitration in London. We can see a sub-

12. Typical is the statement by one of the Paris leaders: "I think most of us feel relatively comfortable that the English courts do not overreach in their review, and so it has become an acceptable place for arbitration" (int. 132, 7) (see Egan 1994). Of course

stantial group connected to the international-arbitration community. Even within the commercial bar, it is relatively easy to see differences between those who have "taken" to the cosmopolitan international community and those who are more closely bound to English commercial arbitration. Those who take well make a clear distinction in the interviews between types of international commercial arbitration.

The cosmopolitan internationalists emphasize that their major interest is not in domestic arbitrations, nor in commodities, insurance, or shipping, but rather in proceedings akin to those handled by the ICC. Describing the more traditional "English international" arbitrations, for example, one internationalist QC stated, "They're not very international at all. It was a very English, English law, English procedure, English language, English arbitrators, English advocates, everything" (int. 93, 3). Further, "They are very parochial. I mean—I won't mention names—but I could introduce you to people who will say I do international commercial arbitration. Now you could ask them, what do you mean by international? What do you mean? And they wouldn't be able to answer" (id., 8). Similarly, in the words of another, "Those arbitrations are conducted in the historically English fashion. The best examples of those are the maritime arbitrations, commodities arbitrations, string arbitrations, and also insurance. And the third category of arbitrations is what I would call in functional terms the truly international arbitration, such as an ICC arbitration. Or for that matter an arbitration under the LCIA rules here" (int. 91, 3).

In part this is a contest over definitions. International commercial arbitration is prestigious and valued, and the question is what counts as international arbitration.[13] The internationalists emphasize the necessity of the 1979 reform as an opening to more international arbitration, and they tend to favor eliminating the exceptional treatment of shipping, insurance, and commodities. They worry little about any need for public courts to police private justice or to develop commercial law through arbitration with respect to the standard form contracts. Parties should be free, they argue, to settle their cases as they

there were still complaints, for example that it "was a recent and insufficient change" (int. 115, 7).

13. It is interesting that another QC with international interests but more attachment to shipping distinguished between commodities—where only the parties were international—and "international arbitration in the broader sense where not only the parties are international but the procedures have more of an international flavor" (int. 71, 3). The boundary was thus placed somewhat differently. Another similarly situated QC described his arbitration practice thus: "I would say that in these chambers we do mostly what all arbitration work is mostly, what you might call private, international arbitration work, which includes, of course, insurance but also includes the maritime work, and we do a lot of that" (int. 83, 2).

wish, and private arbitration involving commercial entities is quite acceptable (e.g., int. 93). And arbitrators are quite capable of applying national public policies without the close scrutiny of the courts (int. 91).

Showing their implicit acceptance of some of the tenets established by the professors who pioneered in the world of the ICC, these individuals write about arbitration and publish in arbitration journals such as *Arbitration International* and even the French *Revue d'Arbitrage*. And, as will be suggested in more detail below, they have absorbed and in turn contribute to the missionary zeal that characterizes the ICC community. They help to promote international arbitration generally throughout the world.

A very recent example of the attitude of this group is a judgment by Mr. Justice Steyn, then on the Commercial Court. He brought into English law the doctrine of the "separability of the arbitration clause" (*Harbren Assoc. v. Kanson Gen. Insce* (1992), Lloyds Law Report 81). This doctrine, a basic tenet of the international-arbitration community, allows contracts to be referred to arbitration even when it is contended that the entire contract is invalid for one reason or another. Citing a variety of international sources, he emphasized "party autonomy," the importance of keeping matters from domestic courts to favor "the neutrality of the arbitral process," and the need to "facilitate international trade" (id., 93). As a result, the court gave up some of its claim to review cases that involve arbitration agreements.

Finally, it is worth noting again that many of these missionaries of the London outpost take well to the ICC world because, like Lord Wilberforce, they have characteristics that favor membership in the cosmopolitan arbitration community. Prominent examples among those already named come easily to mind. Lord Mustill speaks fluent French and even wrote the early drafts of the Mustill and Boyd treatise on arbitration while in France. Sir Johan Steyn chose to leave the Afrikaner community in South Africa to come to London, and his legal education was in Roman law. Sir Michael Kerr, who served as president of the London Court of International Arbitration, was a German immigrant and speaks fluent French as well. V. V. Veeder, mentioned very often as the most solidly cosmopolitan British arbitrator and counsel, went to school in France and majored in foreign languages at Cambridge.

In short, there is now considerable overlap and cooperation between the English leaders, the ICC, and the various other international entities. They participate together in conferences. The ICC committee in London was chaired by Sir Michael Kerr of the LCIA. David Sarre, the ICC's representative in London, calls frequently on the QCs when he names arbitrators for ICC arbitration. London is now third, to Paris and Geneva, among the cities selected by the ICC for arbitrations where the parties have not selected a site.

According to a prominent member of the London internationally oriented group, London gets "a fair share" of the ICC arbitrations (int. 91, 15).

While cooperating with the other members of the international-arbitration community, the London group also emphasizes the rhetoric of competition. Mr. Justice Steyn concluded his recent article by suggesting that London inevitably is in a global market and can expect potential disputants to "vote with their arbitration clauses" (Steyn 1991). Sir Michael Kerr has pointed out that "the provision of dispute-resolving services—principally by arbitration—has become increasingly competitive" (Kerr 1987, 120).

One strategy pursued especially by those most internationally minded is to push the London Court of International Arbitration as a "flag arbitration center," which can bring attention and business to London and its institutions. By 1985 the LCIA had already been recreated and reformed by the internationalist group. The LCIA even publishes a journal, *Arbitration International*, edited by one of the leading Paris members of the new generation, Jan Paulsson, and the journal contributes to the integration of London with the international community. The LCIA is now often mentioned as one of the two or three "leading" international centers.

The LCIA marketing strategy pays great respect to the ICC. Most obviously, the LCIA has drawn on the same international arbitral community. It has organized "user councils" throughout the world, and the chair and most notable members are persons closely associated also with the ICC. The LCIA's court includes more than ten nationalities with people whose careers were made in ICC arbitrations—insiders in the international-arbitration community. Arbitrators and advocates tend not to turn down listings or memberships in serious arbitral institutions. The listings enhance their status in the international-arbitration community and at home, and help them get arbitration business. As a result, the LCIA has a very impressive list of names associated with it. Finally, in the contest of names, the LCIA has gained considerably by retaining Karl-Heinz Bockstiegel, one of the best known and most active arbitrators in the ICC world and a former judge of the Iran–United States Claims Tribunal, to succeed Sir Michael Kerr as president.

The rules adopted by the LCIA also put it in position to attract international business. The LCIA rules emulate the ICC while seeking to overcome the problems that are the source of criticism of the ICC. The basic rules, therefore, as written in 1981 and modified in 1985, provide strong arbitral powers and anticipate an ICC-type arbitration. Like the ICC, the LCIA arbitrations can be held anywhere and in any language chosen by the parties.

Unlike the ICC, the LCIA does not require a large deposit, and the arbitrators are compensated per hour rather than based on the amount in controversy. Terms of reference are not required, and there is no institutional scrutiny of awards rendered by the arbitrators. Appointments when the parties do not designate arbitrators is much more streamlined as well. The president makes appointments very quickly, unconstrained by the need to wait for a full court to meet or the effort to ensure that business is spread out to national committees equitably. Part of the efficiency comes from a conscious effort *not* to reach out, but rather to employ tested arbitrators known to the president: "Our net is narrower than the ICC," noted one LCIA official (int. 95, 15).

The London community, from this perspective, has made a strong entry into the international competition for ICC-type arbitrations. A closer look, however, suggests that the situation is not so clear. The close position between the QCs, the Commercial Court, the appellate judiciary, and English commercial law, as we shall see, is bound to create difficulties for the complete acceptance of any autonomous private justice system. Indeed, many of the leading proponents of internationalism and competition still place their major emphasis on the Commercial Court as *the* best English judicial product to market in the international competition (e.g., Kerr 1987).

Transformations in the National Landscape of Business Disputing

The importance of the large international disputes sought by the reformers of English arbitration today can now be situated in the emerging structure of national commercial-dispute resolution. One way of characterizing the adjustments made is that disputes are being shifted down one notch to make way for the large commercial disputes. Already the "look-sniff" commodities arbitration, the typical construction disputes, and the non–legal insurance and shipping disputes are handled mainly by laypersons. If the energy of many top commercial QCs turns to large international arbitrations, they will tend to pass the shipping and insurance, now defined as "lesser," back to other barristers or into the domain of lay arbitration. And as the opportunities to appeal even those cases diminish, we could expect less of a demand for the legal expertise that protects an award from a successful appeal. These now relatively less prestigious and lucrative cases are in a sense dumped out of the legal system and the consequent legal supervision. Resources instead concentrate increasingly on a tailor-made justice for the large, transnational disputes.

The elite of legal practice—now defined to take into account connection to the cosmopolitan international-arbitration community—thus is in position to handle the "major" cases, while the "lesser" cases become more industry specialized, more integrated into the lay arbitration world. The major cases, furthermore, can be handled either through arbitration or through litigation in a Commercial Court less burdened by appeals from arbitral awards.[14]

Part of the process of transformation is a blurring of the national categories that had dominated the world of business disputing. The various categories of arbitration are tending to merge into two categories—very large and relatively small—disputes. Reshaping to compete for international cases clearly leads to domestic changes and a blurring of the categories for the high-stakes disputes, including those that are like ICC arbitrations. One of the obvious impacts has been on the Commercial Court itself. In a recent article promoting the virtues of internationalism, Mr. Justice Steyn stated that

> one point is worth emphasizing: a dose of the spirit of international commercial arbitration can only benefit our system of conducting domestic arbitrations. The highly successful recent improvement in the trial procedures of the Commercial Court—the exchange of witnesses' statements, the short, uncontroversial opening and an early statement of the defendant's case—were a *direct* result of the demonstrated success of such procedures in international commercial arbitration. The successful adoption of such procedures in the Commercial Court has in turn led to a radical improvement in domestic arbitration procedures. And we are still on the learning wave. (Steyn 1991, 19)

In many respects, the Commercial Court is actually competing with private international justice (and other public justice systems), and one way to compete is to adopt the successful practices of the competition.[15] The result is

---

14. The potential gap between the Commercial Court and international arbitration will be revisited below.

15. The connection was made explicitly by one of the partisans for internationalism. You cannot entirely divorce arbitration practices from what's happening in the courts, you see, because the reason for that is the same people appear in both. Now the procedures of the Commercial Court in London have been revolutionized in the last three years. The trials that used to take twenty days would take six days now. It is a far more open disclosure of witnesses' statements, and, well, expert evidence has always been disclosed, but generally the rules have all been tailored to shortening cases, much more open system than it ever was. Now you may say, "What's this got to do with your subject?" But it's got a great deal to do with it. Because those same people often appear in the Commercial Court and they appear for instance in category 2 [shipping and insurance arbitration] disputes. And the methods of litigation that they pick up in the Commercial Court, if they foster then what they were used to in the maritime arbitration, then they'll adopt and learn. So you've got to look at the whole legal culture. (Int. 91, 12)

that arbitration and litigation of large commercial cases have come to lose some of their distinctiveness.[16] The shift is toward the international practices.

Indeed, in the last three decades the Commercial Court has attracted a considerable increase in its caseload. In the 1950s and the 1960s, according to one of the judges,

> The amount of work had gone down a great deal. There was very little of it; so much so, that steps were taken in the 1960s to make it more user-friendly, the phrase we'd use today . . . and since the . . . I think it was the late sixties there's been a tremendous upsurge in the amount of work done by the Commercial Court. (Int. 75, 2)[17]

It is no surprise to see that the same factors that promoted an increase in business litigation elsewhere[18]—including in the ICC—also affected the volume of work of the Commercial Court.[19] The Commercial Court is in fact experiencing a workload problem that, according to published accounts, is leading to some serious problems such that the head of the court mounted a lobbying campaign to increase the number of judges.

The rhetoric of the campaign well demonstrates the blending of arguments for arbitration and for the Commercial Court. A recent article in *Legal Business* describes the approach as follows:

> Because London has long billed itself as an appropriate forum for resolving international disputes, the Commercial Court is heavily dependent on foreign parties bringing claims. Since 75 percent of the Commercial Court's cases involve one foreign party,[20] [Justice] Saville knows well that dissatisfied customers can vote with their feet and take their disputes to courts elsewhere. (Dillon 1993, 47)

Justice Saville, in fact, reportedly argued that it was important to the City and "millions of pounds" in "invisible earnings" to add more personnel to the Commercial Court. The argument, in short, was that the Commercial Court

16. We have seen already how international commercial arbitration as practiced in the ICC world has come to resemble "offshore litigation."

17. Reportedly there were some two thousand writs issued, 435 cases given trial dates, and about one hundred trials in a recent year (int. 75, 3; Dillon 1993).

18. See the discussions in the following chapter.

19. One observer made the link explicitly to U.S. developments: "As things have turned out, there is at the moment a colossal pressure on the Commercial Court. The amount of litigation in this country has built up an enormous backlog. I think it comes from America, the litigation" (int. 91, 12).

20. And 50 percent involve foreign nationals on both sides of the dispute.

was not merely part of the general justice system, but rather should be seen as a "service industry" (Dillon 1993, 48). Judges on the Commercial Court reportedly have even suggested that, again unlike the other courts, the Commercial Court could charge relatively high fees and "become largely self-financing" (Edwards 1994b, 61).

Another manifestation of this change in the relationship between public and private comes with respect to the judges themselves. The international dimension of private justice may disrupt the incentive for an eminent QC to elect to become a judge in the Commercial Court. If the QC can gain the same or higher stature as a "private judge," which pays much more as well (or if the role of national judge is relatively devalued), then there is less of a reason to follow the traditional career pattern. It is very early to see if the internationalization of legal practice will have this impact in a very large way, but it is interesting already that a recent article lamenting the shortage of quality judges listed five prominent QCs who reportedly had turned down a judgeship last year. At least two of the names were individuals with high visibility in international arbitration, and three were from what is now Essex Court Chambers (Edwards 1994b, 56).

We have already suggested, in addition, that international commercial arbitration is contributing to the reduction or elimination of barriers between solicitors and barristers. Most obviously, solicitors can become advocates in commercial arbitrations, and several have indeed made a reputation as advocates in that field (e.g., Martin Hunter, Arthur Marriott, and Julian Lew). The rise in the seventies and eighties of "big-business litigation" has given solicitors a prominent role in litigation, facilitated their numerical increase, and contributed substantially to a relative increase in prestige and ability to recruit among solicitors.

These two related factors—the higher status of solicitors and the increased importance of international counsel, who can deal directly with barristers—have also, we were told, contributed to a relative decrease in the "autonomy" of barristers (int. 96). Barristers have traditionally been able to ignore the wishes of solicitors or in-house counsel to make certain arguments in a particular litigation. The "independence" of the barrister was in fact a defining characteristic. It is no doubt more difficult for barristers today to resist those pressures. The special learned and mutually supportive role of the bar in developing commercial law—and legitimating it—could in this manner be undermined.

Internationalism poses a real dilemma for the commercial bar. While it has become extremely prosperous in recent years, the number of members of the commercial bar is small, and the growth of the size of the bar is quite slow.

As barriers between barristers and solicitors diminish, the question is what options are available for the bar collectively and as individuals. One option is to try to compete with the firms of solicitors and the international law firms. The move of Essex Court Chambers outside of the traditional Inns of Court could be seen as a potential adoption of this strategy.

In fact, however, it would be very difficult to compete in large-scale litigation. As an Essex Court Chambers QC stated,

> As you know, the art of litigating is not to have a trial at all. Now you can go I think to ten or so law firms and they're very, very good tacticians. They know how to handle these massive cases. They know how to bring in different experts and consultants and how to manage the team. . . . [T]hese are the skills of man management and handling paper and actually moving people around the world. But solicitors have gotten very, very good at this. Now there's no way the bar has ever had that particular skill or could ever acquire it, because you can see they don't have the administrative backup. If you want to keep people—60 to 150 people—working on a case all over the world, you're actually going to have an enormous administration to control what they do, tell them what to do, to move them around and so forth. (Int. 93, 37)

The strategy of Essex Court Chambers may be seen also to be following another approach. In mid-1994, the chambers announced that it was strengthening its "arsenal of international arbitrators" substantially ("Arbitrators Become Essex Men" 1994, 16). Sir Michael Kerr rejoined the chambers after his stint as president of the LCIA. Karl-Heinz Bockstiegel from Germany and the new president of the LCIA also joined. And Martin Hunter, one of the leading solicitors in arbitration, retired from Freshfields to join the bar and Essex Court Chambers. Two other international figures, Robert Macrindle and Andrew Rogers, joined also as "door tenants" who will use the chambers as a London base. These individuals add to an already impressive group.

The question is how successful they will be collectively competing against, for example, the learned Swiss arbitration boutiques who are well connected to the U.S. law firms. The reputation of the arbitrators in Essex Court Chambers will allow them to continue to prosper, but we cannot say whether this represents a serious new international form or the natural evolution of barristers' chambers into places of semiretirement for senior solicitors or barristers available for particular services like arbitration. What is clear, however, is that it represents a remarkable effort to put together a group with a strong international appeal.

Contradictions of the Commercial Bar

The internationalists at Essex Court Chambers share in a problem that makes it difficult for England to become a more important player in the world of international arbitration. We must start by recognizing the centrality in England of the Commercial Court and the commercial bar that supports it. Virtually every solicitor and barrister in England acclaims the Commercial Court as England's major international asset. As noted above, its caseload has grown enormously, and the majority of cases have at least one and often both parties from outside of England. As noted before, the Commercial Court occupies the same terrain as the arbitrations that would go to the LCIA (or come to England from the ICC).

A 1983 Court of Appeal decision by Sir John Donaldson quite aptly characterized the general view of the Commercial Court: it is the *"curia franca* of international commerce, in so far as that commerce is based on the rules and concepts of English law. . . . [I]t is an international commercial court the overwhelming majority of whose judgments are concerned with the rights and obligations of foreign nationals" (*Amin Rasheed Shipping v. Kuwait Insurance,* 1983; cited in Hermann 1983, 40). The importance of the continuing production of English commercial law through the courts is a key factor in attitudes toward arbitration.[21] The Commercial Court has great national and international prestige, and it is central to what London has to offer the international community; but it remains embedded in the national legal system. Arthur Marriott has proposed that the Commercial Court seek to become a "European Commercial Court" (Marriott 1989, 31) with a chamber of non-English judges, but it is hard to imagine the creation of a truly international court embedded in the English legal system.

A recent case illustrates some of the tensions that are inherent in the English system. The case concerned a rather technical issue—whether the High Court could order a plaintiff in an ICC arbitration to post security for the costs of the arbitration (*Ken-Ren Chemicals* 1994). The Court of Appeal in an earlier case—with a key opinion by Sir Michael Kerr—had made a rule that made it quite unlikely that the court would intervene in such a case. A

21. The role of this law as an international strength is described as follows: The one attraction that I think people have in coming here when they're non-English is that you give the same facts to two different lawyers and they'll come up with the same answer. They won't say that it will depend. They won't say it'll depend on the judge. They can give you the answer. And this is what the English commercial law tries to be. Simply because if you didn't have that system you wouldn't get 99.99 percent of dispute settling you see. Everything would have to fight, because no adviser could give you the answer

new case came up, and the rule was applied by both the Commercial Court and the Court of Appeal. The case then came up to the House of Lords.

While the decision was pending, a veritable who's who of the international arbitration community[22] mobilized and insisted, in an article reported in *Legal Business* in May 1994, that what was at stake was "nothing less than the future of international commercial arbitration in [England]" (Egan 1994, 64). They posed the issue as one of control. Citing also the pre-1979 history, the internationalists complained that "England has shown a marked reluctance to release arbitration from the control of the courts." In the words of Emmanuel Gaillard, a French partner in the Paris office of Shearman and Sterling, "The degree of control which English courts exercise is 'outdated, it's ridiculous' " (Egan 1994, 67).

Despite this campaign, the House of Lords ruled in favor of the appeal, allowing the order for costs. Lord Mustill, one of the strong supporters of international commercial arbitration, set out the analysis and tried to stake out a middle ground between court control and freedom for the arbitration. On the facts, however, a majority of Lords disagreed with the outcome of the Mustill approach and decided to award the costs. The delicate balance between supervision and intervention went toward intervention in this case. Yet the supporters of the decision tried to cast it as essentially supportive of international commercial arbitration. Indeed, the head of Clifford Chance's Commercial Arbitration Group, John Beechey, who acted for one of the appellants, quickly published a "spin control" article in the *Bulletin of the Swiss Arbitration Association* (Beechey 1994).[23]

The question of ultimate court supervision is also at the heart of the current debates that have been under way for several years about a new reform for English arbitration.[24] Lord Mustill and subsequently Mr. Justice Steyn chaired the Department of Trade and Industry's Departmental Advisory Committee

---

with any confidence. So English law, commercial law has a very strong bias toward certainty, and you can't have certainly without decided cases. (Int. 93, 9)

22. Among those quoted in the article were Yves Derains, Jan Paulsson, Julian Lew, Sir Michael Kerr, Emmanuel Gaillard, and Eric Schwartz (currently the secretary-general of ICC arbitration).

23. For example, "It is apparent that the courts have re-stated their determination to be seen as supportive of international arbitrations brought to England" (Beechey 1994, 191).

24. According to an insider, who predicted wrongly on the case on security for costs, On supervision I would say the big question in England, that's the most important. If you want to write about it, the big question is whether the special categories are justifiable, whether they should survive, what's the logical basis for

on Arbitration Law. Under Lord Mustill, the committee, despite some controversy, refused to adopt the UNCITRAL Model Law, which represents a kind
of accepted state-of-the-art among the international-arbitration community.
Mr. Justice Steyn reportedly favors an approach that will move closer to that of
the international-arbitration community. The consultative draft as it emerged,
however, does not move from the basic compromise of the 1979 act, which
kept "special categories" of shipping, insurance, and commodities under some
judicial control ("English Committee" 1994). It remains to be seen what will
follow, but again we see the difficult problem of the relationship between
international commercial arbitration and the courts.

A well-known retired judge described the situation as follows:

> Three-fourths of the judiciary is completely ignorant of anything
> about arbitration. They know nothing and care nothing. They don't
> come across it. . . . I think some in the commercial courts are in favor
> of judicial control—ultimate judicial control—others are not so, just
> by different opinions. I would say . . . the majority of opinion in the
> commercial courts is in favor of some judicial control. (Int. 97, 5)

Many in the commercial bar share this opinion as well.[25]

The real dilemma that leads internationalists like Lord Mustill to assert
some judicial control is that English commercial law is what tends to build
any success that England has as an international-arbitration center and as an
international Commercial Court. An American arbitration expert in Paris saw
this dilemma quite well:

> And I've also participated in a number of the meetings concerning the
> LCIA, and every time somebody gets up and says, you know, 'We

---

it. Is that basis valid today? And what are the views of the users? That, I
think, is the big question. When you turn to the other side, the auxiliary, the
auxiliary powers—I think with one qualification that I'll mention in a moment, the auxiliary powers, supporting powers of English courts, are adequate.
The qualification is this; it is still possible to apply to an English court for security for costs in an arbitration. I told you earlier you can't do it in an ICC arbitration. (Int. 91, 31)

25. For example,
The question is whether you should be allowed in a standard term of your contract to opt out—to agree to exclude judicial review—in those particular cases.
Yes, well, I think I'm marginally against it because people just don't think
about it when they're signing their contracts. I think that '79 actually got the
balance right. But it's not something I feel at all strongly about. It does have
the virtue to lawyers, or as lawyers see it, that you can have a consistent body
of case law developing from the . . . in these areas in maritime and in insurance, which does tend to make a cohesive body of law in London which people
know about. (Int. 83, 14)

have to be fully accepted and get more business. And we have to be more international and not always be talking of ourselves as the London court.' And I think a better response if people say, now wait a minute, people are coming here because they think they should have arbitration in London, they think that English justice is pretty good, they think there are a lot of very very skilled commercial lawyers and arbitrators, so let's play this strength while going to an international audience. And I think that's really what they do. And I think it's true that if you choose LCIA you think that, well if I could very well end up with a . . . as the president of a tribunal a skilled English, commercial lawyer. That's the most likely choice nine times out of ten. And maybe they thought of that when they put in LCIA. And they said, yes, with this kind of a contract that would make sense. It's a commercial contract. I want this law to govern it. I want this contract to be interpreted. That's just what I'm looking for. (Int. 106, 4)

The LCIA seeks to be international, but, like the Commercial Court, depends on English commercial law and the leading experts in that law, retired judges and senior QCs.[26] The arbitration experts recognize this strength,[27] which at the same time limits the development of the LCIA as a real competitor to the ICC. The actual number of cases handled by the LCIA is therefore rather small, even if reportedly growing.[28] There is no easy way out of this dilemma, which makes the ambivalent position of the courts quite understandable.[29] It is not only that the courts and commercial bar are limited in what they can accomplish internationally. It is also that the courts remain the dominant institution with respect not only to practice but also to academic

26. According to an insider, "It was Michael Kerr's policy in the LCIA to appoint barristers" (int. 85, 4).

27. Another recent example is an effort to develop a City Disputes Panel for financial disputes. Even though the rules were drafted by a committee that included Arthur Marriott, the article describing the service reported that "most hearings will be tried by a chairman with judicial experience." Not surprisingly, Robert von Mehren, a New York arbitration expert, observed that the service would not appeal to U.S. clients unless it was more international—"unless U.S. lawyers sit on panels" ("Dispute Service for London" 1994, 2).

28. No one has claimed more than thirty to forty cases per year (int. 94, 39). One English expert reported in 1992, "The London court has had something like sixty, I believe, eighty-seven [arbitrations]" (int. 82, 6).

29. One of the best-known international arbitrators thus recognized, "Well, they think that questions of law should only be decided by judges and that giving the judges the power of control over arbitrations enables—and this is right—enables a corpus of commercial law to be built up through reported cases. And I think that's an absolutely valid point. It doesn't exist in any other countries at all" (int. 97, 6).

learning.[30] The rhetoric of competition between arbitration centers is therefore somewhat misleading. The competition is mainly between English law and its competitors in different laws and dispute resolution forums, including the ICC.

Yet the rhetoric and activity around the LCIA and the acceptability of England as an arbitration forum also matters. The one success that all commentators attributed to the 1979 reform was that it ended the "ICC boycott" of London for cases where the place of arbitration was not designated. Thus for ICC arbitrations, London became the third most popular venue behind Switzerland and Paris. And, whether or not London gets around the dilemma of its elegant commercial law, it is clear that the rhetoric and activity around international commercial arbitration have played an important role in transforming the landscape for the handling of business disputes.

30. The English, for example, have a rich tradition in public international law, but at least until very recently, there has been very little effort to invest in an international law for private transactions beyond what is found or potentially used in the Commercial Court.

8

In and Out of the Multidoor Courthouse: Internationalization and the Transformation of the Landscape of Business Disputing in the United States

The internationalization of legal practice, as seen through international commercial arbitration, is helping to transform the landscape of business disputing in the United States in two senses—how disputes are handled, and how legal doctrines and principles are developed to regulate business practices. Lawyers from the United States, as seen earlier, have become major players in the principal international legal developments. What we see, however, is that it is not a matter of a simple convergence between practices in the United States and at the international level. There are important and, to some extent, surprising variations. The litigators who were able to promote the transformation of international commercial arbitration into offshore litigation have been challenged by recent developments in domestic business disputing that in fact stem from the success of international commercial arbitration abroad. "Alternative dispute resolution" has been unleashed and put business litigators on the defensive. Business justice, as a result, is now a wide open and competitive market in the United States, and it appears to be moving away from the domain of law and closer to the domain of business.

Developments associated with the internationalization of legal practice, in addition, are transforming the relative roles of judges, academics, and practicing lawyers in the production and modernization of the law governing business and business disputes. It is not just that the dominant position of litigators and U.S. courts for handling domestic business disputes has been shaken by factors associated with international legal practice. The processes of producing law—and the role of courts in that production—are also changing. As we see from an example from the American Law Institute's Restatement on Foreign Relations, internationalization is promoting law production through an unequal alliance of academics and learned practitioners.

The competitive processes in international legal practice are continuing. Indeed, we can see that both the U.S. promoters of a new ADR different from litigation-dominated arbitration and the U.S. promoters of a new, learned, internationally oriented law are seeking to apply their approaches and redefine the rules at the international level. To date the domestic ADR movement has had relatively little success internationally. It is also early to speculate on the success of the potentially more far-reaching approach of the learned U.S. practitioners. There is some reason to believe, however, that the latter will play a major role in creating the legal framework for the world of business and business disputing in coming decades.

Internationalization and Business Disputing in the 1970s and Early 1980s: The Setting
The United States in the International-Arbitration Community

We begin the story in the mid-1970s. As we have seen, international factors, including the global economic restructuring after the oil crisis and the assertions of newly independent states, played a role in facilitating the development within large U.S. law firms of a powerful litigation arsenal for deployment in business warfare. The litigators were using that technology in international commercial arbitration and in the courts. Their success in representing the contending parties in commercial disputes, however, did not translate into very much international arbitration in the United States or into business for U.S. arbitrators. The arbitrators in major cases were typically from European boutiques, especially from Paris or Geneva. The neutrality of arbitration, in fact, was premised in part on the image of neutrality that this distance from the centers of conflict and power gave to the proceedings (see chap. 4).

Within the United States (as in many other countries), there was a group of individuals who constituted a kind of outpost of the International Chamber of Commerce and the international-arbitration community. Besides the litigators then crashing into the Continental world, there were also a few persons with particular cosmopolitan ties or institutional connections. One group came out of the American Arbitration Association, which had long cultivated ties with those who could be considered their European counterparts. Such ties, bolstered through conferences and honorary organizations, allowed a few individuals in the United States to gain some of the rewards of international arbitration outside of the role of counsel.[1] Others, comprising a few academics with language skills and typically European origins, also were able to enter the world as at least "associate members" in the club (int. 50).[2] And finally, a small number of "notables" of the U.S. legal profession (with ties to government, academia, and private practice) were also able to become occasional arbitrators as well as lawyers for some very large international arbitrations.

1. Examples would include Martin Domke, who came from Germany to the AAA, Gerald Aksen, Robert Coulson, Michael Hoellering, and Howard Holtzmann.

2. Examples would include Allan Farnsworth, Andreas Lowenfeld, and Hans Smit.

The nature of the careers of the latter, however, meant that they would not necessarily remain focused on arbitration.[3] The members of this outpost community, as we shall see, were important in promoting arbitration reform in the United States.

Litigation and the Options for Business Disputing in the United States

Within the United States more generally, as we have noted, business litigation in the courts was prospering (which is indeed why the litigators were so confident in exporting their technologies abroad) (Nelson 1990; Galanter and Palay 1991). The rise of litigation as a major feature of the U.S. legal profession—once dominated at the elite level by "deal makers"—is evident from the fact that the litigation section of the American Bar Association, founded only in 1973, grew quickly into the largest section in the ABA (Dolin and Saylor 1993, 6). Another indicator was the very large number of private antitrust actions found in the federal courts.[4] The market in business litigation was indeed exploding, and business litigators were gaining wealth and prestige (Glendon 1994).

While caseload pressures increased, the only recognized alternative to the courts was the American Arbitration Association. Aside from the courts, we were told, it was in fact "the only game in town" (int. 210, 4). The AAA was quite busy, handling some fifty to sixty thousand cases per year, but the system had at least two problems from the point of view of large business litigation. First, it was designed for relatively small cases, meaning that the processes were quite informal. There was limited discovery, for example, and virtually no reasoned opinions.[5] Accordingly, the AAA did not pay its arbitra-

3. Examples would include Lloyd Cutler, one of the arbitrators in the Greenpeace arbitration, and William Rogers, who was involved in one of the notable early ICSID arbitrations under the auspices of the World Bank.

4. Contrasting the situation in 1992 with that in 1977, the chair of the antitrust section of the ABA stated, "In 1977, private antitrust litigation was rampant. A large fraction of every major law firm was engaged in such work. Most of the urban district courts had one or more price-fixing class actions; some had several. Nearly every decision by a manufacturer to cancel or allow a dealer contract to expire was attended by preparation for being sued. In short, treble damage litigation was a growth industry" (Taylor 1992, 85).

5. The attitude of large-firm practitioners was evident from the following: "For years I have been the critic of the way arbitration has been done in the United States, because most people find it to be a very, very, unrewarding experience. They're unhappy with the results because they believe that arbitrators invariably will split the baby." Further, "The result will not necessarily be understood by the parties. It need not be in writing unless the arbitration agreement provides. It need not therefore spell out the reasons"

tors very much, and it had relatively inexperienced, "amateur" arbitrators (int. 210)—not drawn from the legal elite.

Second, it was relatively easy to avoid an arbitration clause in a contract. All that was required under settled federal law was an allegation that an issue of federal law was involved in the dispute, and the matter would be taken up instead by the federal courts. As a result, arbitration practice generally attracted neither the major law firms nor the most prestigious members of the legal profession as arbitrators. The large-firm lawyers who embraced international private justice stayed away from domestic commercial arbitration.

Business arbitration, it is true, had thrived earlier in the century, according to Auerbach (1983), but its expansive period ended when the New Deal changed the relationship between business, law, and the state (Auerbach 1983; Shamir 1993). Business disputing through arbitration gave way to business regulation through the state and through federal-court litigation. Private arbitration became very much a second-class player in this arrangement. The courts and the state kept commercial arbitration confined in a rather subordinate role.

While business litigation was thriving and litigators were riding high, there were nevertheless some hints of dissatisfaction as early as the 1970s. Those expressions within business were tied to the increase in number and status of in-house counsel, who gained power and responsibility with the increase in importance of business litigation and federal regulation (Rosen 1989). Business was, after all, spending considerable sums in litigation (including litigation related to the tactics of mergers and acquisitions) in a kind of arms race (Caplan 1993). At the same time, the growth of the caseloads, despite the expansion of the judiciary, led to problems of delay exacerbated by an increase in civil-rights and criminal cases. It was becoming somewhat more difficult for business to use the courts effectively.

The increase in the number of judges, in addition, made the judiciary seem less reliable and predictable to in-house counsel, who were beginning to sense their bargaining power and ability to affect the legal system for their interests.[6]

(int. 35, 2–3). As a result of this informality, "Most of the cases in those days were a small . . . I think arbitration is essentially small—I say small—everything's relative—commercial disputes" (id., 6).

6. As stated recently by a partner in a major East Coast firm,
One of these problems is the judges . . . who are appointed. Some clients pick ADR because they don't want to . . . wait three years to get to the judge . . . we have locally. What the law firms are doing through us is saying we need a panel of appropriate judges. We need to be able to say to our clients, we can get you the kind of judge that is the kind of judge you think about when you think about going to court, you know. (Int. 36, 15)

We can express this perspective in several ways. One is that the quality was in fact declining. Another is that business litigants faced a group of relatively more diverse judges from nonbusiness backgrounds, and they feared that the judges would be less sympathetic to their concerns.[7]

By the late 1970s, therefore, the general counsel of major corporations were beginning to organize and to discuss "alternatives to the high cost of litigation." The Center for Public Resources, in particular, was created at this time.[8] It served, one Wall Street partner noted, as a "trade association" for corporate counsel trying to contain the costs of litigation (int. 42, 8).[9] As we shall see, however, the real growth in the power and influence of CPR did not take place until the mid-1980s—when the effects of internationalization provided new openings for business disputing.

The judges were also expressing concerns. They faced a caseload crunch and a growing backlog problem. In the opinion of many judges and commentators (Posner 1985; Federal Courts Study Committee 1990), they had too many criminal cases, civil-rights cases, and social-security claims.[10] Congress was creating all these federal rights and forcing the federal courts to handle them with inadequate resources. Part of the judicial concern was reflected in the

7. One corporate counsel from a major corporation put his perspective in provocative terms: "The judicial system in my view is a little spotty today. We've had various presidents who have appointed people because of quota systems for political correctness. So you're finding your judiciary is spotty. And just the other day it shows that Clinton might be able to appoint as many as four hundred judges. Well, if he follows the pattern that he's using now in filling appointments, attempting to just say, I need a woman here, or a minority there, you're going to have an untried system of judges, which makes it a little difficult to operate" (int. 27, 7).

Some of the same debates and criticisms about the quality of the judiciary are evident in England, despite the strong control of the judiciary and the barristers over business disputing (Edwards 1994b).

8. Much of the early work of CPR was around the "minitrial," invented as a way to resolve large corporate disputes in litigation and written about by the inventors in Green, Marks, and Olson 1978. The early CPR work focused on the minitrial (Center for Public Resources 1982) rather than mediation or arbitration. Green and Marks went on to form Endispute, a leading provider of dispute resolution services. Olson became the chair of the ABA's Special Committee on Alternative Means of Dispute Resolution. All these pioneers moved with the changing emphasis in ADR.

9. The clients "have banded together" (int. 36, 7). The executives are saying, "We want something to give us an answer in less time" (id., 10).

10. "Between 1958 and 1988, following decades of extremely slow caseload growth, the number of cases (both civil and criminal) filed in the federal district courts . . . trebled, while the number filed in the courts of appeals increased more than tenfold" (Federal Courts Study Committee 1990, 5). The committee recommended restrictions on some social-security and civil-rights claims.

mid-1970s in "endless conferences and workshops" (int. 211, 3) about case management and how to deal with backlogs. Interestingly, as Marc Galanter has noted, there was almost no complaint at that point about the number of business disputes in the courts (Galanter 1988).

The well-known Pound Conference of 1976, promoted by Chief Justice Warren Burger, thus focused on the problem of too many "inappropriate"—small—cases in the courts, especially the federal courts, and on the need to provide efficient forums for small claims and neighborhood disputes. The topic of alternative dispute resolution for *business* conflicts was simply not part of the agenda. Accordingly, the first ABA entry into alternative dispute resolution and private justice—a direct result of the Pound Conference—was a Special Committee for Minor Disputes created in 1977. The ABA began its work by promoting Professor Frank Sander's (1976) proposal for what later was termed a "multidoor courthouse," but again the theme of alternative dispute resolution had very little to do with business disputes until several years later.[11]

As of the early 1980s, therefore, judges and in-house counsel were beginning to react—from different perspectives—to the costs and amount of litigation. The in-house counsel movement had not focused on mediation or arbitration, however, and the courts were only promoting alternative dispute resolution for "minor disputes." The major players in handling business disputes simply did not anticipate that private justice was the appropriate means for accommodating such conflicts. As noted before, their imagination was limited by the only games in town—litigation in courts, which typically culminated in a negotiated resolution after considerable pretrial skirmishing, and informal commercial arbitration under the auspices of the AAA—thought to be appropriate only for relatively small commercial matters.

Mitsubishi Motors Corp. v. Soler Chrysler-Plymouth (1985)

The pivotal case in the United States in unblocking the limited traffic patterns of court litigation and AAA arbitration was *Mitsubishi*, decided in 1985. *Mitsubishi* was actually not about domestic business disputing, but rather about the willingness of the U.S. courts to make a space for international commercial arbitration. From that perspective, the case was only about

---

11. Indeed, it was possible for Jerold Auerbach, writing in 1983, to describe mediation as follows: "New mediation programs were designed for a predominantly low-income, minority group clientele, confined by race and class to inner-city neighborhoods. Their 'minor' disputes were designated as 'inappropriate for adjudication': valuable court time must be reserved for 'more appropriate cases' " (Auerbach 1983, 124; see generally Harrington 1985).

bringing the United States in line with the reforms that took place in the 1970s and 1980s in the various centers of international arbitration. That is to say, U.S. lawyers succeeded at home through this case in promoting the same essential reform that they had urged in London, Stockholm, and elsewhere a few years earlier—granting international arbitration greater independence from the courts.[12] What this meant, however, was that the U.S. Supreme Court substantially altered the relationship between the courts, the federal government, and the regulation of private enterprise that had been established in the aftermath of the New Deal (Auerbach 1983; MacNeil 1992). This change, as we shall see, was bound to shake up the landscape of business disputing in the United States.

The *Mitsubishi* case began when an automobile dealer in Puerto Rico, Soler, sought to avoid an arbitration clause in its agreement to distribute Mitsubishi cars. The clause provided for arbitration in Japan pursuant to the rules and procedures of the Japan Commercial Arbitration Association. Soler resisted arbitration, asserting that Mitsubishi had violated U.S. federal anti-trust laws. As noted before, settled federal case law from the post–New Deal era held that such an allegation—indeed, any allegation of a violation of federal antitrust, securities, or civil-rights laws—would give a federal court action precedence, precluding enforcement of a private arbitration agreement.

The case was of considerable interest to the arbitration community in the United States and abroad. As we have seen elsewhere, the small group of individuals who constituted a kind of outpost for the ICC world was particularly interested in the reform. Groups on the periphery of the arbitration world tend to work hard to reform local laws both to encourage more arbitration and also to bolster their own entry into the core of the arbitration world. They help to legitimate arbitration in their own legal systems, and they also open up channels to the center and to the leading arbitrators. We find, in addition, that this local missionary activity opens up the possibility of gaining more cases and recognition from the inner circle of the arbitration community. And, as we see in this and other contexts, recognition and connections to the international-arbitration community help raise the status of practitioners generally. For a variety of reasons, therefore, change such as that sought in *Mitsubishi* is typically promoted by an active band of local missionaries of international private justice.

12. Concern with the reform of arbitration was not, of course, new to this case. The small group of U.S. lawyers active in domestic arbitration and in the world of the ICC had played an important role in the adoption of the New York Convention in 1958, which made it much easier to enforce arbitral awards around the world among signatory nations.

According to a leading New York lawyer who was already active in international commercial arbitration, for example, "We were all well aware of the fact that if the United States was going to be a real player in the international arbitration field, it was essential . . . to get a good ruling on whether or not we could arbitrate" (int. 37, 2). Not surprisingly, the American Arbitration Association's amicus brief, submitted "to make sure that whatever [the Court] . . . did, it should at least understand that the United States, as a large trading country, had better not dismiss international arbitration easily" (id., 1), read as a kind of who's who from among the U.S. lawyers interested in international commercial arbitration.[13] The International Chamber of Commerce in Paris also submitted a brief that clearly had an important symbolic value. It made sure that the Supreme Court appreciated just what international commercial arbitration represented.

The Supreme Court, perhaps surprisingly, sided with the international arbitration world against an odd alliance of the Reagan government and the liberal wing of the Supreme Court.[14] The majority of the Court emphasized the needs of international comity, the flexibility of arbitration, and the quality and legal training of potential arbitral tribunals, including the one that had been put together for the case in Japan. The image that informed the judgment was not the domestic image of arbitration under the auspices of the American Arbitration Association. It was the elite image of private justice found in the amicus brief of the ICC.

The essence of the ICC argument was, "look at who we are." Our people, the brief suggested, are the leaders of the legal profession in Europe and the United States, and in this case Japan. The ICC brief gave the unmistakable impression that the academics, judges, and practitioners who served as ICC arbitrators were comparable in status to U.S. Supreme Court judges. The list of recent arbitrators contained in the brief pointedly included the name of Justice Potter Stewart, who had retired recently from the Supreme Court. One informant suggested that the Stewart selection was well known to the Court. Chief Justice Burger—then contemplating his own imminent retirement—had just recently acted to remove any obstacles to permitting retired justice Stewart from participating on an ICC panel. Furthermore, the ICC brief, no doubt sensitive to the concern about the role of judges as arbitrators, may have

13. Among the names were Andreas Lowenfeld, Gerald Aksen, Jack Stevenson, William Jackson, Robert von Mehren, and Joseph McClaughlin.

14. They overcame the traditional argument that had prevailed for decades that, in the words of the dissenting opinion, it was vital to recognize the "extraordinary importance of the private antitrust remedy" (473 U.S. at 655) and the need for public U.S. judges to apply and enforce antitrust law.

exaggerated the importance of judges in the ICC world.[15] In any event, the Supreme Court was persuaded that the fate of these cases could be trusted to an elite form of international private justice (in which they might even participate personally).[16]

The usual explanation for this decision is that the Supreme Court was acting to express the federal judiciary's preoccupation with a flood of federal cases that it could not handle. The Supreme Court, the argument goes, was in favor of any device, including international or domestic arbitration, that could help to divert some of the potential federal cases from federal courts. It is true that subsequent cases expanded *Mitsubishi* to include a variety of federal rights and to make it clear that the decision applied to domestic as well as international commercial arbitration.[17]

The key to the decision, however, is that it could invoke the elite image of international commercial arbitration and the specter of falling behind in international commercial arbitration. Arbitration had to be envisioned very differently to overcome established law and the hegemony of litigation and public courts for major business disputes. No doubt the increased caseload mattered, as did perhaps a relative decline in the prestige of federal rights (Posner 1985), but the international dimension and prestige overcame formidable arguments and a strong alliance of a conservative government and judicial liberals. As we shall see, the international dimension revalorized the image of arbitration from "sloppy litigation" to a potential elite private justice.

International Commercial Arbitration in the United States

Before exploring further the domestic changes unleashed by this decision and the forces behind it, we should note the impact—or lack of it—in facilitating many more international commercial arbitrations in the United States.

15. The brief named as many judges as academics, and it listed only three practicing lawyers. We know from our interviews that at least one of the judges was far from an ICC regular, and we also found that the major players at that time included many more European academics than judges.

16. The list of international arbitrators from the United States on the ICC list, in fact, helped to show the pool of potential arbitrators within the United States. Two practitioners named were individuals from the United States with strong governmental experience in the State Department (Charles Brower and Mark Feldman). One of them was a judge of the Iran–United States Claims Tribunal. The two professors from the United States included a senior Yale tax expert (Boris Bittker) and an NYU law professor with notable experience in the State Department (Andreas Lowenfeld).

17. In particular, in *Shearson/American Express v. McMahon* (1987), the Court extended *Mitsubishi* to domestic violations of securities laws, and in *Gilmeer v. Interstate/Johnson Lane Corp.* (1991), the holding was extended to age discrimination claims.

Certainly there were notable efforts to use the decision's modernization to promote the United States as a site for international commercial arbitration. The AAA, for example, created the World Arbitration Institute in the mid-1980s and promoted it for a time, and New York became the site of a major international conference in 1986. Subsequently the AAA gradually moved to a new set of procedural rules for international arbitrations, which brought AAA rules in line with the standards of international commercial arbitration. Professor Hans Smit and the Parker School at Columbia Law School also began to publish a list of international arbitrators (see Parker School 1992), a journal called the *American Review of International Commercial Arbitration*, and other works of interest about arbitration. Outside of New York, the Southwestern Legal Foundation in Dallas began to offer annual seminars on international arbitration in the mid-1980s as well. New centers designed to attract international cases also began to proliferate in the United States, just as they did elsewhere in the world. Los Angeles provides one example; San Antonio and Hawaii are others.

It is fair to say, however, that the United States and AAA (and especially the new centers) could develop only limited roles in handling international arbitration cases. One leading U.S. arbitrator described the AAA as a "borderline major player" in international commercial arbitration (int. 50, 12). Another pointed out that the AAA gets "a fair number of international arbitrations, but they're . . . not the real big cases. The real big cases they get only because the American party is so economically powerful that they can ram the AAA clause down the throat of its contract parties" (int. 57, 2). There is some evidence of change, but some of the evidence may be wishful thinking. The AAA cases reportedly are beginning to look more like the cases that go to the ICC (int. 50, 14), but perhaps that is in part because these ICC cases may be becoming more routine.[18]

The limited domestic success in attracting international commercial arbitration business, however, is not a new story. As we suggest elsewhere (chap. 13), reforms that give the appearance of powerful international competition are part of a process that favors the traditional centers of arbitration, most notably Paris, Switzerland, and elsewhere in Europe; the traditional institutions, such as the ICC, which after all will administer an arbitration anywhere; and above all the inner circle of arbitrators. Thus, while the *Mitsubishi* case set out to accommodate international commercial arbitration, the repercus-

18. The AAA does continue to invest in building its international caseloads and in its relations with the centers and institutions around the world. The caseload has grown steadily, and there are now some three hundred cases deemed international that are handled by the AAA (int. 39, 9).

sions in the United States have been largely within the domestic legal profession and domestic dispute resolution. The key is that, as one informant stated, international arbitration "is helping our domestic arbitration through the back door" (int. 37, 12). Indeed, as we shall see, international arbitration supported ADR generally through the back door.

Mitsubishi helped to multiply the options available to businesses and their lawyers, recognizing that arbitration did not have to be small, informal, and ill suited for major business disputes. The domestic market for *major* business disputes thus opened up in arbitration and other processes. As one lawyer reported, "After the Supreme Court had broadened and made valid that which years ago they didn't allow—antitrust and securities—there is nothing today that really can't be arbitrated—nothing. Then they [the arbitrations] got to be a lot more complex" (int. 35, 10). In the words of another, looking back on recent changes, "Our growth in this country in big litigation [handled] . . . by some kind of dispute resolution—other dispute resolution—other than the courts is awful new to all of us. It's not that new to the rest of the world from what I gather" (int. 5, 25).

Blurring the Boundaries I: From Litigation to ADR in the Competition for Business Disputes

The situation just prior to *Mitsubishi* offered essentially two domestic possibilities for business disputing. One was through litigation and the courts. The other was the lower-status, less formal alternative of proceeding through the AAA. These were, as noted before, the only games in town for business disputes. *Mitsubishi* took advantage of the presumed international competition for arbitration and the elite image of international arbitration to reshift the domestic disputing terrain. Suddenly, large-stakes arbitration was just as feasible in the United States as it was in Paris or Geneva.

One might have expected the domestic result of *Mitsubishi* and its progeny to be the transformation of arbitration within the United States into precisely the kind of arbitration that was taking place internationally. The expectation would have been that, once the prohibition against arbitrating federal rights was removed, large-firm litigators could "invade" the informal AAA system, which had no written opinions and a relatively nonadversarial style, and transform the system dramatically. There is some evidence that this process is under way, but, as we shall see, the situation is in fact much more complex.

The *Mitsubishi* line of cases permitting federal rights to be arbitrated provided a major opportunity for in-house counsel to shape private justice somewhat differently than the litigators might have preferred if left to their own devices. And the in-house counsel found potential allies in judges displeased by the system that the litigators had given them.[19] Litigators who were big winners in the period we examined in Europe were suddenly having their position challenged in the United States. That is to say, once the Supreme Court and internationalism allowed the serious contemplation of alternatives to the only games in town, the in-house counsel could take advantage of their own power to promote games where they could establish the rules. Many judges, in addition, were unhappy with a situation where they, too, were in many respects at the mercy of litigators who would proliferate pretrial activity, contribute to court congestion, and then settle outside of court. Judges as a consequence were also ready to promote new approaches in and out of the courthouse.

The Emerging Competition in the Market for Business Disputes

The subsequent developments in the United States can be seen by tracing the history of some of the key competitors who have emerged since *Mitsubishi*. Their strategies show both the opportunities and the transformations that are taking place. We begin with the Center for Public Resources, which, as noted before, has been a stronghold for the in-house counsel movement.

CPR, in several respects, looks very much like still another competitor following the model of international commercial arbitration. CPR's approach to the dispute resolution business is thus characterized by rosters of former judges and distinguished lawyers, procedural rules, published periodicals and books, and mechanisms to appoint individuals from the various lists. And while it is clear that CPR wishes to administer dispute resolution processes, its role—again typical of institutions seeking to establish themselves—has been above all in fostering education and encouragement of the dispute resolution processes that it offers.

Furthermore, the CPR rules and commentary for "non-administered arbitration of business disputes" show strongly the influence of international commercial arbitration. The chair of the Committee on Private Adjudication is an

---

19. Lauren Robel identified two views of crisis in a recent article—one by corporate litigants (through their in-house counsel), and the other by the judges themselves, who seek to "enhance the professional satisfaction and prestige of judges" (Robel 1991, 136). They initiated different processes of reform, but there has been a convergence of interests around certain issues, such as the control of discovery and the promotion of court-annexed alternative dispute resolution. The current direction is revealed by a judicial panel created by the Judicial Conference that proposed "new limits on access to Federal courts for Social Security beneficiaries, victims of job discrimination and consumers as part of a long-range plan to cope with huge increases in case load" (Pear 1994).

internationally oriented lawyer with close connections to the ICC world, Gerald Aksen, and, as could be expected, the rules depart substantially from traditional AAA arbitration. They follow international practice, for example, by calling for reasoned opinions by the arbitrators.[20] The reference in the rules to "private adjudication," in addition, makes clear that CPR takes for granted the "judicialization" of arbitration that took place on the international side but not within the AAA. Arbitration is thus considered simply as "private adjudication." These characteristics of CPR track the international pattern quite closely.

Most of the focus of CPR activity, however, is not on arbitration. The corporate counsel behind CPR have concentrated their attention on cutting costs through alternatives to litigation and litigation-like activities. CPR therefore also has Model ADR Procedures for the "Mediation of Business Disputes." The rules permit a certain blending of the rather vague and changing categories of mediation and arbitration,[21] but the emphasis on mediation signals an emphasis on alternatives that move away from formal and expensive litigation.

The CPR "panels of distinguished neutrals," for example, offer names for both mediation and arbitration (or other processes). There are regional panels as well as a national one. For present purposes, we can note that the national panel is composed of at least fifteen former judges, eleven senior academics, and forty-one others. The group includes many private lawyers who have passed through distinguished governmental service.[22] With these blue-ribbon panels and rules, CPR has been very successful in defining the characteristics of business disputing in the post-*Mitsubishi* era.

A recent *Wall Street Journal* article suggests the relative success of CPR

20. CPR, 1990 Rule 13.2. Indeed, the commentary to the rules notes that they are suitable for transnational business disputes (Center for Public Resources Legal Program 1990, 7). Later the CPR came up with specific rules for international disputes (Center for Public Resources 1991).

21. The mediation rules suggest this blending of mediation and arbitration by contemplating a quasi-judicial exchange of documents and information (CPR *Model ADR Procedures* [Center for Public Resources Legal Program 1991], Rule II.E); the possibility that, if the parties agree in writing, the mediator becomes the arbitrator (II.C.11); and the routine expression of opinions about the merits in support of a mediated result (II.C.12). This approach is very much criticized by "pure mediators," who challenge the position of the notable mediator-lawyers.

22. Again reminiscent of the pioneer days of international commercial arbitration, the list is of "grand old men," with only one woman—former federal judge and former secretary of the Department of Education Shirley Hufstedler.

and other competing providers in promoting mediation for business disputes as a way to contain the costs of litigation. The article refers to an identity crisis at the AAA:

> The non-profit AAA's leadership role is being challenged by an explosion of private firms that offer a variety of options for resolving disputes out of court. More significantly, there are strong signs that binding arbitration is being supplanted by more flexible, non-binding mediation as businesses' favorite alternative to litigation. (Pollock 1993a)

While once the only game in town outside of litigation, the AAA is now trying to catch up with the new private competitors and stake out a position in mediation and in large-stakes arbitration. The AAA has made two responses to the problem described in the article. One has been to emphasize mediation more in its materials and presentations. The second has been to establish a new program in early 1993, the Large, Complex Case Program (LCCP), for cases involving more than $1 million in controversy ("Commercial Initiatives" 1993). The keys to the LCCP are an emphasis on mediation as well as arbitration and, above all, the creation of special elite panels of twenty to forty "hand-picked" arbitrators for each of the thirty-six regional districts of the AAA. The news conference announcing the program made it clear that the AAA had signed up many of the notables on the list of CPR, including several retired judges and well-known private practitioners who were former leaders in government.

Nevertheless, it is clearly quite difficult to transform an organization as established as the AAA—and rooted in a relatively informal, mass arbitration for labor and relatively small commercial matters.[23] It is not surprising that one critic of AAA stated that it is "stuck in a model," and therefore dying (int. 210, 21). The rich caseload and institutionalization make it very difficult to adapt to big cases and processes other than arbitration.

Among the private providers in this new and growing market, JAMS, the largest for-profit dispute resolution company in the United States, also merits particular attention.[24] Founded in 1979 (as the Judicial Arbitration Service) by one retired California judge (Knight 1982, 113; Varchaver 1992), it began

---

23. For example, noting the continued importance of the relatively informal arbitration that characterizes most of its cases, the new president of the AAA emphasizes "civility" and the need to avoid "bringing in all the accoutrements of adversarial dispute resolution" (interview with William K. Slate II [1994, 143], the new AAA president). CPR, in contrast, treats arbitration unequivocally as private adjudication.

24. The AAA is nonprofit.

slowly but, aided by California's liberal judicial retirement rules, very serious court congestion, and the federal encouragement of private justice, found a niche. In 1987, growth began to take off, with revenues jumping from $1 million to $24 million per year in a five-year period. An investment bank then purchased a majority share in 1990, and JAMS has kept growing, recently merging with Endispute (which had merged with the Bates Edwards Group, a mediation firm from California), another major provider. Income for 1993 was reportedly about $30 million ("ADR Providers" 1993). The merged entity has some twenty-one offices, with an especially strong presence in California and New York.[25]

The success of these new providers requires an analysis of their major features. In particular, the key to JAMS (and one of its major competitors, Judicate, Inc.) is that it has offered only former judges on its roster of dispute resolution professionals (until its recent merger and the creation of some new panels). The judges both "mediate" and "arbitrate" (Varchaver 1992, 62).[26] The preference for former judges is partly a matter of their experience. The judges can use the management and settlement skills that are important in today's courts. More important, however, is "the aura of official sanction that retired state court judges give to JAMS" (Reuben 1994, 55). This aura, as one private provider stated, has been sufficiently important that, especially in the early days of promoting ADR, only judges would be selected by the parties from the lists of potential arbitrators or mediators (int. 210, 6).[27]

What is striking about JAMS appears also to be part of the appeal of CPR's lists. Former judges have done especially well, holding down many of the places among the small group of very busy mediation "superstars."[28] Former federal judges, in particular, remain relatively scarce and quite in demand—"in the catbird seat" (int. 210, 29) according to one provider. The market strength of former judges is supported by a recent *National Law Journal* article, which states that "ex-judges . . . are still the most popular choice, largely because

25. JAMS has a roster of 250 former judges in five states. According to the *National Law Journal*, 40 percent of the revenues come from personal-injury cases (Donovan 1994, A20).

26. The leading New York provider of services for JAMS, Harold Baer, who has now moved to the federal court, reported that 75 percent of his work was mediation ("Exploring the Issues" 1994, 204).

27. The successful judges, in addition, can shift with the field, affiliating with a variety of organizations just as the international arbitrators do. They can emphasize their ability to recommend a settlement in one setting, for example, or their commitment to "pure" mediation or pure arbitration in another. As one organization or approach gains ascendancy, they can shift along with it.

28. Most requests are for individuals, as in arbitration (Donovan 1994, A20).

clients want an approximation of what they get in court" in mediation or arbitration (Donovan 1994, A1), and by James Henry of CPR, who stated that judges are still "the preferred resource for neutral roles in ADR" (Varchaver 1992, 63).[29]

In this relatively new domestic market for high-stakes arbitration and mediation, therefore, former judges appear to have pioneered. Blurring the lines between public and private, and between arbitration, mediation, and litigation (and recalling the history of the International Chamber of Commerce in arbitration), they have used their reputations and legitimacy to help establish private justice in the service of business. Internationalization, in the first place, provided an opening, helping to expand the possibilities for domestic private justice. In addition to creating an opening, moreover, the international connection enhanced the prestige of this "descent into the market." Most retired judges, especially federal ones, might have thought it inappropriate to serve in private arbitrations when that was a relatively low-status operation. But the link to prestigious international arbitration, which is in fact encouraged by CPR and others' travels and reports of conferences, training sessions, and links abroad, has helped to break down that hostility in a significant number of judges.

The move by judges out of the courthouse doors to fit the requirements of private dispute resolution no doubt also relates to changes that have taken place within the courthouses. As noted before, many judges were already unhappy about the growing caseloads and the difficulty of managing them. They complained about the proliferation of federal-rights and criminal cases (int. 211), and at times—especially in the late 1980s—about their salaries.[30] Some federal judges reportedly had tried no civil cases in a given year (int. 211).

29. It is instructive that one very active mediator-arbitrator for high-stakes matters named one academic, two lawyer-experts in dispute resolution, and six former judges (federal and state) as active in this field (int. 6, 33). An in-house counsel reported using the former federal appellate judge Shirley Hufstedler for a major mediation, noting that "there are people with great capability of being able to explain the holes in the case to the other side," and that "that's where a former judge has some advantage in that they have some standing to say, I've been there before and I know how you would do on appeal" (int. 27, 17). And a third respondent noted the successful mediation by another former federal judge, Frederick Lacey, solving a dispute in one day that would have lasted weeks in trial (int. 35, 16).

30. One retired federal judge, for example, stated, "I know President Reagan appointed a lot of very young men, and they may find with the passage of ten or fifteen years and when they've got young children that are now getting ready to go to college, they may find it difficult, you know" (int. 59, 20). Another who left the federal judiciary said he did it only for the money (int. 211).

The private alternatives allow them, in the words of a retired federal district judge, to "do exactly what I used to do" (id., 10), both in mediation and in arbitration—but for substantially more money and with better working conditions. Judges "trying to get rid of trials," for example, would tell lawyers in the court that certain arguments will "never convince a judge," and they do the same as mediators.[31] As arbitrators, of course, they simply resolve the case. The transition to private practice for these judges, who reportedly never wrote judicial opinions anyway, was relatively easy.[32]

Such private judges, whose ranks are growing even among federal judges,[33] have moved out of the courthouse but taken some of the public legitimacy with them. Speaking and acting as public judges, but paid by private parties anxious to bypass the full costs and randomly assigned judiciary of regular litigation, judges have helped to establish the legitimacy of the new domain of private justice. Any businesses and lawyers reluctant to abandon the aura of public justice can be persuaded by the availability of the top judges in the private sector. The result has been an opening in private adjudication generally and especially in judicially guided mediation. The judges, as we have seen, feel quite comfortable in either setting.

Blurring the Public Position of the Courts

Tailor-made private dispute resolution allows in-house counsel to select from among the favored private judges (generally senior white males respected in corporate circles), who apply their clout and authority to mediate a result, recommend a decision, or just decide a case. The in-house counsel can also control the boundaries of the process and the expenditure of funds to support any litigators involved in the process. It breaks the monopoly of courts and

31. One former judge described his move to private mediation as liberating: "I got tremendous satisfaction from my time on the public bench, with its contributions to the public, and through the formality of courtroom proceedings. . . . And yet, private judging frees you from the bureaucracy that's inherent in the public system. Sitting on the public bench is like watching a baseball game, where inactivity is occasionally punctuated by something exciting. A private mediation is like being in an NBA game, with constant motion and more scoring. You feel like every minute is well-spent" (Stuller 1993, 18).

32. The transferability of the skills is apparent also from the statement of one of the private providers about a particularly marketable federal judge: he was the "best-known settlement judge" (int. 211, 17).

33. "Today, lawyers become judges earlier in their legal careers than they did twenty years ago—and the bench is no longer considered the last stop on a lawyer's professional journey. Recently, more and more judges have resigned in favor of private law practice or even private judging" (Dolin and Saylor 1993, 8). The evidence in the federal court is not clear at this point (Van Tassell 1993).

litigators who might otherwise go their own way to build a case or even respond to the tactics of their opponents. The new processes have little in common with AAA arbitration or traditional litigation.

The public courts, however, are bound to respond to the private challenge. As we see elsewhere, judges can compete either by moving closer to business, essentially going private, or by seeking to find ways—through incentives or jurisdictional rules—to keep business in the courts.[34] We see both phenomena in the United States today, and again the in-house counsel are emerging as key players in the various reform efforts.

One method to promote the courts for large business disputes, seen throughout the United States, is for the courts to dump lesser cases. They may then preside over a court-annexed and controlled system of dispute resolution that leaves at most a relatively few cases to be decided ultimately by the court.[35] The judge serves as a case manager, settlement adviser, and delegator of cases to court-annexed arbitration or mediation.[36] This approach has been the trend in the federal courts in large urban areas. The federal judiciary, indeed, has been supporting many of the efforts of the in-house counsel to make the courts better suited for business (Robel 1991).

The best recent example of this alliance involves proposed amendments to the Federal Rules of Civil Procedure. The purpose was to curb discovery—the main component of pretrial expense and delay—through mandatory disclosure. The Federal Judicial Center and a coalition of in-house counsel were strong proponents of the reform, which litigators opposed quite strongly from both the side of the plaintiffs and the defense bar. The result has been a kind of compromise, which grants local discretion; but the rule remains in place.

34. This difference is seen between the Stockholm approach of allowing public judges to serve as arbitrators and the continuing efforts in London to keep the commercial disputes under the control of the commercial bar and the Commercial Court.

35. There are increasing examples of mediation by judges of appellate cases as well as cases at the trial level. For a report on a "mandatory appellate mediation program" for the U.S. Court of Appeals for the Third Circuit, see "Court-Adjunct ADR" 1994.

36. According to Judith Resnik, the leading academic critic of these trends, "The role of *judges* as speakers of law, as providers of moral guidance and as crafters of shared narratives has been diminished, in large measure by judges themselves" (1994, 1531). She asserts that this change has diminished the "prestige" of the judicial system. Judges are now "sometimes mediators, sometimes senior partners to lawyers on both sides of the case, sometimes counselors to the parties," all of which are skills "no way unique to judges" (1994, 1532). Federal judges have become more "bureaucrats" of the administrative state than oracles of the law (Heydebrand and Seron 1990; Clark 1981). Under these circumstances, it is not difficult to understand how a majority of the Supreme Court concluded that arbitrators could manage and resolve disputes just as easily applying public law as private law.

A second approach is to create specialized courts for business, giving many of the benefits of custom-made, private justice to precisely the litigants who can afford to take their business elsewhere. A recent example of this approach is a special procedure before select judges in Delaware for commercial cases involving over $1 million in controversy.[37] This procedure is designed to compete both with private justice and with specialized procedures in other jurisdictions. In Manhattan, for example, four judges hear most of the commercial disputes filed there ("Outline of Principles" 1994). The Delaware program allows the parties to rely on a small number of acceptable judges and special procedures designed to give them the efficiency—and limited discovery—that they seek in the private-justice sphere. A recent article notes the advantages to business of being able to select judges who have "had extensive corporate experience before joining the bench" (Dick 1994b), to limit discovery, and to take advantage of special procedures.[38]

The third way is for the judges to move even more clearly into the private sphere. It may even be possible for judges to "go private" and remain members of the public judiciary. To date this "Swedish" approach (described in the next chapter) is unusual in the United States, but there is at least one program that is moving in this direction. According to a recent article, Connecticut has created Sta-Fed ADR, Inc. as a nonprofit provider of dispute resolution services staffed largely by senior state and federal judges ("State Initiatives" 1993).[39] A newspaper account of the organization reported that the creation of this entity was "a matter of self defense. In many areas of the country . . . big private mediation providers like Judicate and Jams, Inc. have wooed away top judges by offering salaries that the public sector cannot match" (Johnson 1993). This approach in a very strong sense moves from "rent a judge" to "rent a justice system."

New Dispute Resolution Providers

We have emphasized so far the importance of in-house counsel and unhappy judges working together to use the opening created by internationalization to build a custom-made justice that draws on the particular skills and

37. There is a five-thousand-dollar filing fee for the procedure, which was adopted after a survey of corporate counsel for the major corporations based in Delaware (Geyelin 1993).

38. There is opposition to such courts, at least in California by the California Trial Lawyers, who are opposed to a "special class of litigant" (Dick 1994b, 107).

39. This entity was promoted by senior U.S. District Court judge Robert Zampano, who has been an active proponent of at least minitrials in CPR publications since 1982 (Center for Public Resources 1982, 65).

legitimacy of judges. This sometime alliance should not be portrayed as necessarily stable and secure, however, and indeed there are other forces that are important in the dynamic processes that are transforming business justice. The private judges, for example, have been subjected to considerable attack by new or nonjudicial providers. In addition, while the custom-made processes may keep litigators at bay, the strength of the litigators allows them to find new ways to compete and to use their skills and approaches.

There are many detractors of the ability of former judges to resolve disputes effectively, and the criticisms come from several fronts (Donovan 1994). Indeed, we see a pattern that, in many respects, resembles what we saw in the history of the ICC. The significant difference in the United States, however, is that we see a new generation of mediator "technicians" seeking to displace the more charismatic judge-notables.

The senior judges were important to legitimate these new forms of private justice. As one of the providers noted, it was vital to gain "credibility" for the promotion of "going outside of the court and not to the AAA" (int. 210, 9). After the senior judges (and some other notables) served to legitimate these new forms of private justice for the business community, numerous potential technocrats—not notable or charismatic mediators—have tried to step in to make careers built in part on criticism of the senior generation. We now have many competitors, for example, who assert that judges do not have the right temperament to mediate. We hear that judges are "often ill-suited" to "the friendly persuasion that is key to successful mediation" (Donovan 1994, A1); or that their form of "evaluative" mediation[40] is not really as "pure" as "facilitative" mediation practiced by nonlawyer specialists or as effective as "blended" mediation by lawyer-specialists.

The hostility of many in the mediation community to the domination by retired judges and their "impure" mediation approach is evident in the proposed Standards of Conduct for Mediators drafted by a committee of the AAA, the ABA, and the Society of Professionals in Dispute Resolution (SPIDR) ("Standards of Conduct" 1994). The proposed standards oppose what some mediators call "evaluative" mediators—those who give opinions about the proper or legal outcome of the case (int. 212). The proper mediator according to most of those who seek to be pure mediators is to "facilitate" resolutions, not give advice or opinions.

For present purposes, it will suffice to note that there are now many entrants in the private judging market as arbitrators and as mediators. There are academics, practicing lawyers, and a growing number of dispute resolution

---

40. Jim Alfini (1991) terms this kind of mediation "bashing."

specialists—now organizing increasingly in "boutique" firms (Dick 1994a). They come with different backgrounds and approaches. Some are very close to the domain of law, while others, fortified only with a substantively weak "science of mediation" to promote their independence, can be expected to respond very strongly to market forces. They are bound to be closer to the domain of business.[41]

The situation, to summarize, is vastly different from the period when the AAA and litigation were the only games in town. The field of business disputing is now composed of many competing players, and they are offering a variety of different products varying in their proximity to formal law or to business. In-house lawyers, who now see themselves as managers of litigation and other forms of dispute resolution, and private judges have taken advantage of openings created by internationalization to disrupt the monopoly of litigators and courts, open the courthouse doors, and bring dispute resolution and the legitimacy of the courts outside.

Litigators and ADR

The role of litigators in this competition merits some attention. As we have seen, the in-house counsel were able to create a means to break the monopoly that the litigators possessed over the handling of large business disputes. Judges helped break the monopoly, making themselves available outside of the courthouse controlled by litigators. But litigators are still in a relatively strong competitive position, and they also have invested in nonlitigation alternatives in the field of business disputing. Many litigators now active in ADR received their first push from in-house counsel (int. 42).[42] But the litigators have been relatively quick to diversify and assert that they are good not only for litigation, but also for all the other possible procedures that a client might wish to select.

A growing number of litigation lawyers have thus found ways to turn ADR into an opportunity to create and market another profitable expertise. A promi-

41. A proponent of this more pure—and closer to business—mediation noted that when judges mediate, they act upon the principle that "the judge knows more than anyone else." A good mediator, in contrast, acts on the assumption that the "parties know more about the case than anyone else." The mediator must "find out what each party will do, then get them to move." Mediation is about "the art of the possible" (int. 210, 11).

42. There are others who play professional roles that limit the available tactics of litigators. For example, there are individuals who monitor construction projects in order to be completely prepared for any potential litigation or other disputing procedure. This simplification and professionalization of conflict management allows them to bypass litigators to some extent.

nent litigator thus stated, "One day you will get to the table anyway" (int. 35, 14).[43] His point was that expertise in "the nuances of ADR" could be used to get the matter settled: "Each dispute has a level of options" (id., 8), including minitrials, mediation, or a variety of other approaches, and the litigator-expert in ADR can help the client select from the options.

> People will come to a law firm when they have a problem. They need to understand what their options are. And each dispute has a different level of options. . . . [T]here are some things you cannot use ADR for. . . . The person with the tougher position frankly is not going to go to an arbitration company or ADR company. He wants to know what all his options are. So he goes to a law firm. (Id., 11)

The litigators claim that their advantage over the other competitors is that they have the knowledge about all the alternatives and the resources effective for deterrence or for fighting.[44]

The litigators and their law firms, therefore, are tending to offer products in which they can use their skills of advocacy and forum selection and shopping. If mediation or ADR is conducted for a commercial or corporate client, one prominent ADR expert stated, the lawyer must present the "strongest, best case for the client"; will have to decide how to use the allotted time, say sixty minutes, among witnesses, exhibits, and experts; will have to decide whether to reveal or hold back important documents at an early ADR proceeding; and will have to advise on what is a good and acceptable solution.

It is not surprising, therefore, that law firms can assert that arbitration and ADR are all part of dispute resolution; and at least one major New York firm—Skadden, Arps—has a person who oversees international arbitration and ADR, studying and invoking an expertise about the full menu of forums, laws, places, and now *techniques* that can be used in a contract prior to disputes or after a dispute has erupted ("Exploring the Issues" 1994, 204–5). One

---

43. "If they don't recognize that it is in the client's best interest to resolve those disputes that can be resolved, they will find themselves off to the side. There'll be people who will never go to them, because their answer is always fight. People don't want that. The clients don't want that. They want to know when they should fight and they want to know when they should not fight" (int. 35, 24).

44. "The reason he doesn't go to an arbitration company . . . is because then he is saying, 'I really don't want to fight. I want to settle.' And he feels right or wrong that that's a sign of weakness" (int. 35, 11). The top litigation backup, in effect, allows the party to negotiate from strength (int. 42). And "there will always be a role—always—for the best litigators. . . . Because no matter how much we work on resolving disputes, there will be disputes that can't be resolved" (int. 35, 23). "There will always be plenty of room for all of these gladiators" (id., 24).

now needs to be an expert—the large law firms contend—to understand the tremendous variety of options available to business clients both onshore and offshore. And among the options, as one litigator recently suggested, it appears that mediation represents a growth industry (int. 42).

Reshaping the Domestic Field of Business Disputing

There is now a relatively intense and wide-open competition for the business of business disputes. The competitors are playing on the same turf, but the stakes are not only short-term gains in market share but also the shape of the rules and institutions. Competitors and participants promote their own definitions and the alliances they have formed, seeking to gain predominance for the approach that favors them and what they embody—retired judges, pure mediators, traditional arbitrators, litigators, business courts, legalized mediation. Some competitors are close to the domain of courts and formal law. They emphasize legal principles and what courts might do, thereby reinforcing the power and authority of the legal system. Others, without the capital of legal authority, for example the "pure mediators," are much closer to the market and the business domain.

It is far too soon to suggest which, if any, products will emerge as dominant for which kinds of transactions. The competition between the various players, in any event, builds the field and serves to give it credibility and legitimacy. The relative winners will succeed in making their approach seem the natural and normal one—the one embodied also in leading institutions. Institutions are thus both the sites and the weapons of the struggle.[45] We can suggest, however, that at this point the trend has been away from legal authority and more toward the market and pure, business-oriented mediation.

The domestic landscape, accordingly, is rather different than that found internationally. In this very competitive national field, litigation and judicialized arbitration in the manner of ICC arbitrations are at the moment considered almost passé in comparison to mediation and related forms of ADR. In contrast, as we shall see, within the world of international commercial arbitration, arbitration still reigns as "offshore litigation," and ADR and mediation appear to be uncertain upstarts.

---

45. For example, we see precisely these concerns in the creation of a new section for dispute resolution in the ABA. There was initially considerable opposition from the Litigation Section, which was created in 1973, but Robert Raven, a former president of the ABA and a top litigator in California, succeeded in creating a new Dispute Resolution Section in 1993. Those who can control this institutional place in the competition will obviously be in an important position to define the field and ensure their place in it.

Blurring the Boundaries II: Changing Oracles and Economic Power
The Shifting Domain for the Production of Learned Discourse

There is a closely related story of the transformation of the market for the production of "learned law," with boundary lines blurring and new entrants becoming increasingly important. Again we start with a relatively stable set of actors and a relatively clear division of labor. In this division of labor, we could say that the law firms and their business clientele controlled access to the courts for the production of business precedents (Galanter 1974). They could, in Galanter's terms, play for rule changes as repeat-player litigants. They could also use their lawyers to play for changes in administrative rules and regulations affecting their businesses and competitive positions. In both sites there was a partnership of academics and judges that served to articulate change and maintain the law applicable to business disputes (Dawson 1968; Stevens 1983; Shamir 1993). This approach could be seen as another aspect of the New Deal arrangement noticed already with respect to business disputing.[46]

We have already seen how the increase in the number of business disputes, part of the aftermath of the economic restructuring in the wake of the oil crisis and the influx of petrodollars, strained the available channels to handle them. In the same manner, the economic and political restructuring behind the increased business disputes also strained the ability to produce new law capable of reasserting and maintaining legal order. As it turned out, legal academics, pushed by a new competition in academic ideas, helped promote the importation of ideas from around the university, especially economics departments, and therefore played a major role in reshaping domestic law in the 1970s and 1980s (Eisner 1991).[47]

It is always the case that new market arrangements for national or interna-

---

46. As with the New Deal, which was a time of transition when academics played a central role in promoting the ideas that were able to reshape the relations between business and the government (Shamir 1993), many of the legal academics who began the law-and-economics revolution in the 1960s and 1970s went on to major roles in the government (e.g., William Baxter), the courts (Posner, Bork, Winter, Easterbrook), and in consulting or moving into private practice (e.g., Fischel). Revolutions made initially in learned law—characteristic of times of rapid change, which is increasingly the situation in the international economy—can be traced into the institutions that implement the change and legitimate it over time.

47. After the era of rapid change in the U.S. domestic scene through deregulation, it is interesting that the new consolidation is reflected in a new set of academic and judicial attacks on the "renegade" professors who developed the law-and-economics revolution (Edwards 1992; Kronman 1993; Glendon 1994). This consolidation again parallels the post–New Deal era (Shamir 1993). We expect, however, that internationalization continues to accelerate the pace of change (see chap. 14).

tional business transactions require "up-to-date" rules to govern the markets (e.g., North 1990), and the new rules and institutions must be capable of regulating and legitimating the new situation (Powell and DiMaggio 1991). But as change accelerates through a much more active global economy, and as the international dimension assumes more importance, it becomes all the more difficult for national judges acting as such to play a major role internationally or even nationally.

Learned Practitioners and Academic Lawyers in the International Market

The emerging situation can be seen in an example from the American Law Institute and the Restatement on Foreign Relations. The ALI, formed in the 1920s to facilitate a partnership between academia, business, and the courts, seeks to bring together the most prestigious members of the legal profession in the United States to "restate" the law on particular topics (Stevens 1983). In the late 1970s, in response to the ferment that was taking place in the United Nations and in the activities of developing countries, the ALI decided that the Restatement Second on Foreign Relations (there was no "first"), adopted in 1965, needed to be revised.[48] There were a number of related and controversial issues in the revision, but for the purpose of this chapter we shall concentrate on the law related to the expropriation of private property, which became important in part through the oil expropriations that took place in the 1970s. It provides an example of the kind of lawmaking that we see in "national" international law.

The five reporters—well-known academics—began by noting that "It is difficult, for example, to state in black or even gray letter what is the international law now as regards compensation for expropriated alien properties" (American Law Institute 1980, xviii). They believed the ALI thus needed to update its position. The first draft of the revised and updated Restatement was published in 1980. The final version came out in 1987. During that period, the section concerned with expropriation, which began with the following language, changed substantially:

Revised Restatement, Tentative Draft No. 3, Section 712 (1982)

Economic Injury to Nationals of Other States

A state is responsible under international law for injury resulting from

(1) a taking by the state of the property of a national of another state, when the taking is not for a public purpose or is discriminatory, or when provision is not made for just compensation. . . .

48. According to Richard Baxter, the reporter for the first Restatement, "A look at the 1965 photograph is enough to persuade us that we are not now as we were then.

Comment e, "Just Compensation": The U.S. view has been that under international law, or under an agreement providing for 'just' compensation, compensation must be 'prompt, adequate and effective.' . . . International practice, however, does not conform to that ideal.

This language questioned the "traditional" U.S. standard in the earlier Restatement, which, according to one of the reporters for the earlier Restatement, "went beyond what customary international law requires in its linkages of the American view to a universalistic minimum standard" (American Law Institute 1982, 250). Louis Henkin, the Columbia Law School professor who was the general reporter for the revised Restatement, observed that the earlier language of "prompt, adequate, and effective" was a "red flag" to developing countries. He further noted that "for us to state 'prompt, adequate and effective' in 1982 would be a gross distortion" (American Law Institute 1982, 250). The academics saw the need to confront this issue and suggested a new approach.

The early draft, however, was revised substantially after "an acrimonious dispute" (Norton 1991, 474), returning to a position very close to that of the 1965 Restatement. The revised Section 712 stated in the text, not a comment,

For compensation to be just under this Subsection, it must, in the absence of exceptional circumstances, be in an amount equivalent to the value of the property taken and be paid at the time of the taking, or within a reasonable time thereafter with interest from the date of the taking, and in a form usable by the foreign national. (Revised Restatement 1987, 196–97)[49]

The process of change provides a picture of the production of law in the United States as affected by the internationalization of legal practice.[50] Again, as with respect to the market in business disputing, we see a blurring and transformation of roles in the market for the production of business law. It is

---

. . . not only the substance of the law but also the form and sources of both the international and municipal law of foreign relations law have altered" (1978, 875–76). See generally Rosenblum 1992.

49. The "exceptional circumstances" clause attracted some criticism by those favoring a return to the 1965 position, and the result was that a comment to Section 712 stated that the phrase could not apply in four circumstances: encouragement by the state that was expropriating the property, discrimination against nonnationals, a state takeover to operate a private entity, or an otherwise wrongful taking.

50. We think that a similar picture could be painted of the changes in the ALI project on corporate governance (Elson and Shakman 1994).

clear, in the first place, that judges were not at all active in the Restatement on Foreign Relations. This is no surprise, of course. International law has always had a strong academic and Continental orientation, affirmed in institutional form by the Hague Academy and the presence of the World Court in The Hague. International law even accepts formally a role for learned scholarship as evidence of the creation of "customary international law." We contend, however, that a greater international dimension in "national" law and business accelerates a trend toward a proportionately greater role for academics and learned lawyers—as opposed to judges acting only on the basis of their judicial authority. And we can see the power of the business clientele in using an approach different from that of the litigation repeat player. The approach here is to invest resources in the learned law and the formulation of legal standards.

The early draft, as noted before, began with an academic representation that showed some sympathy—at least as a matter of what the pure law was— for the third-world position being expressed in the United Nations and elsewhere at that time. The critics of the initial version indicated great respect for the reporter, Professor Henkin, but an unwillingness to accept such an independent position. According to one participant in the move to change the draft,

> He's very able and he doesn't understand like so many others that un-
> like the Rule of Law Committee, which knows that it's promoting
> the economic interests of its clients, Lou Henkin honestly believes
> that he is a disinterested servant of mankind. (Int. 26, 14)

According to another, "He was doing the right thing," "in his own mind [distinguishing between] property rights and human rights" (int. 25, 7), and providing a lesser protection for property rights. The academic stance was perhaps too "neutral" to survive.

The challengers were a group of academically oriented lawyers active in the American Society of International Law. They included Monroe Leigh, representing the Rule of Law Committee—a quite elite group of major banks, oil companies, and others who pay a subscription fee to Steptoe and Johnson to invest in positions relevant to international law and their interests. Others included Professor Don Wallace of Georgetown, who is also a practitioner and was chair of the ABA Section on International Law and Practice; a prominent international lawyer from Jones Day in Los Angeles, John Houck; two notable internationally oriented practitioners from Covington and Burling, who had a very large claim for Amoco before the Iran–United States Claims Tribunal, Bryce Clagett and Peter Trooboff. This group formed an ad hoc committee and mobilized their power and close personal contacts in the ABA, in the State Department, and in the Justice Department. As a result, the ABA Board of Governors took a position against the draft, and finally, the attorney general, Ed Meese, even requested delay and change. Part of what gained the attention of these actors was the fear, evidently not without reason, that the Restatement could be used against U.S. interests in the Iran claims tribunal (see Victor 1985, 10). Learned lawyers close to power gained considerable leverage.

According to one of the participants,

> As the Restatement wrestled along, it was concluded in Washington that the Restatement was such an important document that it had to be taken seriously. And you know the average work of academics will not be taken seriously by the American establishment or anybody else. And you know both the Attorney General, Ed Meese, and the acting Secretary of State, Ken Dam . . . both became personally involved in the Restatement of foreign-relations laws. I mean it's quite extraordinary if you think about it. (Int. 26, 11)

In other words, "the private bar landed hard" (id., 42).

All this mobilization of power unavailable to the academics involved in the project was, however, translated into learned debates about the nature of international law. The debates, even if fortified by power sufficient to infuriate the reporter (Victor 1985), were conducted "in a scholarly way" (int. 26, 42).[51] The learned lawyers who participated in the debates—some of whom even had ties to the Hague Institute—carefully explicated reasons grounded in a sophisticated knowledge of international law. The combination of an ability to debate on the learned terrain of the academics and the ability to mobilize economic and political power proved to be a very tough combination. Still,

---

51. They said, listen, this standard of prompt, adequate, and effective is the customary law of the world, which probably was dubious at that time. But even if it's not, there's no counterstandard. . . . If it did not establish itself, no new status has taken its place. And in any event, you are the Restatement of the Foreign Relations Law of the United States. . . . This Restatement doesn't just deal with those purely [international] subjects of law. It often deals with to some extent U.S. state practice. You know it sort of applies to law, especially . . . since you're talking about the domestic aspect in the relationship. . . . You know because international and the domestic is sort of a key to how issues are placed because of international custom, so that was one point. The other point that people liked . . . was, listen, this is going to be used against us, this Restatement. It's going to be cited in the United States–Iran Claims Tribunal, and you have an obligation everything being equal. You know if you have a choice between rules, you cannot just pick the rule which is hostile for the interest of the United States whatever that might mean. . . . So they push like hell. That was the big battle about 712. (Int. 26, 43)

however, the proponents of a return to the traditional U.S. position did not win every vote. What is also interesting to note is that the learned lawyers did not stop with the Restatement. They wrote articles emphasizing their positions and explaining how the Restatement embodies them (e.g., Houck 1986; Norton 1991; Trooboff 1987).

This somewhat unequal alliance between learned lawyers and more "pure" legal academics illustrates a feature of American law accelerated by internationalization. It is the other side of the emphasis on competition among justice providers. The law firms and businesses invest increasingly in the production of rules, cultivating links to outside academics and moving into learned circles themselves. Their ability to play (and pay) for rules by using the resources of their clients, the state, the ABA, prestigious law schools, or international institutions, serves both the interests of their clients and the interest in producing a law capable of governing international business transactions in a new era of international exchange.

From the perspective of the United States, in fact, the international and the national legal markets are growing very close. In one obvious respect, the U.S. business world is connected closely to other countries around the world. Less obviously, the legal practices and approaches of big U.S. law firms are providing an almost general legal language for transnational business transactions. Accordingly, the U.S. entries in the domestic competitions just described are bound to have an impact on future developments in the international domain of business disputing.

Toward a Redefinition of the U.S. Role in the International Disputing Market

We conclude the study of the United States by exploring the possibilities for the immediate future. We have seen already that the U.S. law firms were able to reshape international business disputing more or less in the image of their litigators by using the institutions and personnel of international commercial arbitration. As the landscape of business disputing is changing form in the United States, it is natural to ask whether this domestic transformation—in providers of dispute resolution services and in the production of business law—will also reshape the international domain.

Exporting ADR as a Means to Regulate Transnational Business Disputes

It is clear that the U.S. providers are seeking to go global (even if, in part, to enhance domestic prestige). JAMS, for example, fortified by its recent mergers and diversification in the United States, is seeking to export its offerings in international dispute resolution by forming a joint venture with the World

Jurists Association—a "global association of legal professionals" ("New Organizations" 1993). In the short term, the ambition is to train personnel in both arbitration and mediation at some centers in places "where traditional arbitration has not played a major role" ("New Organizations" 1993). So far, however, the effort by JAMS has been relatively low-key.

CPR, in contrast, has made a much more concerted entry into the European market, and it is worth exploring this effort in more detail. Borrowing heavily from the established names in international commercial arbitration, it has established an International Panel of Mediators ("CPR Selects European Panel" 1993). The title indicates the basic strategy. A conference put on by CPR in Paris, the home of the ICC, confirms the emphasis on "mediation." It has had success with mediation at home, and that is its best potential export.

Not surprisingly, CPR brought no U.S. judges to the Paris conference, recognizing that its credibility in the heart of the ICC world required that it rely on established players in the international-arbitration world and the major source of CPR power, general counsel of major corporations.[52] The major speakers included Gerald Aksen, who described how he would conduct a mediation. His presentation provided a picture of what could be termed "legalized mediation" akin to that practiced by retired judges in the United States. As we have noted, this approach has been relatively successful in business disputing in the past four or five years.

The tone of the conference, however, was very skeptical, and we can provide two basic reasons (see also Werner 1993). One was that the in-house counsel on the Continent are not now organized enough to take control of disputes from their outside counsel (or from those who handle negotiations informally inside the corporate structures). Several speakers who represented in-house counsel on the Continent noted that they would need to organize better to implement such procedures. Stephen Bond, former secretary-general of the ICC, very strongly emphasized the related position that the disputes between businesses from different national settings were not so easily resolved by mediation as were disputes in a national context. Obviously one reason is that general counsel in national settings may know each other and have developed some rapport that can help to control conflict. Another is simply that, in contrast to the United States, the players in international business may not all agree on what the rules of the game should be with respect to trade, the regulation of markets, and the role of the state. International rules are far from being stabilized.

---

52. We find the same recognition in the fact that no former judges participated in the CPR committee to draft rules for the settlement of transnational business disputes.

With the power of U.S. businesses and the strength of ADR in the United States, we can expect some impact of ADR in the world of international commercial arbitration. We have seen efforts in the construction area, for example, and several European arbitrators helped CPR's effort by consenting to be on the CPR mediation panel. Nevertheless, it is difficult to imagine CPR gaining a position in Europe comparable to the ICC. In addition to the reasons already mentioned, CPR lacks an ability to mobilize learned law that can challenge the framework defined already by the ICC.

The ICC, as we have seen, grew up on the basis of Continental professors and the learned law of the *lex mercatoria*. The U.S. players in this area of ADR, in contrast, have relied only on a very practical alliance with rather little substantive legal theory behind it. The theory tends to be theories of practice that, while useful in establishing this domain, have not been able to provide any kind of positive governing framework for business disputes. Lacking a legal framework or means of producing law, the program of CPR is bound to be taken less seriously by the relatively learned international-arbitration community. Furthermore, and more importantly, the lack of investment by CPR and its allies in law makes it unlikely that the technology of ADR can play a major role in providing any substantial part of the general framework for regulating international business relations. If the ICC and its world are going to be pushed aside, it will not be by U.S.-style ADR.

Investments in Law and the International Business Disputing Market

That is not to say, however, that the ICC's basic position is bound to be secure. The question of whether we are entering another phase of international legal practice—an international new deal—will be addressed in the concluding chapter of this book. What we have suggested in this chapter is that the short-term marketing strategy of CPR and JAMS does not appear to be a major challenger to the general framework—forged out of the material of U.S. practices and learned professors around the institution of the International Chamber of Commerce. The further question is whether a new legal framework—associated perhaps with GATT, NAFTA, the European Community, antidumping, and a new set of legal issues that arises from such legal approaches—will be necessary for the 1990s and beyond, requiring new investments in learned law and new institutions. If that is to be the case, we suggest that the kind of learned investment seen in the battle over the Restatement is likely to pay major dividends for the learned Washington lawyers and their allies.

9

Vintage Arbitration in Stockholm

Stockholm has produced what can be termed *vintage arbitration*, built on an extraordinarily well developed system of domestic private justice. Stockholm, like London, was able to bring major assets to the international-arbitration community, attract the interest of the United States and the Soviet Union, in particular, and build on decades of close ties to the ICC in Paris. It was quite natural for Stockholm to become one of the major centers once international commercial arbitration arrived in the 1970s. In contrast to London, however, the Stockholm community has not changed substantially in response to the challenge and opportunity presented by the international-arbitration community and the growth of international arbitration. The vintage arbitration in Stockholm is still primarily domestic, and more importantly, the orientation is mainly domestic. The Stockholm story is nevertheless a rich one, defined largely by the traditional virtues and independence of the notable arbitrators, because it also embodies all the possibilities and processes of international commercial arbitration. Stockholm's expression of the past, to some a golden age of arbitration, makes it a splendid site for genealogical purposes. It contains the prehistory and history of what has developed in the international commercial arbitration community. And we also see the seeds sown—but not yet very advanced—for future transformations in Stockholm and elsewhere.

Private Justice in Sweden

The Swedish system of commercial arbitration, again like London, provides a remarkable example of how private and public can blend. In Sweden, the systems of public and private justice are parallel, not hierarchical. In the current ADR jargon found with multiple models in the United States, Stockholm has a system of "rent a judge." The British system, in contrast, followed the model of "court-annexed arbitration." In London, prior to 1979, a small group of commercial barristers were at the center of a private system of arbitration linked elegantly to the public jurisprudence of the Commercial Court and the appellate courts. Compared to London, Sweden's system brought, and still brings, the public and private equally close, but the result creates no public jurisprudence at all.

The Swedish system can be traced back at least to the private justice of the fourteenth century. Arbitration today is governed primarily by legislation enacted in 1929. It has been interrupted neither by the public regulatory attack on arbitration associated, for example, with the rise of the administrative state in the United States in the 1930s, nor by any successful effort to compete with private dispute resolution through the creation of the kind of specialized commercial courts found in much of Europe after the French Revolution. Public judges at all levels of courts in Sweden serve as the most important private arbitrators. Virtually *all* commercial disputes go to three-person panels of arbitrators akin to those used in typical international tribunals today.

According to this system, the parties or their attorneys each designate one arbitrator, who in Sweden may come from practice, the academy, or from among retired judges (or occasionally from another profession). Attorneys from one of the three major Swedish law firms, with over one hundred lawyers apiece, typically do the appointing in large cases. Their clients would include the important Swedish multinational firms such as Volvo, Saab, ABB, and Electrolux. According to one leading arbitrator, the state of the commercial bar is such that all three of the law firms will be involved in a major case (int. 160).

In the traditional configuration for an economically important case, the two party-appointed nominees designate a sitting or retired judge to chair the tribunal. The chair in lesser cases, in fact, often would be a local judge from the area in which the dispute is set. For the larger disputes, chairs are typically the leaders of the judicial branch, from the top courts, such as the Svea Court of Appeal or the Swedish Supreme Court. Not all chairs are judges, but there is a long tradition of this practice. Arbitration practice was once forbidden to justices of the Supreme Court, but even that changed in the mid-1970s.

The acceptable nominees for chair in high-stakes cases represent a rather small group. According to one arbitrator, some twenty people serve as chairs in such cases (int. 160). Another says that five persons are "generally accepted" (int. 156, 2) as chairs. It is not enough to be a judge of a high court to be selected. Out of the twenty-four Supreme Court justices, at most five currently serve as arbitrators (ints. 151, 159). The most often named leader of the arbitration profession is generally said to be a retired Supreme Court judge, Ulf Nordensson, who is also affiliated with one of the large firms, Mannheimer and Swartling. A couple of judges from the Svea Court of Appeal also chair major cases, and from practice the chairs traditionally come from the most senior members of the major firms. Several academics also take a share of the chair positions in these significant commercial arbitrations. Except for the active judges, these arbitrators may and do serve also as party-appointed members. Sitting judges by convention are given only the "most neutral" role of chair.

The party-appointed group is somewhat larger than the group serving as chairs. Nevertheless, the party-appointed arbitrators are also a rather familiar group, reflecting desires of the parties in big cases to pick "secure people" and to rely on the safety of the "traditional choices": "People get cautious" (int. 156, 2). As a result, in the words of a retired judge, one "always knows the people in the arbitrations," including the counsel and the arbitrators (int. 163, 1). Another said that if he is party appointed, he is likely to confront "an old friend" on the other side (int. 159, 9). An academic arbitrator noted that he hears people say, "I normally use A or B for these cases" (int. 156, 2), and they are reluctant to branch out to the untested. Stockholm accordingly has a rather small staple of top arbitrators.

These top arbitrators are typically quite senior in their careers. Opportunities to serve as arbitrator tend to come "at a fairly late stage of the career" (int. 163, 2). There are exceptions, especially in some of the arbitrations of lesser importance (and perhaps in the numerous cases where arbitrators are charged with evaluating the worth of an equity interest pursuant to a statutory scheme after 90 percent of the shares of a company have been purchased). But it is fair to say that the potential arbitrators for international cases are the pool of top arbitrators in general, composed of the profession's elder statesmen—senior judges, retired judges, senior attorneys, and leading professors.

That pool, while small, has virtues that can serve well in domestic or international arbitration, as noted below. This parallel, private, rent-a-judge system produces, trains, and evaluates arbitrators potentially able to branch out of domestic arbitration, and several have done so for particular cases. Nevertheless, as will be seen, there are limitations to this system as a private method of promoting international arbitration generally or in Stockholm. Before discussing the international aspects, however, it is useful to assess in more detail the private justice—tailor made for business disputes—that emerges from this kind of arrangement.

First, the system means that judges *as public judges* get almost no commercial cases. This role of the courts is part of a more general phenomenon in Sweden. In contrast to the United States but not unlike other European countries, lawyers and courts as such have not been much involved with the important disputes and decisions—commercial or otherwise—of Sweden's welfare state. Several arbitrators noted that if a business dispute is too important, it likely will be handled mainly by businesspeople and the government, not by lawyers or courts or by legalized arbitration (ints. 159, 160). A prominent senior arbitrator made a related point: the prestige of the judiciary has declined since the 1930s, reflected in judicial salaries that are relatively much lower today than at that time (int. 159). The judiciary has participated very little in the administrative state of the twentieth century, and in fact ambitious judges in training often move into the government rather than remaining in the judiciary; the judiciary has been unable to substitute a powerful role in commercial cases for this diminished role in the Swedish welfare state. The commercial caseload was termed "appallingly poor" by one retired judge (int. 159, 1). Judges as public judges were not permitted to play a central role in business or politics.

Nevertheless, there is a small sector of the legal community that serves business. The three major law firms reportedly provide three-fourths of the legal services to Sweden's business sector, and the arbitration system is today very much dominated by the business lawyers. At least until very recently, the lawyers who advised business clients were the same ones who handled the arbitration of business disputes. In order to recruit the judges to preside over this private justice system carved out by the business community and a small group of business lawyers, however, career judges with no commercial experience must somehow develop into commercial arbitrators. They learn on the job as arbitrators, in part through whatever expertise coarbitrators with more experience might bring. This method is curious, but Swedish commentators can turn the lack of experience into a virtue. The general opinion among the arbitration community in Sweden is that arbitration is "a judicial way of settling disputes," and commercial naïveté may help keep it judicial. Judges must apply the law, not try to suggest "solutions based on commercial analyses of a dispute," as one attorney implied happens in France or England (int. 155, 3). Characteristically, a group of arbitrators insisted in a general discussion that arbitration outcomes are precisely the same as would be outcomes in court (ints. 156, 157; observations by participants at seminar presentation by the authors in Uppsala, May 6, 1992).

The arbitral awards are private, however, so they cannot be analyzed generally by the academic community or by other partisans of "legality." We also cannot evaluate the private jurisprudence according to any external, more political, criteria. The public is not a participant in this legal system. It does appear that a kind of private jurisprudence exists, but it is known only to the legal and business community.

The elite arbitration world of attorneys and arbitrators, who are often interchangeable, is in Sweden composed of those who know each other well. Situations arise with respect to standard term contracts, for example, where the same business need for authoritative interpretations arises in Sweden as else-where. The arbitrators know their own rulings, seek consistency at least with their own pronouncements, and may work out common approaches. One arbi-trator reported that, while eating lunch with the panel in one arbitration, he might very well discuss a problem that has come up in another arbitration (int. 156, 1).

Academic arbitrators, it was reported, also pay attention to jurisprudence in another sense. They tend to situate the arbitration in what they have writ-ten or will write in their academic texts and treatises. This method may also bring arbitral jurisprudence subtly into the arguments and advice of prac-titioners and students (int. 156).

Finally, it was reported that, in at least one instance, the Swedish Supreme Court aided the arbitration world. It took advantage of a case involving build-ing construction that found its way to that court. The court reached out in the decision to solve an interpretive problem in a standard contract term that had vexed the arbitration community (int. 156). The public system probably took ‘advantage of its knowledge of the private world to help maintain the private system.

This private justice system undoubtedly serves the business community well. Cases proceed more quickly than through the public judicial system. Business lawyers can select judges whom they prefer and provide pay only for those who actually decide business cases. And the disputes are kept secret except within the relatively small business/law arbitration community. It is probably also true that such a system ensures that the decision makers, depen-dent on a private system that exists for the business community, will probably not drift too far from a legal regime consistent with the interests of the legal business community. Legal mavericks will simply not be selected as arbi-trators.

The system is sometimes criticized for its proximity to business, the se-crecy of its "judicial" decisions, and the practice of judicial "moonlighting." The problem of actual judges serving as arbitrators is especially noted. One of the daily newspapers observed recently that several judges make more money from this moonlighting than they do from their judicial salaries. And some important legal academics point out the difficulties of reconciling this system with the ideal of public justice and even some practical problems such as potential appeals from arbitral awards back to the courts (int. 213). There is therefore some official concern with at least some aspects of this private-public partnership.

But the power of this private justice system—aside from its not irrelevant business support—is that it is dominated by many of the leaders of the legal profession, including those who are in the courts. Appeals would involve potential conflicts, but the network of relationships that would produce conflicts prevents appeals. One strength of this system in fact is that, unlike pre-1979 England, Stockholm could promise that awards rendered in Sweden would not end up traveling through meddlesome courts ostensibly protecting the public interest. The courts lent enough legitimacy through top judges and a supportive historical evolution to maintain the insulation of the arbitral system.

Stockholm's Suitability in the Late 1970s

The strengths of Stockholm as an international arbitration center grew out of the private justice system and the tradition of Swedish neutrality. Together, as will be seen below, they presented to the world a picture of moral authority, and both moral authority and neutrality were embodied in the senior, patriarchal arbitration community. In the late 1970s, when arbitration began to expand, Stockholm quite naturally was looked to by those at the forefront of the expanding arbitration business.

The private justice system, in the first place, was staffed by top judges, senior lawyers, and senior academics who as a matter of course had at least some facility in English. They had already succeeded in domestic commercial arbitration. These individuals provided a pool of potential arbitrators conversant in the most important language and with a recognized authority to resolve, impartially, large commercial disputes. Their decisions were largely immune from judicial attack within Sweden. The elite of the profession was therefore schooled and available for disputes that were bigger and more international than their customary fare.

Sweden also had the advantage of international neutrality in several senses. First, only Switzerland and Sweden, from within Europe, could claim to be neutral in World War II. Neutrality with respect to international political disputes feeds very well into the set of ideas that surrounds international commercial arbitration. Sweden was not too closely identified with any particular block of nations.

Sweden is also a relatively small country. It has enough large businesses to generate some international arbitration work but not so much as to make it difficult to satisfy the often-invoked criterion that international arbitration should avoid the "home" of either of the disputants. In this respect Sweden again resembles Switzerland. Sweden was thus quite available as a neutral forum, although obviously not as accessible geographically as Switzerland.

The moral authority of Swedish legal neutrality draws on a tradition of leadership in international tribunals in *public* law disputes. International jurists from Sweden, going back several decades, helped resolve many highly visible, international disputes between nations; and in the 1960s and 1970s Gunnar Lagergren, a well-known Swedish judge who later became the first chair of the Iran–United States Claims Tribunal and a member of the European Court of Human Rights, occupied the same high-profile position. The activities of these individuals reinforced Sweden as a focal point for neutral dispute resolution that could transcend the politics of the disputants. Swedish jurists established an admirable reputation for good judgment and moral authority in very significant and complex disputes.

This benevolent internationalism had its counterpart in the business world. The Wallenberg family, dominant in Swedish business, not only stood for business morality, but also saw the connection between arbitration and enlightened business practices. The family gave substantial gifts both to the Stockholm Chamber of Commerce, established in 1917, and to the International Chamber of Commerce established the next decade in Paris. According to one source, the Wallenbergs were the single biggest source of support for the ICC in the 1970s, placing Sweden in a very good position to gain from the growth in international commercial arbitration that was then beginning to take place. These connections and assets are reflected nicely in the fact that Gunner Lagergren, the last of the great line of public law arbitrators, is married to a Wallenberg.

Stockholm Confronts Change

Sweden's neutrality and moral authority, coupled with its location just north of the Baltic Sea, made Stockholm a strong potential site for arbitration of what were then called East-West disputes, especially those between the Soviet Union and the United States. Throughout the 1970s, moreover, Sweden's neutral features from the point of view of the Soviet Union were enhanced by a short period when Sweden had interrupted some formal diplomatic relations with the United States. Accordingly, Stockholm had the chance to be put on the international commercial arbitration map with a specific, high-profile, East-West niche. The initiative to develop this niche, however, did not come from Stockholm, nor did it come from the ICC. It came from the United States and the Soviet Union in the early 1970s as they were discussing a trade agreement.

The U.S. interest, according to one of the participants, was to try to "see if we could talk the Soviets into getting away from insisting on the use of the Foreign Trade Arbitration Commission that they had and accept the principle of totally impartial, independent arbitration in a third country under the auspices of some third-country organization" (int. 7, 7). At that time, Stockholm had no major institutional presence in international commercial arbitration.

It had some individuals like Judge Lagergren, who was named at almost exactly that time by the president of the World Court to arbitrate the first of the Libyan oil nationalization cases, and the individual who served as his secretary in that arbitration, J. Gillis Wetter. Wetter had very good ties with the United States, since he had a graduate degree from the University of Chicago and had worked for White and Case in New York in the 1950s.

The Soviets were represented in part by Professor Sergei Lebedev, who was probably already (and still is) the leading figure in Russia in international commercial arbitration and had ties with the United States through his study at the University of Michigan. He in fact persuaded the State Department to bring in Gerald Aksen, who was already an expert in arbitration but had no international ties except that he had helped grade a paper Lebedev submitted to Michigan on the subject. Charles Brower, a State Department lawyer from White and Case (where he returned later, interrupted again for a stint on the Iran claims tribunal) who became very prominent in the arbitration community, helped start the process by contacting Wetter ("Profile of Arbitrator, Charles Brower" 1992). The State Department then organized a visit to Stockholm. The American Arbitration Association, represented by Donald Strauss and Gerald Aksen, joined Howard Holtzmann, an American lawyer who was also close to the AAA.

The Americans propounded numerous questions of the Stockholm Chamber of Commerce in order to assess its suitability as a site for arbitration.[1] The Stockholm chamber's responses, prepared by a committee including Wetter, then became the basis for a book in English on Swedish arbitration, published originally in 1977. This became a guide for foreign users. Swedish arbitration was also modified slightly to make it more agreeable as well to international commercial arbitration. The successful negotiations culminated in 1976 with a recommended clause for inclusion in U.S.-USSR trade contracts, providing for arbitration according to the rules of the Stockholm Chamber of Commerce and listing a well-known group of recommended arbitrators from many countries.

The agreement brought considerable attention to Stockholm as a major center. It is not clear how many arbitrations actually came to Stockholm, but those that did had high visibility, high stakes, and involved politically sensitive disputes. One famous arbitration, for example, that pended for some time before the cold war came to an end, concerned the construction of the American Embassy in Moscow, with Dr. Wetter as the U.S. counsel. The legitimacy of the 1976 agreement no doubt attracted ad hoc and other arbitrations to

1. At the time the Soviet Union was not eligible to participate in the ICC.

Stockholm and increased business for the Stockholm Chamber of Commerce. Other East-West contracts outside of the original trade agreement designated Stockholm, and the Chinese—following the Soviet Union—also found it suitable to agree to arbitration in Stockholm for business disputes between the United States and China.

Despite the attention to Stockholm, it appears that the number of cases handled by the Stockholm Chamber of Commerce itself remained relatively small, at least until two or three years ago (int. 151). The recent increase, moreover, is in part because of the rapid changes in the economy of the former Soviet Union. The last two years, we were told, have seen sixty to sixty-five new cases per year, of which twenty to twenty-five are East-West and five to ten reportedly have the Chinese as one party to the dispute. But at least prior to this growth, it does not appear that the number of cases rivaled Paris, Switzerland, or London. And even the new influx does not challenge the position of the other major sites.

Stockholm has not taken its high visibility and used it to gain a strong position in the international arbitral community. Stockholm remains largely unchanged in what it offers in arbitration. In contrast to the extensive retooling that could be found in London with the 1979 reform, Stockholm has done "well enough" with the status quo. The procedures for arbitration in Sweden are mainly Swedish, the same procedures that would be followed by Swedish arbitrators in domestic arbitration. While the procedures work well, by all accounts, they have a number of idiosyncratic features they make Sweden less user-friendly to those who are from outside the system as lawyers or arbitrators.

Finally, Sweden also has not capitalized very much on the general growth reflected in the caseloads of the ICC. Relationships are cordial between the ICC and Stockholm, but the ICC cannot be seen as a strong collaborator in helping to build up Stockholm. Stockholm mainly has gone its own way with little effort to change image or build alliances.

Why Stockholm Remains Unchanged

Stockholm's apparent lack of change can be traced back to the strength of the system, the very reasons it was so attractive for large East-West cases of great political sensitivity. The characteristics of neutrality, fairness, and a virtue that is sufficient to command the respect necessary to resolve disputes between states are not necessarily consistent with aggressive marketing. There is "a reluctance to market Stockholm" in part because the idea of arbitration is that it is "a service being rendered" (int. 159, 7).

One lawyer who favored more effort thus noted, somewhat critically, that the 1976 agreement "put Stockholm on the map," but "Stockholm could have done a better job developing out of the East-West arena" (int. 152, 3). Another arbitrator stated that, despite recent efforts by the Stockholm Chamber of Commerce, the chamber has been "sleeping ever since" (int. 159, 6) it was founded in 1917. In fact, the chamber does seem to be interested in expanding business. It put together a major conference in 1992 that focused on the situation in the former Soviet Union and the seventy-fifth anniversary of the chamber's Arbitration Institute. The chamber was also behind the new governmental committee to review arbitration in Stockholm, and, despite the ambiguity of the charge by the Ministry of Justice, key figures of Stockholm's international community have power in the committee. The committee has in fact recommended some changes to preserve and marginally improve the basic system (Hobér 1994).

Change could come, but the general impression remains that Stockholm arbitrators have "enough to handle" with the domestic business. They do not feel it necessary, for example, to circulate at the international meetings (int. 159, 7). The chamber is not pushed by its board or the Stockholm community to reach out or plan strategically to compete. The situation, after all, is pretty good for those controlling the system: "No one today feels any need to stimulate activities" (id., 7).

Both the domestic and the international clientele like the safety and maturity of Stockholm arbitrators. There is thus no strong pressure from the users of Stockholm arbitration to open the system up to non-Swedish arbitrators, and this general acceptance bolsters the position of the group now in control. Moreover, there is no strong pressure from law firms, or more entrepreneurial lawyers outside the large firms, to transform the system to bring in more arbitration business. The close links between the courts, the three big law firms, and the domestic private justice system help inhibit any movement for change. The current system is simply too strong to allow any challenge. The current system also does not promote new arbitrators who can fuel change as they work to build their own niches. A shortage of arbitrators, the inevitable result of a system that needs sixty years to grow a new arbitrator, inhibits the kind of innovation and marketing that easier entry into the system would promote.

Stockholm thus does not really compete for business. By definition its arbitration community waits. Individuals are supposed to wait patiently throughout their careers before they are independent enough and distinguished enough to join the group, and members of the group wait until they are elected for a dispute. The investment in the legal science of arbitration, one very important aspect of the international-arbitration community, is likewise relatively limited. The University of Stockholm has an institute that publishes a yearbook and some other volumes on arbitration, but the Swedish community does not publish much outside of Sweden, nor does it have a journal or other outlet comparable to the effort made in, for example, London and Switzerland. Again, Stockholm is not very entrepreneurial, not pushing to capture a larger market share.

It also appears Stockholm cannot count on the ICC or other institutions to help it grow. Both by attracting key East-West disputes, and by the rigorously independent status of Stockholm arbitration, Stockholm's arbitration system has not made for an easy alliance with the ICC. In the first place, the grand old men of the ICC community resented the East-West disputes that went to Stockholm—complex, high profile, large stakes, politically sensitive. Several individuals in Stockholm commented on rumors and hints from the leading Swiss arbitrators that undermined Stockholm by suggesting the Swedish practices were in some sense "soft on communism." The allegation was denied, but the statement that Swedish choice-of-law rules for East-West disputes favored the application of Russian law has been repeated a number of times. One telling remark about this situation was an observation that, while the ICC competed with Stockholm, Stockholm did not really compete with the ICC (int. 151). This situation no doubt disadvantages Stockholm in the increasing arbitration competition.

There may be another problem that affects Stockholm-ICC relations. As noted before, the grand old men of the ICC world in Paris and Switzerland perceived unwelcome competition for East-West disputes. There may also be some tension between the new, more technocratic generation in Paris and the old values of Stockholm arbitration, a tension captured well in Gillis Wetter's well-known criticism of the ICC for "bureaucratization" (1990). There is not today a very large group in Sweden who can find common ground with the new ICC group. It is indicative that, as happened in London before the reform in 1979, ambitious individuals very close to the ICC may prefer to leave Stockholm to make their careers. Thus a former secretary-general of the ICC from Sweden, Sigvard Jarvin, lives in Paris and is not very close to the Stockholm arbitration community. It is true that he is of counsel to a Swedish law firm, but the firm's key arbitration lawyers seem currently more oriented to the ICC than to building up Stockholm arbitration.

For the moment, at least, the leaders of Stockholm's arbitration community feel no particular need to change, and the characteristics that make them attractive as arbitrators—seniority, independence, service orientation—make it unlikely that they will promote initiatives for change. That does not mean that international pressures will continue to be avoided. As one leading arbitrator noted, if Stockholm actually begins to lose its present niche, things could be "quite different" (int. 159, 8). Unlike London in the late 1970s, however, Stockholm has not had any serious fear that it will lose its practically modest but symbolically notable role. But also unlike London, Stockholm does not have the attitude, an outgrowth of the British Empire, that it *ought* to be a key center for the export of law and legal services to the rest of the world. There is competition for this business of arbitration everywhere, but Stockholm for the most part does not compete. It remains available for arbitration and offers a good service, but most of Stockholm will not *go after* a market.

Stockholm and the Genealogy of Arbitration

Stockholm remains an important center, but it is not a setting where major transformations are evident. A close look, however, will see in Stockholm all the elements of both history and of change in the development of international commercial arbitration. Change is slow, but in the present in Stockholm we can detect all the strands that have come together to create the current situation elsewhere. The Stockholm story lets us see the genealogy of international commercial arbitration in one national setting.

First, international commercial arbitration developed out of the practices and people involved in the arbitration of disputes between states. Only persons of impeccable social and moral credentials, the *noblesse de robe* possessing clout and diplomatic skills, were selected to resolve the disputes between nations that have been arbitrated since the nineteenth century. They quite naturally come from small, neutral nations themselves. They lack political affiliations but possess strong diplomatic skills. Such individuals, who can be traced easily into the 1930s in Stockholm, are particularly suited to the highly sensitive matters of public international law. And once such a group exists for those purposes, the members could be used for the big political-commercial cases involving oil nationalizations and the like. The difference is not so much in the skills required as in the fact that one party in the later cases tends to be a private corporation.

The style and demeanor of such patriarchal notables called to arbitrate is distinctive. One anecdote reveals the characteristics of such arbitrators. An ideal "secretary" for a public international arbitration, for example, was reported to be "a man who, when he walks into a restaurant, is automatically given the best table" (int. 158, 3). Such a secretary would have been able to develop himself into their kind of arbitrator. Stature was essential to this generation's effectiveness.

Such arbitrators are senior arbitration "amateurs," again typical of the generation that developed for the oil nationalizations. Arbitration is not a career for them, but rather a duty undertaken after a distinguished career in other areas of public service. Seniority is important because, as noted by a distinguished Stockholm lawyer, only after a certain period in life do individuals have the independence of judgment to decide matters without an eye toward their future careers. One Swedish arbitrator stated this well by noting that arbitrators should be at least sixty, "better seventy," years of age (int. 164, 4). Quite clearly, it takes a long time to produce an arbitrator who fits these criteria. It takes time, a distinguished career, and social standing to gain the stature necessary to become one of these arbitrators.

The amateurs produced by this system do not therefore believe they must be accountable to the consumers of arbitration. They are too independent. Put another way, they ideally act independently of any market considerations. One Swedish arbitrator of this generation thus noted that he had been selected once by a large Swedish corporation as a party-appointed arbitrator, that he had ruled against the Swedish corporation, and that he had never been selected again (int. 158). It clearly was not a matter of concern to him, and it is doubtful that the opinion in the arbitration was written in a way that would make the corporation or its lawyers feel that it ought to give the individual another try. The new generation of technocrats, in contrast, emphasizes their ability to satisfy the consumers in order to gain repeat business.

While the senior notables still dominate arbitration in Sweden, we see signs of change. Academics have played a key role in the international-arbitration community, and academics also serve as arbitrators in Stockholm. Academic lawyers bring the prestige of their part of the legal profession, and they also bring specialized legal expertise. The legal expertise then serves a dual function. It helps to "legalize" arbitration, creating and filling a demand, fostered by an increase in the number of arbitrations and arbitrators, for arbitration "according to law." The judge and retired judges can, at least within the confines of one legal system, also resolve disputes according to law. But academic lawyers help move beyond the charisma and independence of the patriarchal generation, increasing accountability to legal standards.[2] And in Sweden, as elsewhere, we find two branches of the academic profession contributing to arbitration. One group contains scholars of civil procedure, able to rationalize the process, work on the relationship of arbitration to the courts, and address

---

2. While we cannot pursue the analogy here to the ICC, there is also evidence that the generation that we link together as grand old men in the ICC world was also divided at one time between an early generation that offered only charismatic dispute resolution and the academic arbitrators who combined charisma and the law of the *lex mercatoria*.

central questions of choice of law. The other group, much more substantively organized, focuses on contract and commercial law.

Academic lawyers have the advantage also of being able to create a jurisprudence of arbitration that legitimates it more generally. Because of the prominence of academic knowledge in arbitration, and due also no doubt to the secrecy of arbitral awards, academic writing is a key feature of the international-arbitration community generally. Publication builds knowledge, is indispensable in building careers, and is vital also in building centers. Stockholm has invested in knowledge through the institute affiliated with the University of Stockholm, but there is not the sense of the community pushing the science that then goes back into the community. As noted before, Stockholm has not produced an academic know-how that can compete internationally with the world of the ICC.

The lack of a push in publication relates to the question of the younger generation in Stockholm. More writing, especially in English but also in French, is characteristic of those pushing ahead in this field. The new generation certainly exists in Sweden, but it is by no means in charge of the Stockholm arbitration community. This new generation—very well represented in power positions in arbitration in Geneva, London, New York, Paris, and Zurich—is more professional, more technical. These individuals have the ability to advise in the emerging expertise of arbitration, which indeed they helped to create. They do not otherwise bring special charisma or stature from outside their particular expertises. The professional arbitration specialists are typically in their forties, much younger than the senior amateurs.

Part of the expertise of the new generation is procedural—an ability to work with lawyers from any procedural system, and especially an ability to work with the litigation techniques pioneered by the large U.S. law firms. Another part of the expertise is to know the arbitrators and arbitration centers such that cases can be farmed out or brought in quite easily. These professionals are increasingly delocalized, promoting arbitration in different sites but more and more autonomous from the local legal system. And this generation has made a religion out of the needs of consumers of arbitration, promoting user-friendly arbitration and arbitration that carefully responds to all the claims and allegations of each side of a dispute, such that the losing party ideally understands and accepts the judgment. Finally, unlike the pure academics or the pure judges, this generation of arbitration is closer to business and therefore more likely to work business common sense into the legal norms applied to each case. They tend to criticize academics as too theoretical or abstract. The sum of these characteristics represents a much greater market orientation than the earlier generation of international commercial arbitration.

Stockholm so far, as noted above, is not an ideal setting for this generation or for the U.S. law firms that have helped create it. The only U.S. firms in Stockholm are White and Case and Baker and McKenzie. It is not surprising that the young lawyers with this entrepreneurial, technical, profile tend to move to Paris, or to move their arbitration interests to Paris. But the three, relatively large, Swedish firms are beginning to resemble their U.S. and London counterparts. They are also developing a generation within these firms that is not content to wait. It would not be surprising to see this new group, like their counterparts elsewhere, evolving into the future leaders of international commercial arbitration in Stockholm. They represent a possibility within Stockholm, but Stockholm today is a richer source of the imagery of the past—an age of patriarchal, nonentrepreneurial arbitrators valued for their stature and independence of judgments.

10

Social Capital and Legal Capital: Competition and Complementarity in the Market for Business Justice

The examples of England, the United States, and Sweden provide the basis of a preliminary typology of modes of institutionalization of arbitration—at least with respect to Western countries with well-established domestic arbitration practices for business disputes. The basic contrast is between *delegated justice*—identified best with England—and *parallel justice*—identified with Sweden and more generally the civil-law world. There is a striking diversity in the specific relationship between state justice and business disputing, which is reflected in part in the degree of importance of arbitration in the business-law relationship, but the models can abstract some of the general features. Another general feature worth noting at the outset is that in all three examples the capital of *domestic* learning and institutions related to arbitration has had some success, even if rather limited, in finding a place in the market to handle large, international business conflicts.

The first three sections of this chapter will compare the basic features of the two models as well as the more complex variation found in the United States. In light of these three examples of at least some international success, and considering the reputation of disdain for business by the "grand professors" of law and legal professionals in nearly all parts of the Continent, we focus in some detail in the fourth section of this chapter on the question of the relationship between business and law on the Continent and especially in France.

This terrain in particular did not a priori appear to provide a propitious base for the emergence and recognition of international commercial arbitration. It is true that the ICC existed in Paris since the 1920s, but that does not explain why it became a key player in the regulation of business conflicts through law. The great "notables of law," as we have seen, were themselves convinced of the merits of arbitration and capable also of convincing their peers. They succeeded in furnishing enough professional and state resources to allow this embryonic form of international justice to develop and thrive. In retrospect, in fact, this model for business justice that took root in Paris appears to be more a creation ex nihilo than a continuation of well-established practices and institutions.

International commercial arbitration—as this example confirms—is not an extension of domestic knowledge and usages with respect to business justice. It arrives as something new. This constant will be modified later with respect to the periphery of this field of practice, but it is worth underscoring this quite surprising finding. The world of law, after all, is characterized much more by continuity than by ruptures. Well-established legal rules and institutions provide the raw material for change. While the established norms are perpetually redefined and reinterpreted according to the needs and the strategies of the moment, the resultant innovations can be given the authority of tradition. The question, therefore, is why it is different in this field of business disputing.

This paradox provides one of the organizing issues for this chapter, which seeks to interrogate the experience of arbitration in order to reflect on the relations between the legal field and that of economic power. Accordingly, we take a closer look at parallel justice, especially in Paris, and develop a somewhat broader frame of reference. We examine the relations between business and law and the role of the faculties of law in this relationship. It is important to get beneath the conventional understanding of the separation between law and business on the Continent, both to understand the models themselves and to set the stage for a later discussion more precisely about how this new kind of international business justice took root in Paris (chap. 13). We see that parallel justice, especially in France, encompasses diverse combinations of social and legal capital beyond what is traditionally considered to be in the domain of law.

This chapter concludes with a preliminary discussion of a third model of national institutional development with respect to arbitration. Its purpose is to introduce the chapters on Egypt and on Hong Kong, suggesting the relationship between international commercial arbitration and national situations where law and justice have been—one way or another—put aside from the regulation of the state and economic relations.

Delegated Justice

The English example, which applies in varying degrees elsewhere, shows how arbitral justice may function as a kind of delegated justice. The routine administration of commercial conflicts in England is handled by nonlegal professionals, but they are under the legal control of a small coterie of commercial QCs. In effect, the commercial QCs reserve the right to intervene at any moment in the conflicts. They exercise this right in the name of the superior interest of the common law—and also, of course, in relation to their own individual and collective strategies.

This first model is characterized by a rather large—but rather precisely delimited—mutual overlap between judicial institutions and the sphere of business relations. A series of formal and informal understandings and networks of relationships assures a circulation of information, of disputes, and of resources between the two universes of business and law. But the two universes remain well differentiated.

The vast majority of business conflicts, according to this model, are regulated in the shadow of law, but not outside the law, since they are handled by operators who bring at least limited legal equipment to their tasks. Still, however, it is clear that pragmatic, technical, economic, and other considerations figure prominently in the decision-making balance. These intermediaries play the role of *courtier*, seen often in the development of the legal field: they assure a certain diffusion of legal norms, and they also contribute to the selection of a small number of disputes that can be made the object of greater legal investment. The "troubling legal issues" can then contribute to the enrichment and renovation of commercial jurisprudence.

As suggested in chapter 7, this interaction does not eliminate all tensions between the two poles of business and law. The providers of dispute resolution, while complementary in serving the cause of commercial jurisprudence, are also in definite competition with each other. Those close to business and those close to law compete to promote a market standard that fits their own positions. There is, therefore, some movement back and forth. Phases of "legalization" and "judicialization" alternate with campaigns that condemn the excesses of legalism in support of a "nicer" and less formal approach to the management of business conflicts. Such criticisms can be found recently in England (and elsewhere) under the banner of ADR (even if the importation of this new technology in countries outside the United States is limited by the fact that ADR owes much to the specific characteristics of the U.S. situation).

Rather than trying to explain the latest manifestation of this perpetual conflict, it is necessary to see how the successive waves reveal the complementarities and contradictions between the different potential categories of service providers, each of whom represents different forms of capital that can be mobilized in the market for conflicts. The value of legal capital grows and shrinks in relation to social capital, depending on the particular time period, the number of producers available in each competing category, and the types of problems that are posed.[1] These fluctuations in the market are also evidence

1. Legal capital and social capital can be quite closely linked. In the United States, for example, the hostility of the promoters of the New Deal to arbitration may be

of reorientations in the investments of the producers of business peace. As in all markets, the pace and extent of these cyclical changes depends on the ease or difficulty of making reconversions necessary to adjust supply to the demand of new or different types of business conflicts.

Commercial arbitration is set within this dynamic system. Prosperity and the degree of judicial involvement in arbitration depend to a great extent on the place arbitration occupies in the continuing cycle. The relative fluidity of this "English" model for handling business conflicts permits it to adapt relatively easily to external economic changes. Depending on the time period, the system can move closer to the domestic legal pole, or it can move away, giving more assurances to the world of business. Regardless of the particular manifestation, however, the market is defined by the connection and articulation between the two poles of business and law. And as noted before, conflicts and tensions between the different categories of producers should not be seen as inconsistent with a fundamental complementarity.

The ability of even this relatively flexible system to adapt to major changes, however, remains quite limited. It is a complex and ultimately fragile mechanism, liable to "seize up" from the pressure of multiple intervening parties with opposing interests. The slightest disruption of the market in business conflicts, as we have seen, requires a renegotiation of the compromise between these different parties. Renegotiation, furthermore, is no easy matter, since each of the contending parties defends its own territory; and innovations are badly received. In a situation of relatively fragile compromises, innovations appear as almost violent changes, even violations of the norms of the club that managed and gained from the compromise. The English club, indeed, represents a rather hierarchical and regimented milieu combining institutional relations and personal relations—often knotted in the classrooms of public schools. Innovative outsiders have great difficulty trying to gain a foothold in this kind of a setting.

We can therefore suggest that this success in ordinary times of this compromise justice—even if accepted as a tacit consensus—did not prepare it for the radical transformations that took place beginning in the 1960s. The recomposition of the international market of business conflicts, including the emergence of countries from the third world and the growing power of the large U.S. law firms, required something radically different. The reforms in England were tardy and too attentive to the requirements of consensus to be sufficiently radical. A simple facelift was insufficient to transform a complete ensemble

explained both by their desire to privilege state regulation and by the fact that these new arrivals to the legal field were richer in legal capital than in social capital (Auerbach 1983).

of practices revolving around England's secular imperialism—the commercial law. The arbitration system offered by England could not easily gain credibility for major disputes involving third-world countries anxious to gain their independence. Traditions can sometimes be a handicap, even in law. London, therefore, remains somewhat at the margin of the new market.

In a certain respect, the United States suffers still more from this imperial handicap. Its preeminent place in the political and economic domains precludes it from pretending to an image of neutrality. But this factor is not the only reason that the U.S. activity in the field of international commercial arbitration is essentially extramural, conducted by expatriate lawyers.[2] The influence of the United States in this field of practice is of course considerable, but international business justice has not become merely an appendage or extension of American justice. The specific features of business justice in the United States, as we have seen, are closely related to the structural characteristics of the internal market of business conflicts.

The Variation in the United States

Contrary to the English model, where the practice of arbitration is at the heart of the relationship between business and justice, the American Arbitration Association has historically played a relatively marginal role in relation both to the legal field and to economic power. This relative marginality for arbitration with respect to business disputes, while not new,[3] was reinforced by the development, first, of state regulation, then by the rise of business litigation. The growing use of law in the major relationships between businesses and between businesses and the state, then more recently the increase in the use of judicial systems by litigators serving their clients' instrumental ends, kept arbitration apart from major business conflicts. Arbitration was seen as a kind of cut-rate justice, appropriate only for small claims requiring

2. After all, the placing of the United Nations in New York has not prevented it from becoming one of the principal forums for the expression of the demands of the third world.

3. While we are lacking the research necessary to provide a structural history of arbitration in the field of business disputes (for a purely legal account cf. MacNeil 1992), we can offer a few relevant observations. Auerbach in particular underlines the importance of arbitration at the beginning of the twentieth century, followed by its relative demise at the time of the New Deal (1983). This development likely was accelerated when the New Deal mode of business regulation was generalized after World War II, since the leading lawyers of the New Deal rejoined Wall Street law firms and put their administrative expertise in the service of business clients. They helped in this manner to keep business disputing close to the domain of law.

a minimal legal investment. This "subjustice" lacked the luster necessary for it to become an international justice for major business conflicts.

As elsewhere, the domestic courts in the United States—around which the field of litigation was constituted—were by definition not exportable on the international scene. The litigators therefore had no choice but to look abroad for alliances that would permit them to exercise, or even impose, their legal practices. From this point of view, as explained below, the weak structure of the Parisian legal field was its principal attraction. Still, to the extent that the basis of this alliance was—and remains—a division of labor and a split of the market between the large Anglo-American law firms and the European judges and professors furnishing custom legal services, it ensured that the elite of American domestic justice—the judiciary in particular—would be unable to play a dominant role in the international market.

In contrast, as we have seen, the international revalorization of arbitration has put in place a process of recomposition of the domestic markets of business disputes in the United States. While that recomposition is far from concluded, we have seen that it has permitted judges domestically to commercialize the authority of the state in the market of private business justice. The process continues, but it is appropriate to return here to the earlier generalization that we have developed especially in this chapter: this restructuring of the market of business justice operates less by a remodeling of old institutions, including most notably the AAA in the United States, than by the invention and homologation of new approaches. What that has meant recently in the United States is the development of a multiform field of quasi-judicial mediation,[4] which has a number of the structural characteristics of the field of international commercial arbitration.[5] Also potentially important, but to date even more difficult to assess, is a new field of learning concentrating on the regulation of international business and state competition and particularly on "anti-

4. This flourishing field of practice in the United States is quite diverse. As elsewhere, the different groups of producers seek to promote the particular approaches to the administration of conflicts that correspond precisely to the specific combination of legal and social capital that they are able to mobilize. As already suggested, the types of mediation are divided between a pole that is more legal and one that is closer to business. Even the forms of legal mediation vary substantially, including the various forms of "rent a judge." The rapid development of this market is telescoping diachrony and synchrony. Instead of succeeding each other in response to different relations of forces at different times, the different approaches and techniques coexist and compete with each other.

5. The notable exception is the substantial learned investment constitutive of international commercial arbitration.

dumping" practices.[6] Large law firms in Washington, D.C., have played a major role investing in this potential new field of business disputing.

Parallel Justice and the Swedish Example

Returning to the examples, the second major model of arbitration is the civil-law model. Here the worlds of law and business coexist—but only by pretending to ignore each other. The Swedish example illustrates this duplicity very well. Arbitration functions in Sweden as a kind of parallel justice. We find the great notables of the Swedish justice system functioning in a somewhat hidden and unofficial market of private justice, in effect commercializing the authority available to them from their positions as judge, professor, or leader of the legal profession. As in the English model, arbitration in Sweden serves as a place of exchange between law and business. But in this case, the terms of trade are far more uneven.

Circulation in Sweden proceeds essentially one way. The merchants are able to take advantage of the legitimacy of the law that "moonlighting judges" personally embody. But the reputation of the courts suffers, since large economic conflicts are essentially put aside; and the private market of justice contributes very little to the renovation and revitalization of the law. It is easy to see why this mode of regulation of business conflicts has been unable to support a thriving international-business justice. The Swedish approach is missing two ingredients for the enterprise of institutionalization and revalorization of arbitration: a learned investment that builds—and builds on—Swedish practices; and an institutional visibility that can give international credibility.

This first description of the general models permits a better understanding of the national obstacles that stood in the way of the development of international commercial arbitration as an international-business justice—which had to take place, after all, on some *national terrain*. Even if in different degrees, the practice of arbitration in the previous examples suffered from a very devalorized image. In the U.S. and English examples, it tended to appear as a routine, even cut-rate justice. And in the Continental tradition, the unofficial, even hidden, form of justice is hardly celebrated.

---

6. This recomposition of the U.S. legal field, and the international investment of a certain number of protagonists of the internal market, could lead to a new arrangement on the market of international business disputes. The general rule that we have proposed with respect to institutions for the administration of business conflicts is also valid for the ICC. The growth of the market will be accompanied by the creation of new competitors, with a profile corresponding more to the new geopolitical structure of the international market (see conclusion, chap. 14).

The relatively low level of prestige does not prevent the existence of an arbitration practice for business disputes, but it prevents its further development. It was as if arbitration was permitted to survive in the shadow of the official justice system only if contained in the narrow niche to which it was assigned. Further expansion and development would have disturbed the ambiguous relations between lawyers and economic power. The autonomy necessary to legitimate a more expansive business justice requires a distance—or, more precisely, the public perception of distance—with respect to the vulgar logic of business and commerce. Here, as elsewhere in the legal field, the legitimacy of law and justice is poorly served by a too strict or too visible involvement with power and money.

The relative disqualification of these domestic forms of arbitration is an example that affects all such vulgar legal practices—including that of the *huissier*, the business agent, the main-street lawyer, or the ambulance chaser. Such practices are too openly implicated in social relations, without having made the symbolic investment necessary to transform them into relations of *law*. For international commercial arbitration to develop, then, required a revalorization of the field of practice through internationalization and intellectualization. As we have suggested, efforts coordinated by a small group of European academics and high-court judges, well introduced into the elite of the world of international business, succeeded in taking this vulgar savoir-faire and reinventing it as a learned and cosmopolitan legal practice. How this could take place in Paris is the subject of the next section, which begins with a closer look at business-law relations on the European Continent.

Further Investigations of Parallel Justice, Particularly on the Continent

To understand the dynamic of this process of learned promotion, it is necessary to enlarge the terrain of analysis. We must further take into account the diffusion of legal learning and the extraordinary diversity of the modes of administration of business conflicts (see Ellickson 1991). Business conflicts in general, we suggest, are resolved as much in the shadow of power as in the shadow of the law; and indeed, the two are not necessarily contradictory.

The starting point is the recognition that the Continental legal field, contrary to an ideological image reproduced in sociological discourse, is not limited to a small group of republican lawyers and "legal aristocrats" (Osiel 1989) equally preoccupied with maintaining their distance from vulgar business practices. To the contrary, we are convinced that many possessors of economic power on the Continent—including especially people in business—are, in fact, able to mobilize legal or quasi-legal authority, even if at times only indirectly.

Intervention in economic conflicts is one of the prerogatives and also one of the instruments of the power of these individuals who bridge law and economy. These individuals accept the formal disconnection between business and law—and may not be labeled as lawyers—in part because it allows them both to gain credibility in their interventions in business conflicts and also to protect a certain right of control.

Their interventions in business disputes require that we expand our definition of parallel justices to consider other practices—each reflecting the specific combination of social and legal capital that the service providers have at their disposal. At the same time, the multiplicity of the approaches that compete in this market—considered broadly—of business disputes is favorable to the proliferation of new enterprises for conflict resolution. The French situation is in this sense opposed in key respects to both the English and Swedish models, because in those sites the market is strictly controlled by a small group of relatively homogeneous producers—the commercial bar and judiciary in England, the small senior arbitration community in Sweden.

The diversity of the players in Paris, in contrast, creates a free space where all forms of alliance are possible, both locally and, even more, internationally. The opening to the potential international business in commercial disputes certainly accounts for much of the spectacular growth of the ICC. But this success was only made possible because the tremendous diversity in the local legal field allowed the development of the alliance—between a small group of notables of learned law and large law firms—that took place in and around the ICC.

The almost instant attraction between the grand professors and the merchants of law may appear a priori paradoxical—at least, if one holds to the professional ideology that condemns commercialism or interference from political power in order to affirm the autonomy of law. But behind the facade of condemnation of the market we can find multiple ties between the universe of business and that of law. Paradoxically, there may even be closer ties on the Continent than elsewhere.

The Faculties of Law and the Reproduction of Social Capital

In order to clarify this point, several complementary developments must be explored. Since it is contrary to most conventional wisdom, we elaborate here our understanding of what lies beneath the professional ideology of condemnation of commercialism. The sociology of legal professions has had a tendency to neglect the important role that scholarly institutions play in the reproduction—and the legitimation—of the property-owning fractions of the dominant class.[7] This role is not limited to the landed oligarchy and the rural bourgeoisie, but these two groups have furnished the core of recruits to the faculties of law (Karady 1991; Charle 1983). It is necessary in any event to look carefully at these groups to explain the aristocratic ideology and the denunciation of the market expressed by so many legal professionals.

The Continental cult of disinterestedness, after all, works well for inheritors and for rentiers, worried more about honorific than immediate material profits. It permits them to embody the ideal of unworldly justice, meanwhile disqualifying competitors who are less disinterested, because less materially endowed. New arrivals confronted with this prevailing definition have no choice but to bow to the ideology of renunciation. The most ambitious arrivals may even seek to follow the high-risk political strategy of valorizing this ideology.[8]

The *héritiers* of the landed bourgeoisie have succeeded more than others in shaping their professional ideology to make it conform to the image they wish to give, but they are not the only ones to have invested in legal learning. The success of the law faculties depends precisely on the fact that the education is at the same time generalized and technical. Indeed, the weak scholarly offerings of these institutions respond rather well to the educational needs of large fractions of the property-owning classes. The diploma that the universities delivered under these conditions was the equivalent of a "statutory right to the bourgeoisie" (Bourdieu and Saint Martin 1978, 22). It offered them the advantages of a scholarly title without challenging the essentials of a predominantly familial mode of production.

The families of rural notables were anxious to reconvert a declining patrimony—but intact social capital—into professional titles. At the same time, the degrees from the faculties of law served the bourgeoisie of business, seeking to increase the legitimacy of their economic power and add to it the supplementary credibility of scholarly titles. The implicit condition was that the institutions producing the titles not seek to substitute their own values and, above all, meritocratic selection in place of the logic of the transmission of family capital.

We can thus understand the weak commitment to the pedagogy of legal

7. At the same time that it privileges the bar, it also reflects the domination of North American academics who tend to minimize or ignore questions of social class (Dezalay 1995).

8. But also with great gains, as was the case in the nineteenth century for the republican or nationalist fraction of a certain number of European professional groups (Karpik 1992; Karady 1991). They took this ideology seriously and used it to gain political power.

study that reformers have condemned from the nineteenth century through to the present. Observing the German faculties of law after World War II, for example, Dahrendorf noted with some surprise the lack of interest—even the disdain—of students for legal learning (Dahrendorf 1969). This observation is paradoxical only according to professorial discourse, which proclaims these legal systems as *professorenrecht*. For the most part, however, the professors belong to a meritocracy of new arrivals who have no choice but to "take the law seriously." The *héritiers*, on their side, are aware that the best careers are not made through the formal law. They are more matters of personal relations than of a strict learned technique.

The faculties of law are able to combine the personal and legal in this kind of situation. Hartman (1995), for example, in his analysis of a "slow erosion of an elite," begins to explore these issues in relation to law graduates in banking. He suggests that law graduates seeking to become leaders of large banks needed to adopt a strategy of rapid diversification away from the bank departments that specialized in litigation. The idea is that diversification was necessary to allow them to advance beyond their legal training. We might ask, however, whether the phenomenon has a somewhat difficult explanation.

Given the role of the faculties of law in the reproduction of the establishment, the successful strategy of law graduates[9] could be seen as in fact predetermined by their social origins. They were bound not to be confined to litigation. This explanation holds particularly for banking—an economic branch traditionally considered the noblesse of business. The financial sector has long been predisposed to place a high value on a title that translates the family lines of the bourgeois class or, at least, attests to conformity and respect for its customs. Whichever the explanation, this example and many others[10] suggest that, at least at the level of elites, it is more accurate to speak of the *interpenetration*, rather than the break, between the legal field and that of economic power.

The group of economic leaders with this pedigree—mainly in business but

9. This success is today more threatened by the competition of other technical knowledges better adapted to the role of financial engineer—and perhaps also elsewhere by the relative democratization of the faculties of law, which means that the diploma no longer automatically gives the right to bourgeoisie status.

10. In France, at the beginning of the 1970s, one-fifth of the leaders of the large enterprises were graduated in law (Bourdieu and Saint Martin 1978, 22). And, despite the increasing importance of *les grandes écoles* (Ecole Nationale d'Administration, Polytechnique, and "Science-po") in the market for the education of the *patrons d'état*, the proportion of law graduates was hardly inferior to the proportion of law graduates in the large enterprises controlled by the state. In other civil-law countries, the proportions of law degrees were even higher.

also in government—can thus profit from a double membership and a double influence—even if not considered members of the legal profession by professional ideology or professional organizations. It is true that, outside of their formal studies, which were not that rigorous, this group does not evidence a great zeal for legal learning and legal techniques. Nevertheless, these leaders are not excluded or made marginal in the legal field. In the first place, we can expect them to have some degree of legal competence on at least the questions that are near their economic interests. Further, while they learned relatively little law in the classrooms of the law faculties, they typically were able to acquire and cultivate good contacts with the producers of law. They know enough about legal categories to be able to use their contacts to find experts capable of translating the specific preoccupations of the economic leaders into the field of pure law.

This interpretation of the world of business in the civil-law world returns us to the topic of parallel justice. It suggests that business may avoid the courts in part because it has the ability to short-circuit them. The business leaders economize on jurisprudence by investing in lobbying or in doctrinal consultation (Bancaud and Dezalay 1994). Working through professor-lawyers as intermediaries, they are able to exert pressure to influence the interpretation of norms—even to obtain their redefinition—to conform more to their interests.

These interventions in the development of law have the advantage of being more discrete—and also often more rapid—than the jurisprudential strategy of "repeat player" described by Galanter for the United States (1974). Furthermore, contrary to an ordinary litigant dependent on the executory force of legal decisions, these economic leaders are able to mobilize a full range of resources to exploit any legal gains that they obtain. They are able, for example, to incorporate gains automatically into the contracts drafted by inside or outside counsel. Their principal advantage, however, is that they can act easily and successfully on different terrains. If the legal terrain is unfavorable, for example, they may always promote the authority of "commercial customs," or they can mobilize their capital in social relations.

New arrivals—or at least the most ambitious among them—typically lack the social capital and fluency in the customs of those with the most established presence in the market. Challengers, therefore, have few options but to promote the value of legal arguments and judicial strategies. They may condemn the ensemble of tacit customs and personal relations as a disguised form of collusion or protectionism. Excluded from the local business establishment, the new arrivals rediscover the merits of courts and even "forgotten" legal practices in the name of free trade and economic freedom. As we have seen in many settings, the choice between a legal strategy or even recourse to courts and informal arrangements (which may be the product of amicable pressures) is all a matter of tactic and context. We see these different possibilities in the following subsection.

A Compartmentalized Market

Contrary to a model widespread in the sociolegal literature, the rule of law is not inconsistent with a strong role for personal relations in the regulation of economic activity. Competition between each of these strategies for handling business conflicts in fact contributes to the compartmentalization of this market through a pluralism of approaches that ignore (or pretend to ignore) each other. Each group promoting its approach to business conflict resolution defines itself in opposition to the others; and it then seeks to convince its potential clients that the choice of one strategy precludes others. The specialists of arbitration, for example, pretend that real arbitration is incompatible with the practice of mediation. The promoter of various "alternative justices" may unite together against formal justice or, when competing among the alternatives, promote the distinctiveness of particular approaches.

Those who treat different modes for the resolution of conflict as autonomous systems succumb to the temptation to join in the competition. A more complete and accurate description of conflict resolution requires an accent on the manner in which the different offerings complete, oppose, and redefine each other. Neither "relational capitalism," built supposedly on personal relations, nor legal or judicial regulation of the market, exists by itself. They represent only positions in a constantly changing package of players and approaches. The available mix at any given time offers a vast assortment of tactical possibilities, which can be exploited by practitioners representing diverse combinations of legal competence and social capital.

In this same manner, the field of arbitration contains multiple networks anxious to mark their differences to best market what they have to offer. Arbitration, in fact, is often presented quite overtly as a kind of market where the clients are able to choose from a palette of potential arbitrators according to the nature of their problems, their affinities, and above all their strategies. The parties—and their advisers—thus choose their terrain, their arms, and the rules of the game that will govern their confrontation. A party may opt, for example, for an arbitrator who specializes in law or one more familiar with commercial practices. The choice may be of a strong personality who will settle the dispute, without much concern for party sensibilities, or of an individual who has built a reputation as a conciliator. Finally, as in poker, one may raise the stakes by choosing as arbitrators—or as lawyers—superstars of arbitration.

The competition in providing business justice leads to a compartmentalization of the market that the state judicial system is powerless to control. Indeed, it is a victim of this compartmentalization. Justice is in effect shattered into pieces, divided between the different places or networks of power that claim to have a role in the regulation of economic relations.

The diversity of forums, techniques, and operators, indeed, reflects and reinforces the competition that reigns in the field of business enterprises. As noted before, there are very close connections between business and law in the Continental model of parallel justice. This business justice possesses very little autonomy in relation to the holders of economic power—each is in fact fortified with its own custom-made justice.

We can thus identify the different ways of taking charge of conflicts by mapping more or less the places of power in the economic field. The majority of approaches combine, even if in differing degrees, legal capital and social capital. We shall begin by returning to banking, which, especially on the Continent, has a set of characteristics that is quite revealing. First, while the density of jurists is most elevated in the banking sector, banking is also the sector of economic activity that requires the most relational capital. Holders of social capital obtain value for it in the banking sector. The great business banks have defined themselves as heads of networks of influence going well beyond their financial participation. They have utilized their capital of information, personal relations, and services to "limit their financial participation to that which is strictly necessary to assure mastery in the position of financial engineer" (Bourdieu and Saint Martin 1978, 43).

The learning and practice of the law are inscribed perfectly in this ensemble of technologies of power. The diploma of law guarantees membership in a *noblesse des affaires,* supported through lineage to business and a set of customs and behaviors that provide cohesion within the dominant class. The banker-jurists in this setting are able to add to the worldly ease that comes from their social status a mastery of the techniques and forms that represent the strong suit of those lawyers who would seek to be intermediaries. When contracts are negotiated, or renegotiated after difficulties have arisen, they can draw on their legal credentials and skills.

Because of the privileged position of bankers and the broad economic and social information at their command, they are often called upon to intervene in conflicts that emerge within their zone of influence. This activity of informal mediator is also a strong source of power. Like the justice of the peace in the feudal era, the strategically placed mediator in this system becomes an inherent part of the authority of the aristocracy of business. Legal capital in this model is not opposed to, but rather is confused with, relational capital. It reinforces and prolongs the relational capital in changing economic circumstances.

The example of banking provides a pattern repeated in the institutional settings that are the most public and political in the world of business. They also serve to reveal—and to produce—business cohesion. Professional organizations, most notably the chambers of commerce and industry, tend to bring out the more "legal" and "social" dimensions of the world of entrepreneurs. Like the bankers described above, the leaders in these settings owe their position less to the importance of their economic capital than to a social capital composed of personal relations and academic titles that are themselves more social than technical. Quite naturally, these places of power are also preferred places for the administration of internal business conflicts. In order to exercise this quasi-judicial power, the notables of business have at their disposal institutional means of pressure—whether to promote peace or exclude noncooperators. As elsewhere, some control over networks of information often permits them to intervene before the conflict situation becomes too acrimonious. The very success of this mediation also contributes to its legitimacy.

This quick panorama of the places of power—and of potential intermediaries—in the field of business would be incomplete without mention of the network constituted around the *state* administrative apparatus: notably around the institutions concerned with industrial planning, coordination, and regulation. In effect, while relatively new, these circles of power have encroached upon—and perhaps supplanted—their predecessors, whose center of power is the private economic world. This role is especially evident in countries where the interventionism of the welfare state has favored the emergence of state capitalism.[11]

In settings where economic power is found in strict symbiosis with political power, the leaders most visible in the world of business are often those most familiar with the apparatus of the state. The situation described earlier with respect to the economic establishment repeats itself a fortiori for the new *noblesse d'état* and of business. Even more than their predecessors, from whom they are in any event often the *héritiers*, they owe their power and their legitimacy to their social capital, especially the academic titles, which have become even more prestigious and selective. In France, for example,

---

11. Recall that in Sweden, informants reported that very serious disputes were likely to be handled by businesspeople and the government.

this upgrading of degree requirements provoked a relative devaluation of the faculties of law in relation to the *grandes écoles* of the state. The most important of the schools in France became the Ecole Nationale Administrative, the base of recruitment of the *grand corps*.

This relatively unique French situation, which leads to a relatively lesser role for law degrees in maintaining the dominant class, should not be interpreted as the reason why new institutions of power are outside the law.[12] Certainly, the holders of the new credentials reject the jurisdiction of the ordinary courts, but these new technocrats, who have built and embodied the "law of the state," have taken care to borrow the forms of legal procedures to which judicial institutions owe their legitimacy. This new French generation of leaders, with both economic power and the authority of the state, have in fact constituted themselves as a kind of custom-made justice that is parallel to the civil courts[13] while escaping from their control.

This new kind of parallel justice retains a kind of monopoly on the market for handling economic conflicts. Its promoters intervene sometimes as judges (for all the proceedings linked to state intervention) and sometimes as mediators, playing at the same time on the networks of solidarity (which are particularly strong among those of the *grand corps*) and on their formidable means of pressure. More than ever, there exists a close connection between legal and economic power. France thus no longer fits the particular model of law degrees and business, but it fits very well the general pattern of business and law.

In sum, contrary to the usual image, business is not distinct from the legal field; it is simultaneously inside and outside of it, according to the strategies and the interests of the moment. Business has in fact constituted for itself a custom justice that the authorities of the legal field have only a weak right to supervise. And this de facto autonomy does not prevent business from drawing on the authority of the law or from investing on its terrain. While protecting their distance from the legal field, the holders of economic power have effective access, without the need to submit to the rules of the judicial game applicable to citizens with ordinary conflicts.

Business justice therefore exists in the countries of the civil-law tradition, but the relations between varieties of private justice and state courts are left

12. Even if this is the reproach that characteristically is addressed by the bar to them (cf. "The law of the state against the state of law"). Lawyers are all the more critical when they experience what they perceive to be a dispossession.

13. Even if this administrative justice is made autonomous to the civil tribunals, there exist nevertheless a number of bridges between the two. The same offices of lawyers—where the elite of the profession is found—hold a monopoly of representation before both the Conseil d'Etat and the Cour de Cassation.

quite ambiguous. The varieties of private justice function in a parallel manner, in the backstage of public court systems from which they borrow considerably in terms of vocabulary, techniques, and personnel, and even more of legitimacy. The space for private justice, which is divided up and competitive, is where international commercial arbitration developed in the civil-law world. The logic is exactly the same, adding simply another kind of private justice to the market for business conflicts. The success of arbitration, in fact, comes from the compartmentalization. Arbitration appears as one of the rare places where the different forms of legal and social capital marketable for business conflicts can be circulated and exchanged overtly.

In addition, since the international business community lacks the homogeneity found on the national scale, it cannot be as content with the "moral sanctions" that characterize the less "legal" forms of business mediation. There is a relatively greater need to mobilize the authority of law. This demand for legal authority also creates opportunities for the business of professionals of justice—lawyers, judges, and professors—who had increasingly been kept away from the places of technocratic power where economic conflicts were handled. The internationalization of the market for conflicts permits the notables of the legal field to reenter a field of practice where they had been marginalized and their knowledge and learning devalued. They thus profit from the relative disqualification of their main recent competitors, the "jurists of the state" tied to national state-business relations. In this manner, paradoxically, the development of this private justice appears as a strategy of return game on the part of judicial institutions: the reconquest of lost terrain from the bureaucracies of the social state.

This reconquest remains more formal than actual. It is seen, for example, in the deference that arbitration institutions pay to judicial authorities. Further, the pattern we see in arbitration tends to involve at least a few well-placed legal notables who can assure a discrete but effective liaison between the two forms of justice. The judicial hierarchy then supports and symbolically authorizes considerable autonomy for arbitration.

From this perspective, it is a matter of the weakness of the legal field—its fragmentation and the marginalization of judicial institutions—that explains the success of arbitration in civil-law countries. This paradox has as its counterpoint the weakness, indeed almost nonexistence, of a business bar in the countries of Continental Europe, notably France. That absence explains the ease with which the Anglo-American multinational law firms were able to take hold of this new market at the expense of local practitioners.[14] Born on

14. It does not appear that the Parisian bar has profited very much from the implantation of the ICC in Paris, except, perhaps, from the symbolic point of view of favoring

the margin of the legal field, in the civil-law world, international commercial arbitration can thus be seen as predestined to develop into an offshore justice dominated by lawyers from elsewhere.

Putting Aside Justice in Favor of Private or Technocratic Arrangements: A Third Model

In the preceding model, the dividing line between the different varieties of private justice and state justice serves to maintain the legitimacy of the latter. At the same time, this division of labor fits perfectly the interests of the holders of economic power. The holders of power are able to maintain control over their conflicts but benefit also from the oversight at a distance of the state justice system. This arrangement also promotes the legitimacy of judges and courts, since the separation helps the formal legal system appear independent of the world of business. The rarity of judicial intervention gives it symbolic value in the eyes of merchants. In short, the seeming absence of law actually permits legal participation in the economic field. Formal absence allows a more subtle presence.

In contrast, in the third model, justice is in fact absent. Lacking independence and credibility, its role is confined, at best, to playing bit parts in the administration of economic conflicts.[15] The discredit of judicial institutions most often is only a reflection of the weak position of lawyers in the field of power. The reasons can be multiplied for this kind of situation. There is first the hostility of a certain number of authoritarian regimes to law and a legal

---

its opening to international legal practice. Could it have been otherwise? The example of the Swiss is not probative since Switzerland possessed numerous advantages—its image of neutrality, but also its long tradition of a business law practice—that permitted it to take advantage of the networks of arbitration and the proximity of the ICC, while limiting the encroachments of foreign law firms. Sweden offers a counterexample. The relative stagnation of the market of international arbitration could be attributed in part to the strict control that local professionals have maintained over this field of practice. The large Anglo-American law firms prefer to orient their clients toward places where they are freer to exercise their talents.

15. It should be noted that, even more than the preceding models, this model cannot be identified with one country or group of countries in particular. Even in the countries where justice is most subordinate to other powers, there are efforts, even if timid, to affirm some degree of autonomy. Conversely, it is true that even those states with a long tradition of law still have channels by which holders of economic power can weigh very heavily on the scales of justice. The presentation of this model serves then to draw attention to evidence too often forgotten: since it is a social construction, the place of law and lawyers in social relations can be put into question. The model also shows the place of arbitration when law and lawyers do not play more than a marginal role in the fields of economic or political power.

profession tainted by its foreign origins and clients. The aim of social revenge is added to a nationalistic logic to justify a veritable hunt for lawyers, or, at least, their removal from positions of power. As nicely stated by Osiel, law and lawyers "wilt quickly" when removed from the centers of power (1989).

Another reason for the weak position of lawyers is that economic and political power may be closely intertwined, as in Communist regimes and many countries of the third world. Even when the two groups are distinct, as in Southeast Asia, where the Chinese diaspora controls the essential part of the market economy, the result is nearly the same (see chap. 12). In losing their political role, lawyers lose a good part of their value in the eyes of economic leaders.

This process of a social decline of law quickly becomes cumulative. When the market of law shrinks and is devalued, the younger generations of those best endowed with social capital—familial, academic, or relational—orient their careers and their learning toward new places of power and new avenues of promotion. Law's role in the creation of forms of social relations and their legitimation, in the development of ways to mediate conflicts, and more generally, in the functions of intermediary and broker, is reduced in favor of other forms of authority.

These activities, annexed to business, which constitute a large part of the market for law, are not necessarily linked inextricably to the mastery of a knowledge and a technique that is specifically legal. As shown earlier, and despite what lawyers might like to believe, they require social capital as much or even more than technical competence. And when the social capital diminishes, or when lawyers are dispossessed, they lose the relations of prestige to which they owe much of their authority. Accordingly, the technicians of law are confined to a role of bit part in the field of power, or, even worse, to low-level tasks. Marginalized, they quickly become pariahs avoided by others.

This disqualification of law and lawyers tends to appear all the more flagrant because other places and technologies of power are quickly reconstituted elsewhere, supported by party or bureaucratic structures—even reactivating clientele or family connections. The economic operators learn quickly to bypass law when they are provided with substitute products through which they can exercise more direct control. The difference, in any event, may only be nominal. The new "products for social peace" may be put on the market by senior jurists, or their *héritiers*, having reconverted themselves at the opportune moment—now dressed up according to the new state of social relations, for example as apparatchiks or as experts in planning for economic development.

This putting aside of law and lawyers varies in extent and duration from one country to another. This marginalization, at the extreme, may even be of sufficient duration to appear as if the product of cultural determinism. Obvious examples are found in Asia, where the economic success of "capitalism in the Asian model" has made cultural explanations quite popular. The hostility of the Asian entrepreneurs to law and to courts is attributed to the Confucian tradition, which privileges conciliation as the method for resolving conflicts. The extraordinary prosperity of this relational capitalism in Asia is said to prove that the utilization of family networks and relations of clientele— termed *guanxi* in Asia—is superior economically to legal approaches to the regulation of the market economy. Combining these two propositions, the authors of this theory of Asian capitalism suggest more generally that the Confucian culture represents an alternative to legal regulation and that it prevents the export into Asia of the Western culture of the rule of law.

The claims on behalf of Asian culture are somewhat excessive.[16] In privileging the *longue durée* by inscribing it into culture, the historical context in which this specific form of relational capitalism developed is neglected. By building enterprises that were familial and paternalistic, the Chinese were able to adapt and prosper in an often hostile environment, and they did not have any mastery of law (Wong 1988). History shows, however, that when the alternative of law existed, as in the mixed international courts of Shanghai, the Chinese merchants had little hesitation to use it. They brought proceedings to Western courts to challenge the tacit customs—and the forms of mediation— that were imposed by the Chinese guilds to protect their monopoly profits (Lee 1993). Merchants open to change and aware of how to use Western techniques, especially through service as compradors for foreign firms, were quickest to use these courts for their own advantages.

The respective positions of law and corporatist dispute resolution reflect the relative strength of the different groups confronting each other economically. Each seeks to reinforce its economic position by promoting its preferred techniques for the administration of conflicts. In this Chinese example, the colonial interests favored the creation of mixed courts; and the mixed courts contributed to the dismantling of the corporatist structures that contained economic activity. The result was to the greater profit of foreign capitalists and their local allies.

16. Perhaps because it is a matter of a rhetorical argument where the stakes are not merely academic. The interrogation on the "nature" of Asian capitalism and the reasons for its success are at the center of an ideological debate: it touches at the same time the comparative efficacy of different modes of development—the market economy versus state planning—and questions of political legitimacy—the opposition between the Western and "Asian" conceptions of the rights of man.

This episode shows well that economic and political confrontations have their analogues on the terrain of the administration of conflicts. We can also point to a similar phenomenon—even if the dynamic is reversed—occurring around the same time in Japan. Haley (1991, 89) shows that after a first period of very rapid judicialization of land conflicts, the Japanese military intervened in an authoritarian manner. The military sought to promote a return to conciliation, which conformed more to its nationalist ideology and populist strategy. Like belief in the law, the distrust of law is a social construct that may frequently take the form of political indoctrination.

The respective positions of relational capitalism and legalized capitalism reflect less the impact of cultural traditions than the balance of power between those social groups that play the law and those supported by other mechanisms of power and legitimacy. This battle takes place simultaneously on two terrains, that of economic competition and that of political struggle. The first determines the resources that each of the adversaries will be able to mobilize. But the second is even more crucial, since it is there, in effect, where the homologation and institutionalism of the different mechanisms for the administration of conflicts is decided.

On the political terrain, moreover, the holders of legal capital possess some important advantages. More than other social activities, politics is organized according to legal rules. The majority of countries wish to be democracies and invoke the rule of law—at least formally. Because the state is by definition a legal construct, state actors tend not to favor informal methods for the resolution of conflicts. There are exceptions, especially when legal legitimacy is itself put aside by an authoritarian regime in the name of communism, populism, or developmentalism (Castells 1992).

This situation, unfortunately, has indeed occurred rather frequently. And once jurists are marginalized in the field of power, they are unlikely to find support for a strategy of legalization of conflicts. This depreciation of law occurred in Europe, but it occurred especially in countries of the third world where the law has been, quite appropriately, identified with the colonial tradition. Local implantation of law was recent and fragile, with the legitimacy of lawyers coming from outside the local setting. Notables on the periphery, often quite near to the comprador bourgeoisie, were often victims of nationalist or communist movements.

The relative putting aside of law in the Asian mode of administration of conflicts similarly owes as much to political factors as to the Confucian tradition. The cult of consensus has an impact, but the elimination or disqualification of lawyers also leads entrepreneurs with little choice but to bypass the law. Again, however, this state of affairs is by definition transitory. The prosperity of these Asian economies leads them to internationalize, and by the same process to rediscover the law. The imperialism of the market passes the baton to symbolic imperialism. And this process holds for the range of authoritarian regimes where the law and arbitration represent kinds of enclaves linked to internationalization.

The loss of credibility that judicial institutions suffer under these regimes affects quite evidently their capacity to intervene in the field of business. The authority of the arbitrator is reduced when it is subject to the orders of other powers, whether military, communist, or nationalist. Nevertheless, even the most authoritarian of regimes cannot neglect its credibility on the plane of international economic relations. Unless living in autarky, this option of avoiding law is less and less available. Even strong powers are constrained by internationalism this way to play the card of arbitration—as much on the national as the international setting. As we have seen, the jurisdictions of domestic arbitration provide domestic alternatives to international arbitration outside of the local setting.

On the other hand, this strategy implies adopting the strategy of fighting fire with fire: In order to preserve their sovereignty—and also a certain right of supervision—these authoritarian governments must provide sufficient autonomy and power to the national institutions of arbitration. This is the price to pay to avoid the general opprobrium for the justice of the state. The Soviet Union, COMECON, and China, for example, created arbitration institutions that were recognized by most observers as having a real concern for equity and independence. Perhaps precisely because of such concerns, these institutions had to prove again and again their autonomy, especially in the eyes of foreign users, who are often also their homologues and correspondents in the field of international arbitration.

Lacking power to support themselves on state court systems of uncertain legitimacy, or on a national legal field that is practically nonexistent, the local specialists of arbitration have a tendency to take their references and their models from abroad. These institutions become a kind of extraterritorial enclave of legal and judicial regulation in these "states of nonlaw." By a very different road, one ends up with a process of relative autonomization of arbitral justice that is quite near to what we have described in the preceding model.

11

International Legal Practice as Ghetto or Beachhead: Cairo and the Problems of North and South

Cairo is located geographically and culturally at the south of the north and at the north of the south. It is not an accident that Egyptians occupy top leadership positions at the United Nations, the World Bank, and the Arab League.[1] Cairo, a cosmopolitan capital of more than fourteen million people, including between 100,000 and 150,000 lawyers, inevitably represents a strategic place to address north-south and Arab-West issues, and we can expect a similar role in international commercial arbitration. Cairo can be studied on its own and for its role in bringing together different positions about law and about international commercial arbitration. It thus provides a focal point for exploring Islamic law in relation to arbitration, and for the ways that third-world considerations might be part of international arbitration. North-south arbitration since the 1970s has made up a very large part of the arbitration business, especially the business of construction disputes. There has been much discussion in Egypt and elsewhere about whether arbitration has been somehow biased in favor of the developed countries (Sornarajah 1989). The Egyptian story will therefore address the more general issues that find a meeting place in Cairo.

This discussion will be organized around a specific concern: the role of Cairo as a potential leader in the practice of international conflict resolution through arbitration. The question has two parts: first, the potential role of the Egyptian legal profession in the market of international transactions and conflicts; and, second, the potential of Cairo as a center for arbitration. This formulation of the Cairo issue may not have been foremost in the minds of the individuals we interviewed. Nevertheless, the activities in Egypt and in particular Cairo one way or another revolve around the potential role for Cairo as a leading international legal center. Cairo, we shall point out, has many characteristics that make it a good candidate for a leadership position in international legal practice. It has an abundance of important arbitrators with excel-

---

1. Boutros Boutros Ghali of the UN, Ahmed Esmat Abdul Maguid of the Arab League, and Ibrahim Shihata, general counsel of the World Bank.

lent language skills and an ability to operate in the transnational environment. When we asked respondents in Europe and the United States to name arbitrators outside of those areas, we invariably heard the names of one or more Egyptians. This degree of recognition is unique outside of Europe and the United States. It is quite difficult for someone from outside the northern centers to gain this measure of acceptance. With those advantages, we could suggest that the 200–250 internationally oriented lawyers in Cairo represent a strategic beachhead for major expansion as world trade develops.

Yet, as we shall also suggest, neither the outstanding reputation of the arbitrators, nor the quality and success of the transnational legal practices built around the leaders in arbitration, will be easy to translate into a bright future for Cairo as a leading international legal center. In the terms we have used elsewhere in this study, the capital that provides the strength of the Cairo position will be difficult to convert and build upon in the changing environment of transnational business disputing. Cairo still depends on a haute couture model of French—classically civil-law—legal practice, and it is difficult to build on that model to gain a greater share of international business from outside Egypt or the new private businesses within Egypt. Several hundred lawyers may thus represent more a ghetto than a beachhead. Our discussion will highlight the structural features that will shape the future of this cosmopolitan elite (and its successors).

Cairo as a Legal Center for North and South and for the Arab World

The strategic place of Egypt in general and Cairo in particular has already been noted. Unlike most of the Arab world, Egypt has a long tradition of lawyers in public life (Brown 1995; Reid 1981), and it has a very strong tradition also of a civilian legal system tied closely to Paris. Leading professors prior to 1952 and the Nasser revolution almost invariably capped their Egyptian legal education with a graduate degree from France. The system and the links to Paris, indeed, were sufficiently strong to outlast the British colonial rule of Egypt. As in other civil-law systems, the law professors occupy the leading positions. They comment on the decisions of the courts, and the courts rely on the comments and treatises based on the comments—the doctrine— for their own decisions. Professors consult with businesses privately, but the consulting practice keeps them up-to-date rather than cutting into their production of law. Given the high social prestige of the civil-law professor, it is not surprising that most of them come from cosmopolitan families already with high social status. In this regard the Egyptian legal system circa 1950 resembled quite well—even in exaggerated form—the French legal system of the same period.

The Egyptian professors stood and may still stand at the top of most of the legal systems in the Arab world. One of our respondents stated that Egyptian domination of the Arab legal world "was, is, and will be" (int. 187, 3). Another emphasized the "moral authority" of Egyptian lawyers (int. 200, 3). There are several reasons for the strength of the Egyptian legal profession. First is the influence of the Egyptian civil code, modeled mainly on the French and drafted by Professor Abdul Razzak Al-Sanhuri. Enacted in 1948, it became the model code for many other Arab countries, including Iraq, Jordan, Libya, Syria, and Kuwait (El-Ahdab 1990, 122). Second, the decisions of Egyptian courts and the doctrine generated by Egyptian scholars have exercised a great power over the other Arab countries, including those already named and others, such as Algeria and Tunisia. When their own courts have not resolved an issue of law, the other Arab countries often look to see what the Egyptian courts have done.

One reason for the look to Egyptian precedents in the Persian Gulf region is that many, if not most, of the judges are imported Egyptian lawyers. While there are growing numbers of local citizens with legal training, Egyptians remain in large numbers throughout the judiciary in at least Syria, Kuwait, and Saudi Arabia (ints. 137, 79, 206, 193). This role does not necessarily bring high status in these countries, since lawyers are not especially well respected (they are termed "guest workers" by Saleh 1992, 539), but it does lead to further importation of Egyptian law. In addition, many of the law-trained individuals in the Gulf countries received their education in Cairo or Alexandria (also Lebanon), reinforcing their ties with the Egyptian professors.

Finally, many of the leading Egyptian law professors have been to the Gulf countries as visiting or more or less permanent instructors. After Nasser's revolution, in particular, the law and law professors fared poorly in Egypt. Many leading professors and practitioners went elsewhere until the *infiteh*, the end of the Nasser era in 1972. A fairly typical example was a former professor now in practice in Cairo, whose career took him to teaching assignments for several years each in Khartoum, Beirut, and Riyadh (int. 193). Many professors went to Paris or London or the United States, but many also took advantage of the openings in the Gulf region generated by the oil boom. While this hiatus in the power and influence of the law professors within Egypt created problems that plague the legal profession in Egypt today, one consequence was to further enhance the cosmopolitan character and subsequent influence of that generation of elite professors and lawyers.

The leading Egyptian lawyers, most of whom are or have been professors of law, typically came from elevated social backgrounds, had a familiarity with the French legal system, usually spoke both French and English in addition to Arabic (even lecturing in French in law school classes), and produced an influential body of scholarship. Not surprisingly, their encounters with the developing international-arbitration community in the 1970s and 1980s brought them access to that world and to the world of international business. As in Switzerland, the Egyptian arbitration setting is dominated by the law professors. They are the recognized experts in Egyptian law, and therefore Arab law, and that gives them an advantage in north-south cases that, most often, involve at least some question of interpretation of local law.

The professors also provide the nucleus of the international legal community in Cairo. In the words of a successful nonacademic, the community was "built around the professors" (int. 197, 9). There are roughly eight or nine law firms, and no more than 250 lawyers, involved in international business transactions. Most of the firms have one or two leading individuals and a host of subordinate lawyers akin to assistants in the faculty of law. Rarely are there more than 10 lawyers in total in the firm. The well-known professors or retired professors provide a point of entry for foreign parties seeking to do business in Egypt. There are also some law firms that depart from the professor model. There is, in particular, an office of Baker and McKenzie led by two Egyptian partners; the Shalakany office, which has over 40 lawyers and will be discussed below; and the office of Zaki Hashem, which for unusual reasons remained a contact point for foreign businesses throughout the Nasser period. Even the latter two have aspects in common with the professor model. Both are dominated by one leading individual—typically close to or over a retirement age—of high social status, cosmopolitan training, and education: "Even the big firms are really one person" (int. 207, 1). This kind of organization, as we shall see, is difficult to perpetuate.

Finally, the existence of the Cairo Regional Center for International Commercial Arbitration represents another card that Cairo's international legal community can play. The center was established by the African-Asian Consultative Committee in the late 1970s, and it has an impressive facility and the financial support of the Egyptian Ministry of Justice. It is staffed by Dr. M. I. M. Aboul Enein, who aggressively promotes the center and arbitration in general. Given the criticisms of potential biases in Eurocentered arbitration, and the growth in international trade, it is reasonable to expect that Cairo's caseload will grow. Reportedly, as of mid-1993 there had been some forty-two filings in the life of the center, but it is not clear how many of the cases have actually gone to the stage of argument and decision—or how many are truly international. It is hoped by the Cairo community that the long-awaited passage of a new Egyptian arbitration law, modeled on the quite liberal UNCITRAL model law and effective in May 1994, will have a positive impact (Aboul Enein 1994, 129).

Our focal point, therefore is on the role that this nucleus of international lawyers can play in the legal ordering of transnational business involving Egypt and also the Middle East and North Africa. Cairo could become the regional center for arbitration involving disputes between parties from these countries as well as disputes between such parties and others from outside the region. The difficulties of developing such a role come in part from Cairo's international position and in part from the domestic situation in Egypt. Each of these areas will be explored.

Cairo, Arbitration, and the Arab Legal World: Between East and West, North and South

Cairo's international lawyers speak the same language as their counterparts in North Africa and the Arab countries of the Middle East, share a religion, and share an interest in encouraging a greater participation of Arab lawyers in international commercial arbitration. We found, however, that the lawyers from the Arab countries outside the Persian Gulf spoke a somewhat different language about international arbitration than the lawyers from within the Gulf countries, and both differed from the more "legal" position of the Cairenes.

Joining the Arbitration Community

Before focusing on the differences, however, it is important to see how Arab countries (as well as Iran) have more or less bought into the system of international commercial arbitration as the preferred method to resolve disputes that reach the stage of litigation. The connection between Egypt and the international-arbitration community can be traced to leading professors of international law, including Mouhsen Chafik of Alexandria and Ahmed Sadek El-Kosheri of Cairo. Professor Chafik was quite active in UNCITRAL, including the drafting of the arbitration rules and the model legislation that after a decade has finally been enacted into Egyptian law. Professor El-Kosheri became known for his academic work in the 1970s and particularly prominent in arbitration circles after his representation on the side of Kuwait in the Kuwait versus Aminoil arbitration in the early 1980s. It is fair to say that, given the stature of the Egyptian professors and their links to Paris, it was quite natural that they would be among the first from the Arab world to be invited into the international-arbitration community. The same could be true for academic lawyers in Lebanon, who were also well connected to Paris and the French legal establishment.

The situation is more complicated in the other countries about which we have information. As noted before in our case study of an Algerian arbitration

(chap. 5), the Algerians had agreed with the French after Algerian independence
to set up an arbitration tribunal for any conflicts over the oil industry. French-
educated academics in the field of public international law, probably influenced by developments around the ICC, helped shape this institution, which
was the first Algerian adoption of arbitration for potential commercial disputes.[2] While the tribunal never had to be convened before it was terminated
in 1965, its existence helped foster negotiated resolutions of disputes, and it
was felt by both sides to be a success.

The existence of this arbitral institution also led to further arbitration
clauses in contracts with foreign corporations (who could bargain for what
France had). After some bad experiences in arbitration under these later clauses
and some legal efforts to reject arbitration, Algerian lawyers determined that
they must work within the Paris-centered system of arbitration. They settled
on a bargain supposed to ensure the application of Algerian law and arbitration
in neutral sites, such as Switzerland. They became heavy users of the ICC and
retained an American law firm for their legal work.[3] While the attitude about
arbitration was generally pragmatic, Algerian state companies were quite willing to be plaintiffs as well as to defend claims. Several Algerians, most notably
Judge Bedjaoui, now of the International Court of Justice in The Hague, are
now major players in the international arbitral community.

Libya's relatively recent integration into the world of arbitration was by a
similar pragmatic route (int. 121) with links to Paris. There was not a legal
profession equipped to handle international litigation or arbitration in the
1960s, but there were some individuals who had studied law in France. Again
the first experiences with arbitration were not very positive. By 1970 Libya
had already sought to invalidate arbitration clauses in contracts entered into
by any of the Libyan ministries (El-Ahdab 1990, 445). The Libyans found themselves involved in arbitrations almost exclusively as defendants. They objected
to the fact that the state companies were treated as simply private commercial
entities, not public sovereigns with different contractual status. They had

2. The tribunals were "mixed"—one French arbitrator, one Algerian, and one from
a third country.

3. Sonnetrach initiated at least four ICC arbitrations in the 1970s and 1980s, against
Trunkline LNG (Panhandle), a U.S. company (*Platt's Oilgram News*, April 2, 1984;
Petroleum Intelligence Weekly, April 9, 1984; and *Middle East Economic Survey*, April
9, 1984); Enagas of Spain (*Platt's Oilgram News*, July 10, 1984; and *Middle East Economic Survey*, July 23, 1984); two U.S. companies involved in liquid natural gas transportation, TLC and PEPL (*Platt's Oilgram News*, April 25, 1985); and Chemico, a subsidiary of Aerojet General (*Business Week*, June 4, 1979, p. 77). In 1979, Sonnetrach was
involved in fifteen cases before the ICC (*Business Week*, June 4, 1979, p. 77).

difficulty responding to notices of arbitration sent to state entities rather than to the ministry of justice charged with defending arbitrations. And they found it difficult also to deal with the documentation and expertise that was necessary to put up a cogent defense.

Nevertheless, confronted with substantial price differentials in contracts that precluded arbitration versus those that allowed it, the Libyans were forced to take the economical approach and allow the arbitration clauses. Libyan lawyers learned how to gain some concessions and even assert strong counterclaims in the arbitration process. And, even though Libya did not participate in the oil arbitrations concerned with the Libyan nationalizations of the 1970s, Libyan lawyers did have to help defend all the litigation that took place outside of the arbitrations. One knowledgeable observer reported that the Libyan department of foreign litigation was set up in response to the legal tactics used after the oil nationalizations (int. 70, 13). They learned also that they could draw on the services of U.S. law firms to help them defend themselves. This decision led to the American law firm of Curtis, Mallet in New York, and the firm was used to defend against litigation arising out of the oil nationalizations. Soon thereafter, according to an article in the *American Lawyer*, Libya became the largest client of the firm. The partner assigned to Libya gained enough clout in the firm to become managing partner. Despite the popular image of a country of outlaws, it is clear that Libya has learned to play the legal game—using arbitration as a plaintiff and willing to comply with the judgments by arbitrators against it.

Finally, as with respect to Algeria, there are individuals who have made it into the center of the arbitration world. The best-known individual from Libya in this field is Judge Khaled Kadiki of the Libyan Supreme Court, who was educated in France and gained experience in the 1970s defending arbitrations for the Ministry of Justice. He wrote in a recent article, "The earlier hostility of some Arab countries against international arbitration was not due to a contradiction between arbitration and the principles of the Shariah but was rather the outcome of unpleasant experiences certain countries had encountered in the past." He suggested that now arbitration has become "a constant practice and a major instrument of international trade for Libya because their business partners trust specialized institutions such as the ICC" (1992, 42).

Lawyers like Judge Bedjaoui and Judge Kadiki fit very well with the legal culture of the ICC. They are legal scholars, have French legal educations, and even live much of the time in Paris. They provide critical links between the core of the ICC and their countries, and they help to encourage both arbitration and interest in arbitration in their countries. They have been active as well in promoting further scientific interest in arbitration in the Arab world, which is why they and others were part of a major ICC symposium in 1992, "International Arbitration in the Arab Countries."

The situation in the Persian Gulf countries is rather different, at least with respect to Kuwait and Saudi Arabia, where there was no legal profession to begin with at the time that oil brought them into the world of international business. In Kuwait, for example, the royal family drew on foreign lawyers, notably Freshfields in London, for help with the concession agreement in the 1940s, when Kuwait was a protectorate of the United Kingdom. English law had applied in Kuwait in certain circumstances, and the Sharià in others, depending on the defendant, but there were no lawyers. After independence in 1961, Kuwait brought in Professor Al-Sanhuri to draft a constitution and civil code (called a commercial code in order not to formally displace the Sharià as a civil code), and then the judges and all other necessary personnel, as noted before, were imported. The pay was sufficiently high that it was easy to recruit Egyptian and other lawyers and judges. For legal help with petroleum matters, Kuwait relied primarily on foreign lawyers and a small in-house staff led by a British-educated Palestinian, Isa Huneidi, who had come to Kuwait to work initially for Kuwait Oil when it was owned by British Petroleum and Gulf.

The Kuwaitis have also learned to use foreign law firms from the United States or England for major litigation or arbitration cases located outside of Kuwait. That again does not mean that Kuwait has been enthusiastic in its attitude toward arbitration. The problems arising under construction contracts led to a string of arbitration losses in ICC cases in the late 1970s and early 1980s, and a 1981 law sought to prevent further arbitration clauses. The only exceptions to local law and local courts were cases where Kuwait lacked sufficient bargaining power to resist the call for an arbitration clause. And in arbitration, when the parties could not agree on an arbitrator, the law provided that the third arbitrator in Kuwait would be a member of the judicial branch, typically Egyptian and dependent on the state treasury (Saleh 1992, 544).

For local disputes involving foreign companies, the lawyers are again mainly an assortment of imports from within the Middle East and from elsewhere. We can expect that in these settings the local lawyers will turn to the Egyptian professors or legal precedents to help them determine the law. There are some lawyers who are actually Kuwaiti citizens, but they have not acquired an international reputation for their activities in law. A legal career is not high in prestige, and it has not attracted the kind of cosmopolitan individuals who can move easily to the stage of the ICC core in Paris. The Kuwaiti business people tolerate and use lawyers for their business deals, but they seem to bypass Cairo and Paris to go straight to the business-oriented lawyers in the United States and England. We have not found Kuwaiti lawyers who are visibly promoting the ideals of international arbitration. The international legal culture has not found a place within elite Kuwaiti society. Only the business culture has taken hold.

The Saudi Arabian situation is even more revealing. We start again from a position where lawyers did not exist as such until 1970, and the profession has not gained much prestige since then. Responding to the perceived needs of international commerce in the early 1970s, the Saudis created an Institute for Public Administration in Riyadh, and its mandate was to teach law. The institute notably was not labeled as a law school, even though it was staffed with law professors from Cairo. The students were reluctant to study law. There are now Saudi lawyers, and many were educated in Egypt and able to maintain their links with Egyptian professors.

Saudi Arabia also accepts international commercial arbitration now in at least certain circumstances (Saleh 1992, 545). Commentators, however, suggest some serious problems that hinder its effectiveness, such as court interference (Saleh 1992, 193). There are also some Saudi lawyers now connected to an international legal practice and arbitration. The Saudi lawyers in the arbitration world, however, describe themselves more as *hommes d'affaires* or *hommes de confidance* than as pure lawyers (int. 137). And the Saudi lawyers associated with law firms in Saudi Arabia were frequently described as more business than law. According to one Egyptian lawyer who had spent considerable time in Saudi Arabia, big business came all of a sudden to Saudi Arabia, and "everything, including the infrastructure, was unprepared" for the sudden change. What can a Saudi lawyer do under these circumstances when confronted with an international problem? "Call on lawyers from all over." The "owner" of a law firm then becomes essentially a broker for work done outside the firm. The situation is that the owner has the legal business, but not the know-how (int. 193). In the words of another lawyer, Saudi Arabian lawyers profit mainly through "commissions" (int. 201, 27), and another stated that Saudi firms have "other interests" and take a cut—as an "intermediary"—of any work that they send to Egypt or elsewhere (int. 207, 2).

In both the Gulf and the countries to the west of Egypt, local lawyers have found a way to gain access to first-class legal representation, and they also accept on pragmatic grounds the basics of international commercial arbitration (Saleh 1992, 550). But the attitudes on each side of Egypt are otherwise rather different. On the west of Egypt, the attitude is more Continental, as at least local leaders in the profession—typically educated in Paris—promote arbitration and its values. They are embedded in the cosmopolitan legal culture. At the same time, it is more "political" than the attitude found in Egypt, with more concern for "balance" within the tribunal (int. 101, 1). In the Gulf, the legal culture is virtually absent from local power and prestige, which goes with wealth and business. The tendency of the "lawyers" is to invest directly in the legal services of Anglo-American law firms who are closer to business than their Parisian counterparts.

The criticisms from the West are worth describing in more detail. Judge Mohammed Bedjaoui of the International Court of Justice, for example, recently wrote an article detailing the lack of appointments of chairs from Arab countries in international arbitrations conducted under the auspices of the ICC (1992). Out of 212 chairs or solo arbitrators appointed by the ICC between 1986 and 1990 in cases involving at least one Arab party, only 33 were from Arab countries (and out of that group 9 were from Tunisia and 12 from Lebanon—and 2 from Egypt) (15–16). There is thus a call for a more "balanced" arbitration, built on the recognition that the arbitration decision depends more on the composition of the tribunal when the parties are not "comparable" (Bedjaoui 1992). Critics of the ICC from this perspective thus suggest that there is a double standard: Switzerland is neutral in a dispute between parties from Italy and Algeria; Algeria would not be considered neutral in a dispute between parties from Libya and Switzerland (ints. 121, 101).

Another frequent criticism of a politicolegal nature is that the system of international commercial arbitration gives little respect to the distinction found in civil-law countries between administrative law and private law. Contracts with state entities, which typify many of the contracts that are involved in north-south arbitration, are treated differently than private contracts. Arbitrators from common-law countries tend to be ignorant of this characteristic, uninterested, or dismissive. The result is that the state is treated as just another commercial entity.

The latter criticism merges with a broader one found throughout North Africa and the Middle East. The efforts of the negotiators from the Arab countries to provide that the contract will be governed by local law may be thwarted by the doctrines of arbitrators that "break the contract from local law" (int. 101, 2). Among these doctrines are the *lex mercatoria* discussed elsewhere in this study (chaps. 3 and 4).

The political emphasis behind some of the leading arbitration experts from countries like Algeria and Libya contrasts with what we found in Cairo. Cairo lawyers tended to minimize any "political" aspect of arbitration (although they did complain that some European arbitrators were biased or unduly reluctant to apply Arab law) (ints. 205, 195). When asked about criticisms of the International Chamber of Commerce for the infrequency of appointment of Arab chairs (Bedjaoui 1992), however, proponents of arbitration from Cairo typically stated that nationalities are not important—only impartiality (ints. 185, 207). A leading arbitrator from Cairo stated that "arbitration is arbitration, no matter the parties; it is always the same and depends only on 'neutrality, impartiality, and hard work' " (int. 193, 5). One lawyer noted that, while he found that some Europeans were biased against the claims of Arab countries, nationality was not crucial. Referring to his own cases, in which he represented foreign clients, he noted, "In all cases, we did not have a chair who was an Arab" (int. 197, 3). Another observed that a governmental defendant should be considered "a party like any other party" (int. 185, 6). When the Egyptian government complained of losing arbitrations, one professor retorted simply that it was "your fault" (int. 205, 6).

The new Egyptian arbitration law is, in fact, modeled after the UNCITRAL model law, which emphasizes the cutting edge of arbitration reform, as defined by the world of the ICC—party autonomy, detachment from the state, maximum freedom for arbitrators. It is essentially the same law that English and Swedish supporters of more internationalism favored, and in each of those cases they elected not to give up their local legal regime. The Cairo Center, in turn, follows the UNCITRAL Model Rules. The Egyptian leaders, in short, have become strong proponents of the existing international-arbitration community.

The differences between the statements of the Egyptians and those of the more political arbitrators and lawyers from countries with a stronger third-world perspective, however, should not be exaggerated. As several Egyptian lawyers noted to us, one of the leading arbitrators in Cairo at a meeting there ten years ago characterized developing countries as "victims" of an "international mafia" of European arbitrators. And one of the most severe critics today outside of Egypt calls for "completing, not competing" with the ICC (int. 121, 5), another for making the ICC a truly "universal system" (int. 135, 6). As noted below (see also chap. 13), this kind of shift is a recurring theme in the outposts of arbitrators, whether in the third world or elsewhere. Nevertheless, the tone in Egypt remains somewhat less "political" than that found among the leading figures in arbitration in such countries as Algeria, Morocco, Libya, and Syria. Moreover, those leaders outside of Egypt have the skills and contacts to promote their position in the centers of Europe, especially Paris. The pragmatic, businesslike approach found in the Gulf countries remains very different from that found in the other Arab outposts for arbitration.

Limitations of the Middle Position and of Arab Unity

Cairo's middle position between the businesslike attitudes found in the Gulf and the more political approach in Algeria and Libya offers some advantages in the selection of an arbitration site, but we can also see a tendency of the international lawyers to bypass Cairo except for specific advice on Arab or Egyptian law.

It appears fanciful to expect the influence of the Egyptian professors to lead to the establishment of Cairo as a major international legal center for deals between north and south. Cairo may not seem political enough for one group, which can go to Paris in any event to make the case for more balanced arbitration, and it may seem too legal for those from the Gulf who do not care sufficiently for the niceties of legal doctrine and jurisprudence.

Whether or not Cairo can serve to promote Arab unity more generally or perhaps through the Arab League, the current tendency, which was exacerbated by the Gulf War, is toward fragmentation. There have been two efforts in the 1980s to bring together the Arab arbitration community. The first was the Euro-Arab Chamber of Commerce, which has existed for about twelve years. It represented the first effort of potential Arab arbitrators to gain the attention of the ICC. The second effort was the Arab Association for International Arbitration, created in 1991. The Euro-Arab chamber has been oriented toward Algeria, although with quite broad representation, while the Arab Association for International Arbitration is oriented toward Egypt and Lebanon. There are twelve Egyptians in the association, and it is led by a Lebanese, Abdul Hamid El-Ahdab. Evidently the second initiative caused considerable resentment by the Euro-Arab chamber when it was launched in 1991. The groups are not holding together, and there are now further new initiatives from Saudi Arabia. One arbitrator talked of being torn by friends pulling for one or the other group (int. 193). This evidence suggests that there is not much unity at this point in the field of Arab arbitration (ints. 101, 193, 135).

A fragmented Arab arbitration community makes it more difficult for Cairo to build on its strategic intellectual and geographical position. A related problem is that the value of the Egyptian capital—learned professors, well schooled in French law—is declining. First, the French model in international trade is itself declining (Dezalay 1992). The civil-law system's academic strength comes from the control over the domain of pure law—national and international. Egypt probably still controls the jurisprudence that guides the interpretation of contracts in Arab states, including the Gulf states, but, as noted before, the lawyers/businesspeople from the Gulf states do not care very much about pure law. Law is not treated as pure, but rather as connected to business and politics.

Second, the keys generally to international legal business today are drafting and structuring complex transactions, and then mobilizing legal resources in the event of disputes. These are the skills pioneered by the large Anglo-

American law firms, and these firms have no doubt eroded the global authority of academic law in the Continental tradition—and largely divorced it from business practice.

Even with this decline, there remains a subsidiary role suitable, and even lucrative, for professors, namely providing legal opinions to help draft contracts or resolve disputes. This role preserves the integrity and learned character of leading professors, but it means that most of the money and control over the transaction or dispute lies elsewhere. Professors trained to believe that the pure law is most important may feel at the center of attention and influence, but their role is clearly secondary. As their capital declines, they may even become disposable. Large law firms may decide to use their own, in-house experts.

These developments suggest that the elite, internationally oriented legal profession in Egypt may slowly lose its market share in general legal services and in arbitration. The apparent paradox is that many of the leading arbitrators from Egypt will thrive because of the general increase in arbitration business (caused in part by the ascendancy of large law firms in transnational business). In an analogous, even exaggerated parallel to the European law professors, the civil-law professors in Egypt are thriving in the roles of consultant and arbitrator, not so much in the more lucrative role of counsel for big cases.

While there are no doubt exceptions, it is interesting that the four countries described above have all resorted mainly to English or American law firms for important disputes. Less wedded to the French legal system, the relevant lawyers in the other countries quickly learned the advantages of megafirms and their style of advocacy in large international disputes. Business and pragmatic reasons point toward this kind of move. There are strong Egyptian efforts, aided by the French government, to revive French law and the French language for international transactions, but the English language and the U.S. (or now Anglo-American) style is still perceived to be on the ascendancy. It is quite revealing that efforts to promote French commercial law have been packaged along with the teaching of the English language.

Problems in Building a Strong Transnational Legal Profession in Cairo: Dilemmas of an Egyptian Luxury Good

An analysis that focuses on the internal situation of the Egyptian legal profession reveals some of the same problems. The capital that the international group in Cairo has to offer draws on the prominence of the professors, on their cosmopolitan skills acquired from family background and education and travel abroad, and on their expertise especially in the civil-law system. Most of the individuals who have made names in Cairo and Alexandria in the field of international commercial arbitration have precisely these characteristics. They now have a prominence also in the international dispute resolution field, but the question is whether that prominence can be translated into a powerful international legal practice in Cairo (which will in turn lead to more arbitration business originating in Egypt). Egypt has a large domestic market. A program of privatization should lead to a greater role for law firms and for legal services, but the question is whether increases in international trade herald a major expansion of the rather small, and aging, international legal profession in Cairo.

More precisely, there are two related questions. First, is there a strong enough demand for the services offered by the lawyers who inhabit the international legal community in Cairo to support an increase in their number and importance? Second, could the legal community of Cairo, numbering already over one hundred thousand, generate sufficient lawyers to support a substantial expansion in the size of the international sector? These questions are not abstract economic matters. They depend on the way legal services and the legal profession are structured in Cairo—that is, because of who the profession is and where its members come from, in relation to other components of the legal field. Cosmopolitan Cairo lawyers occupy a particular position and offer a particular product. We begin with the supply-side question.

The Supply of Suitable Lawyers for Transnational Legal Practice

Most of the international law firms, as noted before, are organized around the prominent professors (El-Sharkawi, El-Kosheri, El-Kholy). Other firms tend to have similar organizations, according to which the firm is typically dominated by a senior, high-profile, high-status man (Zaki Hashem, Kosheri, Shalakany, Sharkawi, Mansour, Fouad Riad, ElKholy). According to one lawyer commenting on this phenomenon, these are not strictly law firms, and "they will fade away when the principal partner dies" (int. 197, 9). Another lawyer in a professor-led firm referred to one of the rival leading firms as "solo really" (int. 205, 3). And a third stated that "even the big firms are one person really" (int. 207, 1).

The first problem is simply that of replicating the leaders of the firms, whether they are professors or individuals trained by grand professors. The Nasser period from 1952 until 1972 represented a sustained attack on the power and prestige of the legal profession in what had been a golden era. The elite families had sent their children to preparatory schools that emphasized the English and French languages, and they often attended the law schools in Cairo or Alexandria, which were highly respected in the civil-law tradition. The result was the creation and maintenance of an elite legal profession comfortable in the corridors of power. The residue of this elite represents the leadership of the legal profession and the law schools in Cairo today. But the system changed under Nasser (see generally Reid 1981). Elite lawyers often left the country, and law schools lost their prestige as the private economy gave way to public companies modeled more or less on the Soviet model (Reid 1981).

The law schools no longer attracted many individuals of cosmopolitan and elite backgrounds. They typically studied engineering, medicine, or commerce. According to one law professor, every year it was necessary to further simplify the teaching, and the classes became huge (int. 205, 4). Reportedly it was even a Nasser policy to make law schools the haven for the worst students. The law schools have not recovered from this transformation, and as a result there is not much of a pool of individuals who will be acceptable to the current international legal community. As numerous respondents stated, the international legal profession is quite divided from ordinary Egyptian lawyers. Indeed, to underscore the point, the organized bar is currently led by Islamic fundamentalists. And the Cairo Regional Center for International Commerical Arbitration is "totally detached from the local bar" (int. 208, 1).

Despite the five thousand (int. 207) (from one school) or more law students graduating each year, all the Cairo international firms have great difficulty in recruiting. There is not, in the words of one relatively junior partner, "any system to build a second generation" (int. 207, 2). According to another prominent leader, there are many applications to join the firm, but "the quality is not there" (int. 197, 8; also int. 195). The graduates, we were told, "just don't have that analytical mind" necessary for a high-quality practice. The few who are recruited—not infrequently sons and daughters of the prior generation of elite lawyers—are sent abroad for further experience and training (ints. 197, 194). One lawyer said it was easier to take appropriate individuals from other careers and send them to law school than to take the run-of-the-mill law graduates. The problem of language is a particular obstacle in recruiting for these firms, but language is also a surrogate for class and cosmopolitanism. The elite practitioners have defined themselves in a way that makes it very difficult to reproduce. The new generation of elite lawyers is very small indeed.

The Demand for Luxury Legal Services

The problem of the demand for the services is evident from the fact that the international law firms represent almost exclusively foreign clients (ints. 197, 194, 207) who wish to do business with an Egyptian state company. The lowest figure reported to us by this group of firms was of 90 percent of the clientele from outside Egypt (int. 194). Not only does this reliance on foreign demand reinforce the separation of this group from the rest of the legal profession, but also it suggests a relatively limited potential for growth. Baker and McKenzie has a relatively small but apparently successful law firm in Cairo, but Sidley and Austin abandoned its local office after a few years. Several lawyers noted that business was pretty good because only about a half dozen firms serve the foreign clients (ints. 194, 208), but another noted that the "volume" of business was small enough to require firms to have ties with many foreign businesses (int. 207, 1). We also heard the complaint that the "market has not developed that well" (int. 188, 5), and that, in another's opinion, the market was "shrinking, not expanding" (int. 206, 4). Limited to foreign companies doing business in Cairo, general business, not surprisingly, is not growing rapidly.

One crucial aspect of the problem relates to the "luxurious" category of these legal services. The purchase of luxuries—French fashions, haute cuisine, fancy law—requires that a taste be developed for them and that there be sufficient capital to pay for them. The state companies rarely seek the assistance of the Egyptian international lawyers or the transnational law firms used by the richer countries described earlier. They generally use their own lawyers, aided by translators, to enter into international contracts. For most transactions, "The cost is prohibitive to hire one of Cairo's international elite practitioners" (int. 197, 5). More generally, in the words of one partner in a firm, "quality of legal services is not the most important element" in the Egyptian setting for business deals (int. 207, 2).

Lawyers may be very smart and successful, but there is no particular demand for high quality as defined by the international legal community. The international lawyers thus have few clients from privatized businesses, local entrepreneurs, or state companies. The international firms are organized primarily to provide elite services to companies that appreciate and are willing to pay for such services. In Egypt that means foreign entities.

Dilemmas and Emerging Egyptian Models

None of the law firms expect to survive economically on arbitration alone, either as counsel or as arbitrator. They need to rely on a staple of national and transnational business relationships (which will also lead to arbitration business). It is not at all clear that the Egyptians appreciate or can afford the legal services provided by their vintage legal elite and the law firms that have grown up around them. And even if the demand grows substantially, there remains the problem of finding enough lawyers with the background and training necessary to be invited to participate in one of the legal practices described above. The professorial, cosmopolitan elite in Cairo thus appears to be more of a ghetto, confined and limited, than a beachhead able to expand a legal practice in its image.

One cannot predict the future, but the nature of the dilemmas and the possible futures will become more apparent if we discuss the models of law practice that now exist in Cairo. Each reveals aspects of the legal field in Cairo and the potential sources for change. These models will be presented largely through verbatim quotes from interviews, but they should nevertheless be seen as ideal types, intellectualized versions of a complexity in which each inevitably shares characteristics of the others and constantly changes in any event. The selections of quotes suggest the ideal type, but the reality is more complex.

1. The established models. There is no need to spend very much time on the first two models, beginning with the model of the law professor firm. It will suffice to reiterate a point made earlier. In international transactions, the expertise offered by the Egyptian (or French) professors is losing its value. The professors can be called upon to give opinions on the law, and Egyptian lawyers have the capability to ascertain the law of any of the Arab countries, but the most valued know-how today is not expertise in pure academic law (Dezalay 1992). Such expertise may provide a ticket to get into the large arbitrations, but the major work of the arbitration will typically be done outside of Cairo.

The Anglo-American model is clearly gaining ground. While relatively small in terms of numbers of lawyers, Baker and McKenzie has evidently been successful. One option for the Egyptian community is to affiliate with transnational law firms. The elite professors and practitioners, however, are resistant to the notion of becoming subordinate to large firms centered in London or the United States (or even Paris). Those firms, in fact, do not tend to value academic expertise highly except as an entry into the high status of the local profession. There are, however, plenty of rumors suggesting secret alliances, and it is quite conceivable that we could find a pairing of Cairo's firms with their much larger counterparts in other major capitals. What this means is that some individuals and firms will fall into line with the shifting balance of power, but the result would be that they lose their distinctive identities. They would become small branch offices of big firms centered elsewhere.

2. Reconstructing the professional elite by challenging the prevailing models. We found at least one law firm trying very hard to reconstruct the Egyptian professional elite. It sought to avoid the limitations both of the professor model and the specter of being swallowed up by a large multinational law firm. The firm seeks to reconcile business entrepreneurialism with the existing professional hierarchy. As might be expected, only an established insider, a scion of a leading legal family, could attempt such a transformation from inside. The individual who built the firm, Ali Shalakany, arrived at the family law firm after a career encompassing very different activities. Not socialized to "the way things are done," he has given considerable thought to the problems of international law practice and the limitations of Egypt's traditional hierarchy. He stated that the firm had to be restructured to connect it better to the global market, to multinational corporations, and to local bases of support. Without restructuring, he suggested, the Egyptian practitioners of international law "may be bypassed by modern legal developments." He suggested that the academic elite was "dying out," yet it was clear that he was seeking to save the notion of an elite legal profession, even if no longer dominated by the professoriat.

We shall describe the kind of practice his law firm has adopted, but it is interesting to note first how the innovations were greeted by the other groups among the international legal profession. According to Mr. Shalakany, the local bar and the law firms "do definitely dislike us." We found indeed that several of the professors had very little to say that was favorable about this individual or his law firm. One described him as primarily concerned with public relations, not really practicing law, and another hinted strongly of some problems associated with him (ints. 205, 195).

The work of the law firm is, like the other internationally oriented practices, dominated by foreign clients (90 percent multinational corporations, 6 or 7 percent Egyptian, and 3 percent other Arab). The approach to the multinational clients is quite interesting, building on the firm's "semi-monopoly position" among only about "five firms" capable of handling the business in English. "Citibank, Bank of America, American Express—we have all of them as clients. It happens here because of lack of competition."

"It started with Daimler-Benz when GM came in." It would be "unprofessional" to accept the business without both parties agreeing, which they did. The firm is organized to handle this multiple clientele: "Each client has one client manager," and there are "groups organized around specialized fields of activity, such as banking, construction, manufacture, tourism, and other key areas of economic activity." The multinational corporations think this method of practice is "normal, a context with which they are familiar." One by-product is the accumulation of tremendous expertise since, after all, "we have a large number of banks." Not surprisingly, Mr. Shalakany wants "to translate" this learning and expertise into written form.

If forced to litigate or arbitrate for one of the multinational businesses, the firm creates a "task force" that devotes full time to the case. But the big arbitration cases use arbitration as a "tactical weapon to reach settlements":

they "never go to judgment." Professors are helpful, but "we tell them what we need, since we know the legal issues better. . . . We are exposed to more cases" and "can study in depth." This treatment of arbitration contrasts with the ideal of law professors, resolving disputes with elegantly reasoned opinions. It resembles more the attitude of the large English or American firms.

Shalakany's attitude toward local business was that it needed another ten years to develop, but he expressed "faith in a new class of entrepreneurs."He noted that there is an underground economy of private enterprise: "Nasser created millionaires from contractors through their dealings with the public sector" and gave them "room to maneuver"; and this money is available to invest in local business. Tourism and restaurants, for example, will ultimately require and employ the services of large local law firms. But the strong development of private enterprise requires further development of the "technical, managerial sector," which could get a considerable boost if some of the many Egyptian businesspeople and academics who left during the Nasser period were attracted back to Egypt. To this end Shalakany supports an initiative to start a private university, which could address that problem and also help the problem of recruiting that all the internationally oriented firms face.

With respect to recruiting, he shares the opinion that the law schools produce no suitable people. The law graduates have "the lowest possible abilities and social skills." Moreover, "A lawyer who joins the firm is not immediately useful." In order to gain proper cosmopolitan training, lawyers who join the firm are sent abroad with scholarship help from the French and English and heavy subsidies from the law firm. In fact, the law firm recruits individuals who have not even gone to law school, paying them to attend law school in order to later join the firm. Again, a new private law school—perhaps the old French model taught in English—provides some hope.

In order to avoid dominance by a transnational law firm, one idea Shalakany mentioned was to create a pan-Arab law association. It would build connections without a merger, and it would also be possible to affiliate with a "midsize" French firm. In that manner the firm would gain the benefits of ties to the center in Europe without posing a threat to the U.S. firms. Too much of a threat might bring competition or an offer impossible to refuse.

These kinds of links would fit the ideal of a new elite in law, rebuilding Cairo's position as leader in the Middle East. Although in a sense fighting the traditional elite, his activities would if successful recreate that elite and enable it to survive in a new form. In order to succeed, he must create both the demand for and the supply of elite legal services—and then avoid being swallowed up by a large foreign firm that takes advantage of the new market. Making a virtue of necessity, however, he may create an entirely new model;

a new kind of legal product, a hybrid between business consulting and existing transnational law firms. Like an accounting firm, this law firm might advise multiple clients and use that information to serve each one better. We cannot do more than guess whether this represents a viable new option, but clearly this ferment is evidence of the obvious need to innovate for Cairo to maintain a preeminent role.

3. *Challenging the professional elite.* The innovations described above, while quite radical in Cairo, seem tame in contrast to an approach taken by an outsider—an American lawyer-entrepreneur with multiple offices but headquartered in Cairo. There are similarities: both lawyers are "breaking the tradition" and "making enemies," but the American's innovations, if successful, are potentially a greater threat. There is much more entrepreneurialism and risk, and a rather different image of a lawyer. It is worth examining this "carpetbagger" not because he necessarily will change the Cairo scene, but because he shows again what kinds of models can emerge in crises. The accepted legal conventions are shaken up quite a bit in this model of practice.

This lawyer defined his mission as to focus precisely on the underground economy and the need to "turn black money into white," using the "undeclared millions of dollars" of "hidden millionaires." The method is to set up a law practice, advertise, and obtain information on the "wealth, problems, and people." "We start as a law firm and then branch out." Clients and others "get to invest" in business opportunities in which he participates. The ostentatious wealth that is evident around this office and individual helps give confidence to those with the money to invest. Rolls Royces and the like are "special effects tools" that go with the requisite "fully diamond-studded Rolex." The sources of such investment funds are for good reasons not investigated. If government aid is skimmed as the source of wealth to invest in particular projects, for example, "we don't really care. . . . You don't know for sure. . . . You suspect but have no right to." You "put the money to work." He does avoid "drug connections." But lawyers are "not the moral police of the world." One of the key aspects of the practice is to be able to "park $16 or $17 million" in Granada or the Isle of Man. "Nobody will know my clients. . . . I charge for this service."

With entrepreneurial rather than legal elite aspirations, this firm has no great difficulty in recruiting. It advertises for applications to a "good, strong, legitimate American company." There are reportedly twenty-three full-time Egyptian lawyers in the firm and a group of some thirty-one to thirty-two Americans who rotate between the offices in Africa and the Middle East. Two American lawyers work full-time; one has another full-time job with a U.S.

governmental entity. The Egyptian lawyers need training, but the goal is not much more than reproducing a few trappings of elite lawyers and assertiveness: "You need to make them bolder." For their image they receive proper "transportation, two or three suits, briefcases, and beepers." They also are told to frequent the foreign libraries where they "get more confidence, meet more clients." The pay for these Egyptian recruits is low, but more than they would get from an Egyptian firm (300–500 pounds plus bonus, versus 150 pounds per month). As predominantly local lawyers without some of the elite sensibilities of the Cairo bar described before, they can even handle criminal-defense cases. For the image as well as the ideal, we "work with Amnesty" and offer "free legal services to those who cannot afford a legal defense." Law professors are useful, but in a rather subordinate way: "We use them for research" and especially use their students who can do the research "cheaply." The purely "legal" side of this work is therefore kept down in price and not placed at the center of the firm.

The reason for less pure law is clear. The methods of making deals and resolving disputes involve a heavy reliance on personal relations. The way deals are put together can sometimes be complicated, perhaps with special payments, but "if they have struck a deal, I don't want to know about it." There are three or four people between this entrepreneur and any special arrangements. The firm can "use these people" and put together a "cocktail of contacts" that can produce a deal. Arbitration clauses are used, and the firm is not afraid to file lawsuits or arbitrations. Indeed, all potential claims are "filed initially"—it is important that "the client feel protected." But they avoid taking cases too far. The formal law is invoked only as a sideshow. No one wants the "big mess" that could occur if a case gets to court; "no one goes anywhere." The lawyer's job is "find a catalyst" to resolve the dispute. This requires calling on personal contacts. The Egyptians have respect for "ministers" in the government, "sports heroes, singers," a "weakness for big names." He can "always find someone who can talk" from the "roster of people we have on our list." Contacts are important even if somehow the matter does go to court: "we make phone calls, find out about the judge, set it all up, see what it takes, then send an associate."

The competition with this firm is not really the legal practitioners in Cairo or elsewhere. There are several "trading companies," with their own lawyers, who similarly link together hidden capital and potential investments. This lawyer claimed, however, that the Cairo operation is the only one "based on law." The law is not the key part, but it is part of the presentation and kit of the services provided.

We shall discuss some of the implications of this approach below, but note that, as reported, there is no difficulty in finding recruits nor in linking its services to the private market in Cairo. The method simply avoids or transcends the normal constraints of transnational legal practice tied to traditional elite values. Of course, this approach may go too far, may too much alienate important leaders in Cairo to gain a place in the legal hierarchy, but it is not so clear that this entrepreneur really cares about finding such a place. Even that traditionally valued status is challenged by this manner of practice.

There is considerable ferment within the legal profession in Egypt, and that presents an opportunity and challenge to restructure the positions and values in the legal field. New definitions of legal service can emerge, or new professional hierarchies can be created. The four models both relate to each other and compete for a larger share of the field. Each occupies and develops a position that seeks to gain by offering a distinctive kind of profile—U.S.-style multinational firms offering one style of business law, the Cairo professorial elite another, the elite challenger a third, and the business outsider a fourth.

Arbitration will be affected by these contests, since they help determine even how many private clients will use legal services sophisticated enough to call for arbitration, how such arbitrations are settled or fought, and whether Cairo is central or peripheral in these developments.

General Themes

We have taken the Cairo story to a point where we can see the dilemmas faced from the perspective of our basic organizing theme: can Cairo's international legal profession build on its strengths and assume a leadership role in law commensurate with its strategic position in geography and politics? We now will expand our discussion and highlight some of the fundamental themes.

Revisiting the History of Arbitration

As international commercial arbitration takes hold in settings distant from the centers in Paris and London, it tends to replicate the history of the transformations at the core. We get almost a caricature of Europe—in which, indeed, the leading local lawyers have very close ties to Europe through education and even residence. There is a generation of "grand old men," who get into arbitration through academic or other achievements. The leading senior arbitrators in Cairo tend to sound very much like the leading Swiss or Parisian (or Swedish) senior arbitrators, and their law firms even resemble the Lalive firm in Geneva. They emphasize, for example, that "it takes time" to become an arbitrator (int. 205, 6); there is "no shortcut in professional work" (int. 193,

7). They complain that young people with some language skills in French or English think they are arbitrators—they try "to do in three years what you have done in thirty" (id., 7). The elite, as in Switzerland, does not worry as much about building a local arbitration institute or center as about finding a place in the world of the ICC. The Cairo arbitration center, however, continues to fuel the many individuals trying to enter this arena, and in any event the grand old men identify with transnational, not local, practices.

There is also a generation that seeks to make the enterprise of arbitration more general, partly to facilitate greater entry into the field and therefore more acceptance. Not surprisingly, the effort to root the Cairo regional center in the legal culture of Cairo leads to some resentment among the professorial elite, because it means that "unqualified" individuals—particularly in a place where patronage is still quite significant—are given arbitrations. We thus find many of the same tensions that we saw in the story of the ICC, even exaggerated through the new models of legal services we examined. But again, successes of more entrepreneurial practices within Cairo or brought to Cairo from outside can lead to the proliferation of arbitration clauses and arbitration. Thus the Cairo elite may be declining relatively, with no new generation to take its place, but its members retain sufficient stature to thrive, as arbitrators and experts. Indeed, they may do better for longer than their counterparts in Europe, since the mix of law, religion, and patronage in Cairo slows down the process of rationalization. As noted below, "rationalizers" have not gone too far in undermining the claims and capital of the charismatic grand old men.

Access of the Periphery to the Core and of the Core to the Periphery

A story of competition in arbitral centers and rules might be told about Cairo. There are now many notable arbitrators, and the Cairo regional center could be seen as a more Arab-oriented, third-world-sensitive offering than that of the ICC or London. This story, however, would be mistold as pure competition. The better image is not one of carving out a share of the market, but rather of expanding the market and opening a channel to the central institutions and arbitrators

The Cairo story is typical of those found at the outposts of arbitration. The early movers into the international field—often through an almost coincidental brush with arbitration—build on that connection locally and seek also to gain a stronger place in the ICC world. They may start as outsiders. We know, for example, that the impetus offered initially for the Cairo regional center was a desire to offer a real alternative to Europe that could be sensitive to the needs of the third world. This was the reason for the Asian-African Legal

Consultative Committee's effort in the 1970s both in Cairo and in Kuala Lumpur. The history of the regional center reported in the center handbook provides the story:

> Experience has shown that arbitration held under the auspices of these institutions [located in the West] were [sic] unduly prolonged and costly and procedures adopted by certain associations of trade at the time worked unfavorably to the interests of nationals of the developing countries. (Regional Center n.d., part 2).

Now, however, the Cairenes preach the virtues of the present system of international commercial arbitration, essentially as practiced at the core in Paris and London, and help to gain converts to this form of dispute resolution. They also work to gain local judicial acceptance for arbitration and for the legislative reform that was required to upgrade the local law to the UNCITRAL Model Law—the state of the art. These activities gain legitimacy *for arbitration* locally and legitimacy *for local leaders* in the centers of arbitration. They help quell fears raised by the leading arbitrators in Europe that, for example, Arab arbitrators are too "political" or not "independent" enough (Lalive 1984, 350–51).

It is not surprising that Professor Kosheri, the best-known Cairo arbitrator and member of ICCA, was at one time highly critical of the ICC, nor that later he was "the first to confront" a position taken by the Egyptian court of cassation that undermined international commercial arbitration (int. 197, 2). As several lawyers suggested, no doubt with a touch of envy, he was critical of the arbitration mafia until he joined it (int. 198). The result of such activity—by no means unusual in the outposts where arbitration gains a foothold—is that the leaders in the outpost get closer to the core, with resultant symbolic (and often material) rewards. The price they pay, however, is that they open up direct lines to the core from Cairo (or other outposts) and give up much of their distinctive identity. They do not in fact compete, but rather, as noted before, help to "complete" the arbitration community.

The Cairo regional center, therefore, seeks acceptance by the core institutions and arbitrators. This center increasingly offers a service that closely resembles, at a lower price, the service offered elsewhere in the international-arbitration community. The "third-world" impulse that helped to lead to the establishment of the center is nowhere evident in the current depictions. And it is not surprising that, according to one insider to the Cairo center, other Arab countries do "not use" the center, "maybe preferring Paris" (int. 208, 2). Another lawyer stated that local lawyers "prefer Paris to Cairo" (int. 199, 2), and the leader of a businesslike firm stated that he "preferred Paris" as a "first choice" because of the ease of enforcement of an ICC arbitration held there (194, 5). A state company lawyer underscored this point by referring to a list of fifteen top arbitrators who would be acceptable as the chair of an important arbitration—none were Egyptians.

We cannot have good statistics on this issue, but it is clear that the opening up of Egypt has the effect of helping big arbitration cases to find their way to the European centers. We can further suggest (and explore more theoretically in chapter 13) that the successful arbitrator or arbitration lawyer also tends to get attracted to the center. Again not surprisingly, many of the Cairo arbitrators (and others from Arab countries) spend considerable time in Paris, and some even have offices there.

A further example in Cairo is the effort to set up an Islamic Arbitration Center at the University of El-Azar. One might expect such a center to promote the need to include more Islamic law within arbitration, leading to results more consistent with that law. In fact, the story is no different than the one just told. The first impetus was to offer a real alternative, but, in order to build legitimacy in the international community, the proponents of the new center now emphasize how Islamic law will really lead to no difference in outcomes. Islamic contract law is reportedly the same in practice as that found in the civil systems, and even the *lex mercatoria* can be applied in any arbitrations that may make their way to the Islamic center. The unmistakable theme is that almost all the differences—except perhaps the prohibition of interest—can be eliminated to gain international acceptance.

The outposts give up their distinctive identities as fundamental alternatives, but of course there remain differences—in price, in legal expertise, and in the institutional details. The result is not so much real competition with the core, however, as the creation of more alternatives and more choices within a generally accepted framework. We see, in fact, the continuing development of one aspect of "arbitration expertise"—how to know and use the differences between places, institutions, and arbitrators. There is competition, but the "competitors" cannot get into the field without buying the basic rules developed and maintained in the ICC world.

Making It by Faking It

The noise created by the efforts to reform laws and gain attention and legitimacy for international commercial arbitration gives the appearance of considerable arbitration activity, whether it exists or not. To some extent the activity is misleading. It takes a long time to build an arbitration practice or center. It takes less time to write, engage in professional controversies, attend conferences, and learn to speak the language of arbitration.

With respect to Cairo, we found mixed descriptions of how much real arbitration activity takes place at the Cairo regional center. But there is no doubt that there are many conferences, workshops, and training sessions. One characteristic of such sessions is that leading figures in the world of arbitration are brought to Cairo, adding stature to the Cairo center, gaining attention to Cairo, and not incidentally letting Cairo have a look at the stars of the core—available for important, high-stakes cases.

Observers of this activity are bound to bolster the impression that arbitration is the natural way to resolve transnational business disputes, and the more people who have that impression, the more the market will grow. It is in the nature of a self-fulfilling prophesy. This phenomenon—not unusual in professional activities—is one of "making it by faking it."

The ICC core, we can note, sits on a huge amount of "legitimacy capital." It draws on the grand masters of arbitration and elite members of the legal profession from many different places. In the sometimes shadowy world of international capital and disputing, this access to legal prestige—legitimacy—may be the only immediate payoff for those who buy into the ICC world. In most cases it still takes a long time to grow an arbitrator and perhaps longer to grow an arbitration in a new arbitration outpost. There must be a perception that a new center is viable, a willingness to name it in an arbitration clause, and then a dispute. The long period of waiting offers only symbolic benefits, but the fancy symbols of arbitration can provide a window dressing for other more immediately profitable activities.

Lawyers who may not even get money from arbitration can present themselves through arbitration to the international community. They can hide some of their less appealing and prestigious activity in the shadow of a reputation in the field of international commercial arbitration (int. 175, 30). In Cairo, for example, there were a number of references to "licensing" and the requirements necessary to allow a foreign company legally to do business in Egypt (int. 207). The "carpetbagger" we described earlier also advertised an expertise in international arbitrations, but in fact his main work was putting together deals. In Paris, among some of the Arab lawyers from outside of Egypt, we found the best examples of this phenomenon (which is difficult to investigate directly). One individual noted simply that through arbitration contacts he gained a valuable Middle Eastern client from one of the oil-rich countries who needed help in investing in Asia (int. 135).

This phenomenon is by no means limited to lawyers from the periphery. We were told in Switzerland, for example, that much of the profitable activity in Geneva during a time when arbitration was emphasized was simply the routine opening and servicing of Swiss bank accounts for individuals conceal-ing their assets. It is probably fair to say, however, that there is more inter-change between law and other ways of making deals among cultures that are less legalized in the Western sense.[4] As we suggested before, the situation outside of Europe is not fundamentally different, only a kind of caricature of practice in the centers of the legal world.

One Arab lawyer we interviewed referred specifically to other Arab lawyers with arbitration reputations in Paris who, he suggested, were mainly promot-ing their business deals (int. 135). A lawyer we interviewed from the Gulf who was active in arbitration circles referred to himself as primarily an *homme d'affaires* or an *homme de confidence* (int. 137). He puts together deals for those who want to do business in the Gulf or do business in the West from the Gulf. He even invoked arbitration to get his commission from someone he helped to purchase junk bonds. He noted that his main role is to see that contracts work out, however, and that requires informal personal relations more than formal litigation or arbitration.

The significance of the luster created by involvement in the arbitration community was mentioned explicitly by another individual we interviewed in Paris. He described his work as more *relations personelles* than law. His main role was as "coordinator" for investments for clients who want to invest from or into the Arab countries. He could not say just how much arbitration work he did, but he "would like to develop it." He emphasized that there is a "quality of people" in arbitration, an *"elite juridique"* (int. 128, 3). It has a "certain moral prestige" in addition to the satisfactions from the work; "it gives you a certain aura of importance in the legal community" (id., 3, 4). He lamented (but obviously recognized the temptation of) the practice of putting *international arbitrator* on calling cards. He also worried about the desire of everyone to "get a piece of the cake" in arbitration (id., 6).

This feature of arbitration is evident in another example. We were told that the nucleus of the Euro-Arab Chamber of Commerce was actually a group of Arab lawyers in Paris who were set up to investigate whether companies seeking to do business in Arab countries had relations with Israel (int. 135). Obviously it was more attractive to constitute these individuals into a group to promote Arab arbitration. Indeed, it is even possible that the unattractive activity was enabled to continue *because* of the legitimacy of arbitration.

4. David Sugarman provides an excellent historical example in England of how solic-itors played a very similar role in gaining access to wealth and opportunities to make money through the provision of their legal services (Sugarman 1995).

Arbitration provides a reason to travel, to hold meetings, and to extend contacts.[5]

What is also evident, however, is that these lawyers who may use arbitration (and their legal credential) to camouflage some of their business activities join a network of individuals linked through arbitration. They get to know each other through this connection, and it serves to spread the influence of arbitration and bring them other notable international contacts. From one perspective, this phenomenon simultaneously upgrades the network and promotes arbitration and the internationalization of law. It is interesting that even those who profit under the legitimacy of arbitration can be critical of greedy arbitrators who undermine the image of the system (int. 128).

Returning to Cairo, we can describe the way international legal practice covers unofficial or underground activity, but we must also see how that cover transforms the nature of that activity. The detailed interview of the American lawyer-carpetbagger gives a very good basis to examine this process, which is another version of making it by faking it. Homage to the law helps to make the law.

There is a considerable amount of unofficial wealth in Cairo. The wealth is found among individuals in the government and elsewhere. In addition, there is much wealth that is not in an easily marketable form. Much that is valued and valuable in the economy remains based to a great extent on social connections and "cocktails of contacts." The hierarchy is based not on position in the capitalist system, but rather on role in the political party (as in Nasser's bureaucratic system or the Soviet Communist Party) or in aristocratic families (as seen also in the Gulf royal families).

We also know that modern capitalism has been embraced officially and is, in any event, transforming the Egyptian economy. The individuals with political capital or social capital from the clientele system can see what appears inevitable in the long or medium term. The more general market economy will undermine their positions. As might be expected, they will try to convert their positions into more generally marketable forms of capital. At the same time, they will cling to their former situations—try to maintain their value as long as possible—to enhance the conversion rate.

They can accumulate capital to some extent by rationalizing and formalizing their informal power. They naturally rely less, for example, on reciprocal

5. In fact, we can suggest that this network of dealing around arbitration is analogous to the earlier period when lawyers organized around the legitimacy and activity of the courts could both build the legitimacy of the legal system and use their contacts and personal relations with other lawyers to engage in other kinds of brokering activity that may or may not have required the courts.

favors over long periods of time—an exchange that keeps the position and power of those at the top of the hierarchy. Rather, they use their position to gain monetary reward, whether by sharing in investments, consulting fees, or simple baksheesh. The dilemma for them, however, is that the official system permits no easy outlet for the wealth accumulated by these kinds of transactions. We therefore find a vast underground economy with no direct road into the official capitalist system. The law firms of the Cairo professional elite will not invite this business. It is literally beneath them.

The American carpetbagger, however, and presumably others like him with or without legal training, rationalize the underground economy and at the same time help to promote the official market economy. They mix the resources of the underground economy with the institutions above ground. There is more formal banking and accounting, and there is even a dispute resolution system built on the network of contacts. The state system of dispute resolution cannot be used, but the use of contacts "on our list" can be as effective. The money goes through parallel, unofficial bank transactions and then is put to work in entrepreneurial initiatives. Thus the process helps to create entrepreneurs and a new generation of lawyers and bankers to serve them.

The systematic use of the contacts from social hierarchies outside the official market system, however, is bound to use up those contacts. Individuals who have standing convert their standing increasingly to cash, but explicit cash transactions undermine their social authority and make them appear dependent, the mouthpieces of foreign businesses. The market values take over. The logic of this sequence of events is thus to foster the values of the official market and the transnational rules and institutions that promote and sustain it. The shadow banking and shadow law hides but brings to the surface money and business for official banking and official law.

Indeed, we can speculate that the next step, as seen in Italy, is for the custodians of formal law to investigate and denounce the corruption of the system that places an informal market value on social contacts and political positions. An investigation and prosecution of the offenders then paves the way for still another stage in the rationalization of the economy and polity under a legal regime.

From Community Private Justice to Offshore Private Justice

With respect to arbitration, we can see a parallel story, the move from unofficial, informal private justice to formal, official private justice (Hay 1975). Many of our respondents in Paris and Cairo described an informal private justice found in the traditional Arab world. This justice exists in the form of vendettas, but also in forms of conciliation (Saleh 1992). In disputes discussed among families in front of a local notable, it is still customary to write blank checks for the notable to use at his or her discretion (int. 198). We also heard in Paris from an individual who reported of many "ad hoc" arbitrations, where he as arbitrator may already have known the parties and simply sought to resolve the dispute (int. 128). Such a system, as noted above, depends on social hierarchies and connections to succeed.[6]

To the extent such a system is breaking down through the spread of capitalist legal institutions and markets (e.g., Islamic Arbitration Center), official arbitration provides another way to have private justice. It can be the legalized private justice through arbitration and negotiation that is found in the world of the ICC, or even more so that of the rather comprehensive rent-a-judge system for commercial disputes in Stockholm. To some extent arbitration is simply a substitute for litigation in such systems—a parallel court. Discussions of special commercial courts, including in Cairo, point to the same end.

It is doubtful, however, that "formal" arbitration in Cairo has completely left behind the system based more on social hierarchies. The move to formally rational decision making is very much a process. Arbitration is almost by definition located between formal law and other means of regulating relationships. We should not forget that, despite all the rhetoric of sameness between the ICC and Cairo, arbitration in Cairo is probably still less rationalized than most ICC arbitration (Saleh 1992, 204). The less rational element cannot be eliminated; it continues in some ICC arbitrations that, for example, require the stature of the "grand old men." But the point, finally, is that the move from informal private justice to formal private justice is less complete in Cairo than in Geneva or Paris. Since the charismatic qualities of grand old men tend to be in greater demand when arbitration depends more on personal than rational bases of legitimation, it is not surprising that arbitration in Cairo helps to keep the careers of grand old men flourishing.

Conclusion

The general theme is that Egypt and indeed the other countries of North Africa and the Middle East are increasingly being brought into the international legal system. The conversion to arbitration, however reluctant in some cases, opens up new channels to the central core of arbitration, builds a network of arbitration boosters, and makes a kind of renaissance for charismatic

6. Investment in technical processes such as mediation or negotiation can in fact help social groups or business groups fight against the universals of the law, since the lack of autonomy of such approaches can make it easier for "business" or "social necessity" to be taken into account in the resolution of disputes.

arbitrators otherwise in retreat through the trend toward legal rationality. The "making it by faking it" around arbitration and around international legal practice has the effect, described earlier, of building an international legal profession and bolstering the role of the law. Despite the power of Islam and Islamic law, reflected in strong resurgences of fundamentalism, the institutions of the international market economy increasingly bring converts to a world religion of law. These phenomena necessarily affect the structure of the legal field in Cairo and elsewhere. This field is bound to change in response to transnational developments. The irony in Egypt, however, is that the existing legal elite, found in international law firms, recognized throughout the world and built around leading academic lawyers, faces daunting obstacles if it is to maintain its position and power.

12

Law at the Frontier: Hong Kong and Transitions from One Imperialism to Another

For more than 150 years Hong Kong has been a site where East and West meet, and in particular where the East has met Western capitalism. The British took Hong Kong from China at the behest of opium traders preaching the virtues of Adam Smith and the free market against Chinese emperors who sought to interdict trade they thought harmful to their subjects. With the return of Hong Kong to China coming in 1997, it is difficult to predict how the law and the legal profession will emerge from the change. On one side, there is an English colonial legal system dominated by the English language and a legal profession oriented toward London. On the other side is a rapidly changing Chinese legal system. Hong Kong's six million people may be the beneficiaries of a new legal synthesis between East and West, but their history and the trend of developments make it easier to predict some form of legal domination—a shift from one imperialism to another. An autonomous legal system offers some security for the Western values of democracy and the rule of law that many Hong Kong solicitors and especially barristers have assimilated, but, again, the prospects for that autonomy are rather uncertain.

The story of Hong Kong arbitration—our point of entry into the issues of Hong Kong legality—is a chapter in this larger story of law and the legal profession in Hong Kong. The future of arbitration is clearly dependent on the future of law. There is an arbitration center that is well funded and in very capable hands, and there are very good reasons to expect it to continue to operate successfully after 1997. The first challenge for arbitration, however, is to move from a relatively peripheral position in Hong Kong business and politics to a more central one. But even that level of success would raise other issues. The futures could be radically different, depending on the way that the legal system and the legal profession take shape. Hong Kong arbitration could develop its own strong identity, supported by a legal system with some autonomy from the rest of China, or it could become a branch office of the general Chinese arbitration system.

Any report on "contesting legalities" in Hong Kong must confront the question of the role law plays generally in social and economic life in Asia (see Jones 1994). Unlike the situation in the other countries that we have studied, including Egypt, law has never gained a strong position in Hong Kong or China in regulating the state or the economy. Formal law, as is often said, is only in its infancy in the People's Republic of China, and Hong Kong—at least Chinese Hong Kong—is also said to be relatively unlegalized. The typical explanation is cultural. *Guangxi*—or networks of personal relations—are said to define Chinese (or sometimes Asian) business relations whether in China, Hong Kong, or wherever the Chinese have set the tone for business developments.[1] The primacy of personal relations comes ostensibly from the Confucian tradition and its hostility to conflict, law, and lawyers.

We cannot do a complete study of business disputing,[2] but an examination of the dynamic situation in Hong Kong and China in law and arbitration allows us to see that this cultural explanation is far from adequate.[3] *Guangxi* is a specific historical product that can change and is changing. It certainly exists, and as ideology it has numerous proponents, but *guangxi* coexists increasingly with other "legal" approaches. The career patterns of those we interviewed and the responses to our questions show that law has gained ground in both China and Hong Kong.

A fascinating feature of the recent Hong Kong story, in addition, is that it is both about a growing role for the legal profession and law and about tensions between different and competing legal orders. Both dimensions are part of an internationalization in which the multinational law firms, especially those from the United States, have been key players. A characterization of Hong Kong's position as between British and Chinese domination is therefore accurate, but incomplete, since the possibility of a U.S. "symbolic imperialism" through law and business is also quite present and visible.

This chapter will proceed in four parts, focusing on the specific history that gave Hong Kong and China their structures with respect to law. The first part will focus on the very weak position of law that emerged out of the original colonial traders who set up and shaped the structure of Hong Kong society, and that characterized also the situation of the Hong Kong Chinese.

---

1. The same representations about culture and law are also made, in different terminology, about Japan and Korea (cf. Fallows 1994).

2. We will report much about business disputing that we learned from our interviews, but we lack direct access to the world of business within the various Chinese communities. We did ask questions about changing business and legal developments, and we can advance some propositions, but our look is biased by our limitation to sources that operate easily in the Anglo-American legal world.

3. For a powerful critique of the "orientalism" found in the cultural explanation of the Chinese family firm, see Greenhalgh 1994 (based on research in Taiwan).

The story will shift in the second part to the Chinese mainland. The Hong Kong and Chinese stories are, in law as in politics and economics, strictly connected. The third part will then bring these historical developments to the present structure of Hong Kong, focusing on the dilemmas that confront the belated efforts to build an independent "state" and "law." The fourth part returns to our subject of international commercial arbitration, relating the history and current structure of Hong Kong legality to the prospects for international commercial arbitration in Hong Kong.

Hong Kong and Law's Marginality
English Colonial Merchants Set the Tone

The English influence in Hong Kong promoted not the rule of law, but a paternal system in which law played a very marginal role. Hong Kong was taken by the English in 1841 to serve as an entrepôt to facilitate trade with China. "Traders," therefore, had "the greatest stake in the colony" (Chan 1991, 9) and defined its character. Made famous as taipans of companies that still exist—Jardine, Matheson, and Co., John Swire and Sons—the traders, who built their positions in the opium trade, had little use for law throughout most of the history of Hong Kong. Seeking to turn their wealth into status, they worked to recreate in Hong Kong the paternal lifestyle of English country gentlemen, with clubs, horse racing, high society, and an emphasis on family connections. Law served only as a kind of ornament for the gentlemanly lifestyle.

The colonial government, dedicated to trade, protected the traders and their form of relational or family capitalism. The trading elite became the mainstays of the administrative machinery that governed Hong Kong both formally and informally (Chan 1991). Conflicts in this very small colony could be resolved through personal interactions maintained through such social organizations as the Hong Kong Club or the Jockey Club, or through family favors extended over time. Law was not considered necessary for conflict resolution.

If there was ever a demand for formal law, moreover, the colonists could look toward London. The barristers and solicitors there were higher in status, better educated, and more authoritative than any local lawyers. The local members of the legal profession were neither numerous enough nor independent enough to rival the London professions. Indeed, until very recently, the only way to qualify for the practice of law was to do so outside of Hong Kong, under the rules of the English legal system. The hierarchy was thus reinforced by formal rules.

The status of law suffered further since neither the expatriates who came to Hong Kong nor the locals who gained the titles of lawyers worked to build an independent legal profession. They came prospecting for wealth (note the example of the carpetbagger from the previous chapter). As one observer noted in the late nineteenth century, professionals came to Hong Kong "with the intention of retiring from the Colony at the first convenient opportunity" (Chan 1991, 34, quoting Shepherd 1893). Building a Hong Kong professional society was not a priority for anyone.

While legal institutions were put in place by the colonial regime, they were largely marginal, even decorative. The justices of the peace, for example, were notables rewarded with a title and status, but the office did not create an independent legal power. Justices of the peace belonged to the same merchant elite that controlled political power in all its manifestations in Hong Kong. The network of institutions that gave Hong Kong its basic system of governance and business simply did not distinguish legal authority from other forms of authority. Lacking sufficient lawyers for an interest in an independent professional class (int. 225), legal practice was quite marginal, low status, and subordinate to business.

The descendants of the opium traders therefore continued to have little to do with the law in their business relations. They produced no strong local legal system and practically no state. Lawyers existed in name, and there was a colonial court system modeled on the English; but power and authority came from elsewhere than the law. It came from the networks of personal relationships organized around the great taipans and their business organizations. The formalities of law, in short, had very little to do with the governance of Hong Kong or the business relationships centered there.

Law's Marginality and the Hong Kong Chinese

The Hong Kong Chinese also did not promote law through most of Hong Kong's history. We do not need to invoke the cultural trump card of the Confucian tradition, however, to see why the Chinese reinforced rather than challenged the factors that kept colonial business and governance personal and informal. The Chinese population had very good reasons to settle into the same pattern. When the Chinese merchants gained economic power equal to that of the expatriate taipans late in the nineteenth century, it was no surprise that they maintained the same kind of relational, familial capitalism. The institutions were not exactly the same, since the English clubs were not open to the Chinese; but the Hong Kong Chinese produced another set of informal institutions and became justices of the peace in support of essentially the same patrimonial system (Chan 1991). The differences were in appearances. The English expatriates sought to replicate the society of country gentlemen, while the Hong Kong Chinese dressed themselves up as mandarins to note their elite status. The aristocratic trappings were in any case merely components of the merchant society.

Within the merchant society, however, the Chinese merchants in Hong Kong found themselves in an ambiguous position. They were situated, after all, between two competing empires. They typically built their economic power by playing contradictory roles and building complex alliances characteristic of colonial outposts. As captured in Clavell's novels, they often served the taipans explicitly as their compradors, translating both the language and the ways of doing business between the Chinese and the Europeans (Clavell 1966, 1981); yet, while occupying this subordinate role in the service of the taipans, they also built their own powerful business organizations. They promoted the European traders and their own, obviously related, form of trade.

Their links to the Chinese and to the Europeans placed them in a precarious position. When their wealth finally earned them representation in the administrative machinery dominated by the taipans, they again had to play a double role. They spoke for the Chinese while working within and for the system that subordinated the Chinese. No doubt this difficult and ambiguous role was easier to manage through networks of personal relations than it would have been if brought explicitly out into the open. There was little incentive to formalize this position through an emphasis on law. Their positions and power depended on the maintenance of a relational capitalism built on ambiguous and informal networks.

The specific history of the Chinese pattern of emigration and persecution further militated in favor of an emphasis on personal and familial ties. The Chinese immigrants in Hong Kong suffered from the occupation of the Japanese, the Chinese civil war, persecution as a minority throughout Southeast Asia, and, later, the Chinese Cultural Revolution. The sense of precariousness that must have surrounded existence in Hong Kong made the security of family ties even more attractive. The strategy of closure is a strategy of survival.

The histories of the expatriate English and the Hong Kong Chinese, in sum, support the quite marginal position of law in business and politics in Hong Kong, and for most of Hong Kong's history, there was no impetus to change. None of the potential candidates for a movement toward legality had any incentive to promote change in that direction. There were of course lawyers, but the numbers were very small. Even by 1971, there were reportedly only about 150 solicitors, half of whom were of Chinese descent, and there were only about twenty-five barristers (int. 231, 3). The fact that the legal system operated in English, with judges appointed mainly from among the English community on the basis of their role in the government, made the legal system even more remote from the Chinese-speaking population. The "imported state" (Badie 1993) in Hong Kong was mainly a gloss on the personal and familial relations in a merchant-dominated society.

The merchant class in Hong Kong—Chinese and European—has remained the dominant group from the establishment of Hong Kong society until the present, using essentially the same institutions that sustained their power in the nineteenth century (int. 225). They have had little use for law (int. 231, no litigation among Chinese), and the legal profession historically has done little to carve out any independent role. Persons trained as professionals became successful for most of Hong Kong's history by moving into business—turning barristers or doctors into merchants. There was therefore no "independent professional class" (int. 225), and until recently not even a local system for legal education. There are signs of change, but it is easy to understand the weak role for the law and the legal system in Hong Kong.

Growth in the Legal Profession

The legal profession began to attract more recruits after World War II, including growing numbers from the Chinese population. An increase in numbers does not necessarily lead to the assertion of professional independence, but it makes it easier for such an effort to be made. There were at least two potential sources on the Chinese supply-side. The first source traces from the wealthy Hong Kong Chinese families who emigrated from Shanghai in the late 1940s. Since they had been relatively comfortable with the legal profession as a potential career within the Chinese elite (Lee 1994), they probably generated a certain number of solicitors and barristers from among their children—even if the children had to be educated abroad. Second, the older Hong Kong families, perhaps seeing the potential for professionals serving the new business elite, may also have gained some interest in legal education and legal careers.

At the same time, growing prosperity as an international business center promoted a demand for at least some legal services. The Hong Kong real estate boom that began in the 1960s and 1970s, in particular, caused the volume of conveyencing work to increase dramatically (int. 230). As in the English system, solicitors were heavily involved in conveyencing, and it was potentially quite lucrative. Indeed, the real-estate boom provided the anchor for some very prosperous Hong Kong Chinese law firms and their variety of ancillary business practices.

The expatriate firms, including the Deacons firm and Johnson, Stokes, and Master, were also able to gain work in real-estate transactions. They, however, were more oriented to litigation[4] and the service of English interests in Hong

4. "The contentious business is primarily expatriate" (int. 216, 1).

Kong (int. 231) than their Chinese counterparts. Legal practices grew, but there was still not much of a commercial sector within the bar or the solicitors branch. There was perhaps an increase in demand for commercial litigation in the 1970s, but the business typically went elsewhere: "English QCs would come to handle the cases" (int. 231, 4).

The most important potential changes in demand, discussed below, became important in the 1980s. In the first place, some of the rich Hong Kong businesses began to restructure themselves and to diversify into the world market. Such business changes, managed often by new generations of MBAs, brought more lawyers, including the Chinese-speaking ones, into their transactions (ints. 220, 230, 235). In addition, legal practice was changed by the development of China trade and investment around the same time. Both these changes internationalized Hong Kong legal practice, further changing the structure of the profession. New transactions and new players transformed the Hong Kong legal landscape.

The American law firms—key engines of legal transformation—came in two waves, first in the late 1970s with the opening up of China trade. The second, which followed a retreat or at least cutback from Hong Kong after the Tiananmen Square incident, has occurred only in the past several years. The first U.S. group represented the pioneers, discussed below, and included Baker and McKenzie and Coudert. The second invasion, along with the British and Australians, came in part to engage in sophisticated financial transactions both for Hong Kong and for China.[5] It is indicative, for example, that Cravath, Swaine, and Moore; Debevoise and Plimpton; Skadden, Arps; and Sullivan and Cromwell are all quite recent arrivals (Page 1994, 27; int. 221). These firms are not the pioneers, and they show that the high end of Hong Kong practice is now much more technical and sophisticated.[6] U.S. law firms now are pushing even to gain the same opportunity to practice local law available to the English (Page 1994, 26–27).

In addition to the major influx of U.S. law firms (and also an increased number of English and other firms), there has been the growth in demand for

5. See Page 1994a; Budden 1993. It is interesting that several sources (e.g., int. 230) noted that one of the leading local Chinese firms, Low and Low, brought in Slaughter and May from London to help with corporate work rather than diversify from conveyencing. They soon regretted that decision and sought to recapture their market share.

6. The big six accounting firms are now settled in Hong Kong after the "first wave" failed (int. 221), and the investment bankers have also become prominent. The close symbiosis between Wall Street law firms and investment bankers is noted by Page: "Many of these moves have been client driven, principally as a consequence of U.S. investment bank interest" (1994a, 27).

Chinese speaking lawyers. According to Page, "The non-official, but neverthe-less prevalent, process of Chinafication, whereby firms are actively building up their Hong Kong Chinese staff, has been recognized as an imperative, espe-cially as Hong Kong's business scene becomes progressively more Chinese in both composition and outlook" (1994, 26). The Hong Kong international legal scene is thus becoming both more technical and more Chinese speaking.[7]

While Hong Kong's legal profession has begun to develop along with Hong Kong itself, the role of *most* practitioners has continued to be relatively mar-ginal, linked generally to relatively routine litigation and real-estate transac-tions used in part as a vehicle to build other ancillary businesses. Again, as noted before, a key question is whether the conditions have become ripe for the development of an independent legal profession. Certainly the number of lawyers has increased greatly in the decade of the 1970s and 1980s. There are now some four thousand solicitors and five hundred barristers (int. 220, 7–8). Probably the social status of lawyers has also improved. Nevertheless, Hong Kong society has been slow to produce any professional class to challenge or complement the holders of wealth. And now, more than before, the question of the role of *law* in China and the role of China in Hong Kong law is critical to future developments in Hong Kong.

Mainland China, the United States, and Hong Kong

The Hong Kong story has never existed apart from that of China. Hong Kong was created for the China trade. The population of Chinese immigrants in Hong Kong gave it the population necessary to build factories in the 1960s, and the entrepreneurs needed to build very large industries. No doubt the fact that China was Communist contributed also to the buildup of Western investment in Hong Kong.

The absence of a strong legal tradition in China is also part of the Hong Kong story. China met capitalism, after all, through the opium traders who promoted Hong Kong initially, and law did not play an important role histori-cally in outside trade. There were places where lawyers and law developed in conjunction with international trade, with Shanghai one well-documented example (Lee 1993). But with no real developed local tradition, the lack of any real distinction between law and social power, and the problems of the identification of lawyers with the West, it is easy to see how the Communists

7. In the words of a legal recruiter in late 1993, "there is now a much greater body of home-grown talent within Hong Kong companies and financial institutions who are happier doing business in their native tongue," in part because "many of the Hong Kong based companies now entering the corporate finance market are traditional family-run enterprises" ("Future Grim" 1993).

could step into the role of hostility to lawyers. China's economic-development strategy then pushed lawyers and law further away in the interests of technical skills and economic development. Again, however, we need not blame hostility to law on Communism or on Confucianism. These ideologies served to reinforce the very weak position that law occupied, but that position resulted from the particular history of China's relations with the West.

The importance of the particular history is also clear from subsequent developments.[8] The new interactions with the West, which began in the late 1970s, are transforming the cultural obstacles to law. The specific features of the new China trade, and especially the interactions with the United States and its law, are changing China and changing Hong Kong. Law has become increasingly important by a variety of measures.[9] Law may begin to rival Communism—perhaps more precisely, the legal profession may rival the Party—as the leading legitimating authority. Law may provide a kind of neutral ground between the competing national elites. As we shall see, there is also evidence that the U.S. version of law and legal practice is of particular importance.

Despite the strategic position of Hong Kong and the pool of talent able to work in Chinese, the Hong Kong legal community was not at first much interested in the emerging China trade.[10] According to one individual who did get immediately involved with China work in the early 1980s, work on China trade was considered "low prestige" within the legal establishment. One reason was that there was perceived to be "no law" (int. 221, 1) in China. Another was that the Hong Kong Chinese, who had the advantage of speaking the language, felt uncomfortable with the People's Republic of China. They or their family members had, after all, left China because of their opposition to Communism. The Chinese on the mainland, moreover, did not match well with the Western and prosperous legal community in Hong Kong (ints. 221, 234). Their "bad table manners" fit poorly with the Hong Kong Chinese. Until a few years ago, when "China became sexy," "no Hong Kong Chinese lawyers wanted to do China" law. Further, the conveyencing-driven prosperity in Hong Kong was not favorable to new and risky legal initiatives in China. It was simply "too easy to make money" (int. 221, 2).

8. And from the earlier history as well (see Lee 1993).

9. Any measurement of the importance of law cannot be very precise. We look at the relative prestige of the legal profession, for example, whether it is a highly desired career; when and what role lawyers have in the state; when and what role lawyers have in structuring economic transactions and resolving disputes; and the related use of legal discourse in economic and political settings.

10. There were of course exceptions, such as the barrister Anthony Dicks, who promoted some interest in China and its legal system.

One example reveals the discomfort of the Hong Kong legal establishment with this "lack of law." One solicitor in a major Hong Kong law firm reported that his first China transaction began when a client of the firm wanted to purchase real estate in China in the late 1970s. The particular lawyer, a Hong Kong Chinese just beginning his career, was quite interested in pioneering in China work, but he had to overcome the profound skepticism of his partners. They had serious problems with the question of law. After the deal was concluded, the partners "solved" the problem of "no law" by asking for a London Queen's Counsel opinion on the transaction. The QC, who of course knew nothing at all of any relevance to the transaction, embodied the legitimacy of the English bar among the Hong Kong partners and their insurers. He had enough sense to say the obvious—that under the circumstances the Hong Kong firm did what it could. This blessing allowed the transaction to proceed as "legal." Twenty-five years later, there still are problems in ascertaining Chinese law, but the expertise in China trade and investment is now critical to the burgeoning international legal practices in Hong Kong (Page 1994).

The construction of Chinese legality over the past twenty-five years has changed both Hong Kong and the Chinese legal landscapes. Relying on some of the accounts related to us in Hong Kong, we shall try to show how the landscape changed. To anticipate the conclusion, we should point out that it is quite remarkable, in retrospect, to see how easily the United States stepped into Communist China and established U.S. legal practices. Even a U.S. legal education has become increasingly necessary to a career in China in international trade and investment. The simple explanation is the most obvious one. The United States was the world's leading economic power, and that fact alone gave considerable power to U.S. legal and other approaches. But the story is much more complex, involving missionary efforts made possible by the organization of U.S. law firms and the kinds of individuals that could be recruited into those firms. U.S. legal practices were not simply imposed, even if U.S. economic power was no doubt important. Law, and especially U.S. law, has gradually insinuated itself into a supposedly rigid legal culture. The activities that led to this rather remarkable transformation—even if partial and uncertain—merit closer attention.

The magnitude and the processes of change can be seen in the details of particular stories. One U.S.-educated Hong Kong Chinese lawyer described the early days of United States–China trade—when there was "no law." The deals took a long time to negotiate, he said—even three or four years for major transactions. There were few lawyers in China, and they were "at the bottom of the heap" in prestige (and independence). Decisions to go ahead with a project were made politically. Lawyers were allowed only to "fill in the terms" (int. 220, 1). Accordingly, the senior personnel negotiating on the Chinese side were "political," with the "technocrats" working on the details.

The only lawyers encountered in the early deals in the Chinese side were either very senior or very junior. One group, which tended to be over sixty years old, came from individuals educated before the 1949 revolution. They were "amazingly good," according to one source, since they at least knew basic contract and property law. The other group was very young, in their early twenties, with no formal legal training. They were typically recent graduates of colleges that had only opened again in the late 1970s. They had "usually studied English" and were often recruited from the "foreign-language institutes." They were now drafted into this rudimentary legal work.

The lawyer-pioneers from the non-Chinese side—and before 1985 *foreign* "meant American" (int. 220, 1)—were "Chinese-studies students," "not commercial lawyers." They were naturally stronger on Chinese than on the law. Not surprisingly, in the words of a Hong Kong Chinese participant aware of the standards acceptable outside of China, they wrote "terrible contracts." The Chinese-studies students were, after all, pioneers "straight out of law school," led by individuals and law firms—notably Baker and McKenzie and Coudert—willing to invest in uncharted legal frontiers.[11]

The first generation of legal behavior in the China trade with the West was therefore more a matter of linguistics than law. Each side worked mainly through language specialists, essentially inventing the law as they went. Certain foreign clients, like Pepsi, wanted their lawyers to "do it legitimately," but that was not easy (int. 221, 2). Foreign lawyers in China had to become specialists in Communist *guangxi*, working closely with government officials, all the while seeking patiently to build up a legal infrastructure. While promoting law, they explained the details of Chinese terrain to their clients. As experts in *guangxi*, they could describe to the West "the role of mayors and governors in dispute resolution," for example,[12] and as legal experts they could explain to the Chinese "why [certain approaches] don't work for clients" (int.

11. Describing Coudert Brothers' Far East practice during that time, Veenswijk notes the number of Peace Corps and similar program participants: "In effect, Coudert Brothers was to benefit from the complex of public and private programs and fellowships, Ford Foundation studies, university-level international studies—that had arisen in the postwar years to address the United States' lack of preparedness for the international involvements it had assumed" (Veenswijk 1994, 366).

12. It is important, according to China lawyers, to recognize that, in the absence of a regulatory framework, the legal process is "only one channel" for the solution of a problem. Knowledge of those channels and contacts is essential, according to these sources, for a China practice (int. 219, 6).

227, 2). The missionaries on behalf of U.S. law had to "help to write the laws" (int. 221, 2) to make sure the Chinese found legal approaches that "worked." Indeed, they were enthusiastic to provide such help. And they spent enormous resources in seeking to find and translate unpublished laws and regulations—in effect, making them more public and official (Veenswijk 1994, 405).

There is now much more of a legal infrastructure, but there are still a variety of approaches in China trade and investment. The precise mix of law and *guangxi* varies according to a number of specific factors. According to one expert, the role of law is still quite marginal in most of the rather considerable Hong Kong Chinese investment in China, which took place mainly after 1989 when the United States pulled back in response to the Tiananmen Square incident. Most of the Hong Kong companies, we were told, "get along" pretty well with the Chinese. These companies, for example, still operate for the most part as if lawyers should not be brought to negotiations, since their participation indicates "distrust." They see a lawyer only when "the deal is done," checking only to "make sure it's legal" (int. 221, 3).[13] They do not wish to risk a deal with arguments about such unlikely risks as force majeure. For these Chinese-Chinese transactions, therefore, it may be fair to say that there is a "different mentality" than that promoted by Western lawyers (although the same mentality exists in many business relationships outside of China as well).

There is also evidence of change. While the small Hong Kong businesses dealing with China still tend not to use lawyers,[14] the larger enterprises may not be content only with *guangxi.* The new generation of business leaders in Hong Kong has succeeded their fathers in the leadership of the large family companies. Typically graduates of MBA programs in the United States, these leaders are more comfortable with professionals, including lawyers (int. 220). They are much more likely, for example, to employ the long and detailed contracts associated with American legal practice.[15] They use "big law firms, big accounting firms, and big architecture firms" (int. 221, 3).

13. The big Hong Kong companies are thus said to be "more tolerant of ambiguity" than the U.S. companies. They use lawyers only for some "comfort." They count on political security and, as proprietor-run companies, focus on the long term. If one deal works out unfairly with a party, "the proprietor will make a better deal the next time" (int. 220, 4).

14. And in the early period many simply moved across the borders to China to set up their manufacturing plants without contracts (int. 220).

15. A recent article in *Business Week* about the new generation of leaders in Asian businesses thus quoted one father as saying, "We don't use lawyers, we use a simple handshake," and a son as saying, "Personal friendship . . . should not be confused with a business transaction" (Barnathan 1993, 69).

Even by the early 1980s, in fact, some of these young MBAs were "getting into fancy stuff" (int. 220, 3) in sophisticated transactions that drew on the services of the big professional firms. That does not mean, however, that *guangxi* is in jeopardy. While more attuned to legality, these occupants of two worlds "don't upset their father's friends" by overlegalizing a traditional relationship (int. 221, 3). And generational changes may not proceed all at once. The MBAs, we were told, sometimes got too "fancy" with the financial machinations, and the "old men who retired had to come back and put the business in order" (int. 220, 4)—no doubt calling upon their networks and friends to help.

Transactions with U.S. businesses, however, are somewhat different. The U.S. multinationals promote law actively. They "want it all spelled out," and to "double-check" the risks. Unlike the Hong Kong companies, the U.S. companies bring in teams of lawyers—"the more lawyers, the more important the project" (int. 221, 4). The contracts have grown from the pioneering days, and there are clearly very long, detailed, and "hugely more sophisticated" contracts for large financial transactions (int. 234, 17). Nevertheless, the change is not all one way. In appropriate transactions there are also Sinocized contracts with shorter sentences and fewer words, reflecting in part the fact that the Chinese language does not have as many words as English for essentially the same concept (*burdens, encumbrances,* etc.). The point, however, is that major legal technologies are now deployed. The Chinese have become much more sophisticated on the one side, and on the other side the pioneers from the United States paved the way for the very complex legal relationships and contracts that characterize the practices of the law firms for which they established outposts.

Another way to explore the importance of law in China is to examine the development of the Chinese legal profession. It takes lawyers on both sides to build a legal infrastructure and promote legal practices. When trade began again with the West in the late 1970s, the Chinese felt some pressure to respond to the concerns about the lack of law expressed by the investing businesses. As noted before, and with the help of the U.S. pioneers, they had to piece together some law and some lawyers. One formalization of this phenomenon was the creation of such entities as the "legal department" of CIEC, China International Economic Consultants. Subsequently the Chinese also

---

And even the clients who take a traditional Chinese approach to law may change when dealing with outsiders. If "they trust" their lawyer, they use that lawyer as a "trusted adviser" for all aspects of "advising China how to deal outside China" (int. 221, 5).

set up some state-operated law firms, including the C and C Law Office, the Great Wall Law Office, the Global Law Office, and the China Legal Affairs Center (int. 234, 3). The first group of "lawyers" in those offices were the pre-1949 law graduates and those who spoke English but lacked formal training. They learned law on the job and through seminars offered by American and English lawyers. The Coudert pioneers, including Jerome Cohen and Owen Nee, for example, voluntarily taught a seminar on law and trade in Beijing "for two years running between 1979 and 1981" (Veenswijk 1994, 399). The first group of pioneer Chinese was soon joined by new law graduates emerging in the 1980s.

The initial role of the Chinese law firms, according to a Hong Kong lawyer with long experience in China, was "to give comfort to foreign investors" (int. 234, 6). In order to do so, they would "say anything to encourage foreign investment." Since, however, they operated in a system where the "law and policy distinction is very blurred" (id., 5; see Lubman and Wajnowski 1993, 120), they had to maintain good contacts with the government. The law, for example, "might say yes," while the "practice might be no," and vice versa (int. 234, 5).[16] Not surprisingly, many of these important new lawyers in fact came from the government. The legitimacy of the government came in this way also to bolster the authority of these lawyers. But, as noted before, the main purpose of these lawyers initially was to serve the state by promoting information that would encourage investment.

These law offices became the nucleus of the Chinese commercial bar, and the commercial bar is increasingly important. The demand for commercial legal services is such that there has been considerable turnover—even a brain drain—among these lawyers. And those who were able to gain the expertise and legitimacy of a legal education abroad, typically in the United States, are especially in demand. One Hong Kong lawyer said that a pattern within China was "promote, defect, emigrate" (int. 221, 6). Many of these lawyers also take part in exchange programs with law firms, including, for example, the Hong Kong offices of Baker and McKenzie and Clifford Chance. They are actively seeking the expertise offered by the Western law firms and profiting from it in China and elsewhere.

Amid this growing attention to and prestige of law, there is now some evidence of the emergence of a more independent (from the government) legal profession built on the experience of foreign-oriented legal offices in Beijing and Shanghai. Recently, for example, these state law firms have been joined

16. A lawyer in one of these law offices noted the need to "be in touch with personnel and contacts," since not all was "in accord with the law" (int. 237, 6).

by a number of legal cooperatives in the major cities. These firms, reputedly, are "close to being private" (int. 234, 4), with flexibility on fees, with profit sharing, and therefore with much higher incomes than the state law firms can earn. For obvious reasons, we can predict growth in this sector if it is allowed to continue relatively unregulated.

As might be expected, these developments also bring a change in the professional approach. While the original foreign-trade lawyers in China, as noted before, sought first to promote investment, they reportedly have a different self-definition now. They recognize that their "first duty is to the client" (id., 6). Indeed, sometimes their advice may even be too discouraging and legalistic, especially if they are relatively recent graduates too captivated by the formal law and lacking any real *guangxi* connections. The fact that many Western businesses will now even go "directly" to Chinese lawyers for assistance in a transaction in China (ints. 237, 234) provides evidence of a sufficient faith in the commercial lawyers' independence. No doubt the number of such respected advisers who are "perfectly dual," in the words of one lawyer (int. 234), is still quite small, but the incentives suggest that other ambitious Chinese will seek to follow this path.[17]

The demand for these lawyers is strong and the market is growing. Of the sixty to seventy-five thousand lawyers in China, only about two thousand at most have any real experience in international matters (int. 237). The currently most desirable careers for high-school students are reportedly all oriented toward business—accounting, finance, law, and management, in no special order. Among the relatively privileged "children of cadres" who display sufficient talent, therefore, one of these career choices could be expected. If someone is admitted to law and has a facility in English (which may come from being the son or daughter of a cadre),[18] that individual will go into "foreign and economic law." If not, there is a different and much less prestigious

17. It is not only a matter of prestige. Lawyers in the United States–China trade can get paid $100–150 per hour; Chinese lawyers earn $2 for criminal and family work (Lee 1994, 7–8).

18. We do not mean to imply that only the children of Party cadres are players in this activity. Indeed, it appears that many of those who invest strongly in law are from what has been called the "Class of '77," the group who first gained access to the universities through competitive examinations after the Cultural Revolution. Many went on to graduate work in law and other disciplines in the West. According to a recent article, they offer a competing network to the children of the Communist elite ("China's New Elite" 1995), and "China's progress in building a modern legal system also depends on '77ers" (49). It will be interesting to explore the activities of this network, which while less endowed with the social capital of the scions of the party, can combine its investment in the autonomy of the law with the opportunities of internationalism.

faculty of law for civil and criminal law. The graduates of the foreign- and economic-law faculties then compete for the top jobs, which, until the recent private competition, were those in the state law offices. Social status, cosmopolitanism, and Party connections bring further status to this small sector of the Chinese legal profession.

The new attitude toward law is also evidenced by Chinese pronouncements today, "Don't lock lawyers out," which contrast greatly with an older (Confucian or Communist) ideology, "Chain the lawyers to the tree outside the courthouse" (int. 234, 10). But the major changes are seen only within the commercial legal elite, not at the local level among the local courts. It is still the case, according to several sources, that Party and governmental influence is quite important at that level (int. 230). As one observer stated, there is still a "heavy hierarchy" and considerable "executive interference" despite some progress to date in "legal development" (int. 230, 43). There is, in short, still a "thinness of Chinese law and the concept of legality in Chinese society" (Lubman and Wajnowski 1993, 120). This problem of independence, of course, relates to the relatively low status of ordinary lawyers and judges. Only the commercial lawyers—drawing on government experience and connections— have the legitimacy of the Party embodied in their authority.

This sketch of Chinese legal developments shows the key role of the large law firms, led by those from the United States. Chinese lawyers look toward the United States for an elite legal education and for their legal legitimacy, work in the offices of the large law firms, use that knowledge to gain advancement in China, and not surprisingly, build up a legality and a legal practice in China that fits well with that offered by the large firms of the West. This Chinese group both promotes and consumes the sophisticated legal practices and business relationships that draw on their services and skills.[19] The growth of China trade, with investment in China doubling every year since 1991,[20] provides a ready market for these practices. As legal practice grows in China, of course, it also grows in Hong Kong.

The developments in China also show the potential for a legality that is not only linked to the West and especially the United States, but also is building autonomy from the government in China. The ties to the Party bureaucrats, both through family connections and career patterns, are actually aids to the construction of autonomy. In the international sector, where the

19. The double role was recently noted by Lubman and Wajnowski: "Chinese lawyers are often helpful in explaining to their Chinese clients requirements of Chinese law about which the Chinese side had been unaware or had regarded as negotiable" (1993, 121).

20. Not to mention Chinese investment in Hong Kong.

law is high prestige and connected to elites, the legal profession can assert its autonomy. Among the ordinary courts and lawyers, weak ties to Party elites build not autonomy but subordination.

Now we turn again to Hong Kong, which is poised to move from a British colony to a major Chinese capital. Hong Kong is much more developed in law than China, but the core of its development is English. Hong Kong's law, unlike China's, is also evident in politics, not only in trade and economic relations. But the political side of Hong Kong law is relatively weak, as we shall see, and it may simply merge into the Chinese legal developments just described.

Hong Kong and the Legal Field Today

The picture of Hong Kong today can be seen in two parts. First, we shall focus on law and politics, examining the role of the legal profession in constructing a "state." Second, we examine business law, focusing on the arrangement of forces seen in securities regulation.

Lawyers in Politics

Hong Kong lawyers from the Chinese community have become very important in politics. Beginning in the 1970s, the governor of the colony began to appoint at least one formal representative of the legal profession to serve on the legislative council. This appointment policy evolved to a situation where the profession elected one of its members to serve.[21] At the same time, the organizations of the bar and the solicitors began to speak out about the rule of law, democracy, and the independence of the judiciary (int. 235). Service in this representative capacity, as part of the legal profession, has helped to produce a political leadership from among the Hong Kong Chinese legal profession.[22] These individuals, in fact, represent the leadership today of the political parties promoting the rule of law and democracy in post-1997 Hong Kong.

This politics has come with an effort to develop a distinctive identity—not Chinese, not English—that can complement the identity Hong Kong has cultivated as a financial center. This project requires the work of persons who

21. Martin Lee, for example, who is now the leader of the United Democrats of Hong Kong Party, was chair of the bar, 1980–83, was the appointed representative to the legislative council, 1985–91, and became elected at that point. His party is the most important one at present, winning twelve of the eighteen seats at stake in the legislative council.

22. The Tiananmen Square incident no doubt helped mobilize this group into action and gained support for their views (int. 235). It also precipitated an open break with China.

identify with Hong Kong—"Hong Kong animals" in the words of one activist (int. 235, 5).[23] This effort has some difficulties, magnified by the hybrid legal system that characterizes Hong Kong. As one active solicitor from the Chinese Hong Kong community stated, the effort to promote independence—"real autonomy"—has required that the lawyers "educate themselves" (id., 2). They have had to find "benchmarks" for the autonomy of law. For example, one idea has been to "codify" the common law in Hong Kong to avoid the prospect of "losing everything" when the English common law would no longer be the basis for Hong Kong law (id., 2). Similarly, they have sought to "detach" "human rights" from "politics," thereby leading to much better and more secure protections in Hong Kong and to more autonomy for law (int. 235, 7). In seeking to promote the rule of law and judicial independence, these activists have had also to be "more open," and "more international." They have built ties, for example, both to the U.S. human-rights community and to lawyer organizations outside of Hong Kong (int. 226). And they vary in their approaches—some aggressively pushing democracy, others trying somewhat more moderately to shore up the "rule of law" by building the autonomy of the existing system.[24]

In order to succeed, the Chinese Hong Kong lawyers must use their "Englishness" against the Chinese and their "Chineseness" against the English. That is, they must emphasize the values of the English legal system within which they have developed against any Chinese takeover in 1997. They must build a politicolegal state, organized according to Western values. And, when necessary—prior to the English agreement to give Hong Kong back—they must emphasize the importance of the Chinese language and links to China against the English colonial regime.[25]

This project of constructing an independent legal state is difficult to realize. Reminiscent of the double-agent role of the compradors of the past, it requires the politicians to play a mediating role in law between the English and the Chinese. But the weakness of the English position makes the mediating role very difficult to play. Given the weakness of the English, in fact, it is under-

23. Several of these individuals have also been active with respect to human rights in China, including Martin Lee, who was also the founder of the Hong Kong Alliance for Democracy.

24. It is interesting that David Li, the director of the Bank of East Asia, a lawyer, and an individual with close ties to the Hong Kong elite and U.S. businesses, promotes the "judiciary's independence" as vital to Hong Kong's continued prosperity, and to its future role in Greater China. But he distances himself from the belated efforts of Governor Patten to promote democracy (Page 1994b).

25. One informant stated that the group that now is most hostile to China did in fact push for closer ties in the early 1980s.

standable that the politicians playing this role responded to questions about relations between the English and the ethnic Chinese in Hong Kong as if there had never been any tensions (ints. 226, 235).[26] It is almost as if they were trying to prop up the English side (Mirsky 1994).

Further, with the strength of the Chinese, it is no wonder that the bar and the solicitors' branches are "schizophrenic" (int. 235). The membership, we were told by the relative activists, wants the profession "collectively" to play a strong role in promoting the rule of law in Hong Kong, but "individually" it is difficult to "get away" with a strong position. Lawyers want "others to stand up" (int. 235, 4) rather than risk their own careers. Even the U.S. law firms in Hong Kong, according to one leading activist lawyer, will always pick "business" over "the right thing" in Hong Kong (int. 226, 3).[27] There is too much hunger for the business of the Bank of China and other Chinese companies (int. 226), and too much fear of retaliation after 1997.

Another problem with asserting independence is that most of the members of the bar are far from prosperous, despite the relative growth of commercial practice since the early 1980s (int. 231). Indeed, top law graduates have been more likely to go into the law firms than into the chambers of the bar. There are, of course, many very wealthy senior barristers, and "many Chinese barristers became politicians" (id., 6). Nevertheless, as one of the wealthy ones observed, it is "unrealistic" to expect those who are "scratching a living" to give much support to the "core value" of "independence" (int. 230, 9). Similarly, it is unrealistic to expect much concern for the legal system and the state among the expatriate community. We must also recall that most expatriate lawyers are not invested in Hong Kong as the place for their career. They come for a few years and aspire to return home.[28]

26. Compare the observations of other respondents: "Two years ago it was unprecedented for English firms to take in a Chinese lawyer" (int. 230, 7); "Even now Hong Kong Chinese cannot be partners in a U.K. firm" (int. 221, 7). And see Abel 1994, 745: "When someone leaked a Freshfields internal memo revealing that the firm considered its Chinese lawyers unworthy of partnership in the Hong Kong branch, the local profession was outraged."

27. According to a leading human-rights advocate in Hong Kong, they have heard "hardly a peep" from the expatriate community about human rights in China (int. 228, 3). The main activity is among Asians and the Hong Kong University Law Department, which is a "bastion of human rights activity."

28. The nature of the expatriate community in Hong Kong is changing. The recent emphasis on China has meant that top recruits either have facility in Chinese or high-tech international financial lawyering skills. Note the "frantic musical chairs" described in a recent article ("Hong Kong Silver" 1994, 27). This trend has provided opportunities for the Hong Kong Chinese and for expatriates with language skills and presumably a longer-term commitment to Hong Kong. For example, "four of the last five lawyers to

Two further obstacles to the development of an independent politicolegal system are time and the lack of learned law. The English did not invest in the development of an autonomous legal regime. They maintained the courts and the practice of law as subordinate to England. They also invested very little in legal education, requiring until relatively recently that practitioners graduate from English law schools. The law schools in Hong Kong that now exist are staffed mainly by expatriates, and, again, there is not a strong system of Hong Kong legal scholarship that can help construct the requisite legal autonomy.

Business and Law: The Reform of the Stock Exchange

The story of the stock exchange is interesting because it captures one aspect of the transformation of business and law in response to internationalization. As Neil Gunningham (1990) showed, the closing of the Hong Kong Stock Exchange the day after Black Monday in 1987 reflected the failure of the regulatory system; and this institutional failure related to a clash of business approaches. The Hong Kong market was constructed out of two competing stock markets that operated very differently. One was dominated by the old British elite, the other by Hong Kong family-run businesses. The merger also incorporated the large international brokers serving very large investors, but the exchange remained controlled by the founder of the Chinese exchange and the small brokers who were part of the family system. It thus reflected a local, family orientation, not the norms of the cosmopolitan legal culture.

The closing of the market was the only closing in the world among major markets, and it was condemned universally among the international financial community. The incident led to criminal prosecutions and to a serious effort by the administration to reform the system. Clearly it was important to have the confidence of the international financial community if Hong Kong aspirations to remain a major financial center were to be realized.[29] The failure of the existing system, moreover, required a reorganization of the legal mechanisms for policing the market, which in turn led to changes within the Hong Kong legal profession.

As noted before, some of the Hong Kong Chinese law firms that have been highly successful in conveyencing are also close to business, and the securities

---

be offered partnerships at Deacons have been Chinese speaking" ("Future Grim" 1993 14). This means that there are more Chinese Hong Kong lawyers in some of the traditionally expatriate firms, but their approach to Hong Kong "legal politics" remains to be seen.

29. Hong Kong businesses had "never wanted outside capital" before this time. The American firms "won't play" unless there is "some level playing field" (int. 217, 4).

markets and real estate have also been closely connected (int. 221, 4). One of the successful lawyers in "China work" profiled by the *International Financial Law Review* in 1993, for example, was described as "part of the Chinese old boy network" and with "wide family connections . . . [his] family owns one of the largest local stockbroking firms." Interestingly, the article notes, "the firm is yet to make any substantial inroads in the emerging securities work in spite of . . . heavy involvement in the local securities industry" (Budden 1993, 6).

The reason for the lack of substantial inroads may relate to the problems of the family brokerages in the closing of 1987. According to an English lawyer, "Hong Kong law firms were implicated in the closure" of the market (int. 234, 15). The colonial government thus turned to English firms to reshape the regulatory structure.[30] Firms like Clifford Chance and Herbert Smith were also employed to "clean up" after the securities problems; there was "no real enthusiasm for Chinese firms for this litigation" (int. 214, 2). The particular vehicle for the government to investigate and reform the securities industry was the Independent Commission against Corruption (ICAC), which existed before but "came into the picture" (int. 230, 11) in the securities cleanup. In short, there was a transformation from the closed world of family businesses to the openness and anticorruption (which goes with transparency) of international legal and financial practice.

The Hong Kong legal system, as noted before, is between China and England, with the United States a growing part of the picture. Hong Kong needs its own identity, but it must satisfy China and the business criteria that are now taken for granted in international transactions. Having shed some of its provincialism and looking toward the future in securities, the Hong Kong exchange decided that its "future must lie with China" a few years ago (int. 230, 12). It sought to persuade China companies that they should place their securities on the Hong Kong exchange. There were some formidable challenges, again requiring that some law be "built up." China in fact had no company law at that time (see Torbert 1993), which meant that the Hong Kong committee promoting reform had to help draft workable regulations.

The committee negotiated with governmental officials from China who, while quite intelligent, had not even finished primary school, had no money for hotels in Hong Kong, and had no access to legal advisers while negotiating. According to a Hong Kong participant, they had technical advice only from

---

30. And according to one English solicitor, the resultant reform, enacted along English lines, "gave a huge advantage" to English firms in this field in Hong Kong. They were able to gain a much higher percentage of securities work than competitors (int. 234, 15).

young lawyers in China who served as "experts" (int. 230, 16). These young experts, now in the Chinese Securities Regulatory Commission, were graduates of U.S. law schools with experience in New York law firms. That background clearly had some impact on the arrangement.

The result of the negotiations was agreement on the disclosure requirements and an innovative development in securities arbitration. Noting the "huge gap" that still exists between the two legal systems in the courts, and the need for remedies for securities problems that both the Chinese and Hong Kong could agree to, the negotiators decided to build on the successes of international commercial arbitration in both China and Hong Kong. According to one individual close to the negotiations, "Arbitration was the only way to bridge the gap between the two places" (int. 230, 14). They created a mixed panel of potential arbitrators, and arbitration rules permit either Chinese (the Chinese International Economic Trade and Arbitration Commission) or Hong Kong arbitration and even shareholder-derivative arbitration—a remedy associated especially with litigation in the United States.

The borrowing of some of the U.S. technologies no doubt helped make the system acceptable to the international investor community. The major investment banking firms sought to get involved very actively in the listing of the first nine Chinese companies on the Hong Kong exchange (int. 230). The U.S. firms, nevertheless, tried to persuade the Chinese to "go straight to New York" and "forget the Hong Kong exchange" (id., 19). But "China saw the long-term benefit of listing in Hong Kong." Hong Kong was able therefore to gain some commitment by the Chinese to the Hong Kong exchange.

The building of an internationally oriented exchange, which required a new set of players and new rules, made it acceptable to the international community. It attracted the large investment bankers and large law firms. At the same time, however, it paved the way for both Chinese and Hong Kong businesses to bypass the exchange—located on the frontier or periphery—and go straight to the Western centers. And once these channels are opened, the United States does well in the competition.

According to a recent article, written from the perspective of a London "pitch," "New York and NASDAQ are fast becoming the alternatives to Hong Kong for a listing. Of the 22 Chinese state companies that are expected to be listed, at least five have been targeted for New York, yet there is still no news for London" (Kholi and Heath 1994, 10). The article reports London's efforts to persuade the Chinese to look more toward London. The theme of the article captures the problem of London and, to some extent, Hong Kong: "London officials discovered that virtually all the Chinese exchangers had management and expertise indoctrinated into the US way of thinking. . . . [T]here was a culture that Wall Street was the ultimate model and that in terms of listings of Chinese companies the US was the place to go."[31] This "cultural snag" illustrates the combined power of the U.S. investment bankers and U.S. law.[32] Moving to Hong Kong, needless to say, opens channels to and from New York.

Preliminary Conclusions

The Chinese-U.S. legal alliance points to a major role for Hong Kong as a financial and legal center. Law firms and financial powers are returning to China despite the remaining uncertainties about the shape of Hong Kong after 1997. At present, it appears, both the Hong Kong legal profession and the Chinese legal profession are becoming increasingly oriented to the legal practices of the leading international law firms and to advanced education in the law schools of the United States. As each becomes more international, it also strengthens the links between the international legal practice of the Western centers and that of the Eastern frontiers. And the Western centers have some important advantages in the resultant competition, including the fact that it is fought on their terms.

This orientation of Asian lawyers to the West, similarly, does not necessarily mean that the Chinese educated abroad or hired by the leading law firms will blend into the "legal culture" of the large law firms. Quite a few of the respondents in Hong Kong, both from the Chinese and expatriate side, noted the difficulty of fitting into the U.S. law firm settings (int. 237).[33] There are certainly a growing number of Chinese partners, but it remains to be seen how many there will be and whether they change the culture of the firms or simply bolster the symbolic imperialism of U.S. law.

Formal law and legal practice are not taking the place of *guangxi* in Asia for the regulation of business relationships. Personal ties and legal formality coexist and can be invoked by virtually all the players in this setting. The Chinese-studies lawyers and other pioneers who went into China early learned

31. The chief of the China Securities Regulatory Commission, Liu Hongru, said in mid-1994, "It is imperative to select some enterprises for direct listing in the United States because it is the world's largest capital market which has the highest liquidity and provides the best protection for shareholders" ("China to Focus" 1994, 3).

32. It is further interesting in this respect that two lawyers from Skadden, Arps have recently been hired by U.S. investment banking firms in Hong Kong.

33. For example, one Hong Kong Chinese lawyer noted, "It is difficult to integrate Chinese lawyers," since they have been brought up in the China system. It is "easier to bring in a U.S. lawyer who speaks Chinese" (int. 221, 7). An expatriate who speaks Chinese stated, "If a Chinese lawyer is a partner in China," he or she is still "unlikely to make it outside of China" because of "culture" (int. 234, 1).

very well how to function where there was "no law."[34] And we know that recent Chinese law graduates are quite likely to emphasize formal law in their dealings with China and with foreign clients. Indeed, the large-firm lawyers in Hong Kong who work with China emphasize the virtue of "problem solving" as opposed to an emphasis on legal formalism (int. 234; int. 221, 1 ["hands on"]). A close examination of business relationships, we expect, would reveal a very diverse mix of the personal and the legal. The mix is changing, and the rules of the game are part of the stakes in the competition among approaches.

Nevertheless, we would expect some movement toward more formal law and in particular the U.S. variant. The role of the international lawyer in this sense both enables and responds to business efforts to become more international, to restructure as new generations take over the largest family businesses, and to make more sophisticated deals and financial arrangements. The success in equating this U.S.-style practice with "sophistication" and "internationalization," and the rewards that it offers in status and compensation to practitioners, has led to considerable success in exporting the model. One way of looking at the China and the Hong Kong stories, in fact, is to see the continuing role of double agents and compradors. They serve as brokers between two systems while promoting the long-term dominance of one.

Finally, the relationship between this elite corporate practice and democracy and human rights remains to be seen for both China and Hong Kong. We need especially to know more about China for any assessment of the strength of such forces there. We can in any event see that the democracy movement in Hong Kong is linked to the United States and England, but not well connected to the international business lawyers who are so important in both Hong Kong and China.[35] The human-rights movement in the United States has sought to link human-rights progress to trade with China, and it has had some success in this respect in the past; but it is quite clear that China feels able to resist any such pressures for the moment. The aspirations of the movement for "legal autonomy" and democracy in Hong Kong therefore appear to be isolated from movements in China and from the international law firms.

Arbitration in the Space between Business and Politics

One feature of *arbitration* is that it is a broad enough term to encompass very different experiences. What distinguishes arbitration from other ways of

34. One Hong Kong Chinese in a U.S. firm noted the crucial importance of "being patient" and "keeping up relationships in China" during the period when trade dropped in the late 1980s (int. 221, 2).

35. But they profit quite a bit, in fact, from work generated by the China trade and international business lawyers.

processing disputes is not very much contested today, but even the stable procedural features—binding decision-making by a neutral third party specifically empowered by the contractual agreement of the parties—do not tell much about the specifics of any given arbitral process. The role of formal law and formal procedures, the approach of arbitrators, the characteristics of arbitrators, and the kind of decision making are all subject to enormous variations. It is instructive, therefore, that agreement on "arbitration" was seen as a way to "bridge the gap" between Hong Kong and China (int. 230, 8).

The unifying analytical feature of commercial arbitration is that it occupies a space between business and politics. The decisions may be more or less anchored in formal law or more or less sensitive to political considerations, but any place along the continuum may be accepted as legitimate as long as the parties are willing to accept the decisions as such. The mechanism of arbitration, furthermore, allows for change over time as perceptions of authority and legitimacy change, and for flexibility to meet the needs of different situations.

The parallel stories of commercial arbitration in Hong Kong and China are therefore both different and similar. This relationship is very similar to the one seen in the stories of law in both places. We suggest, in fact, that the success of international commercial arbitration in either of the two places depends in the long term on a successful movement toward an autonomous legal system. In that sense, all the preceding discussion relates to the question of the success and the characteristics of arbitration as it takes shape in Hong Kong and China. Again, as we shall see, the question is whether Hong Kong will be simply a subordinate player to Chinese arbitration or whether it will develop an independent status as a major center for international commercial arbitration.

Hong Kong

Reform of arbitration in London precipitated the creation of the Hong Kong International Arbitration Center (int. 224). The new attorney general, John Griffiths, QC, revitalized the Law Reform Commission and charged it with the topic of whether to adopt the 1979 English Act. The chair of the committee to study the situation, Andrew Li, was a young and very well connected barrister.[36] The committee decided to go ahead with the reform, with some modifications such as a greater emphasis on conciliation, and it was enacted into law in 1982.

---

36. His brother, David Li, is a lawyer who chairs the Bank of East Asia, and his uncle was the individual who ran the stock exchange and suffered the criminal consequences.

Prior to that time the attorney general set up a second committee, chaired by David Hunter, QC,[37] to examine the question of whether to set up an arbitration center. The committee included some very powerful businesspeople, including a key representative of the shipping industry in Hong Kong, Helmut Solman. The committee decided to go ahead, secured some private donations, opened in 1985, and survived until able to secure an endowment from the Hong Kong government in the late 1980s. After Hunter stepped down, Neil Kaplan, a participant in the earlier work, a high-court judge, and subsequently the "construction and arbitration judge," became the chair. An engineer from the construction industry with long experience in arbitration and the Chartered Institute of Arbitrators, Peter Caldwell, became a full-time administrator in 1989. The center has maintained a relatively high profile in the international-arbitration community, holding many conferences and educational programs, proselytizing around Asia and beyond, and adopting the state-of-the-art UNCITRAL Model Law as well as provisions for alternative dispute resolution.

In many respects, the center is remarkably successful. Its relationship with the government and its resources allowed it to move to extremely desirable office space in late 1994. Its caseload has grown appreciably. Statistics for 1993 report 139 cases, of which 50 are construction, 42 shipping, 23 international trade, 9 insurance, 3 securities, and 12 others (int. 224). The center is well run, conducts many seminars for Hong Kong and for Chinese from the PRC, and is anchored in Hong Kong by a very active branch of the Chartered Institute of Arbitrators, with over one thousand members (int. 216; Poppy 1994, 50).

As the statistics indicate, the center has been especially successful in construction and shipping. Both settings reveal how the phenomenon of internationalization has affected disputing processes. In the field of shipping, for example, nearly all the contracts are standard form contracts with arbitration clauses. Nevertheless, according to one knowledgeable observer of the shipping industry, there were virtually no disputes during the boom years of Pacific Rim shipping in the 1950s and 1960s. Problems in long-term contracts with the Japanese companies were handled informally, "over sake." When one unique problem surfaced, for example, the Japanese company could not even find a copy of the contract (int. 236).

Disputes in shipping have long been handled by arbitration in New York and London, and the shipping community played an important role in the early

---

37. Hunter had been a commercial lawyer in London and was quite familiar with construction work and arbitration (int. 231).

years of the promotion of international commercial arbitration. As shipping changed gradually into the mid-1980s,[38] there were new players and a "new set of people looking at how to resolve disputes" (int. 231, 5). The new players have a "great effect on shipping," with a "more international outlook on dispute resolution" (int. 231, 5). New law firms were also arriving in Hong Kong. Arbitration gained in importance, and the role of London led to complaints about how "expensive and slow" the arbitration process was there. As noted before, one of the key Hong Kong shipping persons had been active on the committee to set up the new center, and he managed to use influence with a general shipping organization to gain more opportunities for the Hong Kong arbitration clause.

As a result, the number of shipping cases has grown, and there are now several well-known arbitrators who concentrate on shipping arbitrations. Nevertheless, they note that for very large arbitrations in Hong Kong, the arbitrators and the counsel tend to come from London (int. 236, 6).[39] Other big cases tend to be handled in New York or London, where there is much more choice for arbitrators. Another handicap for Hong Kong is that the opportunity to publicize the cases and the work of the Hong Kong arbitrators is limited by the control to date by the other centers of the publication of opinions.

There is a similar story with respect to construction. For several reasons there was virtually no litigation or arbitration in the construction projects until the late 1970s. One reason was that "the Hong Kong contractors" were "ready to fight only recently. Before, they would settle" (int. 218, 1). Another was that most of the major construction was through contracts with the government, and the contractors did not want to endanger the prospects for future business.

One arbitration in the late 1970s, brought by a foreign entity in Hong Kong against the government, broke through the hesitation to arbitrate against the government. Other arbitrations followed, and now construction arbitration is quite well established. Most of the members of the Chartered Institute of Arbitrators in Hong Kong are from the construction industry. The importance of construction, furthermore, has been translated into some quite innovative provisions for the giant projects associated with the new airport.

38. The world "became more troubled" with the problems of oil shipping and competition by Onassis and others. The Europeans had a "different mentality" (int. 236, 1). One result reportedly was that some members of the great family shipping businesses simply left the business rather than stay and compete under the new, ungentlemanly conditions (int 236., on brother of L. K. Pao).

39. An English solicitor in Hong Kong stated that for an important shipping matter in Hong Kong, the firm would use "an English junior or junior silk" (int. 214, 3).

The reasons for the change in disputing behavior are again complex, but one key reason is again the internationalization of legal practice. "International firms came to town, more aware of their rights in litigation and arbitration . . . not as frightened" (int. 218, 4). In particular, U.S. law firms were "arriving in Hong Kong." Nevertheless, internationalization also opened up new channels to and from London. According to several sources, many of the "megacases still go to London" (int. 231, 8),[40] or if a large case is located in Hong Kong, the arbitrators and lawyers come from London.

To summarize briefly, Hong Kong has developed a niche in international commercial arbitration, but it has at least two problems. One is that the two relatively successful areas of arbitration, shipping and construction, are both still pretty closely linked to London.[41] Hong Kong has its own arbitrators,[42] but the very large cases build on the Englishness of Hong Kong advocacy and therefore draw in a particular London community.[43] The second problem is that this success comes in two specialized kinds of arbitration rather than in building a substantial caseload of other kinds of commercial and investment disputes—which are also more prestigious in the international-arbitration community.

The double problem therefore is to establish a presence in the general cases that characterize institutions like the ICC in Paris and to develop an independent identity as a center. The issue of independence relates to the question of the independence of the Hong Kong legal system. The arbitration system can build on the regular legal system or build a kind of alternative legal system linked to Hong Kong business and politics. This is the strategy, we shall see, that the Chinese in the PRC have followed. It remains to be seen whether Hong Kong arbitration will develop that kind of position, or whether it will

40. One active arbitrator said that "Hong Kong services the medium and small cases" (int. 231, 8).

41. In addition, "Relatively few members of the Chinese bar are interested in arbitration" (int. 216, 1), which reinforces its English character. Note, however, that about 90 percent of the members of the Chartered Institute are from the Hong Kong Chinese community, but they tend not to be lawyers.

42. It is hard to estimate, but one insider suggested that there are probably twenty to thirty arbitrators appointed for Hong Kong arbitrations, mainly in the shipping area (int. 231). Some others suggested that a few individuals arbitrated most of the cases, which is not inconsistent with a broader pool. One American lawyer described a "small group" of "fine men," constituting an "old-boy network" (int. 233, 2). The four names were indeed the people most often mentioned as arbitrators (Caldwell, Kaplan, Pearl, Yang).

43. In addition, according to one British solicitor, despite the UNCITRAL Model Law, arbitration in Hong Kong tends to be conducted in the "English style," with long hearings, discovery, and oral cross-examination (int. 214).

become subordinate to China arbitration.[44] Until 1997, however, the problem of uncertainty is bound to inhibit the insertion of Hong Kong arbitration clauses into a large number of contracts (ints. 214, 233).

Arbitration in the PRC

The Chinese International Economic Trade and Arbitration Commission (CIETAC) has developed a very large caseload. According to a recent article, the number of new cases increased from 37 in 1985 to 513 in 1993 (including 9 maritime). The site of the arbitrations was mainly Beijing, with 115 divided between Shenzhen and Shanghi (Kaplan 1994, 107).

The evolution of Chinese arbitration has been relatively rapid. According to one Hong Kong lawyer in a U.S. firm, the Chinese "couldn't handle" the arbitrations in 1985 (int. 221, 5).[45] In the early days, according to another, you spent "one quarter of the negotiating time on the dispute resolution clause. All the foreign parties wanted arbitration, not the Chinese courts. . . . You could succeed in setting arbitration in a neutral country," for example, Stockholm (int. 220, 9).

Now the Chinese bargaining power is much greater. There is less arbitration outside, and "they have built up their arbitration capabilities." According to an experienced Beijing lawyer, the arbitration panels are "knowledgeable and independent," and, unlike the courts, "no one can exercise influence" (int. 237, 3). The Chinese are seeking to build up CIETAC's "influence and reputation" (id., 3). The Chinese ratified the 1958 New York Convention in 1987. CIETAC is the "most highly regarded judiciary" in China, and appointment to the CIETAC panel is an "honor" (int. 220, 10). The latest revised rules (1994), drafted reportedly with the help of Michael Moser of Baker and McKenzie, a leading China specialist, continue the effort to bolster the status and reputation of CIETAC arbitration. The acceptable list of arbitrators, which is especially important since CIETAC appoints the third arbitrator, has just been expanded greatly to include quite a large number of names familiar in the international-arbitration community.

Two active participants in CIETAC arbitration described the change over time in the arbitrations and arbitrators. The lawyer from Beijing said that they "made some mistakes" in the early years, and the arbitrators overemphasized "compromise" (int. 237, 3). A Hong Kong lawyer with experience over time said that in the early arbitrations, the arbitrators went "straight to the facts" (int. 230, 24). They used very little law in their approaches to arbitration. Now

---

44. An American lawyer suggested that the power of CIETAC may cause Hong Kong's center to "evaporate" or be "gobbled up" (int. 233, 2).

45. The only advice to give then was to "settle the cases" (int. 221, 5).

the situation is changing. For example, there are "choice-of-law problems" that lead to "very lawyerly analyses." In the past two years, in the words of this observer, it has evolved to be more "like an international arbitration" (see also Lubman and Wajnowski 1993, 128–29).

The nature of the arbitrators is also changing, from senior bureaucrats toward more legally trained and by definition younger individuals, especially law professors. The younger ones tend to have had "some exposure to the U.S. legal system," and they are more legalistic and less "practical" than the bureaucrats. The bureaucrats, who are more senior, still tend to be the chairs. It remains, however, an honor to be on the arbitrator list, and that means, according to one expert, that there is a "political" dimension to the choices (int. 220, 5). That also means that the arbitrators are well connected to the Party cadres, and this connection gives arbitration legitimacy in China and facilitates a degree of independence.

The lawyers in these arbitrations, which tend to be in Chinese, can be from different nationalities. U.S., British, and Hong Kong lawyers do appear, although the "British and Hong Kong lawyers always represent the foreign side" (int. 230, 14). The Americans may represent Chinese clients; and some of the lawyers in U.S. firms, including Michael Moser and Sally Harpole of Graham and James, can present cases in Chinese. The Chinese observer stated that there are "more and more foreign lawyers" (int. 237, 3).

It is difficult to generalize on the basis of a small number of interviews, but it appears that the CIETAC arbitration system may be better integrated into the Chinese legal and economic power structure than the Hong Kong center. In some sense, moreover, it is more "international," since the arbitrators and the lawyers tend to come from more nationalities and face a wider variety and larger number of disputes. It is of course true that, in general, Hong Kong's legal system is more developed, which no doubt affects the arbitrations and the quality of the legal decision-making. It is also true, however, that most of the arbitrations in Hong Kong are shipping and construction, which are cases that do not often call for substantial legal analyses. Nonlawyer arbitrators, in fact, handle many such cases in Hong Kong.

Hong Kong's Challenge in Arbitration

The arbitration community in Hong Kong aspires to build a major, independent, international commercial arbitration center. That requires Hong Kong to assert the economic and political power of China and Hong Kong, and clearly Hong Kong is emphasizing its position in the region and its ties to CIETAC (Kaplan, Spruce, and Moser 1994). There are two risks to this difficult strategy. One is that it will help to promote the success of CIETAC at the expense of Hong Kong, which will then become only a subsidiary of Chinese arbitration under CIETAC. It is important, therefore, to promote the legal independence of Hong Kong from China, which we have noted is a formidable task.[46]

It may be indicative that even the Hong Kong solicitors—but not the barristers—were unable to unite behind an effort to convince the Chinese that the new "court of final appeal" should have a strong component of foreign judges. The popular press, at least, interprets this outcome as a loss for the proponents of an independent judiciary (Poppy 1995). Chinese leaders at present may be more willing to tolerate independence in commercial arbitration than in regular court systems in China or even in Hong Kong (see also Kraar 1995).

The other problem, endemic to international institution-building at the frontier, is that the successful development of CIETAC and/or Hong Kong arbitration will serve mainly to reinforce the power of U.S., English, and other large international law firms and the ICC world of arbitration.[47] That is, the reform at the periphery in the name of internationalization and legal sophistication, promoted by lawyers with the best international connections, merely paves the way for the symbolic domination or even imperialism of the institutions in the center, which have, after all, defined internationalism and set the terms of the competition. Hong Kong may become a major outpost for the leading advocates and institutions of arbitration, and it could prosper as a result; but the rules of the game and major players would be defined elsewhere.

46. It is interesting that Mr. Justice Kaplan has recently resigned from the bench and moved to a position in Hong Kong with the U.S. firm of Debevoise and Plimpton. His explanation for the move shows the perception of a relative decline in the local justice system and ascendancy of the United States–ICC world of international arbitration. According to an article in *Legal Business*, Kaplan stated that "there is no drop in status or influence from judge to arbitration" (Poppy 1994, 53). The article suggested that "Kaplan's defection to the private sector serves as a reminder that the judiciary may be crumbling—from the inside as private practice becomes more and more attractive" (53).

47. Reportedly the ICC is planning to set up an office in Hong Kong (int. 224).

13

How to Construct Neutrality and Autonomy on the Basis of a Strategy of Double Agent

The preceding two chapters illustrate the continuing importance of the relative distinction between center and periphery. In "outposts" like Cairo and Hong Kong (or, in somewhat different ways, Vancouver or Los Angeles), the traits that characterize the practice of arbitration, as well as those that, more generally, characterize the legal field, were developed in the great Western centers. The opposition between center and periphery, however, can be misleading. It is essential to underline also the complementarity and continuity, and then also the similarity between two places in the field of international commercial arbitration.

Legal practitioners on the periphery, like their European or North American counterparts, serve above all as intermediaries—brokers between different social spaces[1] or between different circles of power. In order to appear legitimate, those who are dominated in the field of power must manifest a distance with regard to their protectors. Arms and resources owed to the powerful must be turned against them. The arguments that build the independence and autonomy of the clerks then serve also to rationalize, legitimate, and even limit the power of dominant political and economic actors.

This strategy of double agent is not without risks. The holders of economic power may, themselves, play on this confusion and ambiguity to claim the legitimacy of the law while exercising and controlling the functions of justice. The conquest of autonomy for the legal field with respect to the holders of power—whether political or economic—is not an enterprise for the short term. Autonomy is never complete and must be reaffirmed constantly. But relative success over the long term allows this essential characteristic of the legal field to be inscribed in institutions and mentalities. It then appears to be nearly natural and self-evident.

1. See, for example, the connection between the underground economy and the market of official institutions in the case of the lawyer-"carpetbagger" observed in Cairo. We have also found homologues in the Chinese world and in Geneva, where a great number of practitioners gain much of their revenue through their activity as "straw men" serving to recycle dirty money and furnish a legal facade for a hidden economy.

In contrast, when the institutions on which the autonomy of law rests are relatively young, still revealing the power relations and compromises that allowed them to get established, they are much more contested and contestable. They are more sensitive and more fragile with respect to political or economic risks. Since the legal institutions on the periphery are, by definition, relatively young,[2] they tend to be characterized by a weak degree of autonomy in the field of power. That is not to say that this problem cannot exist also in the centers of Western law, but relatively new institutions are more easily challenged.[3]

This chapter focuses on how this double-agent role of lawyers relates to the transformations that take place on the (relative) periphery. It begins with a general theoretical discussion—based on the previous two chapters—of the role of law in settings where law and lawyers have been relatively devalued or never were of major importance. In the same manner as lawyers in the developed legal centers, but in different—and "symbolically dependent"—settings, the lawyers on the periphery serve as double agents—promoting their own careers and the universalism and autonomy of Western law. They operate in relation to their own countries, the traditionally dominant civil-law world, and the increasingly dominant world of Anglo-American legal practice.

The second section of this chapter underscores that the activities of the double agents on the periphery must be examined in relation to external events and transformations that take place in the political and economic fields. The interaction between those external changes and the internal processes allows arbitration to keep up with both local changes and with changes in the international market. Arbitration therefore serves as a barometer of relations between the economic and the legal.

The third section then begins to examine the general themes as they are enacted in both the growth of international commercial arbitration in new places and kinds of disputes and in the transformations that take place in relation to that growth. We focus, as suggested above, on the personal dimensions of these patterns, seeing in particular how an unequal system of patron-client relations fosters new entry for those who pay their dues at the local level and succeed in distancing themselves adequately from the local structures that produce them.

2. Certainly, there existed numerous legal and judicial forms of regulation before colonization, but, in the majority of the cases, colonization introduced a break of such scope that one can speak of new legal constructions.

3. On this point, Europe has not been spared, but the long tradition of legal investment facilitated a rapid reconstruction of the legal order after the breakdowns associated with fascism.

The fourth section follows by looking more closely at the impact of the competition between national elites and institutions. It suggests that the competition must be explained above all by the role it plays domestically—which then promotes the local transformations we have seen. The section concludes by recalling the role that the multinational law firms play in helping to attack local monopolies and thereby promote the universals of arbitration. While we have been concentrating in this part on the transformations of local hierarchies and relationships, it is important to recall the role of these major actors on the international (and national scenes) (seen especially in chap. 3). By helping to break up local monopolies of justice, they facilitate the development of international commercial arbitration—and law.

Finally, the chapter concludes by building on the analysis of the preceding sections to return to the Western center of arbitration. It completes the story of Paris, suggesting in the first place why it became the beachhead for international commercial arbitration and how international commercial arbitration contributed substantially to transforming the legal field found in Paris. The success in Paris, in turn, became a kind of model of the success that international commercial arbitration had in simultaneously attacking fragmented and compartmentalized local markets and establishing itself as a formidable parallel justice. We include Paris as part of our conclusion to the chapter on how international commercial arbitration is transforming the role of law and lawyers on the periphery, in other words, because what happened in Paris could then happen—and is happening—elsewhere (with local variations).

From the Colonial Double Agent to the Role of Mediator in a Trilateral Game

In order to understand international commercial arbitration outside of the Western legal centers, it is necessary to take into account the international context of dependency that leads to the construction of "imported" systems of law. The lawyers on the periphery accordingly enact their double agency in continuing relationships of clientele. The situation, however, has become increasingly complex, largely in response to the increase in power of a new symbolic imperialism, that of the large multinational law firms. This new system substitutes triangular exchange for the traditional colonial relationship, creating a space where, as we shall see with respect to arbitration, the most cosmopolitan of the lawyers on the periphery have assets that give them a head start in the competition. They are better able to move to construct the requisite neutral place for arbitration—or at least a place that appears as such in the relations between different national powers.

The internationalization of the legal field on the periphery can thus support new strategies of "autonomization." The international credibility of business justice, as we have seen, requires lawyers to show their distance from national economic and political powers. To be sure, the requisite autonomy for international credibility will not necessarily be diffused throughout the legal system. All depends on the positions and the resources that the internationalist fraction of legal notables can mobilize toward domestic reformist strategies. Nevertheless, even if cantonized in the law of business, this embryo of autonomy, in the form of a kind of parallel justice, represents a notable innovation in systems where there has been great mixing—or confusion—between the world of law and that of social power.

This questionable autonomy of law can be seen in systems characterized by a clientelist paternalism of notables, by political authority and legitimacy dominated by investment in the construction of the national state, or by a cultural or economic domination exercised by a foreign imperialism. The relations between these different places and forms of power have not been stable throughout the long processes of colonization and decolonization, but it is precisely the history of fights and compromises between different fractions of dominant classes that has profoundly marked legal constructions. The legal constructions are the product and the instrument of a double agency in the field of power.

Comprador Lawyers in the Construction of Imported States

As a general rule, legal elites in the universe of political and institutional relations have played a role similar to that played by compradors in the domain of commercial exchange. Indeed, often the same individuals—or, at least, the same social groups—play on the two registers,[4] simultaneously or successively.

In both cases, the pattern is roughly the same. The cosmopolitan notables follow their own interests at the same time they serve the interests of their protectors. In Asia, for example, they developed their own enterprises on the margin of the European taipans, for whom they were the agents; and in many places, they have used the learning of an imported ideology (Badie 1993) to

4. According to Tahirih Lee, on the basis of her study of litigation and the courts in Shanghai prior to 1949,

"Compradores," a new type of broker, were one class of Chinese who grew wealthy outside the bounds of the guild restrictions.

Courts played a role in the rise of brokers free of guild control. Compradores frequently filed lawsuits at the International Mixed Courts, some on behalf of their bosses, some on their own. Chinese lawyers also amassed wealth outside the guild structure functioning much like the compradores, as brokers and middlemen. (1993, 1404)

construct quasi-state regulatory frameworks that then serve also as vehicles for nationalist demands.[5] Thus, while being agents of a symbolic colonialism, these institutional importers also set the stage for third worldism—often becoming, however, its first victims when the movements became radicalized and demanded to exercise power themselves.

From Imported Justice to Justice under Guardianship

In the majority of cases, the fall of this cosmopolitan bourgeoisie has signified also the beginning of the destruction of the legal field with which they had been associated. Part of the explanation is that the possessors of imported legal learning were quite often political notables or businesspeople rather than high priests of law. As seen in the case of Hong Kong, for example, legal titles have served primarily an ornamental function for local notables who tended to consider the state—and also justice—as an element of their patrimony. These imported legal institutions were therefore the basis of a double network of clientele. One was simply the network of local protégés of these notable economic or political actors, and the other was more symbolic. The second network connected them to the great European centers of the production of legal knowledge and legitimacy. In this context, we can see that the "legal construction" was bound to be quite fragile. In the first place, the sources of legitimacy were distant, outside of the local power structure; and second, the legal domain was experienced locally primarily as a colonial heritage of privilege (in the strict sense of the term) for the comprador bourgeoisie—on the payroll of foreigners.

This situation of dependence became exacerbated with the arrival of new populist, military, Communist, or third-worldist regimes. Their political orientation made them feel perfectly justified in taking control of institutions that appeared as the potential seat of counterrevolution. In many countries, therefore, as we saw in Egypt, new leaders ousted the notables whose social authority was identified with legal institutions of the ancien régime. Even more important than the personal attacks, however, was the fact that these minirevolutions were able to divide the legal institutions from their sources of legitimacy. The ties with the great European centers of production of legal learning had given these peripheral legal practices whatever small degree of autonomy they had with respect to local authorities. In Latin America, as in the Middle East, jurisprudence relied essentially on an imported doctrine. The new political arrangements cut off this source of legitimacy.

5. From this point of view, more than a century separated the two examples studied. Nevertheless, in Hong Kong as in Egypt, lawyers were at the heart of the construction of the state.

Furthermore, these new "developmental states" (Castells 1992) were forced to rely on other, nonlegal, bases of legitimate authority, such as technical proficiency or economics (Fallows 1994; Wade 1990). The new bases of authority undermined the social position of law and lawyers. Such a process of a loss of influence and credibility, as we have noted before, rapidly becomes cumulative. The decline of law promotes a general *déclassement* of its producers that is accelerated with the change of generations (Reid 1981). The decline in status of the legal profession perpetuates the decline of the legal field.[6]

(Re)Constructing Justice in a Trilateral Market

This disqualification of justice and devaluation of the producers of law in capitalist states situated on the periphery had more than local repercussions. Since the periphery also tends to become the new frontier of the capitalist market, the decline of law necessarily had a very strong impact on international trade.

The weak autonomy of justice with respect to political power, which was also often mixed with local economic power, furnished a powerful rationale for multinational corporations to distrust local legal systems and seek to preclude them from handling any business conflicts. Pointing to media accounts of corruption and influence peddling, often implicating lawyers and courts,[7] dominant players in the economic field could succeed in invoking, if not their own laws and judges, at least some kind of formula like the *lex mercatoria* and international commercial arbitration. Such formulas and practices, as we have seen especially in chapter 4, manifested enough independence from the Western multinationals to gain sufficient credibility to act effectively—even if, when they acted, they tended to ratify the domination of the economic powers.

This disqualification of peripheral justice reinforced a relation of dependence that is simultaneously political and economic. The terms of trade were just as unequal in law as in commercial relations,[8] leading to a quite paradoxical victory for Western law. As it happened, the Western-imposed legal machinery was disqualified through the challenge to a colonial heritage, only to make way for its return through another kind of Western legal imperialism (cf. Mattei 1994).

6. Egypt in the Nasser period offers a striking example, but there are many others. They include Indonesia, a certain number of countries in Latin America, and particularly the countries that came under communist influence.

7. Typical is Cheng 1994.

8. This distortion of trade is especially evident in the case of Hong Kong, since justice remains, to a great extent, imported justice.

This description, however, is too one-dimensional. The details are important and require an examination of the dynamic within the legal field. Indeed, we find in the new legal frontiers the same logic of competition and distancing that has permitted the construction of the field of arbitration. We find also the same combination, again in unequal proportions, of the resources and know-how of legal multinationals with the moral and learned authority of the notables who embody the European legal tradition.

The early investors in international commercial arbitration—from the north and the south—came to their investments with different perspectives. The oil companies and construction multinationals well recognized the need to invest in the law, and even to accept the limits that the autonomy of law imposed on their power. For the leaders of third-world countries or Communist states, the choice was more stark: either they invested in the law, or they faced complete autarky. If they wished to play on the international scene or even to enter into relationships of international exchange, they had to invest in the law, and even to slacken just a bit the strict control that they had been exercising on legal practices and institutions.

The development of international trade therefore permitted a small elite of jurists in the periphery to recover some aspects of the privileged role of intermediary. The situation also presented opportunities for them to play again as double agents seeking to construct—or reconstruct—a space of autonomy. As we can see from the two examples studied, however, this (re)construction of a legal field is not simply a matter of dusting off the predecessor legal institutions. Even if the legal tradition had an ancient national pedigree (as in the case of Egypt), the reconstruction could not return to it. And a fortiori, when there was no tradition to draw on (as in Hong Kong or China), the model presented by colonial history could hardly serve as a guide.

One reason for new models was simply the lack of personnel from the earlier period. Even, for example, in Egypt, where a well-established professional fabric had existed, there hardly remained enough survivors or *héritiers* of the old legal bourgeoisie to constitute the nucleus of this new cosmopolitan legal elite. Elsewhere, depending on the duration of the break and the intensity of the attack on the lawyers by the authoritarian regimes, the same problem of finding survivors exists. As it turns out, therefore, the new lawyers tend to be newly converted—or reconverted from other places in the local hierarchy. China exemplifies this reconversion. The new elite of business law has been recruited more easily from the ranks of the leaders of the state technocracy than from within the legal milieu.

Another reason for transformation is that the earlier mode of production and legitimation of law is in the process of being toppled. Even when the institutions are nominally the same, the systems of positions and paths of exchange have been profoundly disturbed. Within the countries on the periphery, the senior cosmopolitan elite, educated in the European manner, is becoming increasingly marginalized, even eliminated. As we have seen in Egypt, the restoration of the prerogatives of the old *noblesse de robe* can last only a short period. Even when they have been reintegrated back to their positions and their titles, these representatives of the old elite appear condemned either to disappear or to effect a major reconversion. This situation is all the more inevitable because the external world has also changed dramatically. The learned European tradition on which this *noblesse de robe* relied for a good part of its legitimacy has been more and more under attack as a result of the growth of the international legal market (see generally Mattei 1994).

We have seen on the periphery, therefore, a replay of the same battles and the same compromises that have transformed the ICC. The weakening of the sphere of influence of the old urban centers of learned law is even more pronounced on the periphery. These new frontiers, after all, have been the terrain where the competition between capitalisms—and the symbolic imperialisms that are their corollary—is most exacerbated. And, again, we see a shift in the center of gravity from the theory of the European legal centers to the practice of the large Anglo-American law firms.

While the balance of power may have shifted, the competition is still quite intense, and international competition in the market of law has other implications for the countries on the periphery. It contributes to break open the play of relations of clientele that placed the legal producers of the third world in a relation of dependence with the principle European sources of production and legitimacy of law. More than ever, it is true, legal technology remains an imported technology; but the multiplication of the centers of production increases considerably the margin of maneuver for peripheral users who can diversify their sources of supply or play on the competition.[9] There may be more legal imperialism, but the competition between legal empires allows some of the actors and countries on the legal periphery to use it for their advantage.

The development of international commercial trade—and, as an indirect consequence, international legal relations—opens a new page in the relatively young history of the peripheral legal systems. What actually materializes, however, depends to a great extent on the manner in which the new legal elites are able to manifest and manage their distance with respect to the circles

9. Thus, in the recent negotiations on GATT, the Japanese lawyers benefited from the competition between Europeans and North Americans to preserve the autonomy of their national market (Dillon 1994).

of power from which they came. The local and international credibility of the private or public business justice systems depends on this distance.

The simultaneous importance of local and international credibility means that local battles on these new frontiers of law also determine the fate of transnational business justice in the local settings. The cumulative importance of these legal developments stems partly from the fact that the new countries occupy an increasingly important place in international trade and investment. There is also another aspect of the contribution of the periphery to the construction of an international legal order. The claims of the new commercial and legal partners represent powerful levers in the effort to construct a truly international legal space—including the north and the south, serving the dominant and the dominated.

A parallel logic leads the multinationals and the third-world states to invest in the terrain of law—for one, to sacrifice a part of their profits, and for the other, to sacrifice a part of their sovereignty. For such a successful mutual investment, however, it is necessary to have intermediaries to negotiate the reciprocal concessions—and to profit from the process, both materially and symbolically. The intermediaries are also constrained to use these reciprocal concessions to build collectively a neutral place. The various intermediaries, whether from the north or the south, have this same fundamental objective. But the strategies that they put in place are a function of the configuration of powers from which this autonomy must be conquered. Thus, paradoxically, the efforts of lawyers of the third world to construct the autonomy of justice locally are the homologue of the efforts of the founding fathers of arbitration to affirm their autonomy with respect to state judicial systems.

The strategies of the intermediaries contribute to remodel the institutional landscape out of which the strategies are elaborated. In the Western countries, the emergence and the revalorization of the market are at the same time the product and the means of a profound modification of the relationship between the worlds of law and business. On these new frontiers of law and justice, the growth of arbitration—and more generally that of the market of law—is tied to the recognition of its autonomy with respect to the state and state justice. The consequences are therefore quite significant; yet, in both cases, the success or failure of these strategies depends on the efforts of a handful of individuals, united by their common interests and brought to help each other.

At the center and the periphery, these individuals exercise the function of *courtiers* operating at the border between the world of law and that of power; but, to succeed, it is necessary for them first to play their role as master double agents in their own universe. They may, for example, rely on the symbolic legitimacy of the state justice system while at the same time putting it aside in favor of international private justice. Similarly, they may build on the competition between different national producers and the tensions generated by the extreme inequality in the division of social and legal capital. They can therefore build on the need for an image of an international-arbitration community that is both diversified and welded together—able to embody and to produce universal private justice.[10]

Given the position of arbitration between law and economic power, it is not a surprise that the ambiguity and confusion of roles that characterize the relations between legal authority and social power is found in an exemplary manner in the structure of the field of arbitration. We see the virtues of legal idealism combined with the dynamic of the market. The workings of this double agency—merchants of legal virtue—is seen especially through the relationships of clientele that, at the same time, both reflect the north-south disequilibrium and permit it to be overlooked. The internal hierarchy of this community leads its members to disassociate themselves from the local system of power that produced them; at the same time, the close personal ties that knot them together through the process of initiation contribute to the inculcation of legal virtue and to a collective enterprise of distancing from social determinations. As we have noted before, competition in the market for justice constructs a neutral place and produces the universal.

It is important to recognize, however, that competition in a symbolic universe cannot be reduced to a simple logic of the market. The contenders must submit to a process of initiation that requires them to modify—but not moderate—their ambitions. To succeed, they must gradually find a place for themselves in a complex game of exchange in favors, controlled by a small group of great notables and leading bureaucrats. In the closed and secret universe where reputations are made with respect to the field of arbitration, overly aggressive or high-pressure strategies are considered uncalled for. The objective in the competition is less to gain shares of the market than to occupy key positions in the networks constituted around the principle institutions.

---

10. We see this approach, for example, in the statement of Fathi Kemicha at the 1993 ICCA conference in Bahrain.

    No one can deny that arbitral institutions have made a genuine effort on behalf of Arab jurists. The arbitration system of Euro-Arab Chamber of Commerce has granted them parity. Other institutions have guaranteed them some seats within the limits of their own rules. Independent and competent Arab arbitrators do exist but many remain unknown; they should be given the chance to prove their mettle! Such a goal can only be pursued by the concerted action of the main arbitral institutions which, leaving aside concerns about their market share but in full respect of their specificities, could carry out common initiatives. (Kemicha 1994, 234)

Success in this somewhat muffled competition depends much more on sponsors and peers than on clients.

This observation about individuals holds true also for the institutions of arbitration, even when they seem to operate by a market logic—or even to focus on a territory. None of the arbitral institutions, however, can require individuals to affiliate exclusively with them. The best-known individuals, who are also the most sought after, accumulate positions with respect to all the leading places. We see them again and again as conference speakers and on the lists of arbitrators of the numerous national or regional centers. Given this fact, the competition between all the institutions is bound to be in large part rhetorical. It sets the scene for political and publicity purposes, but the rhetoric of competition only fools the noninitiated.

The effects of this promotional activity, however, are quite significant. The outpouring of publicity about arbitration contributes to make arbitration generally known to its potential clients. As discussed further below, it also helps to gain local recognition from those close to the formal justice system, suggesting the possibility that others may take part in it. The promotional activity helps also to define the terms of the competition for the players. As we have seen, competition in the field of justice can only be expressed in terms of credibility. The potential merchants of arbitration are therefore constrained to fight for business only in terms of universalism. Their bids thus serve to raise the stakes in terms of idealism and legal virtue. We thus see again that competition in the market of disputes helps to produce the universal values of arbitration. Private justice not only enriches the promoters. It also produces the law.

A Barometer of Relations between the Economic and the Legal

This competition in the field of arbitration is not the only factor in determining the evolution of practices and institutions of arbitration. The competition is both the product of a changing environment and the means for adapting to it—while contributing also to the further transformation of that environment. We have suggested that the practices and institutions of arbitration are inscribed between two poles—justice and economic power. But the relations between these more or less antagonistic, unequal, or proximate worlds vary enormously. They differ not only among different countries, but also over time.

The changes over time are the product of a process that is nearly imperceptible over the short term. The respective positions are crystallized in state institutions and the mechanisms of reproduction of the dominant class—which define the value and social authority of legal diplomas, for example, in relation to other scholarly credentials. These values and authority change only marginally, even when new arrivals opt for different careers in the field of power. But, as noted before, the process may become cumulative if success leads successive groups to follow the same road.

While change is typically gradual, certain sociopolitical conjunctures accelerate the process through which positions among the dominant fractions of the elite are redistributed. One possible interpretation of very recent events, for example, is that an acceleration of the internationalization of economies, with an institutionalization through accords such as GATT and NAFTA, is leading to an "international new deal" in legal and economic arrangements. Internationalization, according to this line of reasoning, is redefining the means of institutional oversight and regulation of business relations, and setting the stage for growing legalization of business relations. A growing legalization thus leads to a revalorization of legal capital for the management of conflicts—changing the relative position of legal capital in the fields of state and economic power. This legalizing evolution, however, is not the only possible outcome from growing economic internationalization. It is also possible that growing unemployment and a concomitant political instability could lead in certain instances to a return to state interventionism. And in remote or high-risk markets, whether in Asia or elsewhere, the relational (even familial) capitalism described by Braudel for the sixteenth century remains another potential strategy perfectly consistent with the minimization of transaction costs.[11]

These major developments, built on contradictory pressures that may affect different countries quite differently, are bound to have a serious impact on the way in which large commercial conflicts are handled. One effect is to modify the value of legal authority and relational capital that the different players are able to mobilize,[12] whether on the basis of their career and practice in arbitration or in the service of their institutional strategies. Like the arbitrators, the arbitral institutions develop a "trademark" reflecting the experience and the network of relations on which their clientele and credibility depend. The market price of one or another competing institution thus fluctuates in

11. To repeat an earlier observation (see also Greenhalgh 1994), we do not believe that the prevalence of relational capitalism in Asia is simply a given structural or cultural characteristic, as suggested by many of the defenders of the specificity of an "Asian mode of production."

12. Note that these are not only changes in relative relationships between legal authority and relational capital. The value of relations, for example, may also change if a particular cosmopolitan or international network becomes more valuable than a local network of relations or family connections.

relation to political and economic transformations that, while in one sense seeming to pass them by, in another sense make up their components.

The very scarce arbitrators from the Chinese world, for example, clearly profit well from the rapid expansion of the market. They increase both their clientele and their recognition in the inner circles of arbitration. But, at the same time, they contribute to the expansion of the market by helping to minimize the potential transaction costs of business disputes. Local promoters of international arbitration serve not only to open this new market for themselves (and then also to their foreign colleagues). They also contribute to enhance the claims to universality for this mode of administering business conflicts. Their specific involvement enhances universality in one respect, but they also tend to articulate within the larger arbitration community the specific concerns relevant to this new market and its potential clientele.[13] The enlargement of this market occurs as the same time as the improvement—and universalization—of its technology.

The local prospectors for arbitration are, then, valuable to their peers for their double agency on behalf of their local interests and the interests of international commercial arbitration. They find new clients, and they contribute also to reinvent or at least to revitalize arbitration. In short, as it turns out, the personal interests of these entrepreneurs of the periphery correspond perfectly with the interests of the small community of arbitration professionals for whom they are salespeople and missionaries. Again, we see how perfectly inscribed this behavior is in the logic of the field of arbitration. External recompositions in the political and economic context are crucial to the expansion of arbitration, yet the individual and collective strategies within the field contribute to a constant renovation and adaptation that serves also to protect the image of autonomy.[14]

The Division of Symbolic Labor and Collective Apprenticeship in Universals

The relative fluidity of the world of arbitration facilitates its adaptability to change. The great arbitrators can move easily between the principal arbitral

13. One could say the same thing about the ICC and the Euro-Arab market. In many other instances, however, it is a matter of one sector of activity like computers or new "alternative" techniques for the handling of conflicts leading the way.

14. They may also try to slow down or attenuate the effects, for example by supporting the relative autonomy of the field of arbitration and reinforcing the hierarchy of international positions of the great European centers and their network of Western arbitrators. Still, even if it is always possible to play on these contradictions, the strategy of countercurrent represents a difficult and uncertain exercise.

institutions. One way to respond to new demands or to find ways to anticipate them is for institutions to put forward particular individuals—and therefore competences—that can stimulate and serve new demands. At the same time, potential arbitrators with a highly sought expertise can build their reputations and increase their market value by playing on the potential competition be- tween the different centers. Each has a strong incentive and ability to take advantage of changes that enhance the value of particular arbitrators and ex- pertises.

In addition to this horizontal mobility, there is a vertical or hierarchical mobility, and it also applies to both institutions and individuals. The major institutions have relations of clientele with the institutions on the periphery, which serve as outposts for the established international-arbitration market. The insinuation of the networks of local "prospector-informants" into the networks controlled by the noted specialists or their intermediaries in the central institutions also serves to correct the relative lack of openness of this field of practice. Political or economic transformations may rather quickly open new sectorial or geographic markets to arbitral practice, but the new opportunities translate only gradually into an enlargement of the circle of arbitrators—at least as far as it concerns the relatively small inner circle. The introduction of new arrivals, as we have seen, is a very slow process that requires passing several tests—even when it is a matter of a distinguished legal notable presenting all the required personal and professional characteristics. It can hardly be faster when those seeking admission are from the periphery of the international field.

The prospecting and exploitation of new territories is made on the basis of a hierarchical division of tasks that reproduces, or comes close to, the classical civil-law distinction between the practitioner, charged with presenting the facts and putting them in a legal form, and the "jurisconsult," who only pro- nounces on questions of law.[15] As it turns out, the "postulants" or prac- titioners on the periphery serve not only as informants, but also as promoters of the great sages of arbitration. When the stakes are very high, new arrivals recognize that they cannot handle the cases themselves. They appeal to the specialists whom they have met at one or another of the "promotional masses" of international commercial arbitration. This favor calls for others and estab- lishes a patronage relationship that permits the new arrivals gradually to famil- iarize themselves with the usages of the club and to progress in the hierarchy of this coveted and secret universe.

15. This is also the traditional distinction in England between barristers and solic- itors.

This clientele relation can repeat itself at many levels. The allegiances are not, however, exclusive. The relations build further a complex and dense network. It is a pyramid structure where the different stages correspond to the stages of initiation. The networks support and construct an inner circle, essentially composed of the grand masters and disciples of the first generation who control the major institutional bases of arbitration. But outside of this first group, composed of well-known and easily identifiable lawyers and arbitrators, the positions and memberships are much less settled.

The main recruits for the position as entrepreneur-promoter come from the intermediate ranks of the initiated—the reserve ready and available for service in arbitration. Arbitration centers proliferating in places ranging from Vancouver to Kuala Lumpur and covering Bucharest in between seek official status as duly homologized correspondents following the norms of the major centers. They periodically welcome visits from the grand masters who come to spread the word to local practitioners and teach them techniques that are not taught in practitioner manuals or law schools. These local promotional activities, in fact, provide the main international activity of the local promoters, since the number of arbitrations that they handle is rather small. What matters, however, is that these institutions procure for their founders-promoters a title and a passport, identifying them as local notables. This international status, in addition, has a local value, permitting them to enter more easily into the milieus of entrepreneurs and professionals who must be convinced of the merits of this mechanism for administering business conflicts.

As noted before, this process of conversion in the periphery depends on the local missionaries' ability to convince their local hierarchies to accept the creed of arbitration. The local missionaries must play the role of *courtiers* sufficiently well introduced in the circles that organize the colloquia and edit the reviews to find sponsors who will support them with the information that comes through connections with insiders. Learning the new technical, conceptual, or rhetorical advances, in turn, builds the local position of the missionary and facilitates the successful exploitation of new markets. The exploration and development of these new raw materials for arbitration is then a long and complex process, requiring a sustained effort on several fronts. In recompense for their services in the cause of private justice, the new pioneers can aspire to move closer to the inner circle of the great (and well-connected) arbitrators.

As we have seen, the renovation of the milieus of the arbitrators, a corollary of the enlargement of the market, takes place in a gradual manner, through a series of exchanges of favors that reactivate the relations of patronage on which this private justice rests. The centers on the periphery serve as outposts that channel potential conflicts toward the major institutions and the small nucleus of prestigious and well-connected arbitrators who control them. It is only at a later time, after they have passed the required tests, that the new institutions and new leaders can aspire to be recognized as full members of the community of arbitrators.

This process of apprenticeship is, in certain respects, a process of delocalization and distancing from places of origin. In order to gain status in the inner circle of arbitration, it is necessary to be recognized as suitable to intervene in a range of very different types of conflicts. In other words, it is necessary to *construct an authority of universal (or near universal) dimensions.* The success of a career as arbitrator implies then a slow enlargement of competences (real or perceived) and sphere of operation. It is necessary to pass from the position of local notable, able to intervene in a quite familiar domain on the basis of a primarily local professional and social position, to that of an itinerant "superjudge." The superjudge must be capable of intervening far from the arbitrator's social bases and to impose authority over foreign parties without either the support of the state and its legal system or of the local old boys' network. This task is very challenging and difficult in practice.[16] But the process of developing arbitrators with this all-encompassing credibility is essential to the claims of international commercial arbitration to serve in place of an international court system.

It is not an exaggeration to say, in fact, that *the social structures of arbitration are conceived to produce this delocalization (or deprovincialization) of legal legitimacy.* The structures lead and permit some legal notables to exchange their capital of local reputation for a portion of international authority guaranteed collectively by the cosmopolitan community of international arbitration. The terms of trade vary according to the state of the market and the relative positions of the protagonists. The notable in a hot new market, for

16. The difficulty of third-world arbitrators who wish to be taken seriously by the arbitrators and lawyers from the core is illustrated by the following example—as told by a U.S. lawyer:

Back in the early eighties the Indonesians liked to have an Indonesian on the panel. So you've got two arbitrators of truly international renown, who've done many, many ICC arbitrations, and you have a professor of law in the University in Jakarta. He may be a bright fellow in his own milieu but just doesn't have the stature of these other two arbitrators. We would feel occasionally that within the deliberative process the Indonesian's case was not really argued as it might have been. So we were sort of in the process over time of persuading the Indonesians that if you are going to agree . . . to an ICC arbitration . . . , you have to be willing to appoint a prestigious arbitrator. You are shooting yourself in the foot if you appoint . . . the most renowned professor of law in your country, but he's really not known as an ICC arbitrator. (Int. 52, 13)

example, may have more immediate value than a candidate from a more peripheral site.

This process follows fundamentally the same complementary and competitive logic seen in all relations of clientele between masters and apprentices, between the center and the periphery, and between all the great institutions that are at the heart of arbitration. The ideal of an all-encompassing competence and credibility, in fact, is always being (re)constructed, since it can never be fully attained by arbitrators or institutions. The transcendent ideal is even more impossible to achieve in an international context where enduring divisions prevent any real form of general consensus. Given the inevitable difficulty of the task, we can see the vital importance of the arbitration market in continually producing a collective legal authority with universal pretensions. This internal arbitration market allows the producers of arbitral justice—institutions and arbitrators—constantly to exchange forms of expertise and authority and therefore to diversify their capital and the sources of their legitimacy.

It is not an accident that, when asked how to find leading arbitrators from outside of the developed Western world, one U.S. lawyer in Paris stated, "There are some people who've become well known, like [Eduardo Jiminez de] Arechaga, who was a former president of the International Court of Justice, in Uruguay and very active in commercial arbitration in the last ten to fifteen years. You see the ICJ, and it does have some possibilities. You have—I think he's from Kenya—[Keba] M'Baye. You have [Mohammed] Bedjaoui from Algeria" (int. 106, 51). The career that leads to appointment to the World Court is a career that has paid attention to the universals of international law—contributing to the distance necessary also for success in the internal market of international commercial arbitration. The cosmopolitan arbitrator is thus referred to often as "the most French of the Egyptians, or the most British of the Lebanese" (int. 109, 6).

Producing the Universal through Competition between National Elites in the Market of Forms of Legitimacy

The market of arbitration can be seen as a market in forms of legitimacy, and this conception of the market can be used to provide another perspective on the competition between national sites in the 1980s. This competition was fought in terms of the legislation applicable to arbitration, and all the changes purported to have the same objective—to try to attract a greater share of the market of international commercial arbitration. Furthermore, in each case the effort to gain more business implied a reduction in the control exercised by domestic courts over this private justice. In each country the promoters of the reforms argued that it was necessary to go further than its neighbors—and competitors—to attract the floating clientele. Following this dynamic, we can see how "free ports in law" were created—giving the parties freedom to select the applicable process, law, and judges, with a minimum of disturbance by the state and its legal system.

The competition between the major sites of arbitration—and those that wished to be—for shares of this prestigious and promising new market thus served to justify bidding wars in deregulation, leading states and their court systems to give up their sovereign prerogatives (Barnet and Cavanagh 1994). It appears, therefore, that the path of "reform" in arbitration represents another example of a form of competition in the law that is often condemned as a "race to the bottom." That, at least, is a tempting interpretation if we follow only the public-relations image of a fierce fight over a rapidly growing market.

The trouble with the fierce-fight interpretation is that, as we have seen, this field of practice is in the first place a club of initiated where personal ambitions must bow to a collective logic.[17] All the members of this community are perfectly aware that the credibility of this private justice is too recent, and too fragile, to tolerate marketing strategies that are too bold or ostentatious.[18] In any event, the growth of this market is hardly so miraculous as is often believed.[19] It is clear from the experience of the new centers that neither advertising nor perfect arbitration laws will suffice to attract very many potential clients. The clients sought by the new centers, after all, value credibility above all. They keep to the proven values. The question then is why all the

17. We can retain the notion of the market if we define it in terms of a closed market with producers limited as much by their mentors as by their peers. The personal relations within the networks of producers promote a connivance and reciprocity that reinforce the stability of the trade. Furthermore, access is still controlled by the small nucleus of founding fathers who select the postulants as a function of the deference that they show with respect to the values of arbitration. This private justice for merchants is then, in many respects, at least as far removed from the market—and protected from its temptations—as the state justice system. The importance of the financial and political stakes in this type of international dispute imposes a certain vigilance, given the fragility of an institution that does not benefit from state protection.

18. There is hardly any reason for advertising. The prominence and reputation of centers or arbitrators who are better established is such that they need no advertising. And the lack of experience of the new arrivals in a market where competition is in terms of credibility cannot be overcome by advertising or marketing.

19. The few published statistics, as we have noted before, are subject to considerable caution. They mix many small matters with the very large ones. The statistics also serve the promotional purpose of attracting new clients by seeking to persuade them of past successes. We have called this "making it by faking it."

agitation and competitive posturing. Or, more precisely, to whom is it directed?

Our hypothesis is that this propaganda aims as much at potential producers as consumers of this private justice. More exactly, it seeks to transform into allies those who might otherwise be competitors. It aims to convince the legal professionals of the state justice system—judges, but also *avocats,* barristers, or litigators—that arbitration is not so much a dispossession as a supplementary competence, and that they can easily add this competence to the range of expertises they offer to potential clients. This effort of persuasion is probably quite important. These national legal systems do not easily depart from a long tradition of distrust of this private justice—often considered a kind of subjustice requiring court supervision. The strength of the argument for court supervision was further fortified by the fact that such supervision serves also to protect the monopoly of national practitioners in the market for handling business conflicts.[20]

Only powerful arguments can convince the legal practitioners to give up this control and to open the market to foreign competition at the same time.[21] The invocation of "international competition" represents a powerful lever to construct the autonomy of arbitration while contributing to its promotion. The legislative bidding wars between the different countries contribute therefore to opening new territories to this private justice.

The public-relations campaigns also serve to make arbitration recognized within the potential-user community as a means for resolving commercial conflicts.[22] The campaigns suggest that arbitration is the only accepted legal means for resolving large commercial disputes. While it is true, as noted before, that these marketing operations bring more profit to the arbitral establishment than to the new arrivals who organize and finance them, there are benefits for the new arrivals. At the very least, these media campaigns succeed in fulfilling requirements to gain a "right of entry." And even better, the local

20. See also chapter 6.

21. In England, the partisans of reform of arbitration estimated that millions of pounds were being lost to London and its legal profession from the fact of legislation perceived by their foreign counterparts as too restrictive and costly. The same individuals today admit that the estimates, widely reported by the press, were complete inventions. Still, we see similar alarms when the House of Lords was on the eve of ruling on the possibility of using the courts for security for costs in arbitration matters (Egan 1994). Recall also the strategy of the internationalists in the United States with respect to the *Mitsubishi* case. The ICC amicus brief made it very clear that this justice was available to retired U.S. Supreme Court justices.

22. The campaign occurs through the organization of congresses or colloquia where the great notables are received by local notables and businesspeople.

effort may provide a deferred investment, which will bear fruit when—once admitted into the inner circle of arbitration—they themselves benefit from campaigns organized by new generations of entrants.

The efficacy of this tactic stems also from what accompanies this implicit bargaining. National legal authorities do not give up their right to control private justice without gaining something in return. When they consent to recognize arbitration, they benefit in return from recognition by the cosmopolitan community that purports to embody transnational legitimacy. Very often we see that, thanks to this operation of mutual recognition, one or another of the members of the local legal elite is co-opted and introduced into the closed circle of arbitrators—providing also access into the international legal field in the process of being constructed. In return, this new recruit becomes an intermediary between two worlds that earlier had ignored each other. The recruit gives value to the national legal culture in the international setting, while at the same time guaranteeing the legitimacy of international private justice.

This process of breaking the isolation of national legal fields, effected by the practice of arbitration, is seen concretely in the interpenetration between the networks that gravitate around the different national sites and institutions for arbitration. The lists of arbitrators—official or unofficial—proposed by these centers bear witness to this political alliance and concretize it.[23] To be credible, each of these places practices a subtle mixing of the local professionals and a certain number of notable foreigners.[24] This relative opening of the national market is the price paid to justify the universalist pretensions necessary to build the market on the international setting. It is translated at the level of the management of arbitration matters into a complex system of exchange of gifts. The closely policed and regulated system plays a major role in holding together this decentralized justice.

There is a further dimension to the effect of breaking national isolation. Operating at the intersection of national legal cultures, the practice of arbitration challenges national monopolies built in large part on a respective misrec-

---

23. The presence on lists of this or that institution may sometimes be more symbolic than real—although the boundaries between the two are difficult to measure in this field.

24. The list of arbitrators approved for Chinese arbitration under CIETAC is indicative, especially given the language and expertise that certainly must be important to handle an arbitration in China. The list of eighty-one potential arbitrators draws heavily on the core of arbitrators. There are twenty-seven who are from China or Hong Kong, leaving fifty-four from the rest of the world. The international names are partly China experts, but many are generally familiar in the international-arbitration community.

ognition. However limited, this bridge between the cultures opens up the possibility of a confrontation. It can lead to an effective competition, or at least a kind of reciprocal evaluation. The different local elites learn to judge each other. As noted earlier, for example, the barrister can now be measured against the Continental professor or the senior partner of a large U.S. law firm.

More generally, this arbitration market substitutes a real measurement for what had been only an academic exercise. Instead of relying on learned comparativists, who would evaluate the respective merits of the different national legal practices before extolling the virtues of importation of some particular innovation, we can now point to a market. In the practice of arbitration, the practitioners themselves evaluate the respective merits of different national practices when they are confronted with a particular problem or when they are opposed in an international matter. The underlying process has not changed. The proponents of change seek marginal modifications in the rules of the legal game, under the pretext of improving them. But the objectives and stakes are somewhat changed today, since the importer-innovators are also—and perhaps above all—practitioners in the international field for the administration of business conflicts.

There is still considerable learned debate about the respective merits of the different rules or procedures. But, since the learned debate is conducted now by practitioners who are engaged daily in a competitive practice, their entries in the debates tend to track closely the perspective of their interests and those of their clients. Their discourses, as we have seen, are also their tactical options. The learned positions that they defend and the choices that they make in the conduct of a matter are then dictated by the manner in which the different systems of rules and usages give value to the strategic resources that they possess.

The relative weights of great legal principles on the one hand, and arguments of a more pragmatic or political nature on the other, are not the same in all places. The relative weights depend on the social and professional groups that control the institutions involved in the handling of business conflicts. The dominant groups tend to impose their language, their usages, and their scale of values. In other words, *the competition between the great sites of arbitration puts into play their structural characteristics, that is to say, the already precarious compromises between economic and legal power, concretized by the institutions, rules, and usages.*

The diverse and fluid structure of the field of arbitration therefore makes it a privileged laboratory for testing the relative merits of the different mechanisms for the handling of large commercial conflicts. The density of the personal ties and the interpenetration between the different networks also facilitates the diffusion of information. Given these characteristics, it is relatively easy to see why the large Anglo-American law firms have played an essential role. Their clientele of multinational businesses leads them to invest simultaneously on the different national scenes without becoming tied to any of them in particular. This position of privileged outsider permits them to exploit to a maximum all the resources of a strategy of forum shopping. They can pick and choose from among all the various possibilities.

The large Anglo-American law firms also can use this position of strength to remodel the institutional landscape to their advantage. In order to deploy their abundant financial and human resources as well as the particular legal expertise that they already have in handling large commercial disputes, it is necessary for them to redefine the rules of the game. National settings, not surprisingly, tend otherwise to institute, de facto, a quasi monopoly for national practitioners—even for a category of national practitioners.

For example, the practice of "case stated" in England permitted a small group of barristers to dominate this market in large business disputes because they controlled access to the Commercial Court. On the Continent, in contrast, the alliance between grand professors and high-court judges gave value to a kind of legal mediation, wedding doctrinal learning to the charismatic authority of the scholars. In the first case, the large law firms found themselves excluded; in the second, they were doubly disqualified. They lacked charismatic or doctrinal resources, and their major expertise in fact gathering and administering huge case files was not valued by learned jurists quite reluctant to operate on this most unfamiliar terrain. In short, in both cases, these outsiders were able to implant themselves only by helping to break the monopolies of fact or of law. *In attacking these national particularisms, the invaders had decompartmentalized and delocalized the practice of arbitration*—and in each case, introduced it to a more universal practice.

The Offensive of the Multinationals of Law and the Decompartmentalization of the National Arbitration Markets

Without reviewing in detail the examples described elsewhere (see the chapters on London, Stockholm, and the ICC), we can return to the question of why, after all, Paris and the ICC served as the beachhead for the penetration of legal multinationals on the European market of arbitration. This paradox is even more surprising since London had a much longer history in arbitration and was able to mobilize well-recognized and diversified competences in law and in other areas such as banking and insurance. Arbitration, we have suggested, functioned in London in a fairly stable fashion under the control of the Commercial Court. The general approach was characterized as "delegated justice."

In contrast, on the Continent, and especially in France, the position of private justice was much more fragile. It had a somewhat ambiguous status at the margin of the legal field, which was itself quite closed and increasingly marginalized from the field of power. In contrast to the situation with respect to the London Commercial Court, neither the Court of Appeal nor the Tribunal of Commerce of Paris could pretend to exercise any real function of control over the handling of business disputes. There was therefore considerable room to develop approaches to handle business disputes, and there were many efforts to organize this sector of activity. The barriers to entry were relatively low in this fractured institutional landscape. In addition, protectionist reactions were even more limited from the hierarchy of the Parisian bar, since the bar was affected with a disdain for "vulgar" conflicts too close to business.

As a result, commercial matters were not the monopoly of any group in particular. The rare specialist practitioners in commercial law[25] were too few in number to permit them to have territorial claims. The domain of large commercial conflicts was too far from the usual practice for the specialists to try to annex it within their jurisdiction. Until the end of the 1960s, it was therefore necessary to be a visionary or dilettante to be interested in international arbitration, which was more an activity of idealist or speculative legal theory. Only the academics, some judges, and a few atypical practitioners[26] were permitted to interest themselves as amateurs in a technique for handling conflicts—seen as a kind of laboratory to test their idealistic vision of a future international business justice. The unusual combination of these academic visionaries and the openness of Paris helped to allow the International Chamber of Commerce to take root as an institution for international business conflicts.

From a Structural Marginality to Offshore Justice

The distinguished amateurism of the promoters of arbitration for international business disputes allowed them to avoid being discredited as simply commercial and therefore vulgar legal practitioners. They were seen not as

25. Those who were admitted to practice before the Tribunal of Commerce, the *conseils juridiques*, or lawyers for enterprises.

26. More or less convinced or enthusiastic according to the positions they occupied and their personal itineraries. Emigrants like Berthold Goldman (from Romania) and Fredrick Eiseman (from Germany) invested the most and were most identified with this project of construction of a transnational justice.

part of some arrangement with merchants in the shadow of the law, but rather as a learned group suitable for elite participation. Some of the pioneers, in fact, were close to the prestigious circles of international law and the Hague Court of International Justice. Arbitration, therefore, could profit from the connections with these cosmopolitan images and pure law. It could be seen as the prototype for an international private justice.

The "nobility" of these origins was a kind of guarantee of legal legitimacy, putting international commercial arbitration and the ICC in position to claim a brilliant future. This nobility, however, was also a serious handicap to further development. Nobility and the spirit of enterprise rarely go together. Yet the business spirit is indispensable to the growth of what was not simply an ideal of social peace, but was also an enterprise aiming for the market of services to business.

Certainly the pioneering promoters were convinced that their project responded to an increasingly crucial need, given the expansion of international trade and the absence of any other possibilities for international private justice. But it is not enough to have a good idea without the ability to impose it. The technology was not really new, but it had not yet gone past the experimental stage. Major technological, human, and institutional investments were required to render it credible and familiar, both to the legal profession and to the world of business.

The founders were quite limited in what they could do to turn the prototype into an industry standard. They had a certain status as notables, but they were at the margin of the worlds of law and business. And very few of their colleagues were ready to support them in launching an international business justice whose future appeared quite uncertain. After all, very few members of the bar or the judiciary brought together the traits this activity required—an exceptional combination of professional notability, a sense of business, and cosmopolitan tastes.[27] It was therefore necessary to find allies and supporters to develop their enterprise.

As it turned out, the Yankee invaders became providential allies. Their

27. This requirement no doubt explains in part the development of what has been called the Paris-Geneva axis. Lawyers, academics, and judges in Geneva very early played a prominent role in the professional community that was put in place around the ICC. Certainly, Geneva benefited from a long tradition of cosmopolitanism and neutrality. In addition, however, as Siegrist (1986) has shown, the practice of law for a long time was more open to the world of business. It was therefore easier to find practitioners or academics both familiar with business and having academic prominence— qualities indispensable to arbitration but quite exceptional in the civil-law world.

arrival in Paris was not very difficult. The Parisian bar was divided and could not pretend to dispose of the competences necessary to monopolize commercial practice.[28] The bar had neither the will to fight nor the means to form a strategy—both necessary to protect legal territory. It is no doubt true that this situation changed with the beginning of the great ICC arbitrations in the 1970s. Local professionals could certainly see by then the importance of the market that was opening. But, even if they had succeeded in putting together a kind of holy alliance between pure lawyers and business practitioners,[29] the alliance would have been too late to be effective.

The acquisition of expertise and cosmopolitan prestige requires a long-term investment. While new generations in Paris have been able to profit from the implantation of the Anglo-American law offices, mainly by using them to become familiar with the requisite practical learning, the Parisian practitioners of the earlier generation were too late. The head start of the large Anglo-American law firms in Paris allowed them to capture a good part of the market of the large north-south arbitrations generated by the influx of petrodollars. Indeed, they could also use the profits from those conflicts to consolidate their positions in Paris, becoming in fact the principal counselors to large French businesses anxious to accelerate their strategies of internationalization.

The development of international arbitration this way strongly contributed to the transformation of legal practice in Paris.[30] In the first place, it permitted the revalorization of the image—until then very negative—of business disputes. By facilitating the implantation of U.S. lawyers and law firms, it also accelerated the professionalization and judicialization of a field of practice to which the French model of law had conceded only a marginal and precarious

28. The difference with England is great. Despite certain conflicts between lawyers and nonlawyers, the community of arbitration was relatively homogeneous and welded to the practice around the Commercial Court.

29. This prospect is difficult to imagine in any event since the projects for fusion between *avocats* and *conseils juridiques* had just been overturned. France had to wait until the end of the 1980s to succeed in the creation of a "grand profession" of *avocats-conseils*.

30. This influence was not only indirect. It is interesting to note, for example, that President Bellet was always interested in the reform of the professions. In 1963, he was in charge of a mission to go to the United States to study the functioning of the legal profession. Several years later, at the request of the Garde des Sceaux, he prepared a report on the fusion of the professions of *avocat* and *avoué*. Finally, in 1985, at the summit of his career as international arbitrator, he was charged with preparing a report on the place of French lawyers in international competition.

status. The legal politics led to the creation of a kind of free zone for law in Paris, where foreign lawyers could locate and freely exercise their activity, further promoting change. This competition meant that local practitioners were not then able to profit as much as they might have hoped from the opening of this door.

The founding fathers, of course, benefited considerably from the entry of large law firms onto this terrain and the growth of international commercial arbitration around the ICC. The alliance between the pioneers and these new arrivals represented a division of labor to the advantage of each. On one side, the notoriety and distinguished amateurism of the pioneers accommodated perfectly the prestigious—but episodic—function as arbitrator.[31] On the other side, the Anglo-American law firms took charge of assembling and administering huge collections of files (for the construction of infrastructure or the exportation of heavy equipment), which permitted them to support their international expansion and the legions of lawyers and support personnel that they had at their disposal.

Even though the influx of matters pointed above all to the entourage of the grand masters and their immediate disciples, the logic of the field promoted further outreach. As noted before, the logic of arbitration is opposed to all particularist or monopolist temptations. The notables had a strong interest in using their powerful Parisian institutional base to consolidate their international notoriety—and that of arbitration. Accordingly, they distributed their favors in a manner as large as possible—diffusing their learning and extending their network of influence.

Today, with the gradual demise of the first generation of grand notables, who were both recognized internationally and stamped with their national legal cultures, the expatriate character of the Parisian arbitration milieu can only be accentuated. There are now Swiss, English, U.S., and Arab practitioners who are quite notable in the Parisian legal scene. For the most part,[32]

31. Which did not exclude the even better-paid activities as adviser on the law and on the strategy for an arbitration.

32. Except for the Genevans, who are able to maintain a certain distance—at least geographically—from the ICC precisely because of their privileged position in the arbitrations as founding fathers or sponsors rather than clients. This relative distance reflects also a certain attitude of condescension on the part of a small community, well established on an international market where the Swiss image of neutrality suffices to assure credibility. To this significant asset is added the fact that the little world of Geneva specialists is itself a kind of quintessence of the world of arbitration, with its extraordinary density of very personalized ties that facilitate the masquerades and redistribution of roles that characterize the "commedia dell'arte" of arbitration practice.

they first came to Paris to participate in ICC activities, and for many of them it takes a number of years before they can be well integrated into the arbitration community. There is also a relatively younger generation, however, who came to arbitration after an education in the large international law firms or the bureaucracies of the arbitral institutions. These expatriate groups, however developed, circulate quite easily between the principal legal cultures.

In this increasingly cosmopolitan world, the French practitioners who claim only a legal tradition and language competence limited to French appear almost provincial, even outsiders in Paris. While being close to the institutional heart of this field of practice, they perceive themselves—and are perceived—as outside. It is perhaps this sentiment of exclusion, rendered more flagrant by the geographical proximity of the market, that motivates an aggressive and defensive attitude on the part of certain organizations of Francophonic arbitrators.[33] Under the leadership of the "founding fathers," they found ways to serve the noble cause of arbitration, but now they have more down-to-earth preoccupations. It is no longer a question of recognizing this mode of resolving conflicts. Their aim is to promote French expertise and language in matters of arbitration.

The appearance of territorial preoccupations, which these recent French activities exemplify, is hardly surprising. The pioneers did not need to say anything about their own interests in arbitration. They identified themselves totally with the cause of arbitration, and arbitration was likewise identified with them. Their successors are confronted with the reverse situation. Arbitration is nearly banalized and accepted as a matter of course; yet competition is growing with the multiplication of the number of potential producers. It is the price of success.

The work of promotion of this new form of justice has finally brought fruit. It is largely known and recognized. But the missionary zeal has been able to promote more interest in the vocation of arbitrator than there are disputes to arbitrate. And this is especially true in the great centers of arbitration. The existence of a well-established arbitration community and the efforts of institutions such as the LCIA and the ICC make it easy for many to claim this expertise through seminars and colloquia.

33. For example, we can point to the Association de Defense de l'Arbitrage en Langue Français, or the chambers of arbitration created by university lawyers who believe that the ICC has not made sufficient use of their talents. One finds the same sentiment, in addition, even if in a form that is more euphemistic, in the attitudes of those now responsible for leading organizations such as the Comité français de l'Arbitrage.

From the Propagation of an Ideal to the Administration of a Market:
Banalization and/or Americanization of Business Justice

It appears that, after a long sellers' market in international arbitration, the number of potential producers of arbitration has become excessive, at least in great European centers of arbitration like Paris, London, and Geneva. This overproduction of specialists not only increases the competition in the specific market, it tends also to modify the relations that are maintained between arbitration and the more general legal field. After having been considered the culmination of a career in service to law, this speciality now has emerged as one of the means of apprenticeship into the career of international business lawyer. This evolution favors both the generalization of this specific technology and the diffusion of the idealistic and universalistic logic that inspired this private justice. In short, as arbitration tends to become the accepted and normal way to handle large commercial conflicts, its logic becomes inscribed in the career strategies of business lawyers, contributing further to remodeling the field of practice in its own image.

As is the case for all of what can be termed symbolic regulatory regimes, this social invention becomes credible when it succeeds in producing users predisposed to consider its legitimacy as a matter of fact, meanwhile hiding all the work of social construction and all the play of strategies, alliances, and compromises that allowed it to succeed. At the same time, the success of this enterprise transforms it profoundly. In banalizing itself, the practice of arbitration, which had been practically the object of an esoteric cult, became the object of a competitive market—which is of considerable importance in shaping business relationships. This symbolic market, as we have suggested, responds to the double requirement of credibility and efficacy—crucial both to the users and the producers of arbitration.

This international market functions at a double level. For the entrepreneurs, it is a site for the handling of commercial conflicts. For the professionals, however, it serves also as a marketplace that permits different forms of legal authority and social and legal capital to be evaluated and exchanged. This function of exchange is in fact responsible for a large part of the success of this form of private justice in legal fields and social settings that were strongly compartmentalized and cut off from their counterparts elsewhere.

This compartmentalization, as we have noted, has been especially characteristic of the civil-law systems, where breaks and antagonisms are found at all levels of the market in business conflicts. There are antagonisms between different categories of lawyers and between lawyers and the world of business. Also important are the cleavages between other holders of economic power who claim a right to invoke justice, even if they may not choose to exercise it. Each of these and of other groups values the prerogatives essential to its authority over some of the terrain of business justice, but no group could become dominant without jeopardizing its own or the credibility of business justice. With respect to lawyers, for example, too much success in business justice would have meant choosing business practice over the cult of law, money over honor. This compartmentalization of the market of justice, therefore, had serious drawbacks, especially in an epoch where the restructuring of the international market threatened to shatter the different networks of economic power in order to recompose them in a different way.

This situation perhaps explains the facility with which the new dominant groups in the international legal field were able to export their model of justice. That model, while furnishing ammunition for industrial and financial battles, nevertheless tolerates a large margin of maneuver. The flexibility of this approach profits equally the lawyers and the holders of economic power. While contributing to the emergence of an international market in justice, the growth of arbitration *à l'americaine* has an impact well beyond simply providing a substitute for court systems. It not only provides a way to overcome national limitations, but also contributes to breaking down the categories and boundaries in national markets in which the state legal systems occupied only a marginal position.[34]

In mixing the genres and facilitating exchanges between lawyers and merchants, between legal authority and social capital, this new institution opened a space for operation between the worlds of law and business. It also brought into existence a kind of amalgamation of the state legal system and the ad hoc, custom-tailored justice. Above all, the success of this new market of business justice stems from the ability of the hierarchies of law to preserve an image of independence essential to their credibility, while putting at the disposal of economic leaders a strategic practice by which the economic leaders could manage their conflicts, as they wished, but with unquestioned legitimacy.

It is then hardly surprising that the Anglo-American law firms have been among the first to rush into this space between the universe of law and that

34. This description applies also, although to a lesser degree, to English justice. Until recently, legal jurisdictions had only a very limited right to oversee the activities of the City, the heart of the English economic system. On this point, the prerogatives of the leaders of the Bank of England, or those of the high functionaries of the Treasury, were quite equal to those of their homologues on the Continent. They also controlled a tailor-made justice discrete and without appeal. See the example of the Takeover Panel (Dezalay 1992).

of business, opened by the efforts of the pioneers of arbitration. From their point of view, this arbitral justice was, in many respects, a tailor-made justice. The structural characteristics of this new form permitted the multinationals of law to valorize better the complex amalgam of legal authority and economic power that allows them to put the elite of the profession and the most sophisticated legal technology in the service of the dominant groups in the economic field.

14

Reintroducing Politics and States in the Market of International Business Disputing

The history of international commercial arbitration does not come to an end with the transformation of the International Chamber of Commerce into an international private justice with the characteristics of offshore litigation. It is true that, as we have seen, international commercial arbitration is now flourishing; it is the accepted method for resolving transnational commercial disputes. Certainly there are challenges within the general approach, most notably by the recent efforts to promote competing technologies such as mediation or other state-of-the-art alternatives to arbitration or litigation. But the field of international commercial arbitration continues to gain new territories and to bring new converts into this multi- and transnational legal profession; and the internationalizing process in turn transforms the landscapes of national business dispute resolution. The new converts, as we have seen, create business for and extend the reach of the key centers and central arbitrators of international commercial arbitration. International commercial arbitration has become increasingly more universal.

Our account of international commercial arbitration, however, teaches also that its characteristics and success relate to a quite specific geopolitical conjuncture. Of particular importance, we can suggest, were the cold war and the interventionism of the welfare state and of third worldism. International commercial arbitration as it developed around the ICC permitted business conflicts to be handled at a distance from cold-war politics and state interventionism. This conclusion will suggest that the specific factors that gave rise to international commercial arbitration as we know it are changing, and that therefore we may look toward the development of a new international approach to the management of business conflict. If so, the role of the ICC and international commercial arbitration may change quite substantially.

The starting point for this analysis is a recognition that the market of business disputing can be organized around two poles—the jurisdictions of the state and those of the business world. We have not had to pay very much attention to the state as such in the preceding chapters because international commercial arbitration in the past thirty years has operated with the state more or less off to one side. From a longer-term perspective, however, we can recall that arbitration declined initially with the development of the New Deal in the United States and welfare states elsewhere. New regulatory regimes gained power at the expense of more private dispute resolution (e.g., Auerbach 1983). Only later did the new international commercial arbitration develop and help recover private justice in places like the United States.

We now ask if the construction of large regional markets—the European Community, NAFTA—or detailed mechanisms for regulating international commerce—the World Trade Organization under GATT—could also disrupt the landscape and introduce new stakes and even an "international new deal." The restructuring of the international market of disputes would build on emerging institutions such as the European Court of Justice, NAFTA, GATT, and even revived and transformed antitrust regulations. These institutions and approaches offer new opportunities for business. Even if it is not at first apparent, these institutions compete with the International Chamber of Commerce and private arbitration. At the same time, new approaches and institutions may facilitate the recomposition of this field of practice closer to the pole of the state. There could also be new providers of dispute resolution services, and new networks—borrowing, perhaps, from certain sectors within the existing international arbitration community.

International commercial arbitration can be transformed or even replaced because it is part of a larger international *market* of commercial or business disputes, and the market is inevitably unstable. Instability, as noted in chapter 6, comes from the fact that arbitration is constantly pulled between two contradictory poles—business and law. Competition in the products that serve this market produces innovations and changes—but only over the long term. In a market in symbolic goods, it is necessary for competitors to begin by producing their credibility—producing consumers at the same time as the producers are constructed out of sustained learned investment. It may even take generations before the fruits of this investment—if successful—are enjoyed.

The best approach to understanding the potential for particular future transformations in national and international business-disputing markets is to reexamine the political and professional landscape that permitted the ICC to succeed and to ask precisely what features are in the process of changing. In undertaking such an analysis, we focus especially on the learned and institutional dimensions, since those are the places where strategies for the long term can be played.

From this point of view, we can suggest first that the ICC represented, among other things, an alliance between the European grand professors and their disciples from countries at the periphery. It was organized around institutions like the Hague Academy of International Law and doctrines that reflect a typical academic neutrality—exemplified by the *lex mercatoria*. This learned investment served to break the stigma associated with business justice as a second-class justice, and it served also to construct the technologies necessary to equip this new forum. In both respects, as we saw in chapter 3, the very success of international commercial arbitration led to transformations of these initial conditions.

In addition to the academic prominence, the ICC approach had a second aspect that set the tone for international commercial arbitration. It studiously put aside the regulations of the nation-state. The approach employed a private institutional platform—the ICC, which is after all an organization of private businesses—that has no formal ties with states. The ICC could persuasively argue that the arbitration of disputes with third-world or Communist states was simply a matter of private, commercial arbitration. It could therefore avoid or channel elsewhere potential threats by states to the needs of multinational businesses who wished to invest or trade in new markets. Not only could the ICC argue that it was divorced from the interests of Western states,[1] but also that international commercial arbitration was neutral. The academic world of learned law was able to provide the neutral authority through the *lex mercatoria*, and this learned doctrine was validated by the authority of the European grand professors over their disciples in the third world. This authority facilitated the putting aside of potentially threatening third-worldist legal claims.

The ICC prospered on the basis of this structural foundation, and it was able to gain credibility and prominence as an accepted institution. Imitators and competitors, as we have seen, have also proliferated. As we ask what may be emerging in the future, however, we must explore what has changed in the building blocks of the arbitration structure over the past thirty to thirty-five years. We can list a few of the more prominent changes.

First, U.S.-style legal practice has emerged increasingly as the lingua franca of international commerce. The large law firms themselves—not only from the United States, but also from London and several other countries—have set up new international offices, and local imitators spread further the influence of this style of practice. Graduate study in U.S. law schools is now one of the key items necessary to build a valuable resume for a non-U.S. practitioner,

---

1. Personal connections and double roles, however, might still provide opportunities for Western states and officials to have influence in this new game. The interchange between careers in arbitration and the U.S. State Department, for example, suggests that personal relations between the state and private justice could be maintained.

and the spread of U.S. legal concepts and practices has further gained through the symbolic imperialism of the U.S. Agency for International Development and the many U.S.-funded international human rights organizations. The center of gravity, as noted in many places in this book, has shifted toward the United States in legal education as well as in legal practice.

In the same way, the legal picture has been transformed by the increasing dominance of the political and economic model of Western liberal democracies. No longer do we face fundamental oppositions between communism and capitalism, or between various models of authoritarianism and relatively democratic entities. There are certainly differences, including those between Asian proponents of a "different model" of human rights and democracy and prevailing Western viewpoints; but the legitimacy of the basic liberal governing structure for the state and the economy is largely uncontested.

Given these shared characteristics, it becomes for the first time possible to build legal regulatory structures—quasi states—that can frame large regional markets or even gain a place in the global market. The political and economic stakes associated with these structures are sufficiently high, both politically and economically, that by comparison private disputes lose some of their importance, becoming more like bargaining chips than major disputes.

States are at the same time among the key actors and the major stakes of an intensified international competition. State battles that were fought in the past around such issues as the legitimacy of expropriation are increasingly fought on the double terrain of protectionism (the legitimacy of trade barriers) and antidumping (with some new interjections of antitrust and some recurring debates about compensation—e.g., Iraq, Iran). The states are major players in determining the framework and even the quite specific details of the arrangements in multilateral or bilateral investment treaties.

The states, it is true, concede certain of their prerogatives to supranational entities, such as GATT or the United Nations; or to courts, exemplified by the European Court of Justice; or quasi courts, exemplified by the NAFTA and GATT panels. In practice, however, the states have the power to control the appointments of judges to such panels—a practice exemplified already in the more state-centered arbitration institutions like the Iran–United States Claims Tribunal and the International Center for the Settlement of Investment Disputes associated with the World Bank.

These developments suggest that modern trade battles are played in the first place on the terrain of the state—and by extension on that of lawmaking—rather than on the terrain of private justice or the practice of mediation of business conflicts. This change in the hierarchy of the particular settings of business conflict and its handling upsets the relative positions of the possible producers and institutional providers (and also the consumers) of regulation and dispute resolution.

We may see, in fact, a kind of reversal of the *Mitsubishi* case described in chapter 8. In *Mitsubishi*, the U.S. Supreme Court in effect recognized international commercial arbitration's precedence over the national enforcement of antitrust laws. The new order could involve a kind of international antitrust (and, relatedly, antidumping regulated by the World Trade Organization). It could therefore be that, while national antitrust was initially pushed out of the international business-disputing domain to make room for ICC-style arbitration, it comes back in as part of a new international legal order.

States—and among them supranational entities—and state jurisdictions intervene increasingly on the scene of economic conflicts. And the relatively new entities that intervene tend to be jealous of their authority and anxious to build up their regulatory domain. Thus, for example, Brussels and the court in Luxembourg have been cool or even hostile to the International Chamber of Commerce.

As states assume more importance, legal professionals and large enterprises tend to move, almost by definition, closer to the pole of the state, leading to a process of acceleration. Those with ties to the state—as seen in the example of the Rule of Law Committee in chapter 8—are more likely to play the public card in business conflicts. That is to say, their expertise and connections will lead them to channel conflicts toward the state, contributing thereby to the acceleration of the recomposition of the field of business conflicts around the state.

If this line of development continues, the field of transnational business justice will be more closely connected to states and to supranational, statelike entities than it was in the period when the ICC gained its eminence.[2] Major business conflicts would be fought on terrain closer to the states—with the states implicated in the contests and the contestants. We cannot say at this point whether this development will take place, and whether, if so, the world constituted around the ICC and its networks will assume a secondary position. But, as suggested earlier, the history of business disputing shows that change is typically made through the creation of new models and institutions rather than simply modifications of the existing institutions.

The question of institutional "breaks" returns us to the important theoretical distinction between the international legal field and the institutions that we find, such as the International Chamber of Commerce and the *lex mercato-*

2. These supranational entities are like states in the sense that they allow state notables to reinvest elsewhere their specific mix of talents and expertise (Milward 1993, 7).

ria, within that field (Bourdieu 1987). The field represents a space of positions and struggles that produce, render obsolete, or reinvent social institutions. The field may certainly be transformed, but in the absence of major unsettling events like wars or political upheavals, the change takes place according to a social logic and even a rhythm of generations. In contrast, the space occupied by institutions is much more susceptible to breaks and reconversions. Our research focuses on the field—exploring therefore the strategies of individuals and social groups that make up the field—because the breaks and reconversions of institutions only make sense in relation to the transformations in the field that produce them.

This distinction is central to any effort to ascertain the future—and the role of international commercial arbitration in it. For example, if we take seriously the suggestion of an increasing role for states and quasi-state entities in business disputing, one reaction might be to ask what this potential role of the states means for the idea of an emerging *international* legal field or for the development of *international* legal institutions. The problem is that it is relatively easy to imagine the development of international commercial arbitration as an aspect of a growing "international legal field"—and indeed, a growing international legal order—with its own form of private justice detached from the national justice of states. As explained in the preceding paragraph, however, the institutions themselves—what is seen as an international legal order—can change quite dramatically in response to transformations in the international legal field. The institutions can move *toward or away* from states. International does not mean a necessary decline of the role of states.

The international legal field, in sum, should not be seen simplistically (or positivistically) as a putting aside or negation of the national dimension. The relevant research question is not in fact whether the international legal field exists or not. For our purposes, it is a question of whether the tool of the international legal field is useful for examining and analyzing strategic opportunities. The international legal field, therefore, should be seen as a virtual space for battles that may vary in intensity in different places and times—and that have more or less strong echoes in national and local power relations.

Internationalization can in fact best be characterized as the opening of breaches in national spaces that are otherwise more or less closed, at times almost watertight. The opening leads potentially to a redefinition or a blurring of the boundaries established and maintained in the national settings. Internationalization allows individuals and groups to construct strategies that go beyond national space. External alliances, such as that formed between the grand old men in arbitration and the large U.S. law firms, are made possible by internationalization. And these alliances contribute to redefining internal spaces by disrupting hierarchies of values and established alliances. In the United States, for example, the connection with the world of the ICC facilitated the valorization of private justice and then the emergence of a new domestic market in private justice.

The impacts of these strategies of internationalization are felt even more strongly as one moves toward nations on the periphery. Legal actors on the periphery may be quicker to forge international connections and apply them domestically in part because their own legal systems point them toward the center. Constructed by and for international relations of economic and symbolic dependency, the legal systems that have been established on the periphery are by definition rooted in internationalization. Nevertheless, on the periphery and elsewhere, the impact of internationalization is not automatic or determined in advance. It depends in every case on the relative power and relations between the protectionist and the internationalist groups from among legal elites.

Meanwhile, as we have seen, the same strategies that promote the recomposition of the local serve also and at the same time to construct the international (or at least delocalization). But what emerges from this process is not preconstructed or inevitable. The geopolitical center of gravity of the international field depends on the results of power struggles between different national groups who fight themselves on the terrain of the international. The international legal field could be closer to Europe or closer to the United States (or to other future competitors on the terrain of law). It could also be closer (or even limited to) the domain of finance and business law, or it could include other components, including international human rights or the protection of the environment. In short, as with respect to the national legal fields, the international legal field may be limited to an alliance with the dominant groups in power or may provide places for other political forces and other social groups.

The international legal field is after all a field of struggle, which means that different outcomes are possible. Systematic examinations of the networks, alliances, and institutions by and around which the international is constituted provide the best way to ascertain what is likely to emerge from the struggles that take place. But the outcomes are indeterminate. One of the goals of this study and others like it, which explore the ways in which the legal profession and law gain their legitimacy and change over time, is in fact to help individuals see that the hierarchies and categories that make acquiescence to economic and political power seem natural and inevitable are themselves the product of struggles.

Bibliography

Abel, Richard L. 1994. "Transnational Law Practice." 44 *Case Western Reserve Law Review* 737–870.

Aboul Enein, M. I. M. 1994. "An Outline of the Principles of the New Egyptian Law on Arbitration." 5 *World Arbitration and Mediation Report* 129–31.

"ADR Providers: Endispute Merges with Bates Edwards Group as Provider Competition Heats Up." 1993. 4 *World Arbitration and Mediation Report* 292.

Aksen, Gerald. 1990. "Arbitration and Other Means of Dispute Settlement." In David Goldsweig and Roger Cummings, eds., *International Joint Ventures: A Practical Approach to Working with Foreign Investors in the U.S. and Abroad*, 287–93. Chicago: American Bar Association.

Alfini, James J. 1991. "Trashing, Bashing, and Hashing It Out: Is This the End of 'Good Mediation'?" 19 *Florida State University Law Review* 47–75.

American Law Institute. 1980. *Restatement of the Law, Foreign Relations Law of the United States (Revised)*. Tentative draft no. 1.

———. 1982. *Proceedings of the Fifty-ninth Annual Meeting of the American Law Institute*. Philadelphia: American Law Institute.

———. 1987. *Restatement of the Law, Foreign Relations Law of the United States (Revised)*.

"Arbitrators Become Essex Men." 1994. *Legal Business*, May, 16.

Asante, Samuel K. B. 1993. "The Perspectives of African Countries on International Commercial Arbitration." 6 *Leiden Journal of International Law* 331–56.

Audit, Bernard. 1988. "Transnational Arbitration and State Contracts: Findings and Prospects." In Centre for Studies and Research in International Law and International Relations, Hague Academy of International Law, *1987 Transnational Arbitration and State Contracts*. Deventer, Netherlands: Kluwer.

Auerbach, Jerold S. 1983. *Justice without Law?* New York: Oxford University Press.

Badie, Bertrand. 1993. *L'état importé*. Paris: Fayard.

Bancaud, A., and Yves Dezalay. 1994. "Des 'grands prêtres' du droit au marché de l'expertise juridique: Transformations morphologiques et recomposition du champ des producteurs de doctrine en droit des affaires." 12 *Revue Politique et Management Public* 203–20.

Barnathan, Joyce. 1993. "The Sons Are Rising in the East." *Business Week*, December 6, 64.

Barnet, Richard J. 1973. *Roots of War*. Baltimore: Penguin.

Barnet, Richard J., and John Cavanagh. 1994. *Global Dreams*. New York: Simon and Schuster.

Barton, John H., and Barry E. Carter. 1993. "International Law and Institutions for a New Age." 81 *Georgetown Law Journal* 535–62.

Baxter, Richard. 1978. "A New Restatement of the Foreign Relations Law of the United States." 72 *American Journal of International Law* 875–77.

Bedjaoui, Mohammed. 1992. "The Arab World in ICC Arbitration." In ICC International Court of Arbitration Bulletin, vol. 3, no. 1, special supplement, *International Commercial Arbitration in the Arab Countries*, 7–20.

Beechey, John. 1994. "International Arbitration and the Award of Security for Costs in England." 12, no. 2 *Bulletin of the Swiss Arbitration Association* 179–91.

Berger, Klaus Peter. 1993. *International Economic Arbitration*. Deventer, Netherlands: Kluwer.

Bird, Kai. 1992. *The Chairman*. New York: Simon and Schuster.

Bond, Stephen. 1990. "The Present Status of the International Court of Arbitration of the ICC: An Appraisal." 1 *American Review of International Arbitration* 108–22.

Bourdieu, Pierre. 1987. "The Force of Law: Toward a Sociology of the Juridical Field." 38 *Hastings Law Journal* 805–53.

———. 1989. *La noblesse d'état: Grand corps et grande écoles*. Paris: Editions de Minuit.

———. 1991. "Epilogue: On the Possibility of a Field of World Sociology." In Pierre Bourdieu and J. Coleman, eds., *Social Theory for a Changing Society*. Boulder, Colo.: Westview Press; New York: Russell Sage.

———. 1993. *The Field of Cultural Production*. New York: Columbia University Press.

Bourdieu, Pierre, and Monique de Saint Martin. 1978. "Le patronat." *Actes de la recherche en sciences sociales*, nos. 20–21, pp. 3–82.

Bourdieu, Pierre, and Loic J. D. Wacquant. 1992. *An Invitation to Reflexive Sociology*. Chicago: University of Chicago Press.

Braudel, Fernand. 1982. *The Wheels of Commerce: Civilization and Capitalism, Fifteenth–Eighteenth Century*, vol. 2. New York: Harper and Row.

Brill, Steven. 1993. "Lopping Off a Third." *American Lawyer*, June, 5.

Brower, Charles. 1993. "Introduction." In Richard Lillich and Charles Brower, eds., *International Arbitration in the Twenty-first Century: Towards "Judicialization" and Uniformity*. Irvington, N.Y.: Transnational Publishers.

Brown, Nathan J. 1995. "Law and Imperialism: Egypt in Comparative Perspective." 29 *Law and Society Review* 103–25.

Bruck, Connie. 1982. "Libya's Low-Profile Lawyers." *American Lawyer*, February, 30–31.

Budden, Robert. 1993. "Who's Who in China Work." *International Financial Law Review*, May, 6–13.

Caplan, Lincoln. 1993. *Skadden: Power, Money, and the Rise of a Legal Empire*. New York: Farrar, Straus and Giroux.

Carbonneau, Thomas. 1989. *Alternative Dispute Resolution: Melting the Lances and Dismounting the Steeds*. Champaign: University of Illinois Press.

―――, ed. 1990. *Lex Mercatoria and Arbitration*. Dobbs Ferry, N.Y.: Transnational Juris Publications.

Casella, Alessandra. 1992. *Arbitration in International Trade*. Working paper no. 4136, National Bureau of Economic Research, Cambridge, Mass.

Castells, M. 1992. "Four Asian Tigers with a Dragon Head: A Comparative Analysis of the State, Economy, and Society in the Asian Pacific Rim." In R. Appelbaum and J. Henderson, eds., *States and Development in the Asian Pacific Rim*. London: Sage.

Center for Public Resources. 1982. *Corporate Dispute Management*. New York: Matthew Bender.

Center for Public Resources. 1991. *Rules and Commentary for Nonadministered Arbitration of International Disputes*, 4th draft, November 8.

Center for Public Resources Legal Program. 1990. *Rules and Commentary for Non-administered Arbitration of Business Disputes*.

Center for Public Resources Legal Program. 1991. *Model ADR Procedures: Mediation of Business Disputes* (Revised).

Chan, W. K. 1991. *The Making of Hong Kong Society*. Oxford: Oxford University Press.

Charle, Christophe. 1983. "Le champ universitaire parisien à fin du 19ème siècle." *Actes de la recherche en sciences sociales*, nos. 47–48, pp. 77–89.

―――. 1989. "Pour une histoire sociale des professions juridiques." *Actes de la recherche en sciences sociales*, nos. 76–77, pp. 117–19.

Charny, David. 1991. "Competition among Jurisdictions in Formulating Corporate Law Rules: An American Perspective on the 'Race to the Bottom' in the European Communities." 32 *Harvard International Law Journal* 423–56.

Chatterjee, Charles. 1992. "The *Rainbow Warrior* Arbitration between New Zealand and France." 9 *Journal of International Arbitration* 17–29.

Cheng, Philip Hui-Ho. 1994. "A Business Risk in China: Jail." *Asian Wall Street Journal*, April 22–23, 8.

"China's New Elite." 1995. *Business Week*, June 5, 48–51.

"China to Focus on New York." 1994. *International Financial Law Review*, June, 3.

Clark, David S. 1981. "Adjudication to Administration: A Statistical Analysis of Federal District Courts in the Twentieth Century." 55 *Southern California Law Review* 65–152.

Clavell, James. 1966. *Tai-pan*. New York: Atheneum.

―――. 1981. *Noble House*. New York: Dell Publishing.

Clow, Robert, and Patricia Stewart. 1990. "International Arbitration: Storming the Citadels." *International Financial Law Review*, March, 1.

"Commercial Initiatives: AAA Unveils Large, Complex Case Program." 1993. 4 *World Arbitration and Mediation Report* 27.

"Court-Adjunct ADR: Third Circuit Launches Mandatory Appeals Mediation Program." 1994. 5 *World Arbitration and Mediation Report* 178.

"CPR Selects European Panel." 1993. 11 *Alternatives* 66.

Craig, W. Laurence, William W. Park, and Jan Paulsson. 1990. *International Chamber of Commerce Arbitration.* 2d ed. New York: Oceana Publications.

Cutler, Lloyd. 1981. "Negotiating the Iranian Settlement." 67 *ABA Journal* 996–1000.

Dahrendorf, Ralf. 1969. "Law Faculties and the German Upper Class." In W. Aubert, ed., *Sociology of Law.* London: Penguin.

Dawson, John Philip. 1968. *The Oracles of the Law.* Ann Arbor: University of Michigan Law School.

de Ly, Filip. 1992. *International Business Law and Lex Mercatoria.* North Holland, Netherlands: Elsevier.

Dezalay, Yves. 1992. *Marchands de droit.* Paris: Fayard. (Forthcoming English translation, Northwestern University Press.)

———. 1995. Introduction to Yves Dezalay, ed., *Batailles territoriales et querelles de cousinage.* Paris: Librairie Générale de Droit et de Jurisprudence.

Dick, S. Gale. 1994a. "Law Firm Initiatives Propel Growing ADR Use." 12 *Alternatives* 123.

———. 1994b. "Special Courts Now Handle Business Cases." 12 *Alternatives* 97.

Dillon, Karen. 1993. "Out of the Robes and into the Ring." *Legal Business,* May, 46–48.

———. 1994. "Unfair Trade." *Legal Business,* June, 68–74.

DiMaggio, Paul. 1991. "Constructing an Organizational Field as a Professional Project: U.S. Art Museums, 1920–40." In Walter Powell and Paul DiMaggio, eds., *The New Institutionalism in Organizational Analysis.* Chicago: University of Chicago Press.

"Dispute Service for London." 1994. *International Financial Law Review,* May, 2.

Dolin, Mitchell F., and Robert N. Sayler. 1993. "Twenty Years of Litigation." 20 *Litigation* 6.

Donovan, Karen. 1994. "Searching for ADR Stars." *National Law Journal,* March 14, A1.

Edwards, Harry T. 1992. "The Growing Disjunction between Legal Education and Legal Practice." 91 *Michigan Law Review* 34–78.

Edwards, Jeremy. 1994a. "The Five-Million Pound Man." *Legal Business,* November, 46–49.

———. 1994b. "The Good, the Bad, and the Bench." *Legal Business,* April, 51–61.

Egan, Dominic. 1994. "Splendid Isolation." *Legal Business,* May, 64–70.

Eisenberg, Melvin A. 1976. "Private Ordering through Negotiation: Dispute Settlement and Rulemaking." 89 *Harvard Law Review* 637–81.

Eisner, Marc A. 1991. *Antitrust and the Triumph of Economics*. Chapel Hill: University of North Carolina Press.

El-Ahdab, Abdul Hamid. 1990. *Arbitration with the Arab Countries*. Deventer, Netherlands: Kluwer.

El-Kosheri, Ahmed S., and Tarek F. Riad. 1986. "The Law Governing a New Generation of Petroleum Agreements: Changes in the Arbitration Process." 1 *ICSID Review—Foreign Investment Law Journal* 257–88.

Ellickson, Robert. 1991. *Order without Law*. Cambridge: Harvard University Press.

Elm, Mostafa. 1992. *Oil, Power, and Principle*. Syracuse, N.Y.: Syracuse University Press.

Elson, Alex, and Michael Shakman. 1994. "The ALI Principles of Corporate Governance: A Tainted Process and a Flawed Product." 49 *Business Lawyer* 1761–92.

Engler, Robert. 1977. *The Brotherhood of Oil*. Chicago: University of Chicago Press.

"English Committee Issues Draft Arbitration Law." 1994. 5 *World Arbitration and Mediation Report* 56.

"Exploring the Issues in Private Judging." 1994. 77 *Judicature* 203–10.

Fallows, James. 1994. *Looking at the Sun: The Rise of the New East Asian Economic and Political System*. New York: Pantheon Books.

Federal Courts Study Committee. 1990. *Report of the Federal Courts Study Committee*. Philadelphia: Federal Courts Study Committee.

Flood, John, and Andrew Caiger. 1993. "Lawyers and Arbitration: The Juridification of Construction Disputes." 56 *Modern Law Review* 412–40.

"Future Grim for Expat Lawyers." 1993. *New Gazette*, November, 14.

Galanter, Marc. 1974. "Why the 'Haves' Come Out Ahead: Speculations on the Limits of Legal Change." 9 *Law and Society Review* 95–160.

———. 1985. "Settlement Judge, Not a Trial Judge: Judicial Mediation in the United States." 12 *Journal of Law and Society* 1–18.

———. 1988. "The Life and Times of the Big Six; or, The Federal Court since the Good Old Days." *1988 Wisconsin Law Review* 921–54.

Galanter, Marc, and Thomas Palay. 1991. *Tournament of Lawyers*. Chicago: University of Chicago Press.

Gardner, James. 1980. *Legal Imperialism: American Lawyers and Foreign Aid in Latin America*. Madison: University of Wisconsin Press.

Garth, Bryant. 1980. *Neighborhood Law Firms for the Poor*. Leyden: Sijthoff.

Geyelin, Milo. 1993. "Delaware Plans Streamlined Court for Business Disputes." *Wall Street Journal*, December 10, B3.

Glendon, Mary Ann. 1994. *A Nation under Lawyers: How the Crisis in the Legal Profession Is Transforming American Society*. New York: Farrar, Straus and Giroux.

Goldman, Berthold. 1984. "The Complementary Roles of Judges and Arbitrators in Ensuring That International Commercial Arbitration Is Effective." In International Chamber of Commerce, *Sixty Years of ICC Arbitration*, 255–85. Paris: International Chamber of Commerce.

Goodman, George J. W. 1981. *Paper Money.* New York: Simon and Schuster.

Gordon, Robert. 1984. "The Ideal and the Actual in the Law: Fantasies and Practices of New York City Lawyers, 1870–1910." In Gerard Gawalt, ed., *The New High Priests: Lawyers in Post–Civil War America.* Westport, Conn.: Greenwood Press.

Granovetter, Mark, and Richard Swedberg. 1992. *The Sociology of Economic Life.* Boulder, Colo.: Westview Press.

Green, Eric, Jonathan Marks, and Ronald Olson. 1978. "Settling Large Case Litigation: An Alternative Approach." 11 *Loyola of Los Angeles Law Review* 493–511.

Greenhalgh, Susan. 1994. "De-Orientalizing the Chinese Family Firm." 21, no. 4 *American Ethnologist* 746–75.

Gunningham, Neil. 1990. "Moving the Goalposts: Financial Market Regulation in Hong Kong and the Crash of October 1987." 15 *Law and Social Inquiry* 1–48.

Haas, Peter M. 1992. "Introduction: Epistemic Communities and International Policy Coordination." 46 *International Organization,* winter, 1–35.

Haley, John O. 1991. *Authority without Power: Law and the Japanese Paradox.* New York: Oxford University Press.

Harrington, Christine B. 1985. *Shadow Justice: The Ideology and Institutionalization of Alternatives to Court.* Westport, Conn.: Greenwood Press.

Hartman, M. 1995. "Lawyers in Banks, the Slow Erosion of an Elite." In Yves Dezalay and David Sugarman, eds., *Professional Competition and the Social Construction of Markets.* London: Routledge.

Hay, Douglas. 1975. "Property, Authority, and the Criminal Law." In Douglas Hay, Peter Linebaugh, John G. Rule, E. P. Thompson, and Cal Winslow, eds., *Albion's Fatal Tree: Crime and Society in Eighteenth-Century England.* New York: Pantheon Books.

Heinz, John P., and Edward O. Laumann. 1982. *Chicago Lawyers: The Social Structure of the Bar.* New York: Russell Sage Foundation; Chicago: American Bar Foundation.

Hermann, A. H. 1983. "Power for the Judges: Just How International Is English Law?" *Financial Times,* September 22, 40.

Heydebrand, Wolf, and Carroll Seron. 1990. *Rationalizing Justice: The Political Economy of Federal District Courts.* Albany: State University of New York Press.

Heymann, Philip B., and Lance Liebman. 1988. *The Social Responsibilities of Lawyers: Case Studies.* Westbury, N.Y.: Foundation Press.

Hirst, David. 1966. *Oil and Public Opinion in the Middle East.* London: Faber and Faber.

Hobér, Kaj. 1994. "The New Draft Swedish Arbitration Act: Commentary." 5 *World Arbitration and Mediation Report* 180–82.

"Hong Kong Silver." 1994. *California Lawyer,* May, 27.

Houck, John. 1986. "Restatement of the Foreign Relations Law of the United States (Revised): Issues and Resolutions." 20 *International Lawyer* 1361–377.

Hunt, Alan. 1993. *Explorations in Law and Society: Toward a Constitutive Theory of Law*. New York: Routledge.

"ICC Court Reports Increase in Filings, More Diversity among Parties." 1994. 5 *World Arbitration and Mediation Report* 216.

"International Arbitration London." 1978. *Hansards Parliamentary Debates*, May 15, 90–117.

International Chamber of Commerce. 1984. *Sixty Years of ICC Arbitration*. Paris: International Chamber of Commerce.

"ICC Panel Hands Down Second Award in £1.2 Billion Channel Tunnel Dispute." 1993. 4 *World Arbitration and Mediation Report* 86.

Johnson, Kirk. 1993. "Public Judges as Private Contractors: A Legal Frontier." *New York Times*, December 10, D20.

Jones, Carol A. G. 1994. "Capitalism, Globalization, and Rule of Law: An Alternative Trajectory of Legal Change in China." 3 *Social and Legal Studies* 195–220.

Jones, Charles. 1983. *The North-South Dialogue: A Brief History*. London: Frances Pinter.

Kadiki, Khaled. 1992. "The Arbitration Clause According to the Islamic Shariah and the Positive Laws of Arab Countries." In ICC International Court of Arbitration Bulletin, vol. 3, no. 1, special supplement, *International Commercial Arbitration in the Arab Countries*, 35–42.

Kantorowicz, E. 1961. "Kingship under the Impact of Scientific Jurisprudence." In M. Clagett, G. Post, and R. Reynolds, eds., *Twelfth-Century Europe and the Foundation of Modern Society*. Madison: University of Wisconsin Press.

Kaplan, Neil. 1994. "Hong Kong Update: Recent Trends and Court Decisions." 5 *World Arbitration and Mediation Report* 107.

Kaplan, Neil, Jill Spruce, and Michael Moser. 1994. *Hong Kong and China Arbitration: Cases and Materials*. London: Butterworths.

Karady, Victor. 1991. "Une nation de juristes." *Actes de la recherche en sciences sociales*, nos. 86–87, pp. 106–15.

Karpik, Lucien. 1992. "La profession libérale: Un cas, le barreau." In P. Nora, ed., *Les lieux de mémoire les France*, vol. 2. Paris: NRF.

Keck, Margaret, and Kathryn Sikkink. 1994. "Transnational Issue Networks in International Politics." Typescript.

Kelly, J. B. 1980. *Arabia, the Gulf, and the West*. New York: Basic Books.

Kemicha, Fathi. 1994. "Future Perspectives on International Commercial Arbitration in the Arab Countries." In Albert Jan van den Berg, ed., *International Arbitration in a Changing World*, International Council for Commercial Arbitration, Congress Series no. 6. Deventer, Netherlands: Kluwer.

Kerr, Michael. 1987. "Commercial Dispute Resolution: The Changing Scene." In Maarten Bos and Ian Brownlie, eds., *Liber Amicorum for the Rt. Hon. Lord Wilberforce*. Oxford: Clarendon Press.

Kholi, Sheel, and Ray Heath. 1994. "LSE in Bid to Woo China from NYSE." *South China Morning Post*, April 25, 10.

Knight, H. Warren. 1982. "Private Dispute Resolution—a Growing Concern in California." In Center for Public Resources, *Corporate Dispute Management*, 113–24. New York: Matthew Bender.

Kostal, Susan. 1992. "Intel's Enforcer." *California Lawyer*, August, 96–99.

Kraar, Louis. 1995. "The Death of Hong Kong." *Fortune*, June 26, 40–52.

Krasner, Stephen. 1985. *Structural Conflict: The Third World against Global Liberalism*. Berkeley and Los Angeles: University of California Press.

Kronman, Anthony. 1993. *The Lost Lawyer*. Cambridge: Harvard University Press.

Lalive, Pierre. 1984. "Enforcing Awards." In International Chamber of Commerce, *Sixty Years of ICC Arbitration*, 317–59. Paris: International Chamber of Commerce.

———. 1991. "L'independence des arbitres dans le système CCI." 9, no. 1 *Bulletin of the Swiss Arbitration Association* 46–48.

Latin American Bureau. 1983. *Chile: The Pinochet Decade: The Rise and Fall of the Chicago Boys*. London: Latin American Bureau.

Lauterpacht, Elihu. 1993. "Law and Policy in International Resource Development." Speech delivered at the Merchant Taylor's Hall, London, January 25.

Leboulanger, Philippe. 1991. "L'arbitrage international Nord-Sud." In *Etudes offertes à Pierre Bellet*, 323–40. Paris: Litec.

Lederman, Lawrence. 1992. *Tombstones: A Lawyer's Tales from the Takeover Decades*. New York: Farrar, Straus and Giroux.

Lee, Tahirih. 1993. "Risky Business: Courts, Culture, and the Marketplace." 47 *University of Miami Law Review* 1335–414.

———. 1994. "The Internationalization of Chinese Lawyers: Fact or Fiction." Paper delivered to the Law and Society meeting, Phoenix, Arizona, June 17, 1994.

Lillich, Richard. 1993. "The Law Governing Disputes under Economic Development Agreements: Reexamining the Concept of 'Internationalization.' " In Richard Lillich and Charles Brower, eds., *International Arbitration in the Twenty-first Century: Towards 'Judicialization' and Uniformity*. Irvington, N.Y.: Transnational Publishers.

Lowenfeld, Andreas. 1985. "The Two-Way Mirror: International Arbitration as Comparative Procedure." *Michigan Yearbook of International Legal Studies*, 163–85.

———. 1991. "An Arbitrator's Declaration of Independence." 9, no. 2 *Bulletin of the Swiss Arbitration Association* 85.

Lubman, Stanley B., and Gregory C. Wajnowski. 1993. "International Commercial Dispute Resolution in China: A Practical Assessment." 4 *American Review of International Arbitration* 107–78.

Lynch, Dennis. 1981. *Legal Roles in Colombia*. Uppsala: Scandinavian Institute of African Studies.

MacNeil, Ian. 1992. *American Arbitration Law: Reformation—Nationalization—Internationalization*. New York: Oxford University Press.

Margolick, David. 1993. *Undue Influence: The Epic Battle for the Johnson and Johnson Fortune*. New York: William Morrow.

Markoff, John, and Veronica Montecinos. 1993. "The Ubiquitous Rise of Economists." 13 *Journal of Public Policy* 37–68.

Marriott, Arthur. 1989. "Arbitration in a Single Unified Market." Speech given at the annual conference of the Chartered Institute of Arbitrators, October 6.

Mattei, Ugo. 1994. "How the Wind Changed: Intellectual Leadership in Western Law." 42 *American Journal of Comparative Law* 195–218.

Mentschikoff, Soia, and Ernest A. Haggard. 1977a. "Decision Making and Decision Consensus in Commercial Arbitration." In June Louin Tapp and Felice J. Levine, eds., *Law, Justice, and the Individual in Society: Psychological and Legal Issues.* New York: Holt, Rinehart and Winston.

———. 1977b. "Responsible Decision Making in Dispute Settlement." In June Louin Tapp and Felice J. Levine, eds., *Law, Justice, and the Individual in Society: Psychological and Legal Issues.* New York: Holt, Rinehart and Winston.

Mertz, Elizabeth. 1995. "Linguistic Constructions of Difference and History in the U.S. Law School Classroom." In C. Greenhouse and D. Greenwood, eds., *Difference and Democracy.* Forthcoming.

Milgrom, Paul, Douglass North, and Barry Weingast. 1990. "The Role of Institutions in the Revival of Trade: The Law Merchant, Private Judges, and the Champagne Fairs." 2 *Economics and Politics* 1.

Milward, Alan S., Federico Romero, and George Brennan. 1993. *The European Rescue of the Nation State.* Berkeley and Los Angeles: University of California Press.

Mirsky, Jonathan. 1994. "The Battle for Hong Kong." *New York Review,* April 7, 16–20.

Mnookin, Robert, and Lewis Kornhauser. 1979. "Bargaining in the Shadow of the Law: The Case of Divorce." 88 *Yale Law Journal* 950–97.

Moser, Michael. 1993. "Hong Kong Refuses to Enforce Chinese Arbitration Award." 4 *World Arbitration and Mediation Report* 40.

Mustafa, Zaki. 1984. "Public Corporations as Parties to Arbitration: An Arab Perspective." In International Chamber of Commerce, *Sixty Years of ICC Arbitration,* 245–53. Paris: International Chamber of Commerce.

Mustill, Michael. 1987. "The New *Lex Mercatoria:* The First Twenty-five Years." In Maarten Bos and Ian Brownlie, eds., *Liber Americorum for the Rt. Hon. Lord Wilberforce.* Oxford: Clarendon Press.

Mustill, Michael, and Stewart Boyd. 1989. *Commercial Arbitration.* London: Butterworths.

Neal, Philip, and Perry Goldberg. 1964. "The Electrical Equipment Antitrust Cases: Novel Judicial Administration." 50 *ABA Journal* 621–28.

Nelson, Robert L. 1988. *Partners with Power: Social Transformation of the Large Law Firm.* Berkeley and Los Angeles: University of California Press.

Nelson, William E. 1990. "Contract Litigation and the Elite Bar in New York City, 1960–1980." 39 *Emory Law Journal* 413–62.

"New Organizations: 1. New Joint Venture to Establish Dispute Centers in

Manila and other Industrializing Areas." 1993. 4 *World Arbitration and Mediation Report* 295.

Nohria, Nitin, and Robert Eccles, eds. 1992. *Networks and Organizations: Structure, Form, and Action.* Boston: Harvard Business School Press.

North, Douglass. 1990. *Institutions, Institutional Change, and Economic Performance.* Cambridge: Cambridge University Press.

Norton, Patrick. 1991. "A Law of the Future or a Law of the Past? Modern Tribunals and the International Law of Expropriation." 85 *American Journal of International Law* 474–505.

Olgiati, Vittorio. 1995. "Process and Policy of Legal Professionalization in Europe: The Deconstruction of a Normative Order." In Yves Dezalay and David Sugarman, eds., *Professional Competition and the Social Construction of Markets.* London: Routledge.

Oppetit, Bruno. 1992. "Le droit international privé, droit savant." 234, no. 3 *Hague Academy of International Law, Recueil des Cours* 331–434. London: Martinus Nijhoff.

Osiel, Mark. 1989. "Lawyers as Monopolists, Aristocrats, and Entrepreneurs." 103 *Harvard Law Review* 2009–66.

Page, Nigel. 1994a. "Gearing Up in Hong Kong and China." *International Financial Law Review,* June, 26–40.

———. 1994b. "Hong Kong's Alternative Voice." *International Financial Law Review,* May, 48.

Parker School of Foreign and Comparative Law, Columbia University. 1992. *Guide to International Arbitration and Arbitrators.* 2d ed. Ardsley-on-Hudson, N.Y.: Transnational Juris Publications.

Paulsson, Jan. 1985. "Introduction." 1 *Arbitration International* 2.

———. 1987. "Third World Participation in International Investment Arbitration." 2 *ICSID Review—Foreign Investment Law Journal* 19–65.

———. 1990. "La *lex mercatoria* dans l'arbitrage CCI." 1990. *Revue de L'Arbitrage* 55–100.

Pear, Robert. 1994. "Judicial Panel Proposes Limits on Cases before Federal Courts." *New York Times,* December 5, A1.

Pollock, Ellen Joan. 1990. *Turks and Brahmins.* New York: Simon and Schuster.

———. 1993a. "Arbitrator Finds Role Dwindling as Rivals Grow." *Wall Street Journal,* April 28, B1.

———. 1993b. "Lawyers Earn Less from 90's Takeovers." *Wall Street Journal,* September 14, B9.

Poppy, Audrey. 1994. "Private Sector Justice." *Legal Business,* November, 50.

———. 1995. "Sino-Surrender: Hong Kong Law Society Sells Out to Chinese." *Legal Business,* May, 26.

Posner, Richard A. 1985. *The Federal Courts: Crisis and Reform.* Cambridge: Harvard University Press.

———. 1995. *Overcoming Law.* Cambridge: Harvard University Press.

Powell, Walter, and Paul DiMaggio. 1991. *The New Institutionalism in Organizational Analysis.* Chicago: University of Chicago Press.

"Profile of Arbitrator, Charles Brower." 1992. 4 *Arbitration Materials* 251.

"Profile of Arbitrator, Marc Blessing." 1991. 3 *Arbitration Materials* 249.

"Profile of Arbitrator, Jan Paulsson." 1992. 4 *Arbitration Materials* 207.

Purcell, Edward A., Jr. 1992. *Litigation and Inequality: Federal Diversity Jurisdiction in Industrial America, 1870–1958*. Oxford: Oxford University Press.

"Quick and Clean: Delaware's Experiment; Summary Procedure Expedites Litigation." 1994. Roundtable. *Corporate Legal Times*, August, 1.

Redfern, Alan. 1984. "The Arbitration between the Government of Kuwait and Aminoil." 1984. *British Yearbook of International Law* 65–110.

Redfern, Alan, and Martin Hunter. 1991. *International Commercial Arbitration*. 2d ed. London: Sweet and Maxwell.

Regional Center for International Arbitration—Cairo. N.d. *Arbitration under the Auspices of the Cairo Regional Centre*.

Reid, Donald M. 1981. *Lawyers and Politics in the Arab World, 1880–1960*. Minneapolis: Bibliotheca Islamica.

Resnik, Judith. 1994. "Whose Judgment? Vacating Judgments, Preferences for Settlement, and the Role of Adjudication at the Close of the Twentieth Century." 41 *UCLA Law Review* 1471–1539.

Reuben, Richard. 1994. "King of the Hill." *California Lawyer*, February, 55.

Ridgeway, G. 1938. *Merchants of Peace*. Boston: Little, Brown.

Robel, Lauren K. 1991. "The Politics of Crisis in the Federal Courts." 7 *Ohio State Journal on Dispute Resolution* 115–37.

Robinson, Jeffrey. 1988. *Yamani: The Inside Story*. London: Fontana.

Rosen, Robert E. 1989. "The Inside Counsel Movement, Professional Judgment, and Organizational Representation." 64 *Indiana Law Journal* 479–553.

Rosenblum, Jonathan. 1992. "Oil on the Waters of International Law: Controversies over the Revised Restatement on Foreign Relations Sec. 712. 'State Responsibility for Economic Injury to Nationals of Other States.'" Typescript.

Rouhani, Fuad. 1971. *A History of O.P.E.C.* New York: Praeger.

Salacuse, Jeswald. 1991. *Making Global Deals: Negotiating in the International Marketplace*. Boston: Houghton Mifflin.

Saleh, Samir. 1992. "La perception de l'arbitrage au machrek et dans les pays du golfe." In *Proceedings of the Ninth ICC Conference*, Marakesh, May 12.

Sampson, Anthony. 1991. *The Seven Sisters*. Rev. ed. New York: Bantam Books.

Sander, Frank E. 1976. "Varieties of Dispute Processing." 70 *Federal Rules Decisions* 111–34.

Shamir, Ronen. 1993. "Formal and Substantive Rationality in American Law: A Weberian Perspective." 2 *Social and Legal Studies* 45–72.

Siegrist, Hannes. 1986. "Professionalization with the Brakes On: The Legal Profession in Switzerland, France, and Germany in the Nineteenth Century." 9 *Comparative Social Research* 267.

Silva, P. 1991. "Technocrats and Politics in Chile: From the Chicago Boys to the CIEPLAN Monks." 23 *Journal of Latin American Studies*, pt. 2, 385–410.

Siqueiros, José. 1990. "Arbitral Autonomy and National Sovereignty in Latin America." In Thomas Carbonneau, ed., *Lex Mercatoria and Arbitration*. Dobbs Ferry, N.Y.: Transnational Juris Publications.

Slate, William K. II. 1994. "Growth and Leadership in the ADR Movement." Interview. 5 *World Arbitration and Mediation Report* 141

Slind-Flor, Victoria. 1993. "High-Tech Needs." *National Law Journal*, July 5, 1.

Snyder, F., and S. Sathirathai. 1987. *Third World Attitudes toward International Law*. Deventer, Netherlands: Kluwer-Nijhoff NE.

Sornarajah, M. 1989. "The UNCITRAL Model Law: A Third World Viewpoint." 6, no. 4 *Journal of International Arbitration* 7–20.

"Standards of Conduct for Mediators." 1994. 5 *World Arbitration and Mediation Report* 223.

"State Initiatives: Connecticut Gives Final Approval to 'Sta-Fed.'" 1993. 4 *World Arbitration and Mediation Report* 29.

Stevens, Robert B. 1983. *Law School: Legal Education in America from the 1850s to the 1980s*. Chapel Hill: University of North Carolina Press.

Steyn, Johann. 1991. "Towards a New English Arbitration Act." 6 *Arbitration International* 17.

Stuller, Jay. 1993. "Settling for 'Bearable Unhappiness.'" 30 *Across the Board* 16.

Sugarman, David. 1995. "Who Colonized Whom? Historical Reflections on the Intersection between Law, Lawyers, and Accounting." In Yves Dezalay and David Sugarman, eds., *Professional Competition and Professional Power*. New York: Routledge.

Swiss Arbitration Association. 1994. *Profiles of ASA Members, 1994–1996*. Zurich: Swiss Arbitration Association.

Taylor, Robert P. 1992. "The State of Antitrust, 1992." 61 *Antitrust Law Journal* 83.

Torbert, Preston M. 1993. "China's Evolving Company Legislation: A Status Report." 14 *Northwestern Journal of International Law and Business* 1–14.

Trachtman, Joel. 1993. "International Regulatory Competition, Externalization, and Jurisdiction." 34 *Harvard International Law Journal* 47–104.

Trooboff, Peter. 1987. "Reaffirmation of Established International Legal Principles Governing State Responsibility toward Foreign-Owned Investment." In D. Dicke, ed., *Foreign Investment in the Present and a New International Order*. Fribourg, Switzerland: University Press.

Tyler, Tom, and Gregory Mitchell. 1994. "Legitimacy and the Empowerment of Discretionary Authority: The United States Supreme Court and Abortion Rights." 43 *Duke Law Journal* 703–815.

Van Tassell, Emily Field. 1993. "Resignations and Removals: A History of Federal Judicial Service—and Disservice—1789–1992." 142 *University of Pennsylvania Law Review* 333–430.

Varchaver, Nicholas. 1992. "Dispute Revolution." *American Lawyer*, April, 60.

Veenswijk, Virginia Kays. 1994. *Coudert Brothers*. New York: Penguin Books.

Victor, Kirk. 1985. "ALI Puts Off Foreign Relations Vote." *Legal Times*, May 20, 1.

Wade, R. 1990. *Governing the Market, Economic Theory, and the Role of Government in East Asian Industrialization*. Princeton: Princeton University Press.

Weber, Max. 1978. *Economy and Society*. Ed. Guenther Roth and Claus Wittich. Berkeley and Los Angeles: University of California Press.

Werner, Jacques. 1988. "Competition within the Arbitration Industry." 2 *Journal of International Arbitration* 5–6.

———. 1993. "ADR: Will European Brains Be Set on Fire?" 10, no. 4 *Journal of International Arbitration* 45–47.

Wetter, J. Gillis. 1990. "The Present Status of the International Court of Arbitration of the ICC: An Appraisal." 1 *American Review of International Arbitration* 91–107.

Wong, Siu-lun. 1988. *Emigrant Entrepreneurs*. Oxford: Oxford University Press.

Yates, Ronald. 1994. "Union Pacific Adds Coal to Santa Fe Fight." *Chicago Tribune*, October 7, sec. 3, p. 1.

Yergin, Daniel. 1991. *The Prize*. New York: Simon and Schuster.

Index

A

Abdul Maguid, Ahmed Esmat, 219n
Abel, Richard L., 268n. 26
Aboul Enein, M. I. M., 222
ad hoc arbitrations, 6n. 4
African-Asian Legal Consultative Committee, 222, 241–42
Aksen, Gerald, 6n. 1, 152n. 1, 158n. 13, 163, 180, 189
Alfini, Jim, 170n
Algeria: construction arbitration, 107–10, 224; courts, 221; development of legal expertise, 95, 102, 224; hostility to foreign law, 88; legal counsel sought by, 70–71
Al-Sanhuri, Abdul Razzak, 221, 226
alternative dispute resolution, 118n. 2, 199, 275; background for, 154–55; competition with arbitration, 120; court-annexed, 162n, 168; exporting, 179–81; specialists in, 26–27; used by litigators, 171–73
alternative dispute resolution movement, 14n, 44n. 22, 151–52
American Arbitration Association, 5, 52; amateur arbitrators, 154; caseload, 7n. 4, 153, 160n, 164; historic role, 158, 160, 201; institutional duality, 125; large, complex case program, 164; relationship with the International Chamber of Commerce, 11, 107, 152; rules, 153–54, 161
American Bar Association: Dispute Resolution Section, 173n; Litigation Section, 153, 173n; Section on International Law and Practice, 177; Special Committee for Minor Disputes, 156; Special Committee on Alternative Means of Dispute Resolution, 155n. 8

American Law Institute Restatement on Foreign Relations, 151, 175–79
American Review of International Commercial Arbitration, 160
Aminoil arbitration, 69n. 11, 82n. 43, 84–85, 223
Amin Rasheed Shipping v. *Kuwait Insurance*, 146
Amouzegar, Jamshid, 77n. 27
Anglo-American law firms: attitude toward international arbitration, 55–57; emphasis on case law, 41; Gulf business, 228; hierarchies within, 35; interest in arbitration, 103–4; openness to Continental practices, 42; power base, 48; power plays, 51–52, 305; role in the rationalization of arbitration, 33, 37–38, 48–54, 302; technical facilities, 44; view of *lex mercatoria*, 39, 41–42, 90. See *also* U.S. law firms
Anglo-Iranian Oil Company, 67, 77n. 28
antidumping disputes, 181, 202–3, 315
Arab arbitrators, 306; lack of arbitration appointments, 228; neutrality, 229; sidelines, 245–46
Arab Association for International Arbitration, 230
Arab countries: attitude toward *lex mercatoria*, 90, 228; disinterest in pure law, 230; hostility to foreign law, 88; importance of Egyptian legal expertise, 221–23; interest in international commercial arbitration, 223; International Chamber of Commerce links, 225–26; legal counsel sought by, 70–72; private justice systems, 247; role of petroleum industry, 77–80